AF361544

The Quest for Purpose

The Quest for Purpose

The Collegiate Search for a Meaningful Life

Perry L. Glanzer, Jonathan P. Hill,
and Byron R. Johnson

Cover photo courtesy of Matthew Minard / Baylor Marketing & Communications

Published by State University of New York Press, Albany

For information, contact State University of New York Press, Albany, NY
www.sunypress.edu

Production, Diane Ganeles
Marketing, Anne M. Valentine

Library of Congress Cataloging-in-Publication Data

Names: Glanzer, Perry L. (Perry Lynn), author. | Hill, Jonathan P., author | Johnson, Byron R., author.
Title: The quest for purpose : the collegiate search for a meaningful life / Perry L. Glanzer, Jonathan P. Hill, and Byron R. Johnson.
Description: Albany : State University of New York Press, [2017] | Includes bibliographical references and index.
Identifiers: LCCN 2016052227 (print) | LCCN 2017018250 (ebook) | ISBN 9781438466859 (hardcover : alk. paper) | ISBN 9781438466866 (ebook)
Subjects: LCSH: College students—Conduct of life. | College students—Religious life—United States. | College students—United States—Interviews. | Self-actualization (Psychology)—Religious aspects. | Education, Higher—Moral and ethical aspects. | Christian universities and colleges—United States. | Christian education—United States.
Classification: LCC LB3609 (ebook) | LCC LB3609 .G58 2017 (print) | DDC 378.1/980973—dc23
LC record available at https://lccn.loc.gov/2016052227

Contents

Part III
Questing in the University

Part IV
The Heart, Hope, and Soul of Purpose

Illustrations

Tables

Figures

Acknowledgments

We are thankful for the encouragement of family, friends, colleagues, students, and institutions that provided valuable support to us throughout this research and writing process.

Their support allowed us to travel to various universities and listen to the voices of students from around the nation, as well as survey or examine surveys of college students from across the nation. First, we wish to thank the foundations that made this work possible. This work was supported by the John Templeton Foundation under Grant 36656, the Templeton World Charity Foundation under Grant 0060, and the Louisville Institute under Grant 2012004. We also wish to note that these organizations had no role in the study design, data collection and analysis, or final conclusions and recommendations.

We also wish to thank those groups and organizations that helped us gather data or that allowed us to use data they collected. We are thankful for the Gallup® organization and Stephanie Kafka in particular who assisted with our large quantitative data and seventy-five of the national qualitative interviews. In addition, we are thankful for the Higher Education Research Institute for granting us access to data from their College Students' Beliefs and Values surveys. Furthermore, we are grateful to Christian Smith for access to interviews conducted as part of the National Study of Youth and Religion.

A large research project like this also benefits from numerous others. To begin, we are thankful to Lois Mulder, Olivia Copeland, and the staff and students at the Center for Social Research at Calvin College (Tom Sherwood, Katie Talsma, Taylor Soderling, Taylor Libolt, and Michael Kelly) who assisted with the transcription of 110 of our interviews. Baylor's Oral History department loaned us transcription equipment. We are also grateful to various graduate students at Baylor University who helped with this work. Jessica Robinson, helped coauthor chapter 9 and also helped edit parts of other chapters. Brittney Graber helped compose one of the stories in chapter 4. Cara Cliburn Allen edited the full manuscript and offered numerous insights and editorial suggestions that influenced the shape of the final manuscript. Nathan F. Alleman helped cover classes for Perry Glanzer while we undertook some of this research and writing.

We are also thankful for the support of our institutions, Baylor University and Calvin College. Baylor University provided a University Research Committee grant during the 2012–13 academic year. Calvin College supported the project through a Calvin Research Fellowship during the 2012–13 academic, and the Calvin Center for Christian Scholarship provided funding for a workshop on purpose, religion, and college students during the summer of 2013.

Finally, we wish to thank the institutions who granted us permission to include their students for this study—with a special appreciation to the students themselves. Their willingness to add their voices is what made this project possible. Without them we would not have been able to write this book.

This book emerged out of our contemporary experience of seeing students wrestle with questions of meaning and purpose in college. Of course, our interest in this topic was shaped by our own experience as well. Our dedications reflect those who have shaped our own meaning and life purpose.

From Perry—I dedicate this book to my friend Mark Mahler who was there throughout my own purpose journey. Our numerous late night discussions at the cabin in Belton, Texas, and our phone calls helped forge my own sense of identity and purpose throughout high school, my eleven years of higher education, and into adult life.

From Jon—I dedicate this book to my children: Isabella, Lucas, and Kayla. You provide meaning and purpose in my life every day.

From Byron—I dedicate this book to the many faith-based and community organizations whose service to others brings meaning and purpose to countless lives each year.

Portions of this book were previously published in academic journals. An earlier version of chapter 1 was published as Perry L. Glanzer and Jonathan P. Hill, "Why Most American Universities Have Given Up on Human Purpose and Meaning: A Critical Exploration of the Historical Story," *Journal of Beliefs & Values* 34 (2013): 3, 289–99. The two opening paragraphs of the conclusion are derived from Perry L. Glanzer, "Building the Good Life: Using Identities to Frame Moral Education in Higher Education," *Journal of College and Character* 14, no. 2 (May 2013): 177–84. The *Journal of Beliefs & Values* and *The Journal of College and Character* are affiliated with Taylor and Francis (www.tandfonline.com). An earlier version of chapter 12 was published as Perry L. Glanzer, Jonathan P. Hill, and Jessica A. Robinson, "Emerging Adults' Conceptions of Purpose and the Good Life: A Classification and Comparison," *Youth & Society* (2015): 1–19.

Introduction

Searching for Meaning and
Purpose in College: A Dying Quest?

I didn't think that I needed college to help me think about my purpose in life. . . . I don't think that four years in college is going to give you that answer anyway.

—twenty-two-year-old Ivy League student

But universities are not really where we look for answers to our life questions.[1]

—C. John Sommerville, Professor Emeritus

"So, what's the point of it all? Like, why am I trying to get great grades? Why am I trying to win all these competitions?" Andrea, a sophomore comparative literature major at an Ivy League university, recalled asking these questions in high school. As one would expect from an Ivy League student, she relentlessly pursued personal accomplishments. Yet, on her way to climbing the ladder of success, she suddenly realized she had no idea where the ladder led her. She started asking, "Why am I doing art? Why am I doing all these clubs and leadership positions?"

Now in college, she admits, "I'm definitely still trying to figure it out. I don't know." She views all her high school achievements as tainted by ignoble motives or purposes. "Everything I did in high school seems pretty selfish. I mean, I see success or driving toward success as very selfish even though that's what I've always tried to do." The new college environment in which she currently finds herself has challenged her previous purpose, albeit in a manner that she did not anticipate. Being a student who sought accomplishments and measured her worth by success, Andrea encounters the Ivy League experience as one that undermines her sense of value—something she also perceives as occurring with other Ivy League students. "Yeah, I think everyone struggles with it. You go from being the genius at your high school to being, like, 'Hi, you're middle of the pack.'" She finds it leads to certain undesirable vices, "So it's easy to just slip around and be jealous and think, 'Oh I'm not as good as that,' or, 'I wish I had that.'" She envies her friends at other schools who have not faced this particular struggle: "Honestly, I feel like a lot of my state school friends and people who went to smaller colleges are much happier. There's a lot of concentrated excellence [here]." She longs for an institution where "you can just be at the top and feel good about yourself all the time."

Since Andrea now perceives that her past approach to success was unfulfilling and an inadequate basis for her worth, does she now believe there is something more to life? "I definitely think we all have a bigger purpose in life. I definitely think so," she insists. Despite being adamant about the existence of a larger purpose, she admits, "I'm just not quite sure what that is." When asked whether this grand purpose comes from some external source or whether we all individually figure it out, she admits, "I don't know." At most, Andrea has reached a provisional answer that began to form in high school. "I guess the answer I arrived at is: I just wanted to be the best version of myself I could be and also get as much success as I could, so I could make the world a better place." Since personal success no longer seems like a sufficient purpose in life to Andrea, she now believes this additional purpose of helping change the world can almost redeem her "selfish pursuits." The key word is *almost*. She notes, "But I guess if you look at it in the context of I'm trying to get this success so that I can help others, then it [be]comes selfless, *almost*, but I want to say I feel like that's something that I tell myself to make myself feel better."

Searching and Finding Meaning and Purpose:
The New Social Science

Finding meaning and purpose in life are perennial human quests. As Aristotle said over 2,300 years ago, "And if, like archers, we have a target, are we not more likely to hit the right mark?"[2] If we discover what gives our life meaning, then we identify a map we can use to orient ourselves in the midst of life's confusing circumstances. When we find purpose, we obtain a motivation for proceeding in a certain direction that can be used to guide our life within the world of that map. Achieving that purpose, or at least making progress toward it, then contributes to our sense of a meaningful life. Humans have sought to meet these vital needs for meaning and purpose for thousands of years.

While the search for meaning and purpose appears to be a constant throughout human history, there are characteristics about our current time period that make this search different from any other previous time, particularly for college students. We possess more knowledge than ever before about the nature and substance of the search. In fact, though the topic of meaning and purpose has been subject to contemplation for millennia, only recently have social scientists undertaken more systematic study of meaning and purpose by examining ways in which adolescents and emerging adults develop their understanding of these topics.[3]

These studies reveal that a purpose focused beyond one's self proves to be a critical component of positive youth development. Finding and having such a purpose contributes to happiness, identity development, positive affect, hope, resiliency, better school performance, and life satisfaction.[4] Furthermore, adolescents with this kind of purpose prove less likely to drink alcohol, use drugs, be depressed or have suicidal thoughts, and resort to violence.[5] Interestingly, Andrea appears to be at the point of realization that her self-oriented goals have failed to satisfy her, and she is ready to begin an exploration of beyond-the-self-oriented purposes.

What can and should higher education contribute to the development of this kind of purpose? This book explores this question by examining how college students attempt to answer questions of meaning and purpose. In particular, it examines the important social, educational, and cultural influences that shape both their quest and the answers they find.

Ironically, while systematic empirical study has increased in the past five decades, the actual attention to the subjects of meaning and purpose in the curriculum appears to have diminished at all levels of education. Our secularized K–12 public education, the dominant form of education for the vast majority of Americans, largely shuns controversial topics that touch on diverse religious or secular worldviews and philosophies of life. Consequently, it largely avoids the topic of meaning and purpose in life.[6] It is little wonder then that Andrea has not encountered this subject in an educational setting prior to attending a university.

Andrea would appear to be in a perfect position to receive a higher education that explores the big questions about life. One might think that classes that provide a liberal arts education about life's meaning and purpose could open her mind to the variety of possibilities and help her think deeply about this all important question. Yet, Anthony Kronman argues in his book, *Education's End: Why Our Colleges and Universities Have Given Up on the Meaning of Life*, that Andrea will be unlikely to encounter this type of education in her university as well. He claims, "I have watched the question of life's meaning lose its status as a subject of organized instruction . . ."[7] Indeed, one national study found that 62 percent of students reported never discussing these matters with faculty.[8] Kronman maintains that research concerns and political correctness distract faculty and, therefore, universities from helping students in this area.

While Kronman's basic argument likely holds some truth, when we began this study we suspected that the story was more complex. As scholars of sociology and higher education, we knew that the social environments and cultures shaping higher education likely play a role in the attention paid to meaning and purpose. We believed that students' own stories and experiences would help shine light on these intricate realities. Thus, we undertook the research in this book using the lens of students' experiences. We wanted to uncover the complex realities shaping students' search for meaning and purpose.

Consider Andrea's story. In some ways, it would appear to support Kronman's argument. She claims that she has not taken any classes that have helped explore meaning and purposes:

> I mean, I'm in the Intro to Moral Philosophy class. I haven't really done any of the readings, but I don't feel like his goal is to shape that [purpose and meaning], though. I feel like his goal is just to give us an Introduction of Philosophy, which is really boring. I mean it's interesting but I just don't understand why they're debating those things when they can be doing other things that are more helpful.

Part of her negative attitude stems from the fact that the professor to which she refers, instead of exploring answers, appears to focus on challenging her belief in God. For instance, Andrea notes, "In the third lecture he comes up to the podium and he's this big philosophy guy and he's like, 'God cannot provide a foundation for morality' and all this stuff." The lecture, she admits, did not seriously undermine her faith because "I don't understand the class material anyways."

Andrea also claims to have had no extended discussions with professors outside of class regarding these issues. The most contact she has is with "one of my writing professors from last year [who] was really nice and she'll e-mail me sometimes about different things. 'Oh, I saw you at the . . . opera concert,' or something." If she seeks any advice from this professor, it's strictly professional, "it's always, 'hey I'm applying for . . . this writing center position,' or something and she's like, 'oh, okay. Let me write you a letter of recommendation' or something." Again, Andrea's account may possibly support Kronman's claim that "the research ideal has helped undermine deeper student-faculty relationships."[9]

Yet, Andrea's story also gives insight into the multiple ways that her own background, desires, and the larger college environment have all influenced her search for meaning and purpose through paths that go beyond the classroom or contact with faculty. To begin, she never really practiced talking about meaning and purpose with her parents. "I just feel weird talking with them about that," she claims. "I feel like my parents can act pretty childish sometimes, I mean, most of the time I feel like . . . instead of me consulting them for help, I feel like they consult me for help." She complains, "Whenever my mom calls me she'll just give me a report of everything that my sister has done and then she'll ask me, "So what do I do about [her sister]?" Even beyond her parents, it appears that Andrea did not have meaningful adult mentors who would serve as guides as she journeyed toward finding purpose.

Moreover, while universities and faculty members may have some responsibility in shaping whether conversations about meaning and purpose are cultivated on campus, students themselves may contribute to an environment where matters of meaning and purpose are neglected. In Andrea's case, her own resistance plays a role. In other words, part of the reason that Andrea has not found support in a quest for meaning and purpose at her university is that she did not really expect or even desire support in this area. The lack of faculty mentors Andrea mentions above does not bother her. When asked if she is interested in adult mentors, she admits, "Yeah, not really. I don't pursue them." What Andrea understands by adult mentorship is limited to professionals dealing with specific sectors of life, "I guess they have a counseling service and the health center and they have a career services department that I can always go and talk to, but I never do. I should, I should . . ." The same lack of interest and pursuit also applies to her religious identity. For instance, while Andrea describes herself as a Christian and attended a small twenty-person Chinese-Baptist church growing up, church involvement is not something she has pursued in college. The problem, she admits, is that she took her Christian faith for granted: "I never even thought to question [my religious beliefs] . . . It wouldn't have been a problem, just nobody did it."

Now that Andrea is in college, she perceives the larger environment as inhibiting her quest for meaning and purpose. Andrea suggests that part of her lack of interest in finding adult mentors in college stems from the struggles of being a minority. Although Andrea's mother is Asian and her father is Caucasian, she does not define minority solely in ethnic or racial terms. She also refers to other identities pertaining to politics, geography, and religion, ". . . it's really a liberal campus, and I guess I'm pretty conservative. I mean, I'm from the South. I'm Christian . . . things like that." Various challenges to these identities have also provoked instability with her religious identity and faith.

> It's definitely different now. After I came to college, it's kinda like believing in Santa Claus and then all of a sudden you wake up and you're like—that don't make sense! [*Laughs*]. So it was kinda like that when I came to [our university] and after a few months I was just . . . I don't know if that makes sense anymore.

She has not stopped believing in God, but she admits, "I felt like if I . . . kept going the way I was going I would stop eventually. . . . [My university] has definitely made me question a lot of things about my faith."

She confesses that what undermined her beliefs is not what she has learned in class but the peer culture in the co-curricular dimension of college life, "Yeah, friends and just all the prevailing voices on campus, like in the newspaper." The major challenges had to do with "just hearing so many dissenting points of view . . . everywhere. Not just friends. Like in the newspaper or groups on-campus, postering, and stuff like that." She clarifies, however, that exposure to diversity was not the problem; it was that the diversity appeared uneven. "It wasn't necessarily that everyone had different viewpoints it was just the [views different than her own] were the loudest," she says. Now, Andrea confesses that when it comes to her religious beliefs, "I've avoided thinking or talking about it." When asked why, she haltingly admits, "It's just scary. I still believe in everything. I'm just having trouble grounding that belief in some sort of . . . I don't know how to ground my faith in something. I don't know what to ground it in." She, however, realizes that the avoidance strategy is not one she can maintain: "I definitely have to come back to it, and I know that."

The same peer culture also challenges her moral outlook and her relation-ships with others. As an example, Andrea does not find the hook-up culture attractive, but she also finds voices speaking out against it to be silenced. "When people criticize other people's culture, some people say, 'Oh, 'you're slut-sham-ing . . . I don't know. You really can't speak out against any of that." As a result, she feels like the hook-up culture "is prevalent everywhere now." She herself does not participate in the hook-up culture and has a serious boyfriend. She admits that this relationship crowds out other social activities. "I feel that's the reason I don't really have friends [*laughs*] in college . . . we invest so much time in each other." When it comes to purpose and meaning, Andrea and her boyfriend do have occasional discussions and agree on most things, but she notes "he doesn't believe in God or anything like that." If they talk about those topics, it is largely in relationship to their future professional goals. Her boyfriend wants "to go into investment banking and stuff like that because, I don't know. You come onto campus and it just infects you."

Andrea's search for foundations on which to build her meaning and pur-pose could conceivably extend beyond the classroom, but she finds very little guidance in this area as well. In *Helping Students Find Purpose*, Robert Nash and Michelle Murray note the void that many students encounter when struggling to ground their personal search for meaning and purpose. "There are few opportunities on most college campuses—either inside or outside the conventional classroom, and as curricula become more vocational and professionally driven—for students to develop these strong background beliefs and ideals."[10] Andrea's story appears to confirm Nash and Murray's claim. Andrea feels she has no one to talk to about her struggles with meaning and purpose. Her boyfriend does not share her worldview, she does not know a professor who shares her perspective, and she feels like the ethos and environment at her university are hostile to these types of conversations. Astoundingly, she feels alone in her search for meaning and purpose in a university that traditionally has prided itself on being a safe and welcome place to explore answers to these types of questions.

When this becomes the case, discussions about meaning and purpose become odd conversations disconnected from normal academic life. As one twenty-two-year-old attending a liberal arts college told us, "I guess when I hear about people talking about issues of meaning and purpose, it seems like something that stereotypically hippies would discuss on pot." At best, a common context for sharing these struggles could be found on certain campus student groups, such as campus religious, service, or social justice groups. When we asked Andrea about this option, she admits she did not attend a Christian group that interested her, "Yeah, [it] just didn't happen, because I wanted to, but the reason why I didn't go is because it's always on Friday nights, and I always tutor on Friday nights." When asked why she tutors, she admits, "It's good money [*laughs*], and it's fun."

Although not explicitly stated, Andrea appears to still be guided primarily by a particular vision of the good life associated with money, achievement, and success. She admits, "Making a lot of money is my career aspiration," and even confesses, "I know that shouldn't be my goal, but it's always definitely there." She justifies the goal by thinking of using her money for others, "I'm always like, 'Okay, the first thing I'm gonna do is I'm gonna buy my parents a house or something or buy my dad this car and,' I don't know. Stuff like that." Her long-term goals are simply "to make a lot of money for my parents and to have kids. That's it."

When discussing these goals, she reverts back to her old view, so that her university degree functions as one more rung on the ladder to material success:

> I feel like college is definitely important for people from the lower-middle class, because . . . if you don't have that financial backing then at least you have this degree and sort of your version of your financial backing. . . . It's the way you prove yourself—your degree.

In addition, she admits, "It's also really fun! [*laughs*]. It's like four years so you cannot be a kid and not be an adult and just sort of be in that in-between place. . . ." The university, she believes, helps contribute to this atmosphere, "It really coddles you. . . . I feel less responsible here than I did at home." Being in college and having time to figure out one's purpose, she admits "is really a luxury." She, of course, is not complaining, "Being coddled is always nice." Still, she does have some pangs of conscience about this coddling, "I just feel kind of guilty."

Her university, her generation, and her own inclinations, she confesses, have not helped to move in the selfless direction she desires to move. The university, she admits, does not have a "mold-goal." They are not trying to shape students' character beyond "want[ing] us to be as successful as possible and . . . to always question and . . . go out and pioneer." In fact, she contends it fosters a privileged mentality, "I feel very entitled on-campus. I feel like the administration over and over is fortifying the sensitive type. I feel like we're supposed to go out and be entitled and to just take what we need." When asked whether she agrees with this unique type of formation or molding of students' affections, she admits, "I don't know. I'm not sure." Ultimately, she perceives that, like her, the institution is perhaps conflicted about its purpose:

> So, I feel like they tell us that, and it's—you pay and you go out and serve the world. And at the same time, they provide us with all these different opportunities to go and work for a place like Goldman-Sachs or something like that.

She also claims her generation does not help. She complains, "This generation . . . we're so about ourselves—we have trouble thinking about others . . . I don't know. I just look around and I feel like everyone, or at least my generation, is so self-absorbed."

She also does not exclude herself: "Honestly, I'm definitely a part of it." Andrea actually returns to blaming her own desires and longing for achievement. She sees her decision to attend this Ivy League institution as bordering on self-deceptive. She says she justified her decision by saying,

> Well, I'm going to make myself the best I can be and then, when I'm equipped with those resources that I learn at [my university] I can go out and help people. I feel like I was just sort of . . . finding a way to justify that, and not really believing what I was saying.

Although it would appear that Andrea believes helping others may be her higher purpose, she actually concludes at the end of the interview, "I really don't have a clear definition of my meaning and my purpose." Unfortunately, she finds herself alone and lost in her journey. Still, Andrea contends that she is waiting to discover something, "I also feel like there is truth in that we all have a higher purpose and that we need to find it. I think the hardest thing is waiting for it and finding it."

Exploring the Complex Realities

Andrea's struggles to find meaning and purpose stem from numerous factors including her personal desires and longings, family background, friends, faculty interactions, and her particular university culture. These are further embedded in a broader educational culture that emphasizes the acquisition of technical knowledge within a broad affirmation of the values of material success and liberal individualism. These are all further compounded by shifting cultural understandings of what adulthood means and how one successfully reaches it. These factors play a role in making her search for a purpose all the more challenging. Indeed, Andrea's story appears to reinforce the conclusion that universities provide little help in students' search for purpose. In Andrea's case, she does not perceive the Ivy League university she attends as aiding her search. Andrea has not met friends or adult mentors to whom she would look to for guidance about life's purpose or meaning. If Andrea's story is typical, scholars' claims that universities and colleges have largely given up helping students with their search for meaning and purpose would appear to be accurate. How does Andrea's story compare to other university students at different institutions?

This book seeks both to answer that question and to help us understand the challenge of fostering discussions about meaning and purpose within higher education institutions. To conduct this investigation, we used a mixed methods approach to gain insight into how college students currently identify and develop meaning and purpose in life. In all, we rely on six data sets—three of them qualitative and three of them quantitative. We rely most heavily on two sets of semistructured interviews that were conducted for this book (numbers 1 and 2 below). Certain chapters also rely on additional quantitative or qualitative data, most of it not directly collected for this book. For ease of reference throughout the work, we will give each of the data sets a short name in bold below (please see Appendix A for more details about the methodology associated with the gathering and analysis of this data).

1. **75 National Qual**: This set of seventy-five semistructured interviews was gathered by the Gallup® organization from a national sample of college students. While Kronman's book and Andrea's

experience may provide evidence that "our" universities, particularly research universities, have given up on meaning and purpose, we know that university experiences are far from uniform. We sought to interview students from different types of institutions in various regions of the country both in this set and in the next.

2. **110 Targeted Qual**: We gathered another set of 110 semistructured interviews from college students at ten different college campuses located throughout the United States. The ten institutions were chosen to represent a diverse set of institutional identities, with a particular emphasis placed on the religious nature of the institution. We suspected that colleges and universities would vary widely in how they conceive of forming student meaning and purpose, and we wanted to capture these different institutional contexts as we made sense of students' experiences. Recent research has also called for further understanding how students' religious and nonreligious identity may play a role in their own quest for meaning and purpose. To adequately explore this, we made concerted efforts to make sure we obtained students from diverse religious and nonreligious backgrounds.[11] Interviewees were selected from a state research university, a regional public university, an Ivy League university, a Jewish university, an evangelical university, a Mormon university, a Catholic university, a Baptist research university, a Lutheran liberal arts college, and a nonreligious liberal arts college.[12]

3. **NSYR Qual**: One of our chapters (chapter 12) draws on the third wave of in-person interviews for the National Study of Youth and Religion (NSYR), which consisted of 230 in-depth personal interviews with eighteen- to twenty-three-year-olds.

In addition to these qualitative interviews, we also drew on empirical results from three nationally representative quantitative surveys:

1. **Gallup® Quant:** Based on our qualitative findings, we devised a survey instrument for a national survey of 2,503 college students undertaken by the Gallup® organization. These findings are primarily discussed in chapters 6 and 10.

2. **CSBV Quant**: The College Students Beliefs and Values (CSBV) survey is a national study of college students undertaken by the Higher Education Research Institute (HERI) as part of the Spiri-

tuality in Higher Education research project. This data is used in chapters 8, 9, and 10.

3. **NSYR Quant:** We drew on the first and third waves of a national survey of U.S. adolescents (13–17) tracked into emerging adults (18–23), which was conducted as a component of the National Study of Youth and Religion (NSYR). We use this data in chapter 3.

From this mixed methods empirical examination, we gained valuable insights into the complex ways students currently construct and derive meaning and purpose in their lives. We also obtained a deeper understanding about the role that higher education and other aspects of students' social environment, including parents, religion or other belief systems, and communities play in this search.

Our Background, Assumptions, Findings, and Argument

When undertaking this kind of mixed methods research of big questions, we think it is important to share our own background and interest in this project. Professionally, we are social science researchers. Two of us specialize in the study of higher education in particular, and all of us specialize in the study of moral and religious issues. As already alluded to, part of our interest in the question of how college students think about meaning and purpose emerged from Anthony Kronman's provocative thesis that colleges and universities have given up on the search for meaning. As social scientists, we were disappointed by the lack of empirical evidence to back-up his claims. Although we were sympathetic to aspects of his argument, we suspected the on-the-ground experiences of students were more complex.

In this regard, we found a recent book by Alexander Astin, Helen Astin, and Jennifer Lindholm, *Cultivating the Spirit*, to be much more satisfying and helpful.[13] It also provided some of the inspiration for the direction of this particular study. They found that half of students report that "to find my purpose in life" is a "very important" reason for attending college (more than eight in ten report it is at least "somewhat important").[14] In short, if purpose has been exiled from the university, it did not seem to us that students had received the memo. The authors not only provided empirical research to help us understand students' search for meaning and purpose, but they also identified important questions for future study. In particular, they noted, "How particular aspects of . . . students' religious faiths may specifically serve to enhance quest inclinations warrants further focused study."[15]

All three of us are Christians who are employed at faith-based institutions of higher education. Our own experiences working in these environments has led us to see up close the myriad ways that faith-based colleges and universities intentionally shape the institutional and cultural context within which students form ideas about their life's purpose. We also recognize the substantial role that personal background and religious identity play for students in providing the language and social script for developing meaning and purpose. Although we could see these factors operating on our own campuses, we wanted to develop a much broader, more complete, assessment of the interplay between these institutional and individual factors.

Ultimately, we believe that diversity lies behind both the collegiate world's interest in and difficulties with matters of meaning of purpose. One of the reasons discussions about purpose and meaning have received a tremendous amount of attention lately, we argue, is that this approach holds the potential for being a solution to addressing big questions in a way that respects diversity. Now that nearly three-fourths of students currently attend state universities, wrestling with big questions in a way that respects ideological pluralism becomes vitally important.[16] After all, in a liberal democracy we celebrate the fact that we are not coerced into a particular life purpose by the state or an established religion, and individuals can freely create and embrace diverse meanings and purposes.

Campus talk about meaning and purpose also shows greater potential for inclusivity over other approaches that have historically been used in American higher education—such as faith or spiritual development. For example, in recent years spirituality has been the broad umbrella term under which discussions of meaning and purpose may appear in order to sidestep faculty and students who are uncomfortable using the language of faith (since many scholars understand spirituality to include nonreligious students and faculty). Nevertheless, the term *spirituality* still poses problems. The term may very well alienate nonreligious, atheist, and agnostic students and faculty who do not consider themselves spiritual.[17] Tim Clydesdale points out that the use of the term "varies widely" and "means little to the overwhelming majority (more than 80 percent) of adolescents and young adults, who struggle to even define it."[18] He found it unhelpful in promoting conversations and noted "in two exploration programs that deployed it in well-intended efforts to be inclusive, it sent students and educators running for the door."[19] In contrast, diverse types of students, we discovered, have no trouble talking about what gives their life meaning and purpose. They recognize that everyone searches for meaning and purpose and needs to find it. This need to find purpose proves even more important in light of the recent social science research highlighting the benefits of having a certain kind of "beyond-the-self" purpose.

Despite Anthony Kronman's claim that colleges and universities have given up on issues of meaning and purpose, our findings reveal a different story. We find that students experience colleges and universities as a unique place they can have these discussions. Although some students have experienced discussions with parents, friends, and adults before college about these matters, as Andrea's story indicates, they are often quite limited. In contrast, for many students, college becomes one of the primary places where they encounter the freedom and opportunity to consider these questions with peers and mentors.

Still, helping students with this process has become harder due to the peculiar difficulties of higher education in a contemporary liberal democracy. We must recognize that the incredible pluralism within America's universities *does* make discussions about meaning and purpose more complicated and messy, but we would also argue it simultaneously makes them more necessary and interesting. Part of the messiness stems from the fact that pluralism creates diversity at several different levels: (1) the diverse experiences with meaning and purpose prior to college; (2) the diverse emphases on questing and finding; (3) the diverse meanings, purposes, and visions of the good life; (4) the diverse university environments in which students experience this quest; and (5) the diverse influences of students' worldviews on their formation of meaning and purpose. If we are going to talk to students about meaning and purpose, we need to understand and appreciate all of these diverse elements and challenges. We must also recognize and take advantage of the ways that this diversity can both enhance and inhibit conversations about meaning and purpose. In other words, we believe this situation creates unique challenges, but it also provides potential resources that can be mined to enhance these conversations. We briefly summarize some of the points we will be making about these five types of diversity below.

1. *The diverse levels of student experience with meaning and purpose prior to college.* Similar to their academic preparation, students will come into college with a range of experiences regarding their development of purpose. Some will have had extensive prior discussions with parents, peers, and mentors about these matters, while others will have rarely ever discussed meaning and purpose. Just as we have various types of academic support, students may need different kinds of purpose development support.

2. *The diverse emphases on questing and finding.* We will argue that our findings reveal we need to value both questing and finding. We must recognize that some students have found their

meaning and purpose, and others struggle to find their purpose. We should also be aware that if colleges and universities want to foster meaning and purpose development they must help students do three things: explore various meanings and purposes, find and build meaning and purpose, and critically examine those meanings and purposes they currently embrace.

3. *The diverse meanings, purposes, and understandings of the good life of students.* We need to understand the diversity of meanings, purposes, life goals, and conceptions of the future good life students embrace. In this study we sought to explore the possible similarities and differences between these terms by asking students specific questions about each of these concepts: (a) meaning, (b) purpose, (c) life goals, and (d) the good life. In other words, in our research we did not define these words and concepts for the students. Instead, we let them provide their own understanding of the terms through the answers to these questions (for more details about our methodology see Appendix A). The results, as we will see in chapters 5, 6, 7, and 12 reveal that students articulate some important similarities and differences in their answers to these questions that both confirm and depart from past scholarly findings in this area.[20] Most importantly, it is necessary to recognize that meaning and purpose are two different things. Meaning for students is usually understood as something universal, and purpose is understood as something unique to an individual. While virtually every student we interviewed had found meaning, over a third of students claimed not to have a purpose. Students mainly derive meaning and purpose from ten particular purpose/meaning ingredients that fit within three broad categories: Self-Achiever purposes, Relationalist purposes, and Transcendent purposes. The Self-Achievers largely derive their sources of meaning and purpose according to some individual accomplishment, experience, or state of being. Relationalists found meaning through either exhibiting a virtue in relationship with others (e.g., serving or loving) or simply relating to a particular kind of person (family member or friend). Transcendents found meaning through a divine being (e.g., God), religion, or a particular transcendent moral ideal to which they wanted to persuade or move others (i.e., "I want to change the world."). We contend that one job of the university should include helping purposeless students find purpose and

helping Self-Achievers consider beyond-the-self purpose ingredients (from the Relationalist and Transcendent types).

4. *The diverse university environments in which students experience this quest.* Despite what Kronman, Nash, and Murray have argued, we find that within the full range of universities there are still plenty of curricular and co-curricular elements that contribute to discussions about meaning and purpose. We identify these important elements that exist at almost all universities. We also realize that we need to recognize that institutions have different cultures and missions that influence students' quest for meaning and purpose and their experience of purpose discussions. Since public universities must approach issues of meaning and purpose carefully and avoid promoting or favoring a particular ideology or worldview, students expect less help in this area from such institutions (although we are skeptical that public institutions can truly be "value-free"). In contrast, students realize that private, faith-based universities will be interested in promoting conversations about meaning and purpose within the context of their religious identity and in light of religiously transcendent purposes. Not surprisingly, we found these contexts not only influenced students' expectations, but they also made an important difference in students' experiences. The more pluralistic the setting, the less likely students are going to expect to address these issues, the less likely they are to feel comfortable talking about these matters, and the less likely they are to expect their professors to address these matters (c.g., Andrea's experience with her professor). We contend that these realities reinforce the importance of sustaining a system with a wide diversity of universities, including those universities that draw from a common transcendent mission. Such universities are more likely to nurture a culture where trust can be established between faculty, staff, and students that helps cultivate conversations about meaning and purpose.

5. *The diverse worldviews of students.* Finally, we address the extent to which discussions about meaning and purpose prove inclusive of all students (versus discussions about faith development or spirituality). In general, we find that all students explore and support a wide range of meanings and purposes. Yet, there are some important differences in how students engage these matters. The most fundamental difference we discover is between theistic and nontheistic students. Theistic students in general

tend to demonstrate greater support for both questing and finding purpose. We should be clear that we do not mean that one must be religious to have a purpose. The difference is one of degree. We believe our qualitative analysis helps us understand a possible reason for the difference between theistic and nontheistic students in these discussions that we explore in part III.

Overall, we conclude that every university and every student should engage in these conversations, and each can draw on a wide variety of resources to do so. Moreover, we will also argue that universities should do more than provide support for conversations about meaning and purpose. Colleges and universities should encourage students to consider and wrestle with the importance of "beyond-the-self" purposes and conceptions of the good life that incorporate "beyond-the-self" purposes. Yet, if they are going to undertake this task, they must do so with empirical knowledge about students' experiences and not merely general impressions based on personal experience.

The Map and Destination of the Book

To present our findings and argument, we divide our examination into four parts. Part I provides the historical and precollege background context for understanding contemporary college students' development of meaning and purpose. We begin in chapter 1 by providing a historical and cultural analysis of the trends associated with thinking about purpose and meaning in life. In particular, we supply a historical and sociological account of the forces, such as secularization, professionalization, and the marginalization of religion and ethics that transformed how colleges and universities address purpose and meaning. This account differs in a number of important ways from one recent explanation of these forces. In addition, we also recount how young people have moved steadily toward more utilitarian approaches to education and life plans.

Next, we dig into the realities of students' search for meaning and purpose as they begin to figure out their quest. Chapter 2 begins this process by drawing on the wealth of scholarly findings and our own semistructured interviews to overview the crucial stage before students enter college, during which they begin to develop their own views about meaning and purpose. We will examine the role relational experiences with parents, grandparents, friends, youth mentors, religious leaders, and teachers play in shaping how young people report thinking about issues of meaning and purpose before college. We end the first part with chapter 3, which draws on quantitative data from the NSYR survey to identify particular social influences associated with the presence of purpose.

This chapter provides a larger empirical map of purpose for emerging adults and helps to reinforce some of the findings from the previous chapter, as well as anticipate some of our subsequent findings. Not surprisingly, an important finding is that participation in higher education plays a key role in developing purpose for emerging adults.

Part II of the book delves into the topic of how college students think about meaning and purpose. Chapter 4 begins by providing four extended examples of students searching for meaning and purpose. These examples serve as helpful touchstones that will allow us to introduce and illustrate important themes regarding the similarities and differences in purpose construction we found among students. This chapter demonstrates that Andrea is merely one of a broad range of types of students we found in our interviews.

Chapter 5 proceeds to explore the ways college students think about meaning using our 75 National Qual and 110 Targeted Qual interviews with students. We illustrate how the three groups already introduced—Self Achievers, Relationalists, and Transcendents—think about meaning and also provide examples of important subdivisions within these groups.

Chapter 6 examines the answer to the question: What are the types of purpose that inspire young people today? Like chapter 4, we explore possible answers by drawing on the 75 National Qual and 110 Targeted Qual interviews. We discuss three important results. First, students draw from the same categories of ingredients to form meaning as they do purpose. The ingredients for both fit into three categories: the Individual Achievers, the Relationalists, and the Transcendents. Second, although similar in some ways, our findings from the Gallup® Quant data reveal key differences in the way students view these various purpose types.

While young people rarely claim that their lives do not have meaning, over a quarter of our interview participants admitted they had not identified their particular purpose in life. In chapter 7, we provide an in-depth appraisal of these purposeless young adults. We call them the Directionless. Like the Individual Achievers, Relationalists, and Transcendents from the previous chapter, there are various types of Directionless: the Directionless Doubters, the Job Searchers, and the General Directionless. We provide narrative examples that help us understand the various types of Directionless and then discuss what, if anything, higher education may offer to this group of students.

Part III shifts from looking at students' views of meaning and purpose to examining the social contexts that influence their development of meaning and purpose while in college. The two chapters in this section examine how students perceive college influences their purpose development in the curricular and co-curricular realms. In chapter 8, where we cover the influence of the curricular world, we examine Anthony Kronman's argument in *Education's End* that the faculty's preoccupation with research and the leadership's concern with political correctness undermine the university's ability to address issues of meaning and purpose.[21] As we have already alluded to, one motivation for our study is that we suspected that the story is more complicated than Kronman's presentation. Particularly, we expected and designed our study to uncover what unique approaches a wide variety of secular and religious institutions take. What we found, which we report in the chapter, surprised us.

Despite the common perception that students largely discover life wisdom in the curriculum, the actual dimension of college life where students explore matters of meaning and purpose the most is the co-curricular, the subject of chapter 9. This area includes the role of social clubs and other student groups, friendships, romantic relationships, roommates, and the rest of the college experience outside the formal curriculum. Interestingly, this is the area that has empirically been given the least amount of attention. In this chapter, we will draw on our interviews to shed light on the ways in which this arena shapes students' views of meaning and purpose. In particular, we give attention to the factor that made the evangelical institution a rare case of comprehensive purpose development—conversations with faculty outside the classroom.

Part IV delves into the heart and soul of the book and the subject of purpose development. It looks at how students' religious or nonreligious identity, and the religious or secular identity of the college or university they attend, shape this quest. It reveals that the specific religious and nonreligious traditions have a distinct, yet not determinative, influence on how students conceptualize meaning and purpose. Since we found that the most important divide exists between theistic and nontheistic students, whether on religious or nonreligious campuses, we devote two different chapters to these two types of students. Chapter 10 seeks to understand the influence of some of the religious narratives through which students make sense of their quest for meaning and purpose. It reports on the diversity of ways theistic students' particular religious beliefs shape their purpose development. Chapter 11 then discusses the singular way that nontheistic students both celebrate their freedom with purpose development and the particular challenge they face creating purpose in what they perceive as a universe that lacks an overarching purpose.

Chapter 12 addresses what we call the end of purpose and meaning. In particular, it examines the relationship between students' stated views about their meaning and purpose and their conception of the future—including their plans for the immediate future, their overall life goals, and whether they believe in the afterlife. In some cases, a clear disconnect exists between what students describe as their purpose and what they describe as their future plans. This chapter draws on empirical findings from our two sets of semistructured interviews (75 National Qual and 110 Targeted Qual) as well as the NSYR interviews in order to explore the similarities and differences between students' vision of the future and their stated purpose.

The concluding chapter pulls together our main findings in order to summarize what we discovered about the complex ways students develop purpose and meaning and the particular role that higher education plays in the process. We also propose future avenues of research and what scholars and practitioners within higher education might learn from these findings as they work to help students discover deeper meaning and purpose. Of course, the success of such proposals may depend on whether leaders within higher education want to help students on this quest for meaning and purpose and whether students themselves expect and hope for such aid.

Part I

The Context of the Quest

Chapter 1

Are Colleges Giving Up on Life's Meaning and Purpose?

The Historical and Cultural Context

Beyond academic and research excellence, universities have forgotten their main purpose, which is to help students learn who they are, to search for a larger purpose for their lives, and to leave college as better human beings.

—Parker Palmer and Arthur Zajonc[1]

Most students, especially those enrolled in liberal arts programs, have a passionate (if intermittent) interest in the question of what makes a life valuable and fulfilling . . . But like their teachers, they regard the question as a personal one that cannot usefully be studied in a public way.

—Anthony Kronman[2]

An increasing chorus of scholars today laments that colleges and universities fail to help students grapple with issues of meaning and purpose.[3] For example, one recent scholar argued that universities

> have forgotten that the fundamental job of undergraduate education is to turn eighteen- and nineteen-year-olds into twenty-one and twenty-two-year-olds, to help them grow up, to learn who they are, to search for a larger purpose for their lives, and to leave college as better human beings.[4]

Often these scholars claim colleges and universities used to give attention to educating students about life's meaning and purpose, but that today's educational leaders fail to provide help to students eager to discuss these issues. The reasons offered for this failure, though, like the quotes above, diverge.

The purpose of this chapter is to outline the common scholarly narrative explaining higher education's lack of attention to purpose development, examine this narrative critically, and explore three areas where this narrative falls short: (1) explanations of why professors gave up on life's meaning; (2) claims regarding how secular humanists provided and can continue to provide a way forward; and (3) the role that growth, pluralism, and diversity played in the current failure.

To What Extent Was Education about Purpose a Part of Early American Colleges?

Stories of decline sometimes tend to romanticize the past. Because of this tendency, it is helpful to briefly revisit the extent to which scholars believe early American colleges actually focused their educational efforts on developing purpose in students. Since the early American colonists established liberal arts colleges without a graduate faculty of theology, law, and medicine (such as in Europe), the opportunities for exploring these matters resided only in the liberal arts college. Still, the absence of specialized theological faculties did not prevent the generalized integration of theological beliefs within the liberal arts curriculum and the colleges as a whole. Harvard College's early college laws actually stipulated, "Every one shall consider the main end of his life and studies to know God and Jesus Christ which is eternal life. John 17:3."[5] Faculty did not expect students to develop their own conceptions of purpose or to select from a menu of available options. The liberal arts curriculum involved further developing and bolstering one's Christian identity and life purpose. Harvard was not alone. From the founding of Harvard in 1636 to the period before the American Civil War, American institutions of higher education were largely Christian, and their professors shared the belief that they "possessed authoritative wisdom about the meaning of life."[6] Professors were expected to supply students with the intellectual, moral, and spiritual resources to fulfill a life journey with a particular type of meaning and purpose. In this sense, helping students understand their purpose was clearly at the forefront of early American higher education but in a way that would seem foreign to many college students and faculty today.

It should be recognized that this shared endeavor existed in, what was at the time, a radically pluralistic context. The sixteenth-century Reformation had produced deep theological divisions that created an atmosphere of significant theological and metaphysical disagreement over a whole host of religious beliefs. Moreover, colonial and early antebellum America had the most ideologically diverse system of colleges in the world. Nowhere else on the planet would one find colleges supported or started by Congregationalists, Anglicans, Presbyterians, Reformed, Lutherans, Baptists, Quakers, Methodists, Deists, and Moravians in the same region.

Despite this theological and institutional plurality, what undergirded how American colleges approached meaning and purpose in life can be summarized by two shared metaphysical beliefs. First, the leaders of these institutions, even the Deistic founder of the University of Virginia, Thomas Jefferson, shared a belief in what could be considered Judeo-Christian metaphysics: the idea that God set up *both* a moral and natural order and the two are fundamentally inseparable. Therefore, one can discern human purpose through study of the natural order, and one can come to understand the natural order through nature, including human nature. This view tied together the "is" and the "ought" and served to unify the whole curriculum. It particularly shaped the moral philosophy capstone course that students took in virtually every college. In his study of moral philosophy professors, D. H. Meyer observed that the idea that "the entire universe is presided over by a wise, benevolent, and all-powerful deity who has ingeniously contrived the whole operation to serve some moral purpose . . . met little responsible opposition in the early nineteenth century." He also adds, "The belief that man was psychologically adapted to fit into a morally purposive universe seemed, in fact, to have the universal assent of mankind."[7] Where college leaders differed was over the degree to which one could use reason or revelation to discover this moral purpose. Whereas Puritan Congregationalists and Presbyterians tended to distrust human reason and experience, progressive Protestants such as the Quakers and Anglicans placed more faith in both as means of discovering truth and goodness. Deists looked to reason almost exclusively.

Second, although not shared among Deists, Christian educational leaders in America believed human attempts to bear God's image and follow God's moral order required God's gracious help extended through the intervening work of Jesus Christ and the Holy Spirit. Catholics and Protestants, Baptists and Presbyterians differed over the details about how one acquired God's grace, but they did not differ regarding this core belief. One's purpose or meaning involved reconciliation with God and sanctification or recovery of one's true created purpose.

These two foundational beliefs, sustained and nurtured by these communities, proved essential in sustaining the common outlook shared by the Christian colleges before the Civil War, which educated the vast majority of students.[8] Most educational leaders held these two common beliefs and shaped their courses of study in metaphysics as well as natural and moral philosophy according to them.

The Loss of Purpose and Meaning

Although a variety of scholars have discussed what led to the decline of these beliefs and forthright efforts to address meaning and purpose,[9] Anthony Kronman has perhaps examined the topic most extensively in *Education's End: Why*

Our Colleges and Universities Have Given Up on the Meaning of Life. Kronman tells the story in two stages. In the first stage, Kronman's historical narrative points to the rise of the research ideal as the dominant factor that led to the exclusion of questions of meaning and purpose from parts of the curriculum starting in the late nineteenth century. According to the research ideal, "a college or university is, first and foremost, a gathering of academic specialists inspired by their shared commitment to scholarship as a vocation."[10] Teaching, mentoring, and morally developing students becomes secondary in this paradigm. Imported from Germany, this model of the research university, with its emphasis on increasingly specialized knowledge production, eventually displaced the antebellum college model (although not without a fight in some cases).[11] Kronman maintains that the first disciplinary area where scholars abandoned addressing issues of meaning and purpose was science. In the classical curriculum, students in natural philosophy studied how the intricacies and laws of God's created order could lead to an understanding of God's character and larger purposes. Kronman argues:

> By the end of the nineteenth century, the study of nature had been thoroughly disenchanted, in part because of the intensifying demands of research itself, which could be met only if the investigation of the physical world were purged of all moral and theological presumptions. As a result, the physical sciences ceased to be connected with, or have much to contribute to the search for an answer to the question of the meaning of life.[12]

The young social sciences, being created around the turn of the century, which hoped to imitate the scientific approach, would eventually demonstrate the same tendencies. In other words, the first shared metaphysical belief of the early American colleges—the unity of nature and morality—began to unravel.

This led to the second stage of Kronman's story. Since the natural and social sciences gave up addressing meaning and purpose, this change left the humanities to take up the task. Kronman claims that a group of humanities teachers emerged in the late nineteenth and first half of the twentieth century who tried to save the older tradition of addressing the meaning of life in the curriculum or more broadly speaking, "the art of living."[13] The old tradition, however, still needed to be transformed by new approaches and methods. These humanists believed English literature could stimulate the emotions and imagination while provoking one to think about life as a whole. Philosophy divorced from theology could use reason to evaluate the plurality of meaning systems now offered. History could provide a catalog of humanity's cultural achievements. Overall, advocates of this approach, what Kronman calls "secular humanists," believed that higher education could still help one explore the meaning of life even without its Christian foundation and particular view of human fulfillment.[14]

In Kronman's view, however, two movements dismantled the old system and stripped away the power of secular humanism. First, the research ideal and the associated professionalization imported from the natural and social sciences undercut attention to big questions of human meaning and purpose. Second, the "political correctness" of the academy relativized all accounts of life's meanings and disestablished the authority of the Western tradition.

While Kronman's retelling captures part of the story, we believe it leaves out important components. We maintain that we need to think more critically about this narrative and the role that other factors played—including even the role of certain secular humanists—in undermining the university's approach to meaning and purpose.

Why Scientists Gave Up on Life's Meaning

A slightly different story of these important changes is told by Julie Reuben in her book, *The Making of the Modern University: Intellectual Transformation and the Marginalization of Morality*. What Kronman fails to address, but Reuben does, is the important role the emergence of evolutionary models of cultural, societal, and ethical progress played in the late nineteenth century. Influenced by the work of Herbert Spencer, evolutionary models broke out of the confines of the biological sciences. Although these theories presented a serious challenge to the natural theology dominant in the first part of the nineteenth century, they did not remove questions of human purpose and value from the equation. Quite the opposite. When evolutionary theory first appeared, the view emerged that the theory, especially forms of theistic evolution, could actually help with matters of human meaning and purpose. Reuben notes, "Because a wide range of disciplines from geology to sociology adopted evolutionary approaches, many intellectuals believed that these disciplines could be synthesized into an overarching evolutionary philosophy that would offer a comprehensive view of life."[15]

Some thinkers even believed a new evolutionary ethics could be developed and that practices such as eugenics could aid with advances in morality. Orientation courses in evolution were introduced into the curriculum as a means to help provide students with the moral orientation they no longer received from religion. In fact, Reuben observes, "The tendency to find a replacement for religion in an all-encompassing evolutionary theory was common in the late nineteenth century."[16]

This view would find classic expression in John Dewey and James H. Tufts' *Ethics*, first published in 1908 and subsequently revised in 1932. In their view, morality was not found in God's created order, as in the old natural theology, but rather in the ever-changing adaption and evolution of society. They wrote, "A direct influence of science upon morals has come from the general spirit and method of scientific inquiry, and in particular from the doctrine of evolution as presented by Darwin and Spencer."[17] The result of applying evolution to ethics, according to these authors, "places the morals of any given time or people in a perspective that renders them less absolute."[18] Consequently, one cannot refer to a moral order established by God. Instead, one must be a pragmatist:

> The business of reflection in determining the true good cannot be done once for all, as, for instance, making out a table of values arranged in a hierarchical order of higher and lower. It needs to be done, and done over and over and over again, in terms of the conditions of concrete situations as they arise.[19]

In this pragmatic outlook, the research agenda of the natural and social sciences were still tied to notions of moral progress and human welfare. In other words, initially, science and social science professors in the research university had not driven out human purpose; they merely secularized it and approached it scientifically.

Still, by the first decades of the twentieth century, many young science faculty began to reject this model. Reuben remarks that "they began to see the interests of their disciplines in a model of science that stressed the importance of factual description rather than constructive adaptation to the environment and that associated objectivity with the rejection of moral values."[20] This new understanding of science also happily freed the scientists from administrative meddling. This change is where the physical sciences' abandonment of purpose, addressed by Kronman, started to gain traction. Scientists began to become averse to normative ethical questions, including the overall normative question about the purpose of life. We see this historical development as far from inevitable though. These were battles fought in the trenches by faculty and administrators over the very definition of what science would become.[21]

This change had important implications for the course on moral philosophy, a forerunner to many of the social science disciplines. This course was considered the capstone course of the college curriculum and was the primary course where issues of meaning and purpose were directly addressed.[22] From the late 1800s until the 1960s, however, the moral philosophy course, and later ethics courses in general, largely disappeared from the curriculum as a general education requirement with the exception of certain religious schools.[23] The disappearance of the moral philosophy course stemmed partly from the rise of the objective scientific research ideal and also the professionalization and specialization that accompanied it. New disciplines, such as economics, psychology, sociology, and political science also emerged. While initially these fields built on the ethical perspective of the moral philosophy course from which they emerged, they also eventually sought to be more scientific and less freighted with moral concerns.[24] In this respect, the social sciences followed the natural sciences in marginalizing moral concerns from their disciplines in order to establish themselves as more objective or scientific. The disappearance of required natural philosophy and moral philosophy courses that addressed the overall question of the good life led to fewer curricular opportunities for larger conversations about the meaning of life.

Formal ethics courses returned to scientific, social scientific, and professional disciplines starting in the 1960s and '70s, but the professional focus of these courses meant that faculty no longer focused on moral questions beyond the profession.[25] The ethics courses most likely taken by someone majoring in the sciences, social sciences, or related professions, such as nursing or business, would usually consist of courses such as medical ethics, business ethics, or similar professional ethics courses. Unlike earlier moral philosophy courses, which placed the emphasis on developing one's calling within an overarching ethical system, their replacements placed the primacy on the profession and limited focus to the ethical dilemmas that might arise within this bounded context.

Why the Humanities Did Not Save Meaning and Purpose

We also think a closer look at the supposed golden age of secular humanism is warranted. Unfortunately, Kronman somewhat misrepresents the late-nineteenth-century and early-twentieth-century movement of secular humanism. He downplays the fact that some of these efforts were driven less by broad humanistic concerns and more by an attempt to use the university for the national purpose of forming citizens. In Kronman's narrative, the increasing importance of the state in university life receives only a brief mention in his overall historical narrative about the importance of the research ideal for undermining attention to life's meaning and purpose. While he does make passing reference to the 1862 Morill Land Grant Act, which transferred federal lands to the states for the purpose of creating universities devoted to the more practical agricultural and mechanical arts, he fails to follow through on the ideological implications of the nationalization of higher education. By nationalization, we simply mean that the interests and political philosophy of the state increasingly came to dominate the purposes of higher education. While Europe experienced this process before the United States,[26] the predominately private and religious nature of American education led to its delay along with the uniquely American belief that higher education should address the subject of life's overall meaning and purpose in general education.

Whereas before the Civil War the vast majority of students were educated in private religious colleges and state universities were the outliers, a concern with promoting the interests of common political entities instead of denominations led to the promotion of state-sponsored institutions throughout the early twentieth century. As a result, they began educating more and more of the population.[27] This nationalization influenced the United States and transformed the purposes of higher education. Instead of shaping the overall religious identity and purpose of students, universities gradually focused on "education for effective citizenship in a democratic society."[28] Required courses in Western civilization provided a unifying narrative for students without the metaphysical baggage of old theology or moral philosophy courses. Instead, the unity came from a focus on "this worldly" as opposed to "other worldly" citizenship.

If democratic thought provided the common framework, the question eventually emerged for faculty in these state institutions about whether it was even appropriate to address issues of meaning and purpose. In particular, as state institutions more stringently applied First Amendment admonishments to protect the free exercise of religion and avoid religious establishments—or to use the popular language, "the need to maintain a separation between church and state"—faculty became more averse to addressing meaning and purpose.[29] Many educators undertook these limitations with the noblest of goals. Whereas many early state institutions still supported nonsectarian forms of Christianity, educational leaders recognized (or were forced by the Courts to recognize) that America's core principles that prohibited the establishment of religion and protected its free exercise should be applied to state-funded universities in ways that respected non-Christian religions.[30] In other words, the view emerged that state-funded institutions of higher education should avoid indoctrinating students in a particular religion, including specific theological conceptions of life's purpose and meaning. Rather, they should actively recognize pluralism, including a plurality of beliefs about life's purpose. Commonality, instead, should be found not in religious beliefs but in national purpose.[31] As a result of this process, the particular Christian metaphysical commitments (the second of the two metaphysical foundations shared in colonial and antebellum colleges) could no longer be given institutional support in state institutions.

The result was that faculty began recommending a curricular approach that Kronman recommends universities follow today. Similar to scientists who found a substitute for religion in evolutionary ethics, scholars at both secularizing state institutions and private institutions began to view education in the great texts as a secular substitute for religion. As the 1945 Harvard Report on General Education noted:

> There is a sense in which education in the great books can be looked at as a secular continuation of the spirit of Protestantism. As early Protestantism, rejecting the authority and philosophy of the medieval church, placed reliance on each man's personal reading of the Scriptures, so this present movement, rejecting the unique authority of the Scriptures, places reliance on the reading of those books which are taken to represent the fullest revelation of the Western mind.[32]

While many of the proponents of this approach grounded their appeals in references to Western civilization or the promotion of liberal democracy, there was one unique exception. The most well-known proponent of the Great Texts curriculum, University of Chicago president Robert Maynard Hutchins, grounded his appeal to the curriculum in a broader form of humanism that sought to "draw out the elements of our common human nature."[33] Interestingly, this program was actually opposed by leading secular humanists such as John Dewey and Sydney Hook. Dewey believed that Hutchins's reliance on Great Texts and authors such as Plato, Aristotle, and St. Thomas Aquinas and their appeal to "ultimate first principles with their dependent hierarchy of subsidiary principles" proved problematic in that it masked a dangerous form of authoritarianism.[34] Not surprisingly, Kronman does not mention this point when claiming that secular humanists helped advance questions of purpose in the humanities. While there were certainly humanities faculty and programs that align closely with the secular humanist ideal that Kronman paints, the historical narrative, once again, is more complex. Secular humanists such as John Dewey and Sydney Hook did not defend the form of secular humanism that Kronman defends, especially an approach to studying meaning and purpose through the study of great books.

Kronman's claim that humanist attempts to address the meaning of life in the curriculum were undone by the professionalization of the humanities finds wider scholarly support if one only focuses on his claim about the influence of the research ideal.[35] As higher education faculty professionalized, they adopted the attitude described by a contemporary professor when talking about matters of spiritual development and human purpose, "There are many of my colleagues who would say, 'Look, we are at a university, and what I do is math; what I do is history. Moving into this other area is not my competence.'"[36] As humanities departments at universities adopted the modern research ideal, Kronman claims the ideal worked to undermine the values that had sustained both the classical tradition and secular humanism. The focus on original research and narrow specialization, hallmarks of the sciences, became standard procedure in the humanities. The broader goals of enriching humanity and exploring the meaning of life increasingly seemed distant from the day-to-day professional life of college and university faculty in the humanities.

The Contemporary Challenges of Growth, Pluralism, and Diversity

In the late twentieth century, three trends would make a tremendous difference in higher education. First, the number of students attending college and attaining degrees would skyrocket. In 1939 and 1940, only 186,500 bachelor degrees were granted in the United States. After the passage of the G.I. Bill, this number jumped to 432,000 in 1949 to 1950. By 2014, this number would increase to over 1.869 million.[37] Second, the vast majority of these students began attending public institutions. Whereas in the early 1800s the vast majority of students attended private colleges, by 1951 public institutions began educating more Americans than private institutions.[38] In 2014, they educated 73 percent of all students.[39] Finally, the types of students graduating grew more diverse with respect to gender and race.[40] The increase in the number and diversity of students in higher education, as well as the increasingly public context of their education, would pose additional challenges for creating an educational experience addressing meaning and purpose.

With the growth in higher education and the professionalization of the faculty also came the increase in professional schools within universities. Business, engineering, computer science, education, health-related professions, and social work emerged as majors that now graduate a significant percentage of students. Today, the humanities, social and behavioral sciences, and natural sciences only account for a little over 40 percent of degrees.[41] Unless addressed in the shrinking general education requirements, larger reflections about big questions such as life's purpose are often not a part of the curriculum for many preprofessional majors (although they could be). The new professional ethics classes alluded to earlier were also not designed to address larger questions about life's meaning and purpose. Instead, they focused on more narrow ethical dilemmas that arise in the professions. As a result, scholars concerned about meaning and purpose understandably bemoan the "career training orientation of higher education"[42] or "business models of education"[43] as factors influencing the decline in attention to meaning and purpose in contemporary higher education.

Not surprisingly, as the number of professional majors grew, the number of students interested in pursuing practical career goals rather than exploring life's meaning within higher education also burgeoned. One of the most commonly cited statistics documents the drop in the number of students who considered it essential or very important for college to help them develop a meaningful philosophy of life. In 1967, 79.1 percent of college students surveyed considered it essential or very important for college to help them develop a meaningful philosophy of life. By 2014, the percentage had dropped to 44.6 percent.[44]

Despite these changes, Kronman does not blame the students themselves for a decline in an interest in the question of life's meaning. Instead, he focuses on the intellectual culture dominating the humanities. He laments that through the humanities' inordinate support of diversity, multiculturalism, and constructivism, what he labels as expressions of political correctness, the humanities found themselves unable to produce a justification for the necessity of Western literature and values that supported the Great Texts approach. By granting admission to these factors of correctness, professors in the humanities no longer had the confidence to argue their ideas on truth. Now, every source has to be considered equal and pertinent, and a balance has to be achieved by compensating the formerly persecuted minority. As a result, dialogue becomes group representation. Lost, he laments, is "the notion of an old and ongoing conversation that gives each entrant a weighted and responsible sense of connection to the past."[45]

While we would agree that these forces work to undermine the authority of secular humanism, we think he is underestimating their cultural power. By labeling this "political correctness," he fails to recognize the popular epistemological shift that has taken place. We are not suggesting that most faculty, administrators, and students became consistent radical constructivists—although some that discuss solutions to addressing issues of meaning and purpose are.[46] We are simply arguing that the academic community (and the associated foundational assumptions) that supported secular humanism was slowly dismantled over the past half century not merely on the basis of a fad but due to a new orientation to authoritative claims about knowledge.

What Kronman sees as secular humanism's support for the Western tradition was actually propped up by the dominance of liberal Protestantism through the Second World War.[47] The liberal Protestant consensus—the center of American moral and religious life—has not held. It has fallen apart, and this dramatic decline is well documented.[48] In fact, scholars argue we are now entering into a post-Protestant phase.[49] The clock cannot be turned back to when older liberal Protestant assumptions could undergird secular humanism. People, quite legitimately, ask, "Why should we give preference to a history of ideas about the good life and human purpose dominated by patriarchal, colonist, Europeans—what grounds do we have to give preference to this over moral perspectives found elsewhere?" Just because Kronman says we should? Secular humanism cannot simply stand as an authority on its own without the old cultural system that undergirded it.

We have moved from doctrinally Christian, to "ethically" Christian, to secular humanist (which maintains a distinctly liberal Protestant flavor and privileges Christian orientations and modes of thinking), to post-Christian pluralism. Each phase involves a crisis of authority that is resolved by further exorcising the religious ghost of the past. Because of this change, the previous default power and weight of the Western tradition can no longer be taken for granted. This reality can be seen in what one commentator calls the "new epistemology" among students.[50] The old authorities no longer hold sway. This is more than "political correctness." This change involves powerful institutions and cultural narratives that propose approaching knowledge about meaning and purpose within a new epistemological tradition.

Moreover, this epistemological shift was reinforced by several sociological realities: (1) an increasing percent of young eighteen- to twenty-two-year-old Americans were going to college[51]; (2) more and more of these American students were being educated at state institutions,[52] and (3) these new students were also much more diverse with regard to gender, race, and religion.[53] Faced with an increasingly pluralistic student body and country, many faculty and administrative leaders teaching these students believed that subjects such as the meaning of life or spirituality fell outside the purview of a neutral liberal democracy and state institutions of higher education. In order to avoid immoral or unconstitutional forms of favoritism, professors at state institutions (which is the majority of professors) increasingly believed they must avoid matters of purpose and meaning and remain merely presenters and caretakers of an ideological buffet.[54] The environment produced by such developments is likely why Dalton and Crosby claim, "The objectivist secular ethos that is so pervasive in much of higher education makes it difficult for students to explore openly their deep concerns about spirituality, meaning, and purpose."[55] This atmosphere is not only emerging on college campuses, of course. Evidence exists these changes are related to elements of modern Western culture as a whole. The sociologist Paul Froese finds that "modern culture increases the likelihood that an individual will lack purpose."[56] Still, these demographic and cultural changes are often heightened in the postsecondary context, where pluralism and progressive philosophies dominate.

These cultural changes, we would offer, reinforced a uniquely American distinction between private and public. Thus, one finds a higher-education scholar commenting that "higher education is not specifically charged with enhancing adults' ability to function in their private lives."[57] This view could only emerge when a system of higher education becomes funded and governed largely by the state for what are seen as public purposes. When this distinction emerges, politically relevant identities, such as race, gender, and sexual orientation become the identities that receive significant academic attention versus other "private," meaning-related identities and purposes. Religion and spirituality are therefore understood as topics that are "out of bounds" for professors since "the spiritual dimension of one's life has traditionally been regarded as intensely personal and private."[58] We find this outlook supported in some contemporary surveys. Today, among faculty at public institutions, 77 percent disagree with the statement that "colleges should be concerned with facilitating students' spiritual development."[59] Indeed, when it comes to any morally related goal, faculty at public institutions are less likely to understand such goals as very important or essential when compared to faculty at private colleges and universities, especially those at Catholic and other religious colleges (see table 1.1). Clearly, institutional type makes a significant difference.

Also, the approach Kronman proposes for addressing meaning and purpose, "teaching classic works of Western civilization," is not supported by a majority of this group. In contrast, the common moral goal held highly by the

Table 1.1. Faculty Goals for Undergraduates Noted as "Essential" or "Very Important"

	Public Universities	Colleges	Private Universities	Non-sectarian Colleges	Catholic	Other Religious
Teach students classic works of Western civilization	24.8	29.6	34.0	31.1	39.0	36.8
Help students develop personal values	56.5	64.9	69.3	67.1	76.4	78.5
Instill in students a commitment to community service	41.6	51.3	49.5	46.4	58.9	58.4
Develop moral character	61.0	65.3	70.7	67.5	79.7	78.5
Teach students tolerance and respect for different beliefs	75.4	82.5	78.9	82.9	84.1	82.4

Source: Eagan, M. K., Stolzenberg, E. B., Berdan Lozano, J., Aragon, M. C., Suchard, M. R., and Hurtado, S. (2014). *Undergraduate Teaching Faculty: The 2013–2014 HERI Faculty Survey.* Los Angeles: Higher Education Research Institute, UCLA, 32. Used by permission.

vast majority of educators is one associated with what Kronman calls "political correctness"—the need to teach students to tolerate and respect different beliefs. In light of the declining interest of students in this issue, the faculty's reservations about addressing meaning and purpose and spirituality, and the decreasing interest of faculty at public institutions to even handle moral issues in general, it is not surprising that the purpose of higher education is understood as increasingly limited.

Conclusion

In light of all these factors, the challenges to addressing meaning and purpose cannot simply be addressed by reducing political correctness, downplaying the research ideal, and encouraging universities and liberal arts colleges to support secular humanism and teach great texts. We must recognize first that some of the goods we find in the American educational system, such as the growth of a national system of higher education that opens up access for more people, may also contribute to the marginalization of meaning and purpose. Respect for pluralism and the First Amendment within the state university system is clearly important when living in an increasingly diverse society, but this respect may also make conversations about meaning and purpose more difficult (although we would suggest this also makes them even more important for students preparing to find their place within this diversity).

Second, universities in a liberal democracy do not respect the plurality of worldviews within the state system by trading the disestablishment of the old liberal Protestant order for the establishment and promotion of secular human-ism. Indeed, if "secular humanism" is defined the way Kronman defines it (in privileging Western thought), then, the state system *cannot* succeed in this estab-lishment. If we are to reinvigorate discussions about purpose without giving up these goods, we must first gain a deeper understanding of the ways in which the different types of contemporary American universities have found ways to address these issues and to cultivate students' own journey toward meaning and purpose. In some cases, we believe, some of these approaches will rely on specific religious or moral traditions that cannot be expected to be shared by all. Consequently, we must also understand to what degree various approaches are only possible within institutions with a shared moral framework and to what degree certain academic approaches to meaning and purpose are not necessar-ily tied to a university's particular moral or religious culture. Students need to understand that purpose development, including addressing the identities and stories shaping one's purpose, is not merely a private concern; however, plural-ism does make discussions about it more complicated, messy, and necessary.

Finally, we should note that while many professors, particularly at public institutions, have some concerns about addressing students' spiritual develop-ment, most American college professors still share the belief that colleges or universities should help students explore the meaning and purpose of life. In a recent survey the Higher Education Research Institute found that 69 percent of professors reported that it was essential or very important to facilitate students' search for meaning and purpose in life.[60] If over two-thirds of professors indicate this type of support for helping students search for meaning and purpose in life, we believe it is important to discover more about what can help students find their purpose or deepen and critically evaluate their understanding of their cur-rent purpose or purposes. We will be needlessly shortsighted if we fail to listen to their stories of purpose development, which begin before even entering college.

The next chapter begins our empirical exploration of these matters by focusing on students' recollections of the various influences on their development of meaning and purpose. While social scientists have discovered quite a bit about the development of purpose in adolescents, we wanted to find out how students themselves perceive the influence of various social supports such as parents, mentors, and peers that extant research identifies as important.[61] After all, in order to judge the willingness and ability of students to engage in the search for meaning and purpose, we need to know how their lives up to this point have prepared them to begin such an exploration.

Chapter 2

———

The Adolescent Journey

The Precollege Path to Finding Meaning and Purpose

My grandmother was actually the first person I asked, "What is the meaning of life?" and she said it's a very good question, "I don't know, but it's something that a lot of people think about all the time." And then I told her I was going to figure it out, and she said, "Good! Go for it. You can do it."

—Student at Jewish university

In the large public high school . . . I was encountering kids who weren't religious and this was so strange. A lot of them expressed ideas like, "Well this doesn't matter, because like there's nothing after this [life] so you might as well do this." And I had never really thought about this sort of thing. So I questioned a lot of meaning and purpose kind of stuff in high school . . . I did go through a period in ninth grade when I may have been depressed. I was really not sure of what my purpose was. Like what am I doing? I just felt so lost and disoriented.

—Liberal arts college student

"My home has been freaking awesome." Cody's claim is a rather unusual one coming from a college student, and he admits it. "I know that not a whole lot of people have that experience." Cody, a student at a southern public research university, realizes: "I guess my experience with my family shaped me to who I am like today." Certainly, his "freaking awesome" family life influences what he finds meaningful. "I stinking love other people and relationships and big families and lots of people getting together, and it's because I've had such a positive impact with my own family." It also shapes his short-term goals:

39

> And so that's why I wanna work at this summer family camp because
> I love families so much that I want to do whatever I can as a camp
> counselor to love on these families and help foster that same experi-
> ence that I've had.

Brimming with enthusiasm when talking about his home life, he believes the love he experienced at home overflows to his future career plans as well:

> I'm thinking about becoming a therapist, or a music therapist, or
> something so that I can love on these people and show them the same
> love that I've gotten from my parents and my family altogether. So
> I think in a huge way, the foundation on which I've kind of started,
> I think of it in terms of both my faith and how I kind of perceive
> others in relationships. My experience with my family and the love
> they've shared with me has been the foundation that I, now at col-
> lege, specifically have started to build on and personalize from there.

Like Cody, virtually every college student we interviewed could find connections between his or her family experience prior to college and how he or she currently thinks about life purpose. Indeed, among the 110 students we asked these questions, all but a half dozen of the students claimed that their parents played some role in this development. Of course, not all the stories had the same joyful exuberance.

A contrast to Cody's experience can be found in Adrianna's story—an undocumented Latino immigrant attending a secular liberal arts college. She certainly does not consider her family life "freaking awesome." Twice, her father kicked her mother, brother, and herself out of the house during her senior year of high school. Her father also left her with a depressing message regarding her future plans.

> The two first fights where he kicked us out, he would just tell me,
> "Oh, you're going to be the same thing and have an unhappy mar-
> riage (and this and that). Like, why are you going to college if you're
> just going to get married? Here you have a boyfriend since you're
> fifteen years old. You're just going to end up marrying him and not
> even go to school." He would say these things.

In comparison, her mother played and continues to play a much different role: "My mom would just tell me, 'You make sure you do good in school so you can prove your dad wrong.'" In this unique way, she realizes both her parents shaped and continue to shape her current outlook:

And so I guess that gave me purpose. My purpose in life is going to be not only [to] graduate high school but also go to college and stay in college; and so, just to prove him wrong. So, I guess seeing my mom cheering me on, "You better not get pregnant. You better not get married. You better not do this," gave me purpose of why I should even go to school.

Unlike Cody, the family conflict Adrianna experienced in high school profoundly shaped her purpose.

Although Adrianna credits her mother with giving her a strong reason to pursue a college education, Adriana claims she would not have even considered college if not for other adult mentors. Her speech and debate coach played a key role. They met in eighth grade when he came to her English class to advertise the speech and debate team. After the talk, "our class debated and he said, 'I want you to be in my debate team.' And so I said, 'Okay.'" Although they worked on debate, this teacher also mentored her in other ways. "I didn't have the money to buy suits for speech and debate and so he also supported me financially too, to get the suits for debates—nice clothes to look professional." His involvement during her first and second year made a tremendous difference, "Because of that mentor, he introduced me to college. He showed me how to look nice, how to talk, how to debate, and how to defend myself." She claims that without his encouragement, she would not have even considered college.

The connection she experienced with her mentor existed on a couple of different levels. Part of the bond they shared pertained to ethnic identity, "He was a Chicano and he would say, 'Adrianna, there's not that many Mexicans in speech and debate, and we have to change that in this school.' He kind of saw his dream in me." He also introduced her to big ideas. As an existentialist, "he liked to read Jean-Paul Sartre, and so he was always talking to me, 'What's the purpose of life?' So he introduced me to this philosopher, and so I just got interested in him in particular because of him."

Adrianna adds that she also needed additional help beyond her mother and debate teacher. She points to a Boys and Girls Club career coordinator who came to her aid when her father kicked the rest of the family out of the house during her senior year.

> I had to call her, "I don't know where to take my family, where do we go?" She helped us, called the police and this and that. 'Cause my mom was so scared, we eventually ended up going. But she really showed me that she was there for me.

The counselor also extended aid to Adrianna in the educational realm, which she now clearly sees as helping her educational purpose.

> She would proof my essays, and she was a recommender for my scholarships. She really helped me open up about my feelings and about my home situation, because even though my mom was suffering in the relationship, she always taught me, "You never show anybody your weaknesses. Don't talk about what's happening inside with your friends or your teachers cause then they'll just say you're not doing well because of this and that." So I never shared my family or my personal self until I met her [the counselor]. She helped me come out and be more outgoing, to be sharing of my experience.

Due to this extensive help, Adrianna even describes her as, "Like a mom within education is what I call her." As a senior, she believes she is close to proving her father wrong and making her mother and mentors proud.

The Adolescent Journey toward Purpose

As these stories indicate, a student's journey to finding meaning and purpose starts long before college. Indeed, there is evidence that we are natural purpose and meaning seekers from a very early age.[1] Consequently, young adults are often already engaged in this endeavor in some form. Surprisingly though, research about the development of meaning and purpose during adolescence has only recently emerged. For instance, only a little over thirty years ago, researchers noted that they did not know of any studies on the meaning of life in young adolescents.[2] A decade and a half later, a scholar noted, "In general, psychologists have not given the development of meaning and wisdom in adolescence the attention that it deserves."[3] A similar observation about the late start of empirical research regarding purpose has also been noted.[4] Less than fifteen years ago, scholars claimed that one of the important unanswered questions in the literature regarding purpose is "How have young people traditionally been introduced to [noble] purposes?"[5] Fortunately, we now know much more about the answer to these questions than we once did.

Not surprisingly, scholars find that both meaning and purpose develop extensively during adolescence.[6] What proves of particular interest, though, is that the nature of this development is more complex than once thought. Previous thinkers shared the view that acquiring purpose or meaning helped young people navigate and resolve their identity crisis. In other words, these scholars tended to view purpose as something youth developed as a healthy defensive framework in the midst of "danger, stress, and deficit" instead of "a motivator of good deeds and galvanizer of character growth."[7] While Adrianna's story fits this paradigm, Cody's story does not. In fact, family conflict has actually been found to negatively impact adolescents' reports of purpose.[8] Encountering this kind of explanatory weakness has led scholars to address the overly negative approach to purpose development by understanding both the prosocial and negative social forces that may influence the development of adolescent purpose. Indeed, today many scholars find that a healthy adolescent environment is a critical aspect of positive youth development. Finding and having purpose contributes to adolescents' happiness, positive affect, hope, resiliency, better school performance, and life satisfaction[9] and helps students avoid the tendency toward self-oriented or narcissistic behavior.[10]

Scholars find certain positive influences are vital to helping shape students' budding ideas about meaning and purpose and producing these positive results. As one scholar noted, *"whether adolescents' life meaning and wisdom will grow and unfold from being relatively straightforward to being mature and complex will depend invariably on the presence or absence of a number of other intervening and moderating influences and contextual factors."*[11] Some of the important positive influences that help adolescent students develop such a purpose include parents, mentors found in schools, clubs, religious groups and summer camps, and peers (although the impact of peers can vary).[12]

Still, scholars claim that we do not understand the core of this influence.[13] The answer, one group of scholars suggests, can come through questions that focus "on issues of future orientation, goals, and guiding forces that direct a young person through life."[14] In our 110 Targeted Qual interviews, we took this approach. We wanted to hear from students about how they perceived the important guiding forces in their adolescent lives, such as parents, friends, or other significant adults, with regard to the role played in the development of their views about meaning or purpose. Moreover, we sought to explore the important ideological backgrounds shaping this stage. While we do not claim these college students comprise a representative sample, we do believe they provide a beginning typology of the prior contexts that enable and inhibit the development of purpose and meaning among students. They also provide insight into the variety of ways students think, feel, and respond to various social influences when it comes to purpose.

The Diverse Influence of Parents

Lauren and Hao provide two examples of the range of parental influence. Lauren, a student at an Ivy League school, like Adrianna, recalls experiencing substantial family conflict. "As I was growing up, there was always such a conflict between my mother and dad. They always said opposite things. So, I wasn't exactly sure who to believe." Interestingly, instead of choosing sides among parents, she came to a different conclusion: "So I had to find other ways to value what they said and then construct my own opinion from five years old on." At first, she struggled with the weight of this burden and admits that she spent a lot of time in confusion. Eventually though,

> I decided, you know, screw this, I was going to decide what makes sense for me and go with it. So, their relationship definitely engendered this idea of self-design. And not unnecessarily arbitrary, but I had to create my own code, my own set of criteria for what I was doing.

According to Lauren, she consciously decided to find her own purpose in light of the conflicting signals she received from her parents.

Yet, despite her professed independence, her parents still formed her views about purpose and meaning in more indirect ways. She told us, "I was independent. Basically as a kid, my life was my job. My job was school." Surprised, one of us asked, "Why were you like that? I mean, that's unusual. Most don't think that school is their job or their calling in life. What gave you the strong impulse to treat school like that when most don't?" She admits:

> Well, ever since I was little, my mother told me, you know, your focus is on school. And when I started asking her, "Can I have a job?" She would say, "Your focus is your school. Don't worry; I will make the money [so that] you have what you need."

She also acknowledges that her father played a shaping role but in a different, perhaps more indirect, way as well. She contends,

> My dad, he only does his job for the money. For the flexibility of his schedule. I don't want that to be my primary motivation. I mean, it's nice that his schedule is flexible. It's nice to make good money, but if I have to sacrifice that for something I find meaningful and engaging, I'll do it. And he always tells me I could be a doctor if I just did it. But I don't want this to be me.

Lauren also sees her father as an antimodel in other ways. "He doesn't like his job because he feels unchallenged by it. He feels it's beneath him. Like he could've done better. And I want to feel good and push myself as far as I can reasonably go." Overall, although Lauren claims she has chosen her own way, the direction she chose is still influenced by her parents. Her mom directed and enabled her to concentrate on obtaining the education that allowed her to take a different path, and she sees the paths she does not want in the example of her father.

Hao, a public research university student majoring in advertising, provides a contrasting example to Lauren. When describing his purpose Hao starts by telling one of us, "I want to make money." While this comment might lead one to categorize him as a self-achievement-oriented business major, Hao adds an important caveat, "not for myself, but for my parents." In fact, Hao notes, "My life is mostly based around my family." Listening to Hao's life story, one gains a better understanding of why he has made this kind of commitment. Hao's father was studying to be a medical doctor in Vietnam, but he decided to come to the United States for a better life when Hao was twelve. Hao recounts, "He had to pay all this stuff and leave everything behind. When we came over here, we lived in a house with three other families . . . it was really a hard life." This act left an indelible impression on Hao. "He had a meaning in life, he wanted to be a doctor, but once he had kids, like we're his purpose, we're his meaning, so it taught me that family is more than money." This model also shapes his view of meaning, "They gave up everything for me so I want to like do the same thing. When I make whatever I can to give to them. That's pretty much my meaning."

This same vision of self-sacrifice also forms Hao's outlook in other areas of his life. He also shares about possibly starting a charity modeled on the student group China Care, which raises money for orphans in China. The motivation to start a similar group for Vietnamese children came from his previous experience:

> Seeing all the kids in Vietnam who don't have parents—they just live on the street, and it's like, they're kids. When I help a kid out, I feel like, "Oh that's why I'm here." I was privileged enough to have all this stuff given to me, so I just wanna give back.

Unlike Lauren, Hao sees his father as a positive model of someone who chose a path that did not lead to self-fulfillment for his own career prospects but instead created greater opportunity for his family.

It is hardly news that parents play a role in adolescents' development of meaning and purpose. What our interviews reveal that can be helpful is an understanding of two important things about the diverse nature of parental influence. First, purpose does not just emerge out of conflict. Although earlier theorists saw purpose as something that one develops in the midst of danger, stress, and deficit, only six of the students we interviewed, including Lauren and Adrianna, reported that the parental influence upon their purpose involved conflict.[15] In contrast, the majority of students, similar to Hao and Cody, understood their parents' influence to emerge less out of conflict and more out of conversations, a general family ethos, or the parents' example. In this regard, our findings reinforce the contemporary movement to view purpose and meaning as positive assets that emerge out of healthy youth development.

Second, how students perceive the substantive nature of their parents' influence on their developing sense of purpose varies in five different ways. Our interviews provide a variety of examples of the five types of influence (or lack of influence) students perceive as coming from their parents.

1. The Supposedly Laissez-Faire Parents

One group of students perceives their parents as largely uninvolved in helping them with purpose. We call this outlook the Supposedly Laissez-Fair Parents. For example, Erica tells us her parents "have been very hands-off—kind of laissez faire" when it comes to purpose. In Erica's case, her parents' laissez-faire approach actually stems from the failure of other approaches.

> I think that they understood early on—through parenting me for the first eighteen years of my life—that when they tried to control things—that was not a source of encouragement, or that I didn't respond well to those boundaries. And so, when it comes to college, they've been, you know, whatever you want to major [in]. When I took a year off it was, "it's your life, and we understand your decisions." . . . So and I guess that's been their biggest influence: that they really have tried not to influence my comings and goings or whatever.

The reason why we add the descriptor "supposedly" to this label can also be illustrated with Erica's story. Despite Erica's narrative about her parents being hands-off, some of her comments reveal they still attempt to have an influence:

> They've always been very good about sharing the potential risk about things that they see I'm doing, and offering their opinions but in a way that says, "This is how I see it, but you're more than welcome to do whatever you want to do."

Even in this narrative, it is clear that while Erica claims her parents' greatest influence has been providing her with autonomy, her parents are still offering wisdom they hoped would guide her.

In this respect, our sample of college students, including students such as Lauren and Erica who claim not to have had much parental input, differs substantially from another study of adolescents that claimed, "Many parents do not see it as their responsibility to actively help their adolescents form plans for their futures."[16] We found the opposite to be the case among our sample of students. Even when emerging adults make professions of independence from their parents, their own interviews indicate that parents still attempt to exercise influence over purpose development.[17]

2. Encouragement and Effort Parents

A second group of students focus less on how their parents influence their substantive views and more on *how* their parents encourage them to pursue their purpose. We label their experience the Encouragement and Effort Parents. There are two types of Encouragement and Effort Parents. One type encourages students to pursue their passion and be true to that passion. As one student explained it, "I don't think I've gotten any specific direction, but generally, I think I've been pushed just to do what I want to do and be true to myself." This principle works even in the case of disagreement, as one student noted, "They kind of raised me to be genuine and be yourself and to do what you love and what you're passionate about, even if they don't altogether approve of the way that I've done that." Either authenticity (as in the above cases) or happiness, as in this student's case, provides the guiding principle: "My parents have always been really encouraging: To follow your own passions and not do what people expect of you but do what you really want and do what really makes you happy."

Within this second group of students there are a couple of important variations. A number of students primarily see their parents' influence on their views of meaning and purpose as involving expectations of excellence (e.g., "they always expected very highly of all three of us"). One might call them the tiger mom and dads.[18] Students do not perceive them as encouraging a certain career, but they do view them as encouraging a certain kind of effort in one's life endeavors. Or, as one student described what his father taught him, "You give a 110 percent on whatever it is. It really doesn't matter. As long as you're giving it that 110 percent of the time, then I think your life is certainly fulfilled." While this message bears some resemblance to those parents who encourage their children to pursue their passion, it highlights an important difference. Encouragement to pursue a passion is something connected to the specific interests of the children and not to rigor in general. Effort relates to whatever activity the student happened to be engaged in, whether it interested them or not, as this student indicates:

> [My mom's] always saying, "Whatever you do, you have to do it very
> well. So, even if you're going to be a janitor, just do it really well."
> And she always says she's not expecting me to become a janitor but
> just the idea that whatever you do, do it well.

Effort, in other words, is something that these parents (as these students perceive them) insist should remain consistent no matter the endeavor (even if one is not passionate about it). Following one's passion is not dependent on a sense of constant self-discipline. Both, of course, are not about the ends of purpose, but about the process. These concern *how* one goes about developing direction and purpose in life, not the destination chosen.

3. Make a Living Parents

Another group of students view their parents as primarily influencing their purpose by offering advice about vocational choices. Practicality drives these parents, and students perceive these parents as wanting them to follow the jobs that can pay the bills instead of the students' passions. This student describes an interaction with what we call a Make a Living Parent,

> When I first got to college, because we didn't grow up in the best conditions, [my mother] stressed, "Go to college, and make sure you have a good major and get a good degree—that way you can have a good career." We struggled financially growing up and so she wanted to make sure that I went to college that way we wouldn't have that problem in the future. So I feel like that kind of shaped what I chose as a major and honestly as of now, I feel like I chose the best major that was for me, I chose what I thought would get me the best job and that would put me in the best career financially.

This group of students and the message they receive from parents, which the above student clearly absorbed, demonstrate a striking contrast to the Encouragement and Effort Parents as this illustration attests:

> Well, they've always been supportive of, well, okay that's a lie. When I first came to college, I was going to be an art history major and so I wanted to do archaeology and that was like my dream forever, because I really wanted to be Indiana Jones. Then I realized with a little bit of their pushing that that wouldn't really get me a job doing anything that would, like, pay bills. So, I, meaning half with them and half with me, decided to change my mind and do a different major. Obviously, a business major opens up everything so that, I'm happy about it now, but back then it was like "Why are you making me change my life?"

Obviously, Make a Living Parents are much more willing to force certain decisions related to college major, and the guiding principle for forcing such a decision is simply monetary or a vision of educational attainment (e.g., "my mom's a middle school teacher and my dad is a painter, and so they've both really encouraged me to you know, seek out something higher than they achieved"). As one student described her experience with a Make a Living Parent,

> My dad is extremely practical, and so he's definitely steered me away from some paths that I might have taken, especially more artistic

kind of things: "You can't have a career there. You don't need to do that." . . . And so I guess with my dad, he's kind of refined, changed my desire of my purpose to be in terms of, "Do what you want with your life but still support yourself," and kind of have that more pragmatic take . . .

It should be noted that students with Make a Living Parents often appear to have absorbed a rather narrow understanding of life purpose, since they interpret questions about the parental influence on purpose in terms of wisdom or "encouragement" pertaining to a future career choice (as opposed to a general philosophy of life).

4. Modeling the Good Life Parents

The largest group of students claim they experienced and continue to experience what we label the Modeling the Good Life Parent. They recall their parents offering broader teaching or examples about the substantive nature of purpose and meaning. These students not only remember specific advice from their parents, but like Hao, they also perceive their parents as providing positive role models for how they want to live their lives. In some cases, this modeling serves as a substitute for conversations about purpose in life. One student from a Baptist university told one of us, "I think mostly my parents served as good moral role models and pointed me to the right places, but I don't know that I've ever talked to my parents specifically about my purpose in life or anything like that." Another student from a liberal arts college recalled a similar experience.

> They led a lot by example; we didn't broach these, a subject as massive as the meaning of life explicitly, but I think they led by the way they chose to live their lives—the hours they dedicated to my brother and I.

What exactly parents would model varied considerably. As the above student noted, his parents modeled a value for family. Another student from a regional university talked about a different form of modeling that communicated a particular message:

> Seeing how they live, their different actions throughout life, through my twenty years just growing up with them around, seeing how they react and how they act through everything. It's like they're not always just trying to live for themselves. They're really trying to go out and help other people but still sustain the family.

In fact, the most mentioned type of modeling priority involved serving together as a family or emphasizing the importance of relationships. A Jewish student shared that this kind of moral teaching extended to "determining priorities that you develop in your life." He cited as an example:

> With the recession, all the financial difficulties that so many people, including my family, experience, the ideas that there are things that are more valuable than money and physical things, and that how my family and mental, positive mental state of mind are all things that are priorities, and it's not necessarily things that are important, physical or monetary.

Modeling the Good Life Parents are obviously understood in a positive manner. This finding proves consistent with a previous study that found that high school youth identify the positive modeling role of family members as a particularly important role in their development of purpose.[19]

5. *The Religiously Inspired Parents*

The Religiously Inspired Parent or Parents play a role in shaping their meaning and purpose in a religious context. In other words, unlike Make a Living Parents, these parents place the quest for a future vocation or even life purpose itself in a larger story. Cody, the student introduced at the beginning of the chapter, identified the influence of his parents as stemming from this outlook:

> Yeah, my parents became Christians in college and so they raised all of us kids in a Christian household family and all that . . . I guess, just like, because our family's been so tight knit, like it's been so filled with love because of my parents' faith, like the way that they've set everything up in our family has been kind of based on that love that they have from their own faith.

For Cody, not surprisingly, meaning related to his faith,

> Meaning for me is my faith and I ask like, I think that my Christian faith is where I find meaning . . . I think that like meaning in my life is having, like learning more of who God is and how he loves me and how I can be closer in a relationship with him.

Cody viewed his purpose as then emerging from this particular meaning: "My purpose is to love others as I have been loved."

The nature of the Religiously Inspired Parent can be indirect or more direct. In some cases, the student simply attributes the influence of the parents to the general religious ethos of the family. For instance, this Catholic student at a Catholic university recalled how she experienced this type of parental influence:

> I think growing up in a strong Catholic family [purpose] is just something that you place trust in God about, and I think that's something I've taken away . . . I think right now, especially when I'm like, "Ugh, I need a job," . . . I think somehow it's going to work out, and I think God plays a role.

In this case, her trust in God inspired how she deals with the emotional instability during the search for a particular career. At other times, it entails specific types of guidance. Christina, a student from a public research university describes a similar form of indirect guidance:

> My parents are really good about whenever I get bogged down with school to say, "Christina it doesn't matter, we love you if you fail out of college, and we love you if you succeed and get a great job, like that's not what our love is determined on." And that's just like a great example for me of God's love. I don't love you based on what you can do. My love it's not coming from your accomplishments, but it's just because I love you and I created you.

In her case, she experienced a particular character quality of God (unfailing love) while in the midst of pursuing purpose.

The Absence of Helicopter Parents

Overall, our finding that parents influenced students' purpose is not surprising. What proved intriguing, and what university faculty and staff should recognize, is the varied nature of this influence. Some students perceive the influence of their parents as minimal while others understand the parental shaping of purpose as linked through positive or negative experiences, advice, or modeling. We should also note one thing we did not find. Recently, a significant amount of attention has been given to the concept of overinvolved or "helicopter" parenting. Numerous studies have found that helicopter parenting is associated with a variety of negative outcomes in college students such as lower psychological well-being, greater depression and anxiety, a lower sense of autonomy, and less life satisfaction.[20] In particular, one study explained the problems as linked to "the perceived violation of students' basic psychological needs for autonomy and competence," or what student development theorists would likely identify as the lack of ability to self-author one's purpose.[21] Interestingly, we did not find any students who complained about this type of parental influence (of course, students may not yet recognize their parents' style). The closest we found were those students with "make a living parents" who strongly encouraged a particular type of college major. Yet, one could argue that these parents were ultimately concerned with their child's autonomy and self-sufficiency after college.

Discussing Purpose outside the Family: Older Adults

Trinity, a social work major from a public research university, recalls examples of two adults with whom she talked about meaning and purpose. First, she describes an educator: "My English teacher junior and senior year was very much a mentor to me and a lot of us." In this case, the influence largely concerned her future education and career:

> She was very good about helping us realize graduation just isn't the end goal. You have your whole life, and whatever you accomplish here you can still take it other places. She was very good about telling us, "Take a deep breath, everything will be fine." She was like, "I graduated with this degree, and I've done these five completely different jobs." So that's always so comforting to hear and know that whatever, no matter what path you're on right then, you could be somewhere else and it's okay what your history is, really. That was very nice from her.

In addition, Trinity mentions another educator who influenced her, but the nature of the conversation with this mentor was different, since she actually got to know her in a religious context.

> I had my tenth grade English teacher. She led our girls Bible study every Monday. She was a very good role model as far as like relationships with boys, 'cause she had been dating the same guy for like nine years . . . so she talked to us a lot about guys and just how to make sure that our purpose in life isn't to get married, you know, and our meaning in life isn't just to be a wife and a mom and that we have other things to accomplish outside of that, so that was really great.

As Trinity's story reveals, relationships with older adults beyond one's parents can also make a crucial difference in how one thinks about purpose. One researcher notes, "Adolescents' social transactions with adults who encourage them to participate in dialogue and personal valuations set the stage for the growth of personal meaning."[22]

Yet, listening to students, one might come to the conclusion that they rarely talk about these matters with other adults beyond the nuclear family. A paltry 5 college students out of 110 referenced the influence of grandparents on their life purpose. Over two-thirds of our college students did not mention talking with or learning about these issues from other adults beyond their family during high school. Whether such a finding signals an overall pattern among college students would need to be discerned through broader empirical studies. In general, we found two primary contexts where students explored issues of meaning and purpose with other nonfamilial adults during their adolescence: educational and religious environments. In this sense, Trinity's story was representative of our sample.

Scholars studying purpose have suggested that teachers may play an important role in the purpose development of their students, but as one writer summarizing the literature noted, "the empirical research supporting this claim has been sparse."[23] As exemplified by Adrianna's story, our interviews provide some evidence of this influence. Among the students who mentioned being influenced by their teachers about these matters at all, the nature of the influence was, like Trinity, largely in the context of future career options. David, a student at a Jewish university gave the following example:

> We had one psychologist on campus all the time, and I remember speaking to her about like what she does on a daily basis and like, because that was the point where I was starting to get interested in psychology, in early junior year in high school, I think. We started talking about like what she does on campus and stuff like that, and I remember walking away from a conversation thinking "Wow, that's what I want to do." After speaking to her, I realized all the people she helped, and I saw all the things she did, and I noticed it more and more, and I kind of said, "That's what I want to do, I want to help people and I want to be here."

Even for the few who did mention the influence of educators beyond a career, what the teachers provided the students was not discussions about larger matters of the good life but usually something much more specific, such as the confidence to overcome an inhibition. Adrianna's story at the beginning of this chapter noted this type of influence. Chelsea, a student from a Lutheran liberal arts college, shared how a public school teacher provoked a passion for a particular subject and provided a model of how to help others:

> I had this teacher in high school named Mr. Brown . . . he just had a way of opening my eyes up to things that he made me believe that I had the capacity to succeed in subjects I didn't feel that great about. And so I guess someday I want to be someone's Mr. Brown, and I want to be the person that they look to as being the one who proved to them that they, or who let them see that they had the skills to do this or I gave them the confidence to go on . . . he kind of showed me that I can, that learning can be fun if it's the right thing and so I want to be able to show someone else what that feels like.

It is likely that the school environment played some role in shaping the nature of these conversations. Public schools, for perhaps First Amendment reasons related to how religion must be treated, do not appear to be nearly as conducive for fostering conversations about the good life. For example, Emily mentioned conversations with a public school teacher about life's meaning; the teacher (who supervised the school newspaper) largely facilitated these discussions without offering substantive content.

> If we—the students kind of brought it up or had questions or you know, then he would engage and I liked that. I mean he wasn't trying to force anything, wasn't trying to sway us or anything, but if there was an opportunity to talk about it or discuss he would. . . . I remember having a couple other friends on staff that were kind of like, "we don't know what we're doing. What is the meaning of life?" And then sometimes we'd kind of have those conversations . . . he was definitely a model to me of someone who wasn't afraid to talk about those kinds of subjects that sometimes are maybe a little sensitive in a school setting, in a public school setting, but at the same time, I guess you can say he facilitated the conversation but [he] wasn't going to persuade anyone to any one side, you know. "Look at it this way. Look at it that way. Have you thought about this, kind of thing?"

As this case reveals, the conversation was informal, and the teacher resisted setting forth particular ideals regarding the good life. Moreover, in these cases the students did not recall any particular educational high school program that helped them think about these issues beyond informal interactions with teachers.

The role that religion plays in fostering adolescent conversations about meaning and purpose, however, appears to be much more substantive and comprehensive. Usually, it involves talking about matters beyond career choices. Particular types of subcultures may foster these kinds of conversations since over half of the students who mentioned religious mentors came from three particular institutions: the evangelical, Jewish, and Mormon universities. Tim, a student at an evangelical university shared about one such unique relationship.

> I have a couple guys at my church. They were like my youth group leaders for a few years back in [his home state]. And they really poured into my life. We met a lot and had lunch all the time and just like talked about just life and they were guys that I can look to and say, "Hey, I'm struggling with this, you know? What should I do?" I think it's just that they're not my parents and it's just like we've connected—they're both older, they're both like married and have kids, but we just connected. They were my leaders. We hung out, and we connected in a different way . . . I guess, in a sense, they were another father figure. But not like super-father figure. They were other guys that I could look up to and if I'm struggling with something, they're an open book. They're open ears no matter what time of day. Anytime I could go to them, and I knew that.

Tim's intergenerational experience with older adult figures who talked about more than future career paths was unusual. What was clear from many of the interviews is that talking about meaning and purpose with other older adults requires intentionality and a community of purpose, trust, and vulnerability. Cody, whose positive family experience we described above, also identified a positive adult mentor during his youth.

> I had a guy in my church. We didn't have like a high school youth group that all met together generally. We met in different small groups, and so my small group leader was Mike. He was a cool guy. He really liked philosophy and stuff, and I was kind of into that too. We would like have philosophical conversations and stuff. But he definitely shaped me a lot and encouraged me a lot to think about like my faith. And I've always liked music, and he was encouraging in that too, like "you should do what you wanna do. You can write songs or make music and like that's legitimate." I think especially being an oldest kid, you wanna make like quote unquote "responsible" choices and stuff and so sometimes I would be like, "Oh, that's frivolous or whatever" in light of other, more serious pursuits. He encouraged me in that.

These type of small group settings in which youth interacted with other older adults at a deep level not only about their future career but also about how to live a good life appear to be found almost exclusively among those in religious communities.

Discussing Purpose with Friends

Darren, an atheist, grew up in the upper Midwest and attends a religious liberal arts college in the area. He claims that he feels comfortable with his parents and communicates with them regularly. Yet, he admits, "I guess we don't too often go into more serious or deep topics like religion and politics, things like that. We would often talk about day to day things." In fact, while his mom goes to church, he claims, "I'm not sure how religious my dad is."

Darren's lack of conversations with his parents about deep matters such as religion and purpose also extends to his high school friends:

> During high school I had four or five really close friends and generally the things we talked about would focus on either academic sort of things or in more entertainment sorts of things. A lot of us really liked languages, and we would talk about that and just differences between different languages. Or like TV shows, video games things like that, also sometimes, occasionally more serious topics like political ones. But I usually wouldn't feel comfortable being the one to bring the sort of conversations up [about purpose], even though I would enjoy being in a conversation like that.

Darren had plenty of friends, but he was not able or ready to approach the depths and trust level required to approach topics of meaning and purpose.

Jasmine, an Indian American student attending a public research university, provides an interesting contrast to Darren. When responding to our question about her parents' role in forming her beliefs, she shares what might be considered a classic American immigrant story:

> My parents, when they came to America, didn't have anything. They basically worked from the bottom up, and money was always a constant struggle for them trying to establish who they were. And so to see this selflessness and willingness to give up everything to provide for me and my sister has been incredible . . . I would hope that I would be half as good a parent as my parents are.

Despite Jasmine's admiration for her parents, she does not necessarily buy into their two views about life's purpose that she perceives their immigrant experience helped to foster. She sees their outlook as containing certain weaknesses,

> I think for my parents it's all about security, it's about the fact that they grew up without a lot, and that they don't want me to have to go through that, so the easy option would be go to school for a really long time, get an incredibly good job that pays a lot of money and you won't ever have to worry about half the problems we had to go through.

She also notes that purpose for her parents is more than just financial security: "They feel like purpose has to do with culture, and purpose has to do with tradition and family, which I think it does." While she does not dismiss these purposes, she does express concern about how these purposes play out in her parents' lives. For example, she believes that her parents' views have led to an exaltation of Indian ethnicity and culture that she finds problematic,

> Their narrow-mindedness toward our culture is something that I'm not sure that I would have the same outlook [about] with my kids like that, "We are the right way. That being Indian is the supreme—like that's who you are and that's what defines you."

Does Jasmine feel like she can talk about these issues of purpose with her parents? "I mean, we could talk about politics. We could talk about dating. We could talk about anything. It was just the whole concept of religion . . ." It was here where the conversation stopped.

Jasmine's conversations about life's meaning and purpose started during her childhood and later adolescence. They began with an important introductory conversation with a friend when she was eleven, the summer after her fifth-grade year, and then culminated in an important ninth-grade decision.

> I was on the swim team, and my parents worked while I was a child, so I had to go over to this friends' house every day after practice. And one day she just goes, "Do you know there's a God in Heaven that loves you?" And I was like, "What is that? Sign me up for that." . . . But I think that's how I was introduced to Jesus. It was more like a year process, many years after that, through the death of my grandmother, understanding the consequences of sin, and understanding that there is a sovereign God. I don't think it was like a one-day introduction, "Okay, I'm a Christian." But I think it took years of really understanding what Christianity is and what

> does that really mean for people. So I would say my freshman year of high school [was] when I really was like, "Alright this is what I'm doing. This is it."

Looking back she sees how her Christian friends, including her swim practice friend, played an important role in shaping her Christian commitments:

> I think hanging out with the same friends really shaped me a lot. If I had switched friend groups or hadn't been friends with them for a long time, then things would have been different, but I think spending a lot of time with them and just reading the Bible together, I think just doing things that brought us close together enhanced what we believed in.

Together they would spend time talking about their Christian lives and questions such as:

> "What are we doing with our life, like what are we supposed to do in life right now? I'm so confused about everything." And that's a topic we're always talking about, "How can I better what I'm doing right now for God? How can I better, you know my lifestyle choices?" I think our purposes are always changing in terms of how we can be doing things, but I think the overall meaning of life is the same.

For Jasmine, her meaning is now quite clear. "In very simple terms, Jesus Christ, I don't know how to say it any other way . . . I think that, I don't think anything in life for me would be meaningful if it wasn't about loving God and loving his people." For Jasmine, her whole purpose in life is shaped, in large part, by adolescent conversations with her friends about religion. The result of these conversations, however, was the end of conversation with her parents about meaning and purpose that involved religion. Her parents told her, " 'Well if you don't want to be Hindu, then you don't really want your culture,' and so that was kind of a taboo topic for a long time. And it still kind of is."

Among the students we interviewed as a whole, Darren's experience of avoiding purpose discussions among high school friends proved to be more the norm. Only a third of the students reported having significant conversations about meaning and purpose with high school friends. For the vast majority, high school was simply not a time or place when students spend much time talking to their friends about life meaning and purpose. Julie, a student from a Baptist university provides a typical recollection: "In high school and middle school when I was working through this sort of thing, I didn't really have people that I was close enough with to discuss these sorts of things with."

Julie represents an experience from the students who do not have conversations of meaning and purpose with friends. This group of students simply experiences a lack of deep, trusting relationships. The inability to develop this deeper level of relationship is sometimes perceived to be the result of environmental factors and sometimes self-imposed. Like Julie, an Ivy League student named Sandy reported that she really did not have close friends in high school, and she listed both of these reasons:

> Socially it was difficult because there was so much competition. Academically it was difficult just because the level, the standard was much higher, and then I was struggling with my eating disorder as well, so psychologically, I think I was still dealing with my family stuff; my dad had left home when I was in sixth grade, but I mean it carried over into high school, I think, and then I think I just closed myself off. I think that was when I realized, or that was when I felt, that I needed to be independent in order to survive. I can't rely on my family, I can't rely on my friends or you know, [they're] gonna backstab me until you get into college. I just ended up really isolating myself.

The obvious barrier in this case was the lack of intimacy and trust that would allow for such conversations with friends. For Susan, a Latino student at an evangelical university, her mother reinforced this lack of trust. "I had friends, but I didn't really have close friends, um, because my mom always told me, like, 'don't trust no one, not even your own shadow,' so I always had like that, like distance between friends."

A second group of students acknowledge having significant and perhaps more trusting relationships, but they simply were too preoccupied by other concerns in high school to talk about lofty topics like meaning and purpose. Mike, a student form a Baptist university recalled:

> My other good friend from high school, I would talk to him about pretty much anything. Like as far as relationships go, I'd be comfortable talking to them about stuff, but I never really saw any reason or a need to [with regard to meaning and purpose]. I would probably lean toward saying my friends had no role in that.

As Mike mentioned, some of this inability stemmed from a focus on other things and the fact that life's purpose and meaning were not pressing issues at the time. Jacob, a student from a Jewish university, cited a couple common youthful preoccupations—entertainment and sports.

> My friends and I, we talked about TV shows a lot. Football, we loved football. We would really just like hang out, go outside, and play football, watch football, and then just talk. Yeah. It was always movies. We never really talked about our purpose, a purpose or what we thought it was, or anything. Yeah, I mean I guess maybe it was because we just weren't old enough, maybe, to think about it, but at the same time I feel like that's the time you should be thinking about it.

Oddly, among students with a significant commitment to higher education, the big questions were not central in their high school lives. Instead, achievement is often what mattered. One Ivy League student we call Lauren told us, "I wasn't necessarily thinking about what my purpose in life was. I was focusing on academics. I mean, you know, my problem in high school was that I was very high achieving, but I didn't know what I was doing it for." When compared to another recent study of adolescents' development of purpose, our findings are not usual. The study found that in early adolescence peers actually had a negative influence on the development of students' purpose, and in some cases even caused students to lose a sense of purpose.[24] This is a result of peer relationships and peer-related hedonistic activities, which "caused them to lose focus on previously important empathic concerns."[25]

While a minority of students did talk about issues of meaning and purpose in high school, even the nature of these conversations appeared quite shallow. For instance, when conversations were recalled, they usually related mostly to career matters. Katie, a liberal arts college student even claimed that her friends who loved deeper conversations were "a little bit different than the norm." She went on to note, however, that it was not a sophisticated approach to matters of purpose:

> I guess maybe we wouldn't talk so deeply all the time about, like, philosophical issues or religious issues, we didn't even really talk about politics that much, but she, or one friend in particular, would always wonder, kind of, what direction I wanted to go with my life—like career paths, just kind of always like thinking about the future—not exactly philosophically, but definitely just, maybe more of a purpose in life kind of thing instead of a meaning in life.

Indeed, conversations about meaning and purpose that went beyond one's future job were at the far reaches of adolescent vulnerability and only occasionally occurred during special times like sleepovers. One student recalled, "All of their normal defenses are lowered and people start asking what's on their mind and like sometimes you talk about things like girls that you have crushes on. Then other times you talk about other kind of deep things like meaning and purpose." Clearly, meaning and purpose were not usual high school conversations. One could say it was as rare as death for the young. Not surprisingly, it was this kind of death that spurred one adolescent's unusual conversation. Monica, a Buddhist student from a liberal arts college recalled:

> I mean, I remember actually . . . one of my friends, Daniella, she was like the first one that I kinda, we had serious conversations . . . it started out like us talking about our families and I was like, "Oh yeah, I don't know if you knew this, but my dad's sister died when she was twenty-two. Isn't that weird? That's in like five years for us. Can you imagine?" So we'd kind of think about that, like what we would have wanted to accomplish if we were to die at twenty-two.

For most of the students we talked to, however, this kind of perspective and discussion proved rare.

When students did talk about meaning and purpose with friends in high school in the context of normal relationships, the major topic commonly involved religion. Those that did recall conversations with friends about meaning and purpose recalled relationships that involved religious similarities and differences, whether within one's tradition or outside of it, that helped spur deeper conversations about meaning and purpose. When the religious traditions were similar, a trust existed that allowed these types of conversations to occur. Erica, a student at a Baptist university talked about this dynamic.

> With the friends that I had on the soccer team in high school we just talked about pretty surface-level stuff most of the time. I mean, we'd talk about family issues or academic issues, but as far as morally, because I was raised Baptist and they, most of them actually, were not practicing Catholics, and so we had such a difference of religion there that I don't think I was brave enough to approach most of those subjects, because I didn't feel like I was able to defend my views and beliefs. Where, like, with my Christian friends in high school we talked a lot about, you know, "What are we doing here? What's the meaning of life? How are we serving the Lord?"

Overall, beyond conversations with a few trusted friends who had similar experiences or with fellow religious believers, peer conversations during adolescence appeared to be unusual. In general, the situation we found was one expressed by this student when asked about conversations of meaning and purpose, "I don't really remember having conversations like that with my high school friends. I was having one with my family when I was in high school, but I don't think I ever talked about it with high school friends."

Although talking about purpose was rare for students in high school, their journey into college would change that. A variety of students made this observation.

- "Purpose is a very common topic with my friends now, not so much in high school."

- "I didn't really think about like a lot of that stuff in high school, but college I would say, yeah definitely."

- "Only in college, I think before that not too much."

- "Those conversations were probably more in recent years than directly in high school."

It is to the nature and influence of these conversations, as well as the substantive views about purpose that we will turn in the second part of this book.

Conclusion

When the college students we interviewed look back on their early adolescent experience, what they remembered reinforced what earlier studies of adolescents have found. Healthy relationships with parents, mentoring relationships with other older adults, and involvement with faith-based activities play an important role in the development of purpose.[26] Parents in particular play a vital role, although the nature of their influence varies considerably.

The influence may come through basic encouragement, advice about making a living, modeling, or religious inspiration, but it all proves noteworthy to students. Indeed, despite the literature about helicopter parents, students did not express exasperation with parental involvement. Understanding the importance of healthy relationships and the diversity of this family influence, we believe, can help educators and other community mentors understand how to address different parental styles and the gaps, strengths, and weaknesses those styles may produce. In particular, educators steeped in student development theories that emphasize the importance of cognitive dissonance[27] need to realize that students will also benefit from stable communal sources of meaning.

While parents proved influential, one of the surprising and important gaps we found concerns the existence of older mentors or other friends who can help students with their purpose development. When students find these mentors, they usually do so either in an educational or a religious context. In light of the continued decline of adolescent participants in positive youth development organizations,[28] the important question is whether and how these kinds of relationships are cultivated in college. Moreover, since scholars have found that access to supportive peer networks is important to developing a beyond-the-self-oriented youth purpose among purpose exemplars, our findings may point to a major weakness that exists in adolescent support.[29] Providing safe contexts for peer discussions about purpose would certainly fill what appears to be a significant gap. Again, the question is whether the college or university experience can help fill this gap.

The above two questions prove particularly important during this transition period. Sharon Daloz Parks has observed that the journey from adolescence to college in the areas of meaning and purpose can be rough. Drawing on the work of James Fowler and echoing the theory of William Perry, she claims that late adolescent meaning making involves a journey from inherited forms of meaning making espoused by authorities, to a wilderness of relativism, and then finally to the promised land, which involves a "committed, inner-dependent mode of composing meaning, affirmed by a self-selected class or group."[30]

Parks locates when students emerge from the wilderness as taking place between late adolescence to early adulthood. She identifies it as "when one begins to take self-conscious responsibility for one's own knowing, becoming, and moral action—even at the level of ultimate meaning-making."[31] She proposes that late adolescents actually go through a postadolescent period, what today we might call the emerging adulthood phase (which she calls young adult). The young adults discover their sense of self, but they still seek a fit within the adult world. This quest for purpose, and the nature of college students' success undertaking it, is what we chronicle in the rest of the book. Before looking specifically at college students though, we begin our examination of this quest in the next chapter by overviewing the important role that social context and education play as emerging adults make this pilgrimage.

Chapter 3

Mapping the Presence of Purpose

How Identity, Social Context, and Education Matter

A growing body of theoretical and empirical research has focused on what constitutes purpose, on the close correspondence between purpose and identity development, and on the positive correlates of leading a life of purpose. However comparatively little research has focused on how purposes are discovered or how they are pursued over time. Consequently, we know relatively little about how to effectively foster this important construct.

—Kendall Cotton Bronk[1]

If we consider the presence of purpose a developmental asset, then it may prove helpful to find what general social environments nurture purpose. In this chapter, we use a national survey of young emerging adults to generate a descriptive map of the factors that are associated with the presence of purpose for eighteen- to twenty-three-year-olds. What types of factors—such as family, health, religion, education, employment, relationships, and sex—are associated with developing a clear sense of goal-driven purpose during this phase of life?

We want to make clear that in this chapter we are only focusing on the presence or absence of a sense of purpose in young emerging adults—*not* on the substantive content of this purpose in college students (the subject of chapter 6). In this chapter, we simply want to establish which young emerging adults are more likely to end up reporting that they have a sense of purpose in life and which ones are likely to feel that they are free-floating through life without a clear sense of direction. As explored earlier, the psychological literature on purpose suggests that the presence or absence of purpose is important in and of itself. Simply believing one has a sense of purpose in life is associated with a variety of positive life and developmental outcomes such as happiness, successful identity formation, resiliency, positive affect, and life satisfaction.[2]

We also think that having a clear sense of purpose may be *more* important for young people today than in the recent past. The pathways to adulthood have become increasingly variable over the past several decades.[3] Default cultural scripts, which specified an ordering and timing of the markers associated with adulthood, fail to describe the experiences of many young people today.[4] While most individuals successfully navigate this transition, not all are successful. Without the cultural scripts to fall back on, some stall, flounder, or never fully emerge into successful adult life.[5] A sense of purpose can be seen as increasingly important to both motivate and guide young people into stable adult life in culturally unsettled times.

The National Study of Youth and Religion (NSYR) Survey

The survey data used in this chapter is comprised of a representative sample of U.S. adolescents (age 13 to 17) in 2002–03.[6] The same sample of adolescents was then resampled at age sixteen to twenty (in 2005), age eighteen to twenty-three (in 2007–08), and age twenty-three to twenty-eight (in 2012–13). The measures of purpose we are interested in were asked during the third wave of the study, when the adolescents were of the traditional college age (18 to 23). Respondents were asked to assess their level of agreement (measured on a five-point scale ranging from "strongly disagree" to "strongly agree"), with the following three questions related to certain aspects of purpose: (1) Your life often seems to lack any clear goals or sense of direction; (2) You don't have a good sense of what it is you're trying to accomplish in life; and (3) Some people wander aimlessly through life, but you are not one of them.[7]

About six out of ten young emerging adults (age 18 to 23) consistently affirm that they have a purpose—they claim their life is not aimless, goalless, or directionless. Again, we should note that this affirmation of purpose is different than the more restricted "beyond-the-self" definition offered by positive psychology scholars.[8] The results affirm that a substantial minority of young emerging adults at least occasionally feel that their life lacks a clear purpose.[9] What social factors, particularly during adolescence, end up being the most powerful predictors of who consistently claims to have a life purpose and who does not?

To find the answer to this question, we use multivariate statistical analyses. For those interested in the details of how we constructed our models, as well as the statistical coefficients from these models, please consult appendix C. Instead of presenting the raw statistical findings in this chapter, we present all of our findings graphically using predicted probabilities.[10] In other words, we use the statistical models to generate the expected or predicted likelihood of someone with a given set of characteristics to consistently claim that they have a sense of purpose in life. At the same time, we are able to control for potentially confounding factors such as age, race, sex, and parents' income and education. The influence from these factors is eliminated in our predictions. Beginning with the knowledge that roughly 60 percent of young emerging adults consistently claim to have a purpose in life, we can gauge the relative importance of other factors by how much they increase or decrease from a predicted probability of .6—the probability we would expect if we knew nothing more about a respondent.

Demographic Factors

Social scientists often begin with basic demographic characteristics such as age, race, gender, and socioeconomic status because these factors consistently divide our experience of the world in meaningful ways. Our analysis suggests this holds in our case as well. In the NSYR, young women, on average, are more likely to report the presence of purpose in life, as are Whites, and those who come from households with higher socioeconomic status (defined by parents' income and educational attainment). Why Whites are more likely to report the presence of purposes in the NSYR survey while they were less likely in our national Gallup® survey, as reported in chapter 6, is a subject that needs further investigation. Age, perhaps because it already so delimited in the NSYR sample, does not appear to matter very much.

Figure 3.1 (page 68) gives a sense of how powerful some of these factors are in predicting who reports having a purpose in life. For example, a White female who comes from a high-socioeconomic status (90th percentile on parents' income and education) has an approximately 81 percent likelihood of consistently reporting the presence of purpose. On the other end of the spectrum, a Hispanic male from a low-socioeconomic status (10th percentile on parents' income and education) has only a 29 percent likelihood of reporting purpose. Other combinations of variables fall somewhere in between. Because of the high predictive power of these factors and because these factors often correlate with other behavioral and attitudinal measures we might be interested in, all future analyses statistically control for and remove the influence of these demographic indicators.

Figure 3.1. Predicted probabilities from demographic variables (from table C1, model 1)[a]

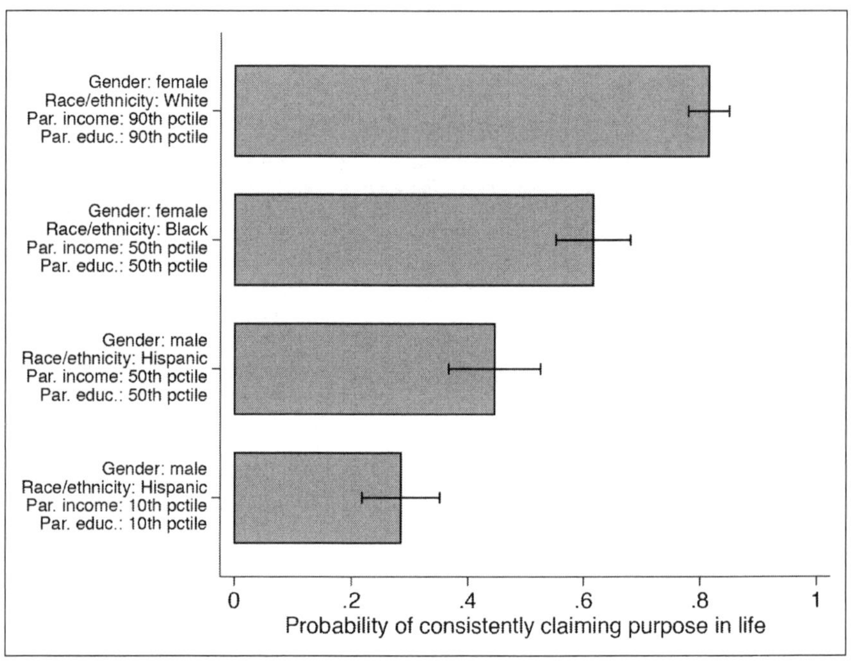

Source: National Study of Youth and Religion 2002–03, 2007–08.

Note: [a]Variables not specified are held at their mean.

Family Structure and Relationship with Parents during Adolescence

Chapter 2 revealed that students' parents were central to their development of a sense of purpose in life. Does this show up in the national survey data as well? To investigate this, we included both a measure of closeness to parents during adolescence, as well as two measures of family structure (whether or not they lived with two biological or adoptive parents during adolescence, and whether or not they experienced at least one parental breakup during childhood or adolescence). The statistical analysis tells us that the reported closeness to parents definitely matters. Adolescents who report being close to their parents are much more likely to report having a purpose in life at age eighteen to twenty-three. Family structure, once demographic characteristics and closeness to family are controlled for, matters significantly less. There is a slight "purpose benefit" to having grown up in a two-parent household, but no discernible impact from having experienced a parental breakup.

As before, we present these findings through predicted probabilities (fig. 3.2). It is clear that these variables do not differentiate who has purpose to

Figure 3.2. Predicted probabilities from family variables (from table C1, model 2)[a]

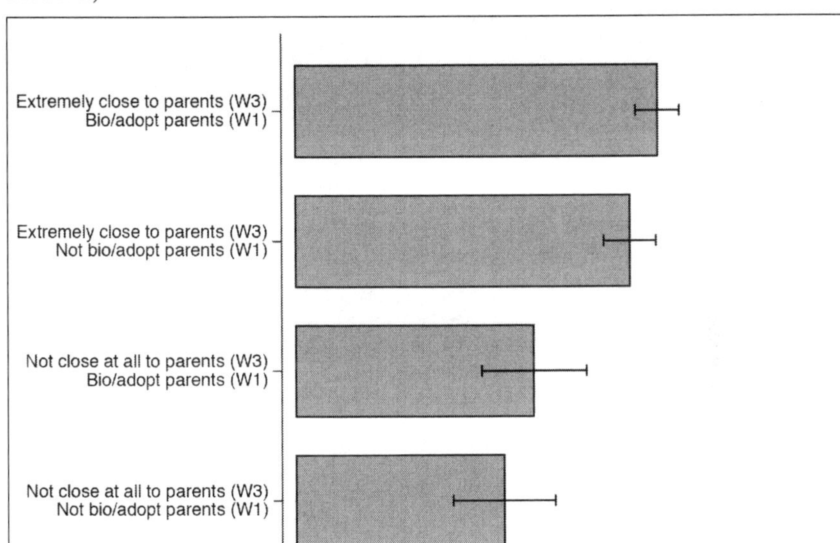

Source: NSYR 2002–03, 2007–08.

Note: [a]Variables not specified are held at their mean.

the same extent as some of the demographic indicators. Still, those who are extremely close to parents and who lived with biological or adoptive parents have a 69 percent likelihood of reporting the presence of purpose, while only 40 percent of those who are not at all close to their parents and did not live with their biological or adoptive parents report the same. This figure also makes it clear that closeness to parents is a more important indicator overall than living with biological or adoptive parents. Feeling close (or not) to one's parents is driving the purpose gap we see in this graph.

Religion during Adolescence

Along with families, religion frequently came up in our interviews as a central component to life purpose. True to its name, the National Study of Youth and Religion surveys contain numerous items that measure youth and emerging adult religion. Although religion is clearly important in the development of a life purpose for many young people, the various measures of religion help us to identify which aspects of faith tend to matter most. Is it religious identity?

Religious community? Spiritual practices? Having a relationship with God? We included measures of religious tradition, closeness to and belief in God, self-rated importance of faith, frequency of Bible reading and prayer, and frequency of church attendance (both of the parents and of the respondent). All of these were measured during adolescence. Similar to what we found with parents, closeness to God during adolescence was the most important predictor of who reports having a life purpose during emerging adulthood. Importance of faith, somewhat surprisingly, had a negative relationship with life purpose, but this was only after all of the other religion variables were controlled for. Apart from these, the only other factor that really stood out was identifying as Jewish. Jewish respondents were substantially more likely to report having a purpose in life compared to other religious traditions.

Figure 3.3 presents some of these graphically. The top bar indicates the predicted value for a Jewish respondent who feels very or extremely close to

Figure 3.3. Predicted probabilities from religion variables (from table C1, model 3)[a]

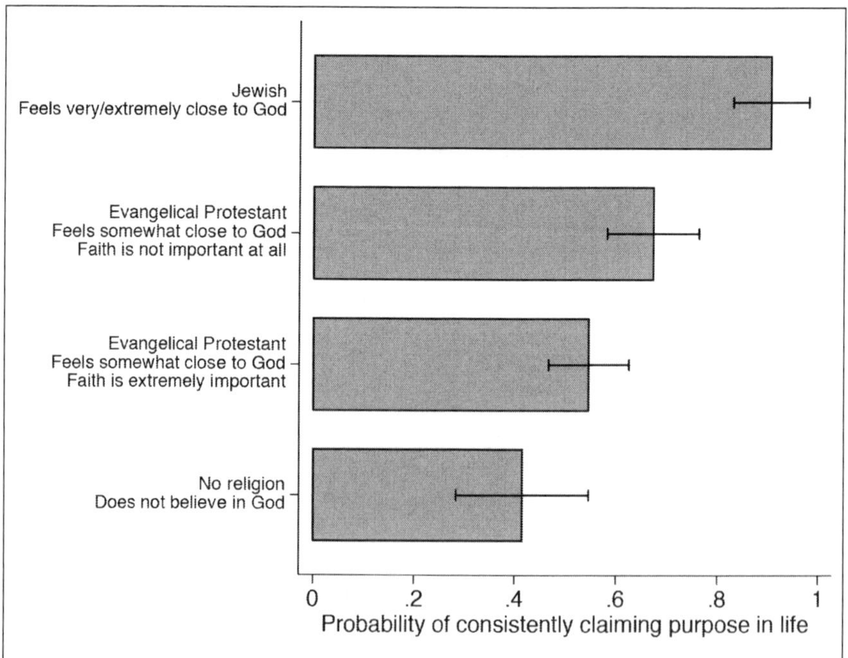

Source: NSYR 2002–03, 2007–08.

Note: [a]Variables not specified are held at their mean.

God. Our model predicts that such a respondent has a 91 percent likelihood of consistently reporting having a purpose.

An Evangelical Protestant who feels somewhat close to God and claims that his or her faith is not important at all has an estimated 67 percent likelihood of reporting purpose. The same individual who reports his or her faith is extremely important only has 55 percent likelihood of reporting purpose once other factors are controlled for. This illustrates the somewhat surprising negative effect on purpose for those who report that their faith is extremely important. Last, those without a faith and who do not believe in God (controlling for other variables held at their mean) have a 41 percent likelihood of consistently reporting purpose. This is 19 percentage points below the mean level of 60 percent for the entire sample.

*Education, Employment, Finances, and Living Status during
Emerging Adulthood*

In this book we focus most of our attention on the development of meaning and purpose during college. Before we delve into the experiences of students, however, it is worth considering how college itself is a factor in developing a sense of purpose in life. When it comes to purpose, do those that go on to college differ in a systematic way from those who do not? The answer appears to be yes. Using a measure of enrollment and educational attainment, we found that those who were currently enrolled in a college or university—of *any* sort—were considerably more likely than those not in college, and much more likely than those who dropped out of high school, to consistently report having a sense of purpose in life. Many young people view their life purpose through a vocational lens (a topic discussed in chapters 5 and 6). Given the increasing importance of college to securing meaningful and stable careers, it is no surprise that college is associated with a sense of purpose in life. To get a better sense of the degree of these differences, we can look at the predicted probabilities in figure 3.4 (page 72).

Those in college are 5 to 10 percentage points above the statistical average of 60 percent. All of those not enrolled in college are below the average. High school dropouts are substantially below the average, with only 33 percent consistently reporting purpose across all three measures.

What about those eighteen- to twenty-three-year-olds who are not in school but are earning money, living on their own, and working jobs? Since these young people are taking on adult responsibilities, we might also expect that they have a clearer trajectory into the future. Our models include measures of earnings, debts, living status, and employment. We find that individual earnings are associated with higher reported purpose, while debt is negatively related to

Figure 3.4. Predicted probabilities from education variables (from table C2, model 1)[a]

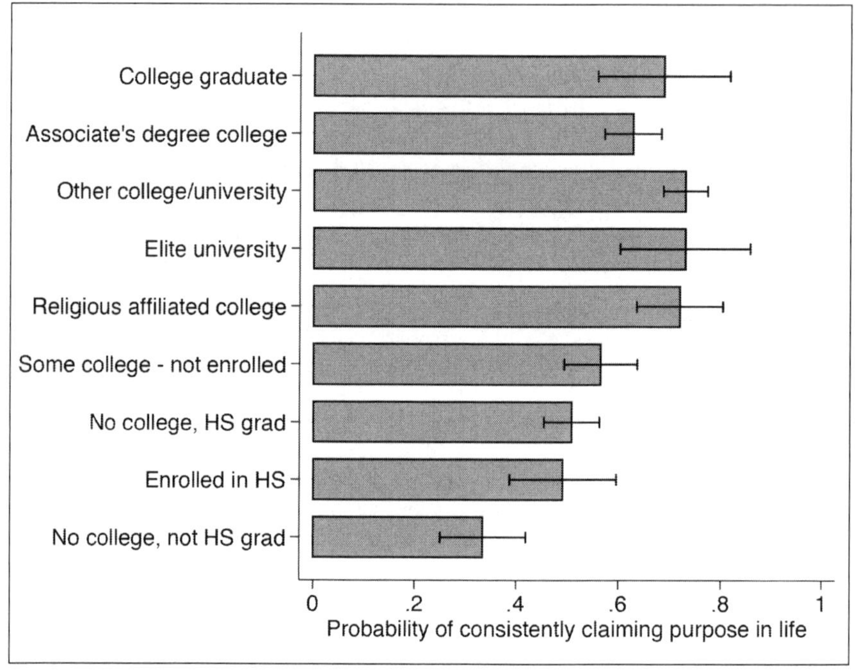

Source: NSYR 2002–03, 2007–08.

Note: [a]Variables not specified are held at their mean.

purpose (although only modestly). Compared to living at home, both those who live in their own place and those who live in group quarters, such as residence halls or barracks, are more likely to consistently report having purpose in life. This latter group is especially likely to report having purpose.

Last, those that are both employed and/or in school (with the larger effect size associated with school) are more likely to report a sense of purpose in life. However, the largest effect size overall is associated with those serving in the armed forces. Once again, we can get a far better sense of the magnitude of these effects from figure 3.5.

Those with high individual earnings (90th percentile), living in group quarters, and both employed and in school have a high probability of reporting purpose (81 percent). Our model predicts that someone in school only (and not working), living in group quarters, and earning the median level of individual income is expected to report well above average levels of purpose (71 percent

Figure 3.5. Predicted probabilities from earnings/employment variables (from table C2, model 2)[a]

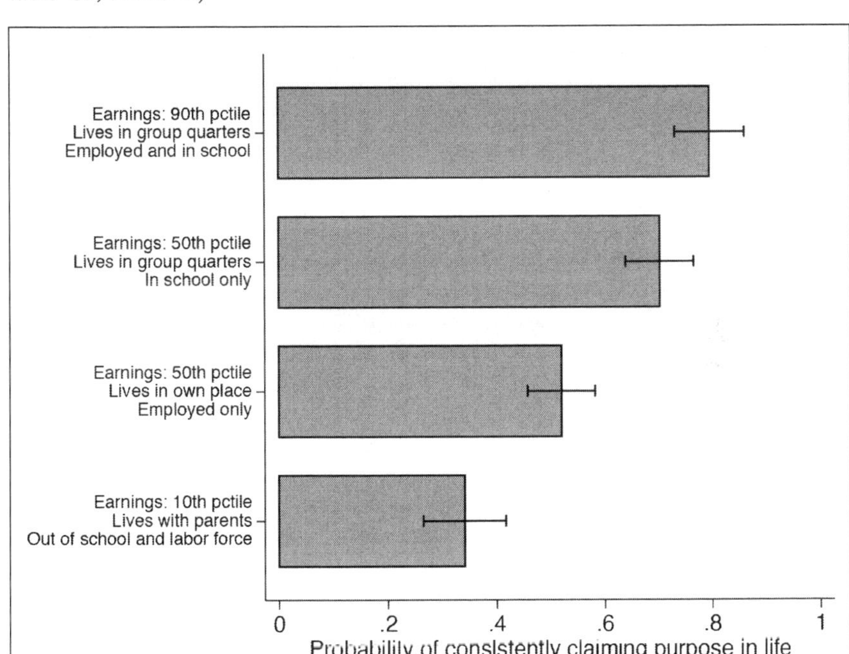

Source: NSYR 2002–03, 2007–08.

Note: [a]Variables not specified are held at their mean.

likelihood). Those working, earning the median income, living in their own place, and not in school are expected to report slightly below average levels of purpose with a 52 percent probability. Last, those living with parents, earning very little (10th percentile), not working, and not in school, have an expected probability of consistently reporting purpose at only 33 percent.

Sexual activity, romantic relationships, and body image are all important factors related psychological well-being, particularly during adolescence and emerging adulthood.[11] Are they associated with a sense of purpose in life as well? We include several measures of sexual activity in our models, including whether or not the respondent reports having ever cohabited (that is, lived with someone in a marriage-like relationship outside of marriage), ever performed or received oral sex, and ever had sexual intercourse. To simplify things, we only include those eighteen- to twenty-three-year-olds who report never having married (this reduces the sample by 7 percent). The results tell us that these variables do very little to differentiate those who consistently report having purpose from those who do not. This can be seen in figure 3.6, which compares the probability associated with someone who has never had sexual intercourse, oral sex, or cohabited to someone who has done all three. The differences are not substantially (or statistically significantly) different from each other. Both groups are near the overall mean of 60 percent.

Body image and health provide a different story. We include a measure of body mass index (derived from height and weight) as well as subjective measures of body image and perceived health. The BMI categories are highly significant in a model by themselves, but once body happiness and perceived health are included, they are no longer statistically significant from the "normal" BMI category. Both happiness with body and self-rated general health are highly correlated with purpose. Additional statistical tests tell us these factors are on par with religion, education, and finances/employment/living status in

Figure 3.6. Predicted probabilities from sex and relationship variables (from table C2, model 3)[a,b]

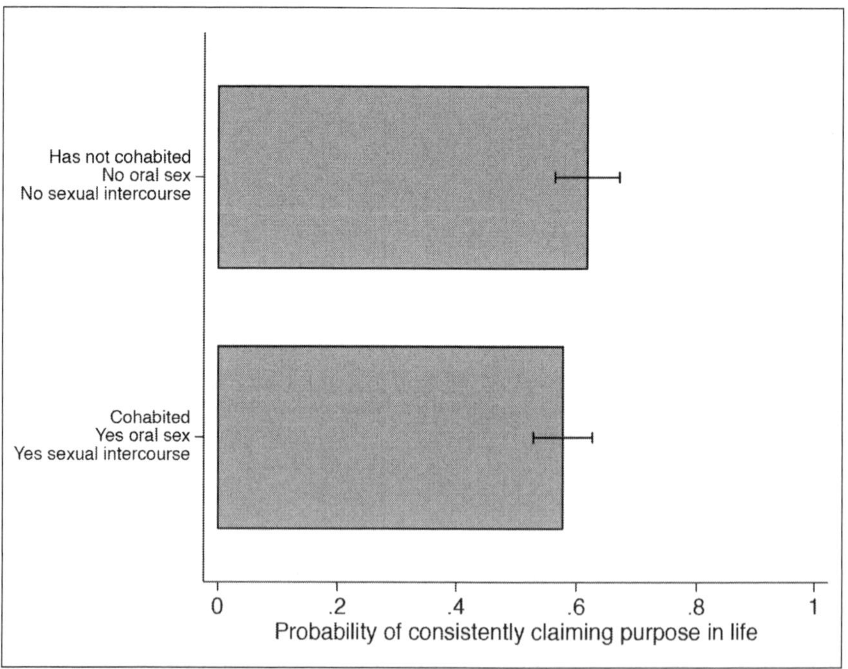

Source: NSYR 2002–03, 2007–08.

Notes: [a]Variables not specified are held at their mean; [b]sample restricted to those never married.

their predictive power. Figure 3.7 illustrates this. Our models estimate that those who are very happy with their body and in excellent health have a 75 percent likelihood of consistently reporting purpose in their lives. Those who are neither happy nor unhappy with their body and report that they are in good health have a 50 percent likelihood of reporting purpose. Those with low body image (very unhappy) and poor health only have a 25 percent likelihood of reporting purpose in their lives.

Deviant Behavior, Prosocial Behavior, and Materialism during Emerging Adulthood

Last, we look at behaviors during emerging adulthood—both those categorized as deviant (to varying extents) and those categorized as prosocial. We expect that deviant behavior, often considered risky or antisocial in nature, will be associated

Figure 3.7. Predicted probabilities from health/body variables (from table C3, model 1)[a]

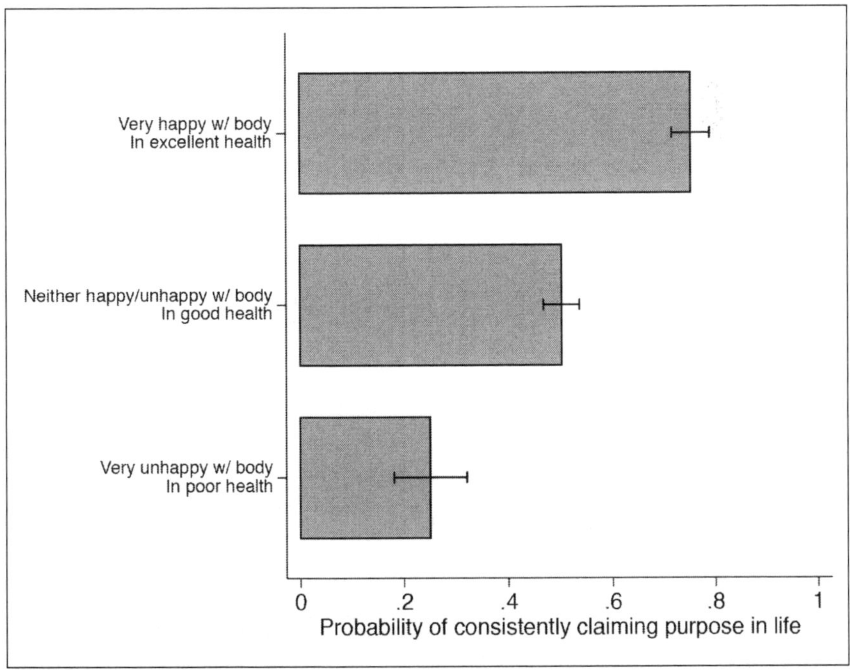

Source: NSYR 2002–03, 2007–08.

Note: [a]Variables not specified are held at their mean.

with lower likelihoods of a sense of direction and purpose to life. On the other hand, we expect that helping behavior, which involves young people reaching beyond their own needs to meets the needs of others, will be associated with higher likelihoods of a sense of direction and purpose to life. We include five measures of deviant behavior during emerging adulthood: binge drinking, cigarette smoking, marijuana smoking, fighting, and pornography use. While all five are associated with decreased reported levels of purpose, we can only be statistically confident in the effects associated with cigarette and marijuana use. Using only the statistically significant variables in figure 3.8, we can compare high cigarette and marijuana use to low use. Those who never smoke marijuana or cigarettes have a 65 percent likelihood of reporting consistent purpose (slightly above the average). Those who smoke cigarettes and marijuana once or twice a month have a 55 percent likelihood of reporting a sense of purpose, while those who smoke these daily (only about 3 percent of the emerging adult population) have a 44 percent likelihood of reporting a sense of purpose.

Figure 3.8. Predicted probabilities from deviant behavior variables (from table C3, model 2)[a]

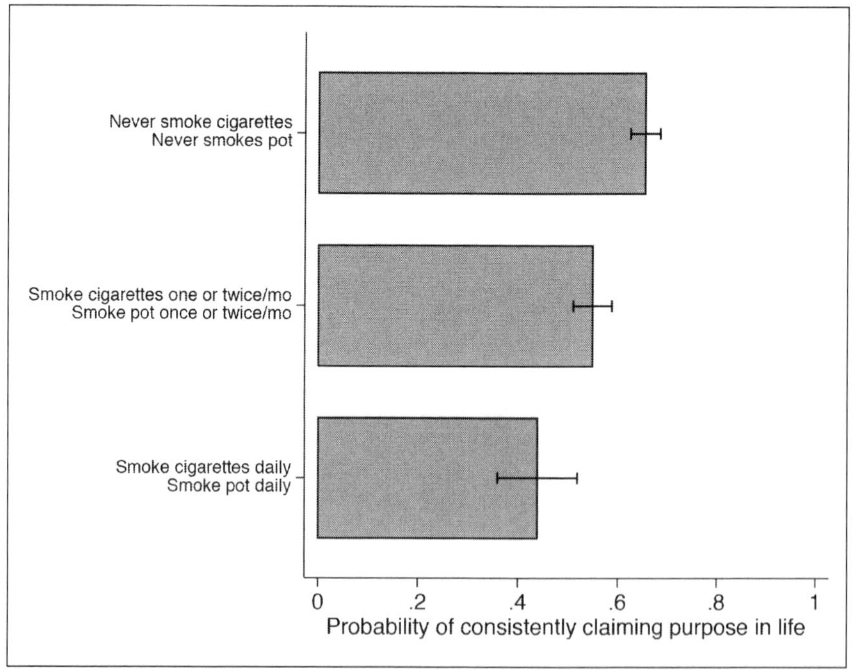

Source: NSYR 2002–03, 2007–08.

Notes: [a]Variables not specified are held at their mean.

We use three measures of helping behavior: donating money, volunteering through an organization, and helping people directly (not through an organization). We can only be confident that the first two are related to purpose, and the overall effect of these behaviors is not very powerful in explaining the presence of purpose. Figure 3.9 shows this. For those who had donated at least 50 dollars and engaged in formal volunteering in the past year, our model predicts that 67 percent will consistently report purpose. For those who did not donate or volunteer the model predicts that 56 percent will consistently report purpose.

The NSYR data contain four measures of materialism at age eighteen to twenty-three. These are measured as agreement or disagreement with the following statements: (1) I admire people who own expensive homes, cars, and clothes; (2) I would be happier if I could afford to buy more things; (3) Shopping and buying things gives me a lot of pleasure; and (4) The things I own say a lot about how well I'm doing in life. Only one of these four variables ends up being statistically significant. One of the variables ("shopping brings me pleasure")

Figure 3.9. Predicted probabilities from helping behavior variables (from table C3, model 3)[a]

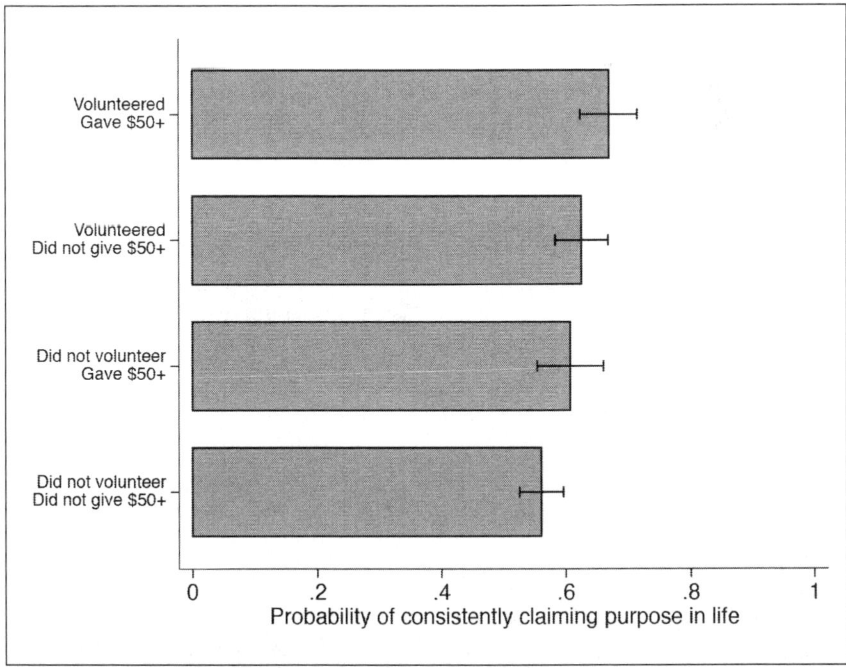

Source: NSYR 2002–03, 2007–08.

Notes: [a]Variables not specified are held at their mean.

Figure 3.10. Predicted probabilities from materialism variables (from table C3, model 4)[a]

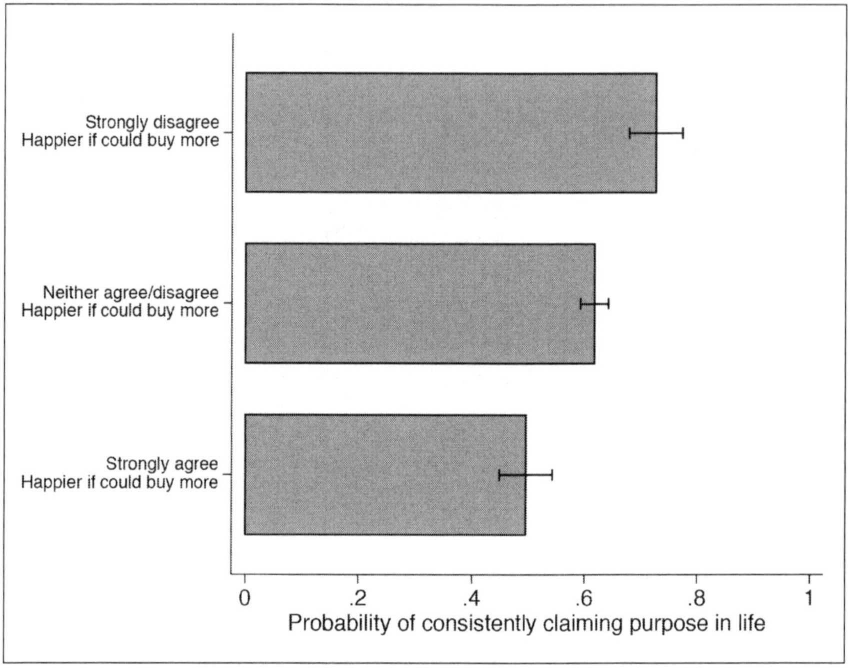

Source: NSYR 2002–03, 2007–08.

Notes: [a]Variables not specified are held at their mean.

actually indicates that more consumerism is associated with higher purpose, but it is not statistically significant. Predicted probabilities are shown in figure 3.10. Those that strongly disagree with the statement, "I would be happier if I could afford to buy more things," have an estimated probability of reporting purpose of 72 percent. Those that neither agree nor disagree with the statement have a predicted probability, 62 percent, near the overall average. For those who strongly agree, 50 percent are estimated to consistently report purpose.

Finally, we ran what might be called the "everything and the kitchen sink" model that includes all independent variables in a single model. A model like this controls for all of the factors simultaneously and estimates the independent effect of each variable net of all the effect of all other variables. We present the statistically significant factors in table 3.1, ordered from largest to smallest effect size.[12] This means that the factors near the top of the list tend to do a better job distinguishing between who reports having purpose and who does not. It is also important to remember that just because a variable is no longer statistically significant in this model does not mean it is unimportant. It may no longer have a clear, direct influence on purpose, but it may have an indirect influence *through* another variable. It is quite plausible that some of these factors indirectly affect purpose through their effect on other behaviors and attitudes.

Table 3.1. Statistically Significant Factors in "Kitchen Sink" Model Ordered from Largest to Smallest Effect Size

Employed and in school[f]
Feels very/extremely close to God[c]
In school only[f]
Other college/university (enrolled)[d]
Self-rated general health
Employed only[f]
Active in armed forces[f]
HS graduate (not enrolled)[d]
Feels somewhat close to God[c]
Jewish[b]
Some college (not enrolled)[d]
Happiness with body
Earnings (W3)
Parents' income
Religiously affiliated college/university (enrolled)[d]
Hispanic[a]
College graduate (bachelors or more)[d]
Frequency of binge drinking
Importance of faith (W3)
Elite university (enrolled)[d]
Would be happier if could afford to buy more
Personal debt (W3)
Not religious[b]
Black[a]
Feels close to parents
Ever had sexual intercourse[e]
LDS[b]
Female
Indeterminate religious identity[b]
Underweight[g]

Source: NSYR 2002–03, 2007–08.

Notes: [a]Reference category is White; [b]reference category is evangelical Protestant; [c]reference category is feels distant from God; [d]reference category is not currently enrolled, did not graduate from high school; [e]coefficient from model restricted to never married (N = 2,263); [f]reference category is not in labor force or school.

Although the entire list of variables in table 3.1 "survived" the influence of the other variables and have a statistically significant contribution to predicting the presence of purpose, the variables near the top tend to have a more powerful effect than the variables near the bottom. What types of variables are these? The most important factors have to do with school enrollment and employment, a sense of closeness to God, and health.

The majority of variables that were significant in the previous models remain significant in this model. And, the majority of nonsignificant variables also remained so. However, there are exceptions. First, although Blacks report slightly less purpose on average than Whites, this did not reach statistical significance in any of the previous models. In the "kitchen sink" model, however, we do find marginally statistical differences between these two groups, with Blacks reporting less purpose on average than Whites. Some religion variables also show signs of having their full direct effect suppressed by other variables. For example, the difference between Mormons and evangelicals is more pronounced (with Mormons reporting more purpose) as well as the difference between those with no religion and evangelicals (with religious "nones" reporting less purpose—a relationship we also found in our Gallup® survey and our interviews). Two other factors whose direct effects were suppressed stand out and are worth noting: the first is the small positive effect on purpose that sexual intercourse has among those who have never been married, and the second is the negative effect of binge drinking.

Several factors were statistically significant in the previous models that no longer are in the model presented in table 3.1. Variables measuring family structure are not statistically significant in the final model, suggesting that feeling close to family members is more important for purpose than the actual structure of the family during adolescence. Two of the religion variables, religious service attendance and prayer, are no longer statistically significant. Interestingly, the negative influence from faith importance on purpose remains. The positive impact of living in group quarters no longer has a direct effect (this is now explained by school enrollment). And last, no measures of helping behavior or deviant behaviors, apart from binge drinking, remain significant predictors of purpose in the full model.

Making Sense of the Findings

What can we say if we take a step back from the statistical analysis and try to make sense of some of the main findings? Let us begin with some of the demographic characteristics. In one sense, it is easy to overlook the precise impact of gender, race, and social class because they are so commonly associated with social division in the United States. Here, we treat them as background characteristics to control for as we conduct other analyses. Taken as a whole, however, they are some of the most powerful predictors of who consistently reports that life has purpose and who does not. At first glance, it seems that women consistently report more purpose in large part because they are not sidetracked by deviant and risky behavior to the same degree as men (see table C3, model 3). However, women are also harder on themselves when it comes to body image and perceived health, which ultimately suppresses some of the true difference between men and women. In the final analysis (table C4), none of our variables can fully account for the persistent advantage that women have over men in purpose during emerging adulthood.

Race and ethnicity also persist as strong markers of identity and status that have real consequences for consistently reporting that life has purpose. In this NSYR survey, Hispanics consistently have 40 to 50 percent lower rates of reporting purpose in life compared to Whites. The direct effect of being African American, in the "kitchen sink" model (table C4), is significantly negative compared to Whites (although more modest than the White/Hispanic difference). And, Jewish emerging adults, both religious and ethnic identity, consistently report some of the highest rates of purpose in life, even after controlling for all other indicators. All of this suggests that a large part of predicting who reports purpose in life can be traced to the role that key social identities play in functioning as salient status markers in the broader society, even net of socioeconomic background and education.[13] These basic divisions can oftentimes be missed when we focus solely on the psychological factors that lead to a healthy sense of purpose in life.

Perhaps the single biggest predictor of purpose is socioeconomic background. Social class, measured by parents' income and education, is strongly associated with who has purpose and who does not. Once again, this is sometimes overlooked in some psychological investigations of purpose in life. We find that purpose is largely associated with the educated and financially well off. Those young people that come from working-class and poor backgrounds are disproportionately left without a sense of purpose in emerging adulthood. Although the idea of emerging adulthood—with its slow, uneven, drifting into full adulthood—has been criticized as a luxury reserved for the privileged,[14] here we find that those at the bottom of the socioeconomic ladder disproportionately experience this sense of aimlessness.

While family income continues to be a strong predictor of emerging adult purpose, the influence of parents' educational attainment is mostly indirect through the emerging adults' own educational progress (see table C2, model 1). College, in particular, is strongly associated with purpose. Being enrolled in college likely signals to emerging adults that they are making concrete progress toward meaningful work and economic independence. For those not enrolled in college, and especially those who never graduated from high school, the reality that prospects for stable employment and living wages are becoming out of reach without a college education[15] leaves a majority without a consistent sense of purpose in life. A 2002 survey[16] finds that nearly all Americans believe finishing formal schooling and economic stability and independence are key markers of becoming an adult. As college increasingly becomes the only reliable pathway to this, we should expect that it would also increasingly differentiate those who report having a purpose during emerging adulthood from those who do not.

Likewise, employment seems to be associated with purpose, although less strongly than education for this age group. Those who are working and not in school are earning money and many will be living independently. Both earning money and moving out of one's parents' household are associated with higher rates of purpose. Interestingly, one of the primary drivers of purpose, apart from work and school, is military service. Like education and work, the military is an institution that gives direction to the lives of young people by providing a broader purpose beyond themselves. Those who are disconnected from these institutions during emerging adulthood are substantially less likely to report that their lives have purpose.

It is rare that social scientific studies look closely at the role that satisfaction with body and health play in the lives of young people. Yet, we find that this is one of the strongest and most consistent predictors of purpose during emerging adulthood. It is important to point out that the *perception* of health and the body is what really matters. Actual body mass index has very little impact apart from these perceptions. Feeling as if one has control over his or her body provides a sense of self-efficacy that seems to provide energy and direction to life (and perhaps a level of confidence). Compared to other key factors (e.g., education, income), this may be one area where targeted efforts to alter emerging adults' overall sense of purpose could potentially be more successful.

Religion, almost by definition, is tasked with the meaning-making and goal orientation that fits the definition of purpose we employ here. But, we find that it matters very much what aspect of religion is being measured. While religious identity mattered (and some religious traditions were more associated with purpose than others), an experience of divine presence was by far the biggest predictor of purpose of our religion measures. Those who felt close to God were considerably more likely to report a sense of purpose in their life when compared to those who felt distant or did not believe in God. We expect that those who feel close to God are more likely to narrate the events of their life as part of a divine plan. This idea that events are not random or accidental, but meaningful in some cosmic sense, can provide the "big picture" reflection on life that is part of the development of purpose. We explore some of these themes throughout the rest of this book, particularly in chapter 10. Unlike our findings in chapters 6 and 10, other measures of religion, such as religious service attendance, prayer, or Bible reading, do not seem to have the same effect. Clearly more research is needed regarding the role that religious service attendance plays in relation to purpose.

One of the most surprising findings was the *negative* impact of those who indicated a high degree of importance of faith. It has to be remembered that this effect is the net of the other religion variables. Still, this is somewhat puzzling. One hypothesis may be that perhaps once felt closeness to God is accounted for, importance of faith can be construed as tightly adhering to a set of religious doctrines and practices without an affective component. If faith is some type of routine formalism, it is possible that this actually discourages reflection on the bigger purpose or meaning of life. Another hypothesis that will emerge from our findings in chapter 10 is that faith may serve as a supporting narrative that allows one greater freedom to search for the particular purpose to which God has called a person.

A number of factors were inconsistently or trivially related to purpose. Families, for example, are important in providing material resources and emotional support, but family structure by itself does not seem to be very important. Of course, experiencing a parental breakup or being raised by a single mother can certainly constrain material resources and can potentially be associated with feeling distant from parents. But, it is important to recognize that it is these consequences of family structure that matter and not the family structure itself.

Sex and relationships matter very little for purpose during emerging adulthood, at least compared to the bigger issues of schooling and employment. Cohabitation, which had a slightly negative effect (see table C3, model 2), completely falls out as predictive in the final model that includes all factors simultaneously. Oral sex and sexual intercourse (restricting the sample to those who have never been married) are also not predictive in the original model. Interestingly, sexual intercourse does become significant, and positive, in the full model once other variables are controlled for. Perhaps sexual intercourse is a proxy for having a significant other, which could contribute to an overall sense of purpose in life. Still, the effect size of this variable is small compared to other factors. This is not a primary factor in developing a sense of purpose during emerging adulthood.

Helping behaviors, such as formal volunteering, charitable giving, and helping the needy directly (not through an organization) were inconsistently related to purpose in life and were not powerful predictors overall. In the final model that includes everything, none of these three factors were significant. The same can be said for measures of deviant behavior such as binge drinking, smoking, fighting, and pornography use. Although they are consistently negatively related to purpose, only some are statistically significant, and their effect size is small compared to some of the other factors we have been discussing. Last, attitudes about materialism mostly do not matter. The one exception to this is the feeling that the respondent would be happier if they could afford to buy more. This is negatively related to purpose. Of course, this question could also be picking up on actual material deprivation and not simply a consumerist drive for happiness. The fact that the other three materialism variables do not seem to matter makes this finding unclear and not robust. For the purposes of this chapter, we simply want to note that these types of factors should clearly be ranked below factors such as family resources, schooling, self-rated health, and some measures of religion as important predictors of purpose during emerging adulthood.

Summing Up

Having a sense of purpose in life is unequally distributed in the young emerging adult population. This chapter presents a "mapping" of purpose during this key phase of the life course. We find that social class, educational attainment, a sense of closeness to God, and perceived health are powerful predictors of who reports the presence of purpose and who does not. These findings are consistent with other surveys that explore whether individuals know their purpose in life or if they see their purpose is part of a larger plan.[17] Other indicators of religious faith, reports of risky and deviant behavior, and attitudes toward consumerism/materialism are less consistent but predict moderate differences in purpose overall. Measures of helping behavior and sexual activity/cohabitation were poor predictors of purpose.

In light of the fact that educational attainment is such a powerful predictor of those who have purpose, it is vitally important to explore how college students encounter the exploration of meaning and purpose. We begin this specific exploration of college students' experience with four extended stories from students at four different years attending four different colleges. The stories help introduce us to the whole range of experiences and influences students encounter as they think about and develop meaning and purpose in college. The chapters that follow then analyze particular aspects of these experiences in greater detail.

Part II

Figuring Out College Students' Quest

Chapter 4

Developing Purpose in the Contemporary University

Four Stories

> To know who you are is to be oriented in moral space, a space in which questions arise about what is good or bad, what is worth doing and what is not, what has meaning and importance for you and what is trivial and secondary.
>
> —Charles Taylor[1]

Narratives claiming colleges and universities have given up on helping students develop purpose, we believe, need to be evaluated in light of evidence. One of those sources of evidence is the stories of students. While Andrea's story in the introduction may confirm aspects of these narratives, our interviews provide a wide variety of other examples from different university contexts. Not surprisingly, the diversity of stories we heard revealed that students' encounters with purpose development do not always neatly follow the declension script.

Students can usually summarize what gives their life meaning or purpose in a few sentences. How and why they arrive at those conclusions, however, proves much more complicated. To help us gain an understanding of how students interpret this experience, we probed students with questions about the various social, psychological, spiritual, and intellectual influences that shaped the development of their meaning and purpose. Most of this book relies on small snippets of these conversations. However, lengthier accounts provide a more complete sense of the texture of students' whole stories and can more fully represent certain types of thinking, talking about, developing, and establishing one's purpose, to which we will refer throughout the book.

These stories illustrate the five types of diversity described in the introduction. First, they illustrate what we already discussed in chapter 2. Students come to college with certain types of diverse experiences that have already shaped their meaning and purpose development. Second, they also reveal that, though much of the literature focuses on questing for meaning and purpose, many students beyond their first year in college claim to have found both meaning and purpose in their lives, and even students who may be searching for purpose do not necessarily consider themselves "lost" on their journey. Third, students articulate a variety of meanings, purposes, and views of the good life and often differentiate between these ideas. Fourth, students experience a wide range of diverse and important curricular and co-curricular influences on their meaning and purpose development—although distinct patterns of influence emerge. These stories highlight some of the most important influences. Finally, these stories illustrate the ways that students' own worldview shapes their journey. Even at a university that might provide opportunities for purpose exploration, students choose to either avoid or embrace these opportunities depending on their current identities and beliefs. Furthermore, a student's worldview often influences whether he or she embraces meaning and purpose making that is "self-authored" or meaning and purpose discovery that could more properly be labeled as "coauthored."

We organize the stories below according to the four traditional years of students. Traditional students are largely the focus of the study (although we did interview some fifth-year students as well).

First Year—Evetta

"I don't know what my purpose is yet; I don't know what I'm supposed to do with my life," Evetta, a first-year student at a secular liberal arts college, confessed to one of us. Yet, despite Evetta's confession, she does not perceive herself as lost on her pilgrimage toward purpose. Evetta's journey to her present college has taken her halfway across the world. Born in a country in central Africa, she immigrated to America when she was eight. In the midst of this transition, her family life proved instrumental in the development of her sense of meaning in a bittersweet way. Her father, a teacher, helped educate her and supplement the teaching she received in schools in Africa and the American Southeast. Not surprisingly, she still looks to both her parents as role models, "I definitely see my parents as people who worked hard to live the good life, to set good examples for us." She also attributes much of her current identity to them: "Everything they did led to where I am today." Tragically, she later reveals, "Freshman year of high school my dad passed away, and so it's my mom and the rest of us."

The influence of her late father still reverberates in how she thinks about life's meaning. "I was really close with my dad . . . Especially after my dad passed away, the things that people say become more important to you." In particular, she recalls a talk that shaped her outlook

> I was, I don't know, fourteen or something. He was talking about the future, 'cause I used to just brush it off and be like, "Who cares? I'm only fourteen. It doesn't matter." But he would tell me, "You're not always going to be able to see things like the way you do. One year from now, things will change." Looking back on that I've been able to see how that influenced the way my life went because once you start living with more of something driven behind you rather than just going step by step, like letting things affect you; then it just creates a different aura about you, a different aura about your life compared to maybe someone else's. Maybe it's not even that their life is different, it's just that you're able to live more fully.

While she could not identify her specific purpose, Evetta does share the general meaning of life that her parents provided, which helps guide her.

> I just feel like my parents have engrained in me, especially through Christianity, that my life is supposed to mean something to other people. It's supposed to be good, moral, and so I feel that sense—like you should be able to leave something behind that says you were a good person, or you helped other people.

Indeed, a shared religious identity was central in her relationship to her parents.

> We definitely talked about religion a lot because my parents are both Christians; so am I, and we would talk about, like, everything else would kind of flow from that. So, if we were talking about ethnicity or we would be talking about schools and what you want to do when you grow up, it would all be centered around Christianity.

She also believes Christianity holds the key to discovering her future purpose.

> I just feel like the more I read my Bible or the more that I fellow-ship with other people, the more I'm able to actually live my life in the way I think God would like me to live it. And so through that, I think, I'll hopefully be able to find my purpose.

While Evetta's parents have helped sculpt her initial understanding of life's meaning and the groundwork for determining her purpose, she also believes that much of her understanding will depend on her own decisions and beliefs. "And so I feel like my parents are instrumental, but they are not the end-all be-all in everything." Evetta uses her sister as a means of comparison to illustrate this point:

> I feel like they [her parents] have helped me, but . . . the individual defines how their life is going to be shaped out and what their morals are going to be; because I can decide that stealing is bad or whatever, but then my sister might not feel the same way or, if she has different experiences than I did or because of her personality or her behavior.

Evetta says her beliefs have grown, in some ways, apart from her parents' beliefs. "My mom, she's really like, sometimes she thinks everything's of the devil—so I definitely don't see things like that."

As an example of another meaning and purpose forming experience, Evetta points to an "eye-opening" trip during high school back to her native country in Africa. "The reason we went back, though, was because, after my dad passed away, all the people in his family wanted to see us—see who we were—and we also wanted to see our family." Her father's job enabled their family to leave Africa and come to America when genocide spilled over into her country. Evetta's extended family was not as fortunate. Many experienced the horrors and tragedies, particularly the women. "I was lucky enough to leave when the genocide happened, and some of my cousins—they weren't so lucky. Some of them were raped or different things happened to them." Knowing that she was spared these horrible experiences gives Evetta a unique understanding of both her identity as a contemporary African immigrant and her future purpose.

> It just really helped me to see that, yeah, I'm not from here and because of that my purpose is different than other people's. . . . Because of that I feel like my life is so different. It's the reason I have to do something, to be successful, because I wouldn't have got a chance to. And so I have to try harder and give it my all.

Following their trip, Evetta's mother impressed on her children how thankful and appreciative she was for their move to America. "Sometimes my mom says that there are so many opportunities here and people don't see that, or they don't utilize all of them. I might have never had these opportunities." Evetta has taken the message to heart. "It can't be something I take for granted. I might have never gone to college, you know; so I feel like it's really important to me to value everything that I've been given."

Evetta never questioned going to college, since her parents expected she would go. Evetta recalls seeing the purpose of college as something more than obtaining a job. She saw college as "really important because it helps you think differently and that was something I wanted to see." She desired to be challenged to think for herself and to investigate the world around her.

> . . . in high school you're still living at home, you're still sheltered from everything, and, like, college is a totally different experience, and so you're able to see, hmm, do I really believe this, or should I change my views to fit what really I actually truly feel, truly believe?

Though her first year of college has been a time of self-discovery and determination, she also sees it as more than this. It also serves as "the way you can get to where you want to go." Consequently, "It's the tool you use to be what you want to be or have a good life—to be able to provide for your family or reach the goals you want to set for yourself."

In response to questions about how classes have influenced her views about meaning and purpose, Evetta notes reading the *Communist Manifesto* for the first time. Issues of social justice began to grab Evetta's attention. "It showed me how maybe there are flaws to the way communities [are] run nowadays, and how people view morality, especially how they treat each other . . . although it was back in the 1800s, even now [the social class gap] is still a problem." She also cites one of her first classes, a philosophy course, that challenged her to examine life's meaning and purpose. She was introduced to conversations surrounding various philosophers, different beliefs, the meaning of life, and ethics.

> That class was really able to help me. I didn't necessarily believe all that the philosophers said, but it was able to make me see what other people believe, see how they came up with these ideas, and if that makes sense to me or if it's too abstract or too out there for me.

The course also delved into the topic of God and morality as well. "It was interesting to see how lots of people can have such varying views on the same topic." Growing up, Evetta had not encountered much opposition to her beliefs from peers. In this class, she encountered a whole different outlook: "I was like the only mostly conservative person—everybody else was very liberal—and the way they talk about God or the way they talk about religion or their morals pertaining to their lives." It was a new experience for Evetta, and helped her "to see how different people can be." She learned to appreciate others' opinions and reasoning without compromising her own. She now appreciates how college "shows you different perspectives, and you can kind of decide if you want to follow that perspective or just stick to your own."

Indeed, since coming to college, Evetta has sought "to have more of an open mind." College has been the perfect environment to be exposed to new ideas and experiences.

> When I came to [this college] I had to decide that this isn't just going to be my lifestyle, it's just not going to be my background, and so I wasn't allowed to do certain things when I was younger, and so I was able to see like people drinking and stuff, and I'd see that and I'd be like, "So why wasn't I able to drink?" And I look at the people around me and see, "Oh, so that's why." And you kind of get like a good idea of why things are the way they are.

College has also given Evetta the chance to "see how different people live and how their morals affect them as well. And so while I've been here, it's just kind of solidified what I was taught when I was growing up." Although some of the beliefs Evetta was taught as a child have been confirmed, Evetta still aspires to verify others. "I just kind of want to see why I believe this, why I believe that."

Evetta identifies the most formative experiences for her views on life's meaning and purpose as her relationships with other students. Through these various interactions, Evetta has encountered people with different beliefs than her own.

> Meeting new people and being more accepting of their differences has been something that has really changed . . . it's been very eye-opening to see why people believe what they believe. You can't just go up to them and change what they believe because it's already in them, but maybe you can help them see things in different ways. And, I think that's been something that I've been able to see—the difference between helping people see things your way if you want to, or changing their views completely.

For instance, through her friendships on campus, Evetta claims she's "definitely talked to my friends about being Christian or having a purpose for your life."

Her extracurricular involvement has also been meaningful to her. In her spare time, Evetta tutors young boys, undertakes a work-study job, participates in a campus Christian group, and attends a local church. However, all of her extracurricular activities combined have proven to be overwhelming and Evetta is currently attempting to reduce her commitments. "I've been trying to like take one off, one at a time, and focus on a few 'cause there's just so much to do all the time—there's no way you can do everything, which is sad." When it comes to conversations about meaning and purpose, Evetta encounters these discussions primarily with the Christian group. "We talk about why we believe what we believe and if that's like, you know, what backs up what we think." For Evetta, these conversations have opened her eyes to the arguments people have for not believing Christianity and strengthened her own convictions for being a Christian. The Christian group has been particularly instrumental, especially during her History of Modern Philosophy class, "'cause at first when I took the class . . . I had to sit down and think about, you know, really why, why would I be a Christian, and I think that's been really helpful to help me see why." In particular, the group has been a good forum for discussion about the character of God. At one time, she struggled with the question, "You can know God exists, but I don't know how you can really know who He is." The Christian group has helped her explore this question. As she states it, they did not provide

> "answer answers," but more like, I don't know, like leading you toward the goal. . . . So, the [Christian group] has been able to help me look through my Bible, talk with other people, and see why we think it pertains to us.

Although Evetta would not claim to have found her particular purpose, she perceives that being a Christian shapes her thoughts about the meaning of life.

> If I wasn't a Christian, the way I would view life and the meaning behind it would be totally different. I wouldn't be living my life for God, I would be living my life for myself and so the intent behind everything would be changed.

She says her actions would be based on selfish desires and attention, rather than obedience to God or the Bible. Thus, Evetta proclaims that her actions "have a bigger reason behind it." Evetta believes that nontheists usually focus on the question, "Do I want to better myself?" when deciding to help someone. But, she believes her actions are based on God's will. "I want to better myself so that I can be more in tune to God, so that I can be a good example for my sisters so that they want to follow God."

In light of her religious understanding of meaning, material goods, achievement, or "worldly" success do not define a good life for Evetta. Instead, relationships and making a positive difference in others' lives remain a priority. In five years, Evetta says if she was "still really close with my family, and I had a job that was able to help me impact other people," that would be a good life. She anticipates getting involved in public health in third world countries, desiring to help others medically, or by working in public policy. "I feel like if I was able to impact other people that would be the best way to live the good life . . . to be fulfilled, at least for me."

Second Year—Jacob

Raised in New York, Jacob attended a Jewish elementary school until sixth grade, where he finished his secondary education at a public school. Throughout his childhood, Jacob's African-born father and American mother maintained a religious household where Jacob adhered to the elements of the Orthodox Jewish faith. They affirmed a "belief in one God," and he notes, "We go to our synagogue every Saturday. Sometimes on Friday night, we celebrate all of the Jewish holidays. We have Sabbath dinner Friday night . . ." Having intimate relationships revolving around faith and family, Jacob says, "I was very close to my parents. I'd tell them any problems I had—really—and I never really kept anything from them." Jacob recalls a few conversations from his childhood in which he engaged his parents in conversation about life's meaning and purpose.

> I remember when I was younger, I asked them, "What's the meaning of life?" and they were like, "I don't know," and they told me I could like look it up online just because it's a very hard question to answer, and it's very philosophical. So I did look it up online, but I didn't really get so far, though. There's a lot of stuff out there about this person says this, this person says this, and I found a bunch of different websites about it, but some of them didn't look so credible, so I didn't really know where to go next. Definitely in terms of purpose of life, though, I've talked to my parents about what I'm gonna do with my life.

When asked what currently gives his life meaning, Jacob cites his family and friends. However, Jacob is less sure of the purpose of life: "growing up, getting married, having a family, I guess, and then, I don't know, maybe changing . . . maybe impacting somebody's life or something in a way that changes who they are, I don't know."

What has shaped Jacob's outlook is also less clear. Jacob's parents and grandparents have served as role models and mentors in his life. While he describes his mother as an influential example in his life, Jacob says, "I never really talked about purpose or meaning or anything with her." Despite the lack of explicit conversations about the meaning of life, Jacob believes his parents played and continue to play a critical part in shaping his understanding of life's meaning. "They definitely raised me to be religious, and there was a period of time that I wasn't, but I feel like that's something that's very important in terms of figuring out what everybody's meant for, the purpose for everybody."

As he entered high school, Jacob says he became "less religious." Jacob felt influenced by other less-religious Jewish friends.

> I migrated toward them, I guess . . . we all shared the same belief, but more toward their practices in terms of what I did on Shabbat because they all kept all the holidays and everything, it was really just using electronics on like computers, TVs, on Shabbat and the holidays.

His parents found out when "they walked into my room when I was on my computer on Shabbat," and "on the Sabbath you can't use electronics."

According to Jacob, his wayward ways changed when in tenth grade he became involved with the National Conference of Synagogue Youth (NCSY). Their motto, "Large enough to be a region, small enough to be a family," impacted Jacob's faith and future. Jacob recalled one conversation with a NCSY friend about purpose. "He said the main thing is, or what stuck with me, was to be happy." Jacob found this advice useful. "It's pretty vague, but at the same time it's very helpful, like do what makes you happy, and don't let anyone tell you that you can't do that."

Through NCSY, Jacob also began what he considers "in terms of purpose, the biggest experience that happened." Jacob met a girl on a NCSY trip, and they became friends and eventually dated. While Jacob states, "We never really discussed a purpose or meaning," he admits to thinking about the topic due to his girlfriend's prior injury resulting from an accident. Living in two different cities, Jacob and she "talked on the phone basically every day." However, due to the nature of her injury, ". . . one week we could talk and then the next week she just was having a terrible week so we couldn't talk. . . ." The ups and downs of communication eventually led to an end of their dating relationship.

> She told me that after these two weeks of talking, or of not talking, it was hard for her to remember . . . the feelings when she was with me after being so far apart and not talking to each other in that time, which I understood.

Despite an end to the romantic relationship, Jacob still kept in touch with his old girlfriend as she underwent various treatments to help improve her condition. "We ended up Skyping like once a week for three hours at a time, and her mom told me that really helped her get through everything." Following her treatments, they rekindled their dating relationship. Jacob's support during her treatments impacted his purpose in profound ways.

> I've talked to her mom a lot about it—and her mom and her dad both have thanked me so many times because I was a huge help in getting her through everything. So I've definitely thought about a purpose in terms of that, and helping her get through it.

Eventually, however, they ended their relationship.

Even though Jacob chose to attend a Jewish university after high school, he initially saw the purpose of higher education as "to get a better job." He currently does not necessarily see receiving an education and obtaining a well-paying job as separate from his overall purpose since, as Jacob put it, "In order to help people, you need to be in a good position yourself financially, . . . so I guess a higher education would give me a better job in order to help people." He also chose a Jewish university, since "I definitely feel like being a religious Jew is something very important in terms of the purpose that they [parents] gave to me."

So far, in his college courses, he has experienced religious conversations surrounding purpose and meaning of life. Classes also help stimulate conversations among his friends. Jacob recalls talking with another friend from a philosophy class about life's meaning, "what he thought about it and what I thought about it, and why we thought we were here." However, Jacob admits, "it got to the point where we were just like, 'I don't know how to get to the next level of discussing this.'" One way that Jacob perceives himself getting to the next level is through the help of his rabbinical teachers. Through his close relationships with his rabbis, Jacob feels "I can just walk up to them" and ask them the difficult life questions, which is "much more helpful." He remembers one Judaic studies class that delved into the topic. "We talked about meaning, and, of course, the answer, or meaning in life, or purpose in life, is to learn Torah, as extolled to me by my rabbi. So yeah, we have talked about it one time." While Jacob has had personal conversations with the rabbis about the meaning or purpose of life, he has not had these "with any of my secular teachers." He says the reason for this difference lies in the personal nature of the relationship, "On Sabbath . . . we get invited to their houses all the time, so we see them outside of school, which is very nice, and we become very close with them." In one conversation about life's purpose with his rabbi, Jacob recalls:

> We discussed our purpose, I guess, I'd say, and the main thing we were talking about was finding the one girl that makes you happy and marrying her, and just being so happy together and making her

happy and, yeah, so finding a wife, I guess, would be one thing we've discussed about purpose.

For the most part, college has served to deepen Jacob's growing convictions about the importance of family, the Torah, and happiness that are rooted in his Jewish identity and beliefs. Consequently, he currently summarizes his future understanding of purpose in those three ways.

> One thing in Judaism we definitely have [is] get married, have children—and getting married is definitely one purpose I see as in the future . . . being Jewish [also] involves learning the Torah, keeping all of the laws, and that helps you be happy.

Overall, Jacob feels that his religion has made it easier to contemplate the questions of meaning and purpose in life as, "with a religion you have some sort of direction." Jacob's five-year goals or direction appear quite conventional. "I actually hope to be married by then, and have a job, and living in a house. . . ." That would be considered a "good life."

Third Year—Troy

Troy attends a regional state university and majors in marketing with an emphasis on distribution logistics and general management. Raised an only child, he wants to make sure that we know one thing about his life: "We've had a dog our whole life." When asked about what gives his life meaning, Troy thinks of recent events that give him pleasure or stir him. "I mean, my friends, obviously, they give my life meaning because I like hanging out with them and having fun. Right now, my grandpa's in the hospital so I guess he kind of inspires me too." Beyond these recent events, he struggles to answer the question. "I don't know. It's a not very straightforward question. It's hard to think . . ."

When asked about what gives his life purpose, Troy hesitates and then lists a number of upcoming goals:

> Um, I don't know. I guess I could say my purpose right now is I want to graduate, get a job, live on my own, maybe eventually get married and start a family. I'd like to travel a lot. See the world. If that's considered a purpose. . . .

Troy indicates a preference for focusing more on immediate concrete realities and specific goals rather than a future overarching purpose.

When probing Troy further to find out the source for his views about meaning and purpose, he points to the instrumental role of his parents. "I would consider my parents models, yes. My dad, definitely. Same with my mom. There's nothing really that I wouldn't want to be like them." Following this up, he points to the role of his parents in setting before him particular career goals: "Both my parents were in business, so that kind of led me toward business, and my parents are both relatively successful so that drives me to want to be successful like them." In particular, Troy focuses on the material aspects associated with this success. "I've grown up . . . I'm not saying I'm rich, I'm just saying, like, I've had nice things and I like nice things, because I've had those in my past, and I'd like to have them in the future too." In fact, he claims, "I would honestly take my dad's job if it was offered to me."

Although Troy claims to want to model his parents in every way, he actually does not model them when it comes to religion. His Lutheran mom works as an administrative assistant at the church. His dad, while raised Catholic, "doesn't really go to church, but I honestly don't know what he believes. He doesn't really talk about it. I think he might believe, I think he does believe in God. But, he doesn't really talk about it." Despite the apparent theism of his parents, Troy admits, "I don't go to church with them. They make me go on Christmas just so my grandparents are happy." Troy did grow up going to church, but he claims, "I hated every minute of it. I was like, 'I don't want to go to Sunday school, I just want to stay home and watch cartoons. I just want to go to sleep.'" In the end, he says, since his attendance turned into a big argument every Sunday, around seventh or eighth grade his mother "just gave up." Troy thinks it happened "once I got my confirmation, which I think was thirteen at my church."

Since that time, Troy recalls that during high school, "Religion just wasn't a topic that I cared about." Now, Troy notes, "I feel awkward talking about it in front of other people. . . . I'm not just going to be like, 'Yeah, I'm atheist.'" The reason for Troy's hesitancy comes from the social stigma he sees associated with atheism. "I don't want them to have a negative view toward me because they're like, 'Oh, he's an atheist.'" When asked how he would currently describe himself if he was given a survey that asked for his religious identity, Troy states he would choose "the 'none' option."

Troy does not point to any influential peer relationships as contributing to his rejection of religion. In fact, he would not point to his peer relationships as playing a role in his thinking about purpose in general. He considered himself a loner at the beginning of high school. Later, he tells us, "I started getting more friends and becoming more popular. So, I guess, yeah, it was mainly people who helped me. And, drinking." Drinking, he claims, helped him with his social life. "Going out to parties. That's, in my mind, the best way to make friends in high school, even though it sounds terrible."

After high school, Troy chose to attend a regional college due to "the features of the campus, obviously it's a good school, and I know they have a well-ranked business college here which was an important factor too." More specifically, though, "I wanted to make money. I wanted to be able to attain those things that I talked about previously." Troy does seem at times to believe in some other purpose for college. He claims, "I feel that if people don't go to college, they don't really make a difference in the world. I just feel like, going to college makes you something, I don't know." While he appears to try to articulate some higher goal, Troy struggles to express what that "something" is. He does finally settle on the idea, "like you contribute to the world by getting educated. Like the advancement of society, too, that's a big part, just moving forward. I mean, I don't want to take out garbage my whole life." It would appear that Troy teeters on the verge of taking a larger view of college's purpose that links to societal well-being, but he still finally settles on the fact that he does not want a low-level job.

When asked about how college courses have helped his purpose, he answers in utilitarian terms. "I came into college knowing I wanted to be into business, but I didn't know specifically what I wanted, and then I declared my major last year." However, when taking classes that might address larger philosophical issues, Troy finds himself disengaged. Although he notes that his ethics class maybe touched on these matters, he complains, "I don't like my ethics class because my teacher is biased." When asked why, he responds, "Well, she's a big, fat, Black woman. And we talked about McDonald's, and she blames McDonald's for America being fat, saying it's their fault for making the food." He does note that one of his classes on diversity helped him, since there were "a lot of meaningful readings in there, obviously about like issues of diversity, like homosexuality, women's rights, Black rights, African-American rights, whatever you want to call them." While not dealing with the meaning or purpose of life, Troy believes they impacted him, "because they really opened up how I thought about different issues. Before, I was more narrow-minded, I guess I could say." Troy would not say that he has had any personal interaction with the faculty other than academic advising. Plus, he admits that "I wouldn't talk to them" when it came to discussing subjects such as life's meaning and purpose. In fact, he would not claim to have any other adult mentors beyond his parents, except for his grandparents.

Troy claims the co-curricular part of college has also helped him with his purpose as he conceives it, "just like the social aspect of talking to people and stuff kind of guided me as well." Beyond this contribution, however, Troy's social life in college has proved rather limited, as have his conversations with friends. He says his romantic life deserves part of the blame. He had a girlfriend for almost two years. "I was always with her, so it's, you know what I mean, you don't have as many friends when you have a girlfriend." The relationship did make him think about longer-term goals, "I wanted to be there for her, and I wanted to marry this girl." Recently, however, they broke up. His response to the break-up has taken what many might consider a common, rebounding tone: "Now, I'm kind of like, you know what, I'm almost twenty-one. I'm going to be single for a while, go to parties."

Currently, though, he mostly hangs out with his roommates who are big into gaming. When asked if he engaged in conversations about big questions such as the meaning of life, Troy admits, "Not really, no. I don't have any friends like that. Well, I had some, but those are the kids I don't really talk to anymore. I'd like to get back to talking to them." When asked if he had any friends he would consider role models of the good life, Troy states, "I don't perceive them as bad or good. I just kind of perceive them as, they're just my friends and we get along and hang out, but I don't like aspire to be like them." Interestingly, Troy took the question to refer to how they dress, "Maybe clothing or something like that, you know what I'm talking about? If my friends have certain clothes then maybe I'll want to like get those types of clothes."

When speaking about not having a religious identity, Troy claims, "College definitely reinforced it." He tells us that classes did not play a role though. It was mainly certain " 'religious fanatics' who start screaming and yelling, 'You're all going to hell if you have loans, debt, gay, premarital sex, use condoms, drink alcohol. . . .' All that stuff." Still, Troy never attended the local atheist club that would come and respond to these preachers. Again, he noted, "I don't need to broadcast or like get together with other people. It's just how I feel. I'm not going to go out of my way about it." In fact, when it comes to religion and purpose in general, Troy reiterates, "It doesn't really make a difference to me. I mean, I'm sure some people are like, 'Oh, God has a plan for me' or whatever, but not me." His philosophy can be summed up, "I just live for my own satisfaction to be happy in life, and I don't worry about what else is going on. I live my life."

When thinking about the future of his life, Troy largely sticks to concrete goals. "I'd like to have a job in downtown Chicago. I definitely want to have a job in the city. . . . I'd probably like to have a girlfriend or a fiancé or a wife. Let's see, I would be twenty-five, maybe not a wife." He also hopes to travel. That way he can say, "So like if someone is like, 'Oh, the Dominican Republic, it's a bunch of poor people or a bunch of losers,' or whatever. I've been there, I know what it's like. I could tell you exactly." He also adds, "I don't like to admit it, but I am kind of a materialistic person. I love cars . . . technology stuff, like computers and whatnot. I like clothes." Troy offers an important distinction though in his mind: "I didn't really buy them to impress other people. I buy them because I like them."

At the end of the interview, Troy does suggest that maybe in the future, "I might eventually become less materialistic and more settled." When asked why, he points to the model of his father who recently told him, "When I was young, I wanted everything, and I bought a bunch of stupid stuff. And now you sit back and you look at it and you're just like, 'I just want to enjoy my life, and I don't need anything extravagant.'"

Fourth Year—Brooke

"Okay, what do we do with all this now? We've been here for four years, we've made these connections. We've made these friends. We've learned these things. Now it's just like, 'What do we do?'" Brooke, a fourth-year psychology major and education minor at a Catholic university shares her thoughts about the future with one of us. She feels a bit torn. On the one hand, one of the things that faces her, like many college seniors, concerns her debt issues, "realizing, you know, after college and stuff, I'll have to start paying my loans." As a result, she wants a career that makes money, but she despises focusing on a career for the point of money, particularly in light of her parents' situation. "Money's a very sensitive topic for them . . . it's just like recently and stuff, and that's what a lot of their separation has to do with, so I try to avoid that when talking with them."

Brooke's reference to her parents' separation indicates another difficult transition Brooke faces. She grew up in a Catholic family with three younger siblings (a younger sister and two younger brothers), and lived in the same place her whole life. "I'm very close to my parents," she admits. Her father worked as the stay-at-home dad, which she appreciated. It made her feel like if she wanted to go and work and somebody else could stay at home, "that's a possibility." As an added bonus, "He cooked pretty well, so I definitely respect that."

Although close to both parents, she confesses, "My mom and I, the last few years, I would say we've sort of, you know, had more arguments." One of the arguments concerned money and her future purpose.

> My mom says, "Oh well, if you work this job, you know you're not gonna make any money" and stuff like that. For me, right now, I've sort of developed the attitude, "Mom, I don't care about money at this point."

Part of Brooke's attitude comes from watching her parents, "Seeing them struggle, fight, stuff like that lately. I realize, 'Okay, I don't want to worry about money. I don't want to put my kids through any of this.'" She adds, "My parents separated, so now my dad is still at our house and my mom is somewhere else."

Her thoughts about money, not surprisingly, influenced what she shared with us about meaning and purpose. When asked about what gives her life meaning, she identifies something different than money or material things: "it's just people, relationships, and things like that." This meaning comes from a certain experience or feeling inside of her:

> I'll have that weird inner tingly feeling when I'm interacting with another person. You make a connection with the person. You realize you could help a person, and just like that, I'm like, "Oh, that's what it's all about."

She believes her purpose flows from this meaning. "I would like to leave a legacy. That there's one person that cared. There was one person that worked for other people. Just sort of be selfless." She compares this perspective to money goals. "Even if I'm not rich and famous, at least, it's like, 'Hey, that person was great. They really felt the human spirit, and they were just, you know, like selfless and giving love,' and things like that." When asked where this vision for selfless, giving love comes from, Brooke admits, "I am not sure. I actually don't know, because I'm not particularly religious. I never really was and now even less, so I don't know if it comes from there." She speculates that it may come from her personality and some privileged life circumstances. "I never really had to think about all the hard things in life, and so I think it was just having this easy, happy-go-lucky sort of thing going on that I could just take time and appreciate those things." Yet, she still admits that she is not quite sure. "I don't know, somehow I realized it's just sort of, love solves everything."

Her career goal flows from this purpose, although it also involves obtaining some professional wisdom as well. "My goal would be to eventually go back to grad school to get some sort of master's, or some sort of certification, to work with individuals with autism or other disabilities." The formation of this particular career goal stems less from her university experience and more from a summer camp experience:

> The last two summers I worked at an Easter Seals camp for kids with special needs—or kids and adults rather—so that sort of sparked my interest. I'm fascinated by it, being a psychology major, I really got into autism and like things . . . it's just like a big topic right now, so they need a lot of people working there and finding out the causes, finding out the different treatments and things like that.

She also encountered times when she experienced that special feeling that gives her meaning:

> There were a lot of frustrating days that I'd be up for, you know, twenty hours and I'd be, you know, so tired and stuff, but then you

get up in the morning and you see all your campers and people that you work with having fun, being excited, having this experience, and that's just, like, "Oh my gosh, like that's it."

Although Brooke is a senior, she would not say her education directly helped her with issues of meaning and purpose. She went to a public school where she rarely encountered the issue. While she believes opportunities existed to explore this matter at her Catholic university, she admits when asked if she has experienced discussions about the meaning and purpose of life in class, "I try and avoid those sorts of classes." By "those classes," Brooke refers to some of the questions explored in philosophy classes. Brooke admits, "I just don't think all that deeper philosophy stuff really is relevant to my daily life . . . I don't even understand how people can just keep going and thinking about these things."

When it comes to extracurricular activities, Brooke also avoids clubs and activities that explore the big questions in life. Still, she is involved with plenty of activities. "I work . . . I'm still on my dorm's sports teams; I do like dodgeball, basketball, and flag football. I am the vice president of the judicial council, and then previously I was involved in my dorm's hall council and stuff." She also likes "hanging out with my roommates, just like sitting on the couch and talking or baking cookies, you know, something that's just, like, it's actually intentionally relaxing." Her activities, however, largely revolve around practical interests.

She does identify mentors, who help her think through the practical expression of what she sees as her future purpose,

> I've met with a couple professors in different fields that I'm interested in, that I've had, just talking about career options and things like that, and what the future of that area is looking like.

For her, mentorship in her future purpose means mentorship in her career.

Despite Brooke's avoidance of issues of life purpose in her classes, and her practical focus on a future career, she still believes that her college experience has somehow changed her outlook on life in general. "I have more of a sense of self, I'm more comfortable with myself; I feel I was awkward before." In addition, she believes she has become less rigid and more tolerant.

> In certain things, I was like, "I'm this person, this is what I do and stuff," whereas now I'm a lot more open and fluid and more comfortable with myself in terms of saying, "This is what I like. This is what I don't like. This is what I want to do. This is what I don't."

In addition to self-knowledge, she believes she also gained a greater understanding of the larger world. "I would say I'm definitely more socially aware of things going on." She attributes some of her beyond-the-classroom learning to the holistic approach of the Catholic university. "They're all about the whole person, like the mind, body, spirit stuff, and I definitely agree with that."

Although Brooke claims she agrees with it, she actually admits that she no longer believes in God and other Catholic theological beliefs. Some of this transition occurred before coming to the university. She notes, "My mom's side of the family is very Catholic . . . my parents met teaching at a Catholic school . . . and so we went to Mass every Sunday morning . . . up until eighth grade, my mom used to teach Sunday school." Still, she recalls that her parents' religious devotion did not appear to extend to their home life. "I don't ever remember having a cross in the house or praying before we ate or anything like that." Moreover, a break occurred when she got older, "after my brother made his confirmation, I would say there was definitely less focus on that." Interestingly, she is not exactly sure why. "I don't know, for whatever reason, either my parents got disinterested or we got disinterested, so it just sort of tapered off and it just, you know, fell to the wayside."

This drop off also occurred in Brooke's life as well. In fact, her drop off in faith appears to mirror her parents' declining interest:

> I would say in high school it just wasn't really important to me, and I didn't really care either way, and now coming to [this university] and seeing how people in this environment, as opposed to my home friends, care about a lot more, actually that made me realize that I just straight-up don't believe in that.

Interestingly, Brooke is not quite able to label herself using certain nonreligious identities: "I don't want to say I'm, you know, atheist or agnostic or anything like that . . . I don't want to label, but at this point I just don't believe in anything, I don't think that there's a god out there." She says of her fellow students, "I mean, I have a hard time still contemplating how an entire body of people, how all of these incredibly intelligent people at [her Catholic university], it's just crazy that they all believe in this thing that you know nobody can prove." Still, being at a Catholic university, she appears to hold back on her atheism: "I would say right now it's like I'm just too scared to say it out loud."

Despite Brooke's incredulity about Catholic theological beliefs, she would not say she is antagonistic in any way. In fact, if she receives social encouragement, she will still respond. "If my roommates are like, 'Let's go to this Mass' or something, I'll go with them . . . because it's socially acceptable." Being a nonreligious person at a Catholic institution, however, has not been too difficult for her. "I mean it's not like it comes up in conversation a ton, like straight-up religion and stuff . . . I only remember one particular conversation where I told somebody, 'Sorry, I don't identify as Catholic anymore, I don't really believe in God.'" When pressed further whether the conversations do not come up or she avoids them, Brooke admits, "I think it's both, but I think the opportunities are here more than anywhere else to bring those things up, and I definitely choose to avoid them when they do come up." Similar to how Brooke avoids dealing with issues of meaning and purpose on campus, she also avoids conversations that deal directly with religion.

Still, she has also found her experience of Catholic education valuable when it comes to the moral components with which she agrees, "like Catholic social teaching I think is great for a lot of reasons, like I've brought it into a lot of the education research I've done. Those things I'm totally onboard with." Overall, Brooke admits that when it comes to social justice issues and issues related to the sense of community found in Catholicism, she still appreciates Catholicism. What she prefers is the ability to pick and choose what she likes from her religion:

> It's individual preference. I'm more of a fan of that. That's why I think that I have sort of abandoned the whole organized religion thing and belief and everything. . . . I think it's more about individual navigation through your different values and stuff.

In fact, when it comes to thinking about purpose, Brooke feels a new freedom. "I definitely feel more liberated . . . I think it's just pick and choose what you want, make up your own ideas, it's you, you know, you're the individual at this point." For Brooke, she wants the freedom to create her own meaning and purpose.

How does Brooke envision the good life she would want to choose to create in the future? She claims that after graduation, "I don't think there's any script or anything . . . I think it's just sort of the time to be selfish, you know, 'What do I wanna do? What am I thinking about?'" She has a variety of bucket list ideas, but she begins with one important emphasis, "So right now it's about me and then, you know, once I know what I'm doing, then I'll think of others." Like many emerging adults, she sees herself delaying commitments to focus on her own agenda. "I want to be working for a nonprofit with people with disabilities, like returning to grad school while I'm working to get a higher degree, or even going back to school full-time to get a doctorate."

She adds travel to this bucket list of things to accomplish, "My parents got married in Vegas, and that was their honeymoon, and that was the last vacation they ever went on . . . I mean I want to travel." Although she does not believe money is important, she does "want enough to be comfortable. I want enough to either rent in a decent area or if it's time for me to start a family, to be able to put a nice down payment on a mortgage." Even at times, she admits that she wishes for that lifestyle, "That would be really nice to have like that second home and stuff." But she resigns herself to the fact that she did not grow up that way. "I don't know what it's like to have a mom stay at home to redecorate the bathroom every few weeks and put up holiday decorations for stuff like Arbor Day." Once she accomplishes some of her goals, she believes,

> If I was set in a job and had a good path going, made a decent living and stuff, I'd be more focused on, "Okay, I'm settled now, now I can be responsible enough to start a family." . . . I definitely do see, yeah, marriage and family and stuff in the future. . . . I want to have a bunch of kids.

By a bunch, she has a specific number in mind:

> I say I want to have five just because, I mean, my mom's one of eleven, my dad's one of eight, and so on my mom's side alone I have fifty-two first-cousins. . . . I don't know what I would do without having a bunch of people around.

In some respects Brooke appears to have been influenced by the Catholic worldview and ethos of her university in indirect ways, but she also has absorbed and taken to heart mainstream cultural narratives about individual freedom and the American Dream. When one of us asked her at the end of the interview if her views about purpose were settled, she admitted, "I'm not too set in it. If I have a husband who comes and he's a big marketing executive and wants to move us in a mansion, I'm not going to be so morally opposed that I'm not going to do it."

The Language, Formative Context, and Shaping of Purpose

These stories make clear that students already bring to campus certain languages, expectations, and moral traditions when they approach issues of meaning, purpose, and the good life. Moreover, as various forms of student development theory remind us, these students are all at different stages when it comes to developing their meaning and purpose. Similar to what was described in chapter 2, some of these students, such as Evetta and Jacob, are critically evaluating but continuing to hold on to their parents' religious tradition and its related purposes. In other cases, such as Troy and Brooke, students may be in the process of rejecting these traditions and creating their own purposes. Still, they have not yet made a commitment among the many competing choices or fully established what Marcia Baxter Magolda would describe as self-authorship.[2]

Students also tend to speak in slightly different ways about meaning, purpose, and the good life. As with Evetta and Jacob, some students have a general understanding of what gives their life meaning, but they may not have yet fully formulated what they consider their purpose in life to be. Others, such as Brooke, have a more established purpose in one domain of life. Chapters 5, 6, and 12 will describe some of these important differences between understandings of meaning, purpose, and the good life.

The unique nature of language tends to become most important when talking about purpose in particular. As our interviews reveal, one finds an important difference between the language used by those with no purpose, those with self-oriented purposes, and those with beyond-the-self-oriented purposes. As chapters 5 and 6 will detail, scholars find that determining a beyond-the-self purpose proves vitally important for flourishing and well-being. What contexts support students' search for such a purpose is important. For instance, while Evetta does not yet have a clearly identified purpose, she draws on her parents' advice and the Christian moral tradition to establish her belief that her purpose should be something that focuses on the well-being of others. Similarly, Jacob relies on his Jewish tradition and leaders to look for guidance in this area. Troy and Brooke appear to fluctuate between an interest and recognition that their purpose should be larger than their own achievements, but they also are attracted to certain elements of American individualism that undermined their pursuit of beyond-the-self purposes.

As chapter 8 will reveal, colleges and universities, as one of the primary shapers of young adults, play a vital role in informing and shaping this purpose development. Yet, the degree to which the various facets of college life—such as classes, faculty and staff, and the co-curricular experience—influence students varies considerably depending on both the institution and the student. Evetta and Jacob find numerous opportunities to wrestle with these matters within classes and through student groups. Troy picks opportunities that he believes might help his specific goal, while Brooke avoids most of these opportunities even though her Catholic university provides them. Of course, the degree to which students take advantage of institutional resources varies considerably. Chapters 8 and 9 will explore in greater detail the various resources institutions provide and identify some of the ones that students choose.

Students also draw on different kinds of moral and religious traditions in different spheres and stages of their lives. Consider the language and moral traditions that Brooke drew on when she spoke about her purpose. Brooke would appear to be quite willing to renounce material goods to work with autistic children in a beyond-the-self endeavor. Her language, however, to justify why she finds such a calling fulfilling relies on the positive feelings she derives from helping people. Outside of her career choice, she also sees her postcollege period as a time to focus on her own agenda (although she acknowledges wanting to engage in significant beyond-the-self commitments when she eventually starts a family). When it comes to religion, she mixes aspects of Catholic values with the language of American individualism. She says she values family (hoping to a have a large one herself), relationships, and others-focused love. At the same time, she feels a strong pull to write her own story and choose her own meaning and purpose. In contrast, Evetta and Jacob appear more willing to retain the particulars of their religious tradition and rely on these particular traditions to help guide their way forward. Chapters 10 and 11 discuss the important difference between these two types of students and the important role in the substantive beliefs shaping the worldview informing the core of one's purpose.

Before talking about the heart and soul of purpose, we need to talk about the basic ways that students think about issues of both meaning and purpose. We will start with language of meaning because, as these stories reveal, though students often derived meaning or purpose from similar sources, they thought of the two concepts differently. Moreover, though virtually every student reported sources of meaning, over a third of students claimed not to have a purpose. The next three chapters explain the differences in how the students understood the key concepts of meaning and purpose, and how students with a purpose and those without a purpose differed from one another.

Chapter 5

Mapping What Makes Life Meaningful

What gives my life meaning? I would say accomplishment. I am accomplishment driven, whether it's, you know, just getting through the day, finishing a test, receiving an award, just excelling in some area in some way—that gives my life meaning.

—Jennifer, secular liberal arts college student

I worked at a day care in the summers and right now I basically volunteer in a kindergarten classroom a couple times a week, and what gives my life meaning right now is watching kids struggle and struggle and struggle with reading or spelling or something and not realize how much progress they've made until that one time the lightbulb goes off [on], and they realize they're doing whatever they thought they couldn't do without help and all of the scaffoldings gone, and they're just like, "Oh I just read that word and I didn't have to look at the pictures!" And that moment, that's what gives me meaning, is knowing that I helped somebody get to that moment.

—Chelsea, Lutheran liberal arts college student

My relationship with the Lord for sure is probably the biggest thing that gives life meaning because [when] you think about when life is hard or doesn't make sense, there is a reason for that. If we believe that we have a bigger God who's omnipresent and sovereign, then you don't have to understand everything of life.

—Erica, Baptist university student

"I think one of the hardest questions was always discussing the meaning of life." Malik, a first-year student at a secular liberal arts college, shares this statement when talking about the difficulties he had discussing big questions with his parents. The difficulties stemmed neither from a bad relationship nor their inability

to address moral matters. As he relates, "We weren't wealthy in a financial sense. We were wealthy in a moral sense . . . and so that was probably one of the cool things about my family." The moral emphasis stemmed from the family's religious tradition. "When I was growing up my family's religion [was and still is] Islam, and so there was a lot of conversation about religion and philosophy and different things like that." The difficulties in talking about meaning derived from something else.

Malik's parents are recent immigrants. His mother and father's extended family came from Pakistan, but his father was actually born in an African country. His mother moved to the same country when she was ten. Malik himself was born in Zambia, but because his dad was not making enough money, and they had family living in the Southern United States, they moved to America when Malik was eight years old. He claims:

> I still consider myself African. And so it's always funny when I talk to people and they're always like, "So where are you from?" and I say, "Zambia." They think [it's] somewhere in the Middle East or Pakistan, and I'm like, "No, it's in Africa."

As a child growing up in this unique context, Malik says he did a lot of inquiring and learning, "As I grew older and I learned more about philosophy and questioning things; that's when my parents were like, 'Oh, no, he's starting to question stuff.'" Some of his queries and conversations concerned the big questions of life:

> So I would always start up these daring conversations like, "so what's the meaning of life?" . . . Sometimes when I would ask questions of a religious nature, my parents would get upset, but they would realize that I wasn't questioning my beliefs just to push myself away from the religion. I was questioning it to become closer to my religion.

The struggle with being able to have conversations about these questions became exacerbated due to his family's difficult economic circumstances.

> My dad works two jobs and my mom works as well, so we're very low income. And so growing up I always had a desire to be, not wealthy or ridiculously rich, but just have enough to survive and not have to work so hard. 'Cause I would see my dad work . . . he wakes up at four in the morning, goes to work at five, comes back at three, rests for a little while, then he goes to work at five until one. So that was his schedule. It was hard for us to see him most of the time.

This difficult and demanding work schedule influenced the type of relationship that Malik could have with his parents—particularly, his father. "We wouldn't see him a lot, and like the moments when he would have days off he would want to rest. So it was hard to have conversations with him [about] things like that." This situation led Malik to want to create a better life for himself and his family, "And so that was always the focus of my life: to have money and to be successful and to really push myself to be the best person I could really be." If he became a rich man, Malik believes, he could enjoy contemplating the big questions of life with his own family.

Understandably, Malik sees this difficult background as making his life different than many of his fellow college students:

> What gives my life meaning? . . . I have a really good friend of mine who's also similar to me—he's a senior and he's very successful and he's very involved in the [college] community. But me and him, we were both talking about what drives individuals like us to just run on such a low amount of sleep or not eat, and just really work hard and really push ourselves. And he said something, "People who have grown up with a golden spoon in their mouth, they never know hunger and they never know desire. They can never really push themselves to their full potential." And so that really stuck with me. And he said, "This is your one opportunity in life where you can move your last name to a different socioeconomic level; like you have that potential here by educating yourself and involving yourself in meeting all these people."

This fellow student's comments resonated with Malik. He realized his past experiences with a difficult financial situation helped drive him to succeed, but they also made some of his decisions challenging. He notes, "One of my struggles right now is realizing whether I want to pursue something I'm passionate about, or if I want to do something practical that will make me money—so it's a challenge." At the core, he sees himself as taking on challenges with his whole heart so that he can find meaning in his accomplishments:

> Like anything I do, I just do it as full as I possibly can—I put one hundred percent of myself into it. I don't like spreading myself thin so even though I'm involved in a ton of different activities, I still put one hundred percent into each one . . . I enjoy seeing what I've given myself to succeed and grow and develop.

Ultimately, what gives meaning to Malik are the numerous achievements he imagines himself accomplishing someday.

Humanity's Search for Meaning

Throughout the eight centuries of the university's existence, students have constantly searched for what makes life meaningful. Yet, only in the last few decades has scholarship on the search for meaning and purpose in general, as well as college students' search for meaning and purpose and the role that higher education should play in that search in particular, received significant scholarly attention.[1] Within this literature, the terms *meaning* and *purpose* are often used together, although in some rare cases a distinction is made between the two terms. One even finds this combination in book titles such as Sharon Daloz Parks's *Big Questions, Worthy Dreams: Mentoring Young Adults in Their Search for Meaning, Purpose, and Faith* (2000); Robert J. Nash and Michele C. Murray's *Helping College Students Find Purpose: The Campus Guide to Meaning-Making*; and Jenny Small's *Making Meaning: Embracing Spirituality, Faith, Religion, and Life Purpose in Student Affairs.*

We suspect that the conflation of these terms in higher education literature could be the result of a discipline just beginning to wrestle with the topic. Higher education scholars are not alone. In fields such as psychology and sociology, the study of this search for meaning and purpose has only recently begun. The reason stems from the dominant originating theories and theorists. As Damon, Menon, and Bronk noted in an influential review of the literature, in mid-twentieth-century psychology the idea that meaning and purpose "could motivate someone to do something, or even shape a person's basic choices about how to live—seemed impossibly soft-headed and sentimental to mainstream psychologists of that time."[2] Instead, the view predominated

> that meaning, purpose, and other such belief systems were the products of more fundamental drives; that they were dependent on the drives for their shape, substance, and very existence; and that meaning and purpose were no more than marginal factors in behavioral development.[3]

What helped change this view was the publication of Victor Frankl's *Man's Search for Meaning* in 1959.[4] Frankl's work helped psychologists and other social scientists recognize the importance of both meaning and purpose in shaping human development. Beginning with Frankl and continuing for several subsequent decades, meaning and purpose were treated as roughly synonymous in the psychological literature.[5] One influential example, James's Fowler's *Stages of Faith: The Psychology of Human Development and the Quest for Meaning*, demonstrates this tendency. Through 359 qualitative interviews with subjects ranging from age four to their early eighties, Fowler attempted to provide a theory about the structure of faith development for individuals from diverse faith traditions and even those who held to secular ideologies. To achieve this broad inclusiveness, Fowler briefly described faith as "the way we go about making and maintaining meaning in life";[6] however, in his research, he also understood it as much more. Later in the work Fowler, defined faith quite comprehensively as:

> People's evolved and evolving ways of experiencing self, others and world (as they construct them) as related to and affected by the ulti-mate conditions of existence (as they construct them) and of *shaping their lives' purposes and meanings*, trusts and loyalties, in light of the character of being, value and power determining the ultimate condi-tions of existence (as grasped in their operative images—conscious and unconscious—of them).[7]

Fowler described this type of faith as universal and not connected to any par-ticular religious tradition. Even atheists experience this kind of faith, which is developed through six different stages.

While some scholars have tested and found some support for this theory,[8] a number of Fowler's critics, however, have expressed problems with this use of the word *faith*.[9] Since *faith* is a religious word that often has specific meanings within particular traditions, it seems confusing to talk about faith development in a universalistic fashion. Craig Dykstra, for example, maintained that Fowler's approach did not "allow for the possibility; however, that what different people and groups mean by 'faith' may be so diverse that it would be impossible to talk about faith or faith development in any general sense at all."[10] Other scholars have also questioned whether Fowler's theory can hold true for diverse religious traditions outside of the Judeo-Christian worldview.[11]

Another problem, in our view, is that if Fowler's scheme is understood as a theory about how human beings develop their views about meaning, this broad language of faith development creates problems if one wishes to talk about com-peting sources of meaning. After all, as Malik illustrates, students may identify with a certain faith tradition (e.g., Islam, Christianity, etc.), but they may not understand the meaning of life as primarily shaped by the tradition. They may actually want and pursue worldly happiness or material gain in ways that defy their own faith tradition's standards. In addition, multiple ideological traditions may compete for a person's allegiance. For example, students may find them-selves having to choose between various religious and philosophical traditions. Fowler's approach makes faith something more monolithic rather than helping us understand the messy details about how students choose between competing or contradictory religious or philosophical traditions of thought or simply dif-ferent sources competing for meaning (family, friends, a career, a nation, etc.).

By using such a broad understanding of *faith*, Fowler's theory does not help us account for the substantive conflicts and contradictions that may be inherent in students' lives and views of the world at large. For instance, Brooke, from the last chapter, narrated her own struggle between the Catholicism of her youth and her current unbelief. We cannot helpfully make sense of Brooke's competing faiths, loves, or sources of meaning if we discuss her faith development, or any student's for that matter, in monolithic terms.

Although some scholars have continued the trend of mixing meaning and purpose language (e.g., one simply used one term to define the other[12]), a number of recent scholars have now called both for more precision in our language about these matters, as well as a more inclusive approach to these discussions. For instance, a well-established group of positive psychology scholars have set forth arguments for distinguishing the two terms, *meaning* and *purpose*. Damon, Menon, and Bronk contend that purpose "has a special developmental role not captured by the more inclusive, diffuse, and pluralistic concept of meaning."[13] In particular, they note that purpose can be thought of as a driver of action, and this role makes it vitally important for healthy or positive youth development. As a result of this important emphasis, most recent psychological research in this domain has focused on purpose more than on meaning, although some scholars still focus on meaning.[14]

Among higher education scholars, however, there is not a clearly developed practice regarding how to differentiate these terms. This is perhaps due to two tendencies. First, the studies mentioned earlier tend to focus on the process of meaning-making or purpose development and not on the actual meanings and purposes embraced by students. Second, higher education scholars have historically tended to focus on one of these concepts. For instance, the work of Arthur Chickering and Linda Reisser focused solely on purpose as related to: "(1) vocational plans and aspirations, (2) personal interests, and (3) interpersonal and family commitments."[15] In contrast, Sharon Daloz Parks focused primarily on students' quest for meaning, which she understood as involving a search for "a sense of connection, pattern, order and significance."[16] Parks later went on to define meaning-making as "the activity of composing a sense of the connections among things: a sense of pattern, order, form, and significance."[17]

As commented on earlier, two recent higher education writers in this area, Nash and Murray, have differentiated meaning and purpose and have composed different definitions that attempt to capture an important difference between the two. They wrote,

> For us *meaning* is all about those interpretations, narrative frame-
> works, philosophical rationales and perspectives, and faith or belief

systems, that each of us brings to the various worlds in which we live, love, learn, work, and worship.[18]

In this understanding, as students draw connections and find patterns, they draw on the *traditions* of meaning-making available in culture. Students may find these traditions expressed in narrative frameworks, philosophical perspectives, and faith or belief systems. These previous connections and patterns help produce a meaning map of the world. Purpose, according to Nash and Murray, pertains to the destinations one chooses within this meaning map of the world. They claim, "*Purpose* has to do with pursuing certain goals, reaching resolutions, seeking results, and realizing particular objectives and ends in those worlds."[19] Although we believe these separate definitions could possibly offer a helpful way forward, we also believe that fundamental concepts in this area of research must be both substantively precise *and* tethered to the phenomenological experiences of individuals. Only after doing this important phenomenological study can we begin to form tentative grounded theories about these concepts and their relationship. Damon et al. have maintained that the distinction between meaning and purpose used in their studies of adolescents is based on the "common-language" usage of the terms among adolescents.[20] We wanted to understand what possible differentiations, if any, proved important among the college students we studied.

While the two terms clearly bear a family resemblance, one purpose of our research was to explore how students articulate and understand both their own meaning and purpose. Consequently, we set about attempting to understand how students understand what gives their life meaning and purpose, if there are any connections between those perspectives, and what the practical implications might be for student affairs professionals approaching these topics.

In our own research, we observe some important differences between how students talked about meaning and purpose. Although Malik's story above is unique, his ability to articulate what made his life meaningful is not. All but one of the 185 students interviewed in our 110 Targeted and 75 National Qual data sets shared answers to the questions: "What gives your life meaning? What makes life worth living for you?" Our findings are not unusual when compared to other studies. In an earlier study of college students, two scholars found that only 5 percent of students claimed to lack meaning.[21] In fact, adolescents seem to identify life meaning early. When the same scholars asked a sample of 116 thirteen- and fourteen-year-olds from California to write about what made life meaningful, only one of those students claimed to have no meaning in life.[22] Students appear able to articulate what makes their life meaningful long before college and the sense that life has meaning also appears to persist through early emerging adulthood. One recent survey found that 80 percent of young emerging adults (18–23) rarely or never experience times when life feels meaningless.[23] Only 6 percent indicated they very or fairly often have that experience.

This finding is one reason we will differentiate how students in the 110 Targeted and 75 National Qual data sets talk about meaning and how they talk about purpose. Indeed, we recommend that instead of talking about helping students find meaning in college, we should instead discuss how college might help students enrich and critically analyze their current views about meaning. The reality is that many students are not searching for meaning; they believe they have already found it. In fact, surveys that find students are not searching for meaning may merely uncover those students who believe they have already found meaning. In contrast, as chapter 6 and 7 reveal, a significant percentage of adolescents, young emerging adults, and college students have a greater difficulty identifying their purpose or purposes. To help understand this point, in the first part of this chapter we categorize students' different sources of meaning. After describing our findings, we examine an important distinction when it comes to how individuals talk about meaning. Finally, we discuss our findings in light of a proposed theoretical framework for understanding meaning.

Differentiating Different Kinds of Meaning and Meaning Cultures

Like Malik, most participants (80 percent) identify one dominant theme that informs their sense of meaning, while only a minority derived meaning from a range of themes. Overall, we find that what gives students meaning consists of ten categories—what we call meaning ingredients. We can divide these ten ingredients into three overarching types, which are listed below.

Type 1: Self-Achievers

1. Accomplishment in general: For example, "My goals, my dreams, my ambitions, my career"; "I think what gives life meaning is just your goals and what you want to achieve and how hard you're willing to work for that."

2. Career: For example, "I guess working . . . I'm trying to get a career started at the job that I work at."

3. Happiness: For example, "I guess it would all string to happiness."

4. Experiences: For example, "I guess going through all the experiences that life brings, traveling, love, just basically experiencing things I haven't experienced before."

5. Creative accomplishments: For example, "My creativity. My ability to story tell and write."

Type 2: Relationalists

6. Family: For example, "My family"; "My son."

7. Relationships/Friends: For example, "Friends and family."

8. Service and/or helping others: For example, "What makes life worth living is what you do for others."

Type 3: Transcendents

9. God or religion: For example, "Overall, for me, it's God, and through Him I can have meaning in my life."

10. Change the world for good: For example, "I'd say the desire to do good in the world and, I don't know, hopefully get myself into a position where I can realize some change."

We should note that the ten ingredients consist of those ingredients referred to by at least two students in our interviews. A handful of respondents did allude to ingredients not addressed here (e.g., "nature," "hope"), but these were only mentioned by individual students. Below we illustrate and describe the different types of Self-Achievers, Relationalists, and Transcendents.

The Self-Achievers

Joshua, a senior political science student at a Jewish University, comes from a unique family of high achievers. His father is a Protestant African-American who is currently a doctor. His mother, a Jewish refugee from the Soviet Union, was a doctor, but when she immigrated in 1989 her credentials were not valid in the United States, so she had to go through schooling in America to once again become a doctor.

When asked specifically about what makes his life meaningful, Joshua lists achievements. He talks in terms of current accomplishments and future accomplishments. His current accomplishments pertain to individual hobbies. "It's very meaningful to me to make music and to learn music, to play on the piano." He then proceeds to describe additional hobbies. "Over the summer, I took Krav Maga—if you don't exactly know what that is it's martial arts—it's an Israeli martial arts so it was . . . it felt very patriotic to just look at it." After these hobbies, he lists something more predictable since he attends a Jewish university: "I guess religion, naturally, has a very meaningful impact on my life." When he catalogs specifics about the religion that were meaningful to him, he lists practices he can accomplish. "I mean, there's prayer in the morning, there's prayer with food." He does the same when discussing school, "And the assignments that I do. . . . I'm writing a paper on duels and dueling in the Russian short stories. I wouldn't say that specific essay is very meaningful but . . . it's also meaningful to have these assignments." When it comes to his future accomplishments he focuses on his career: "I know that I want to go to a graduate school—to continue in education. I don't know if I would go into law or into an academic field . . . or to maybe do both at the same time—get a joint degree."

While most of his accomplishments focus on concrete goals that can be reached in the foreseeable future, he also concludes by mentioning, "And long-term is just to live a good life." He contrasted this goal with a negative, more materialistic option. "I wouldn't put too much focus on business or too much focus on what house I would get or too much focus on any specific thing. I would just try to live well." Interestingly, despite his interest in listing accomplishments, he concludes our conversation with the following thought: "But the main goal is to be satisfied [and] not to go crazy looking for things."

Joshua provides a helpful profile of the student who derives meaning primarily from individual achievements. Self-Achievers, who comprised a little more than one-sixth of the students interviewed, think of meaning as something to be obtained by accomplishment. Emilee, a student we profile in chapter 7, represents a helpful example of the Self-Achiever:

> I guess my studies give me satisfaction. And my ambition, like what I want to achieve in the future. It really stresses me out, but it gives me—I want to go to law school. I want to work in conflict mediation and international law. I want to have an international career.

Within this group, five subtypes exist. There are Self-Achievers who primarily find meaning in (1) achieving certain goals, (2) reaching a certain career, (3) achieving certain experiences, (4) finding happiness, or (5) creating. We call these different subtypes the Goal, Career, Experience, Happiness, and Creative Achievers.

The Goal Achiever mentality can be found in the liberal arts student quoted above, "I think what gives life meaning is just, your goals and what you want to achieve and how hard you're willing to work for that." Although these students are very oriented toward their future goals, they are also attuned to the signposts along the way that indicate whether or not they are on the right track. Even the small accomplishments of the moment can make their lives feel more worthwhile, as long as reaching these goals moves one toward personal achievement.

Career Achievers focus solely or primarily on one of the most significant achievement signposts—a future job. For example, a Career Achiever will share something like the following:

> I'm a ROTC student, so I'm currently a cadet. I'm waiting for my commission into the United States Army as a Lieutenant. You know that gives me drive, that gives me—that's a big part of my identity— gives me meaning.

Given the importance of postsecondary education for determining future careers, a number of students clearly derive meaning from progressing toward their career aspirations.

Experience Achievers are less concerned with traditional economic and educational paths to success than Goal and Career Achievers. Instead, they merely wanted to explore and discover new things no matter the ladder it helps them climb, and they derive meaning from these different kinds of experiences. Still, they see these experiences as contributing to their overall understanding of life. For instance, the following male Experience Achiever illustrates this outlook:

> I mean, for me, it's just always learning new things, seeing new places. It's the fact that there's always something more out there to discover . . . I'm always searching for meaning, and I do think that involves always putting yourself in new places and new situations. I mean, next semester I'm studying abroad in Australia to do that basically. It's to live in a new culture, get different worldviews, and I think by doing that you can formulate a better philosophy.

The Experience Achievers let personal curiosity be their guide rather than well-defined future goals or a particular career path to success.

Happiness Achievers focus less on the broad range of experiences and only on those things that give them a sense of happiness. In addition, they speak less about finishing a task and crossing it off their list, and focus more on engaging in the experience or living in the moment. Chase, a liberal arts student, provides a helpful example of a Happiness Achiever (as well as a Career Achiever):

> I tend to identify the meaning in my life differently now obviously in that, for me, there are activities that bring me happiness. I'm very content when I'm working in the lab, and I'm working on my research. That's a very fulfilling thing for me, but I don't know that I really have a grand overarching sort of statement of my life's meaning.

It should be noted that Happiness Achievers in this category think of happiness in "this-worldly" ways. Others may focus on a more transcendent understanding of happiness linked to God beyond this life. As one Mormon or Latter Day Saints (LDS) male student shared, "My meaning . . . the meaning of my life is . . . happiness. But, more specifically, eternal happiness. That's the meaning." These kinds of students fit better in the Transcendent category we describe later.

Creative Achievers are a small minority that are quite easy to identify. They derive meaning from "creative activity." It might be creating film, art, music, or entertainment experiences. One Creative Achiever at an evangelical university provides a helpful example:

> What gives my life meaning? I would say that I feel like I was put on this earth to . . . I feel like I was born to entertain. I feel like I was born for the stage or for the screen. I'm just so comfortable up on a stage. I feel like I love hosting camps. I love hosting events. I love performing. I love acting. You know, stuff like that. To an extent, I always get a little bit of butterflies before, but once I get up there . . . For an example, there was this time we had to kill some time at a concert, at a high school concert and I was like, "Gimme the microphone!" And I killed probably about twenty to thirty minutes

As a result of these prior successful experiences, this student hopes to pursue this kind of life as a career. Overall, all five of these types focus on the individual pursuit of an end goal that primarily pertains to the student's own accomplishments.

The Relationalists

"I think people make my life worth living," shares Makenzie, a cheerful young woman attending a Lutheran liberal arts college. As a result, she describes her list of meaningful activities in relational terms, "forming bonds with people, with friends, with family members." Moreover, she articulates the motivation behind her major as specifically linked to relational goals. "I'm passionate about psychology, [because] I like to connect with people and I like to help people and have those bonds."

Makenzie's heart for people, she believes, is shaped partially by the deep ties she shares with her whole family. "Like the experiences I had, like seeing my grandparents three or four times a week and getting to see them and have that experience." She contrasts this experience with what she has learned from talking with her friend, as she says, "Their grandparents would live out of state or something like that, and I didn't realize how important it was to me until I thought of the alternative of not being able to see them." Makenzie also observed the difference between her experience-oriented peers and her family-oriented focus. "I started to notice the different family dynamics and what I preferred I guess is what I have." Her friends would go on a vacation with just a mom and sister. In contrast, "I would stay [home]. We'd have the whole family over."

She also describes the way in which her parents taught and modeled, "forming meaningful relationships or authentic relationship with others instead of doing things to only benefit yourself." She shares the example again of her observations of her peers' lives, "a lot of people I went to school with have nannies, or they would have people that would take care of them. They wouldn't see their parents as much." In contrast, she recalls, "I got to see mine a little bit more." She understands that this difference stems from her relational priorities as opposed to a focus on individual achievement. What is important to her is "having that relationship . . . even if you're not the most successful at work, or even if you don't make as much money." What matters is "valuing people." She concludes, "I think that [valuing people] is something that I admire and I respect and that helps me kind of model how I see what's important in the world. Like, helping others when you can and being generous and caring about your family."

Makenzie represents the second group that comprised slightly more than half of our college students. These are what we call the Relationalists, and as the name suggests, this subset derives meaning from their relationships with other people. Makenzie represents two of the three types of Relationalists—those that find meaning both spending time with family and serving others—the Service and Family Relationalist perspective. A third type we label the General Relationalists.

The Service Relationalists consist of those students who derive meaning specifically from serving others and not merely having relationships with others. Julie provides a good example of a Service Relationalist. A neuroscience major, she hopes to go to medical school. Growing up in her family, she recalls, "I'd say we, not directly, like sat down and discussed what is the meaning of life, but in sort of other ways we've talked about it." For instance, they discussed why it is important to work hard and to be an academic. In retrospect, she muses, "I guess that ties into the meaning of life in some ways. Like, if this is not meaningful, then why are we doing it kind of thing?"

While this prior background may appear to make her a candidate to be an Individual Achiever, she shares:

> I guess what makes my life worth living would be like other people. Everything that I do is oriented toward either helping people or connecting with people in some way. So I value the time I spend at the soup kitchen or volunteering for others. In addition, I value the time that I spend just interacting with others and communicating with others and having conversations at the dinner table and stuff like that. Just the interactions with other people are what add meaning to my life. Like without those communicative interactions, there wouldn't be any meaning I guess.

For Relationalists such as Julie, their focus is not directly on individual achievement, experiences, or obtaining a job; those things are merely instruments to accomplish the larger goal of helping someone else. For example, a Relationalist discusses her major and future in the following manner:

> Now that I think about it, it's interesting 'cause it kind of relates to what I would define as meaning in that I really want to help people with my life. I mentioned that I was a Bio Major—I'm really interested actually in going into either the medical or dental professions, [be]cause I really can't imagine my life without it being guided by helping others to be healthy or be better than they think they can be.

Similar to Julie and the young woman quoted above, many Relationalists chose majors in the helping or serving professions such as medicine, psychology, or teaching.

While we will later discuss those who find meaning by seeking to change the world according to some particular vision of the good society, Service Relationalists are different. They want to change people's lives for the better, but they tend not to focus on fulfilling some grand moral vision of the good life. Instead, they are motivated by how others responded to their service. Amber, a student at a Baptist university, provides a helpful example of these contrasting motivations:

> What is the meaning of life? . . . in general, I've always just felt like my purpose is to serve and, I think a lot of people take that to be in a big worldly like, "I'm going to go out and you know save the world kind of service." But that's not me. In anything I do or anything I'm involved in, I want the people closest to me to feel served by me. Whether I end up being a stay-at-home mom or whether I do go

out and try and, you know, save the world or something like that, I want those who are directly related to me, wherever I am, to feel like they can be served by me. So yeah, that's basically it.

It should be noted that Amber does not necessarily reject the notion of changing the world, but she fundamentally understands it as stemming from her heart for service.

The next kind of Relationalists are those who identify deriving meaning from their relationships with friends or relationships in general, what we call General Relationalists. The General Relationalists do not talk about serving others, but they do talk about valuing others. Furthermore, in contrast to the Service Relationalists who are interested in helping people they know personally, the General Relationalists are more interested in getting to know people they do not know. John, a General Relationalist, shares what he found most meaningful:

> The relationships that I make with everyone. I'm a big people person and so I think, for me, just having relationships and meeting new people and learning different people's opinions gives me a lot of purpose. I enjoy just talking to people and arguing with them on politics and stuff like that. That's when I'm definitely the happiest [*and*] when I feel the most comfortable.

Katie provides a good example of someone who contrasts herself to the Individual Achiever approach:

> Okay. I think a lot of what makes life worth living is, interestingly enough, the other people that I love being around. I guess, and I don't necessarily think of myself as a—what's the word—like externally driven person very much. Like, I'm very comfortable with myself and being independent, but I think that a lot of what makes life worth living is the people that I love.

As these examples indicate, the General Relationalists are focused on a wide group of family or friends, and they are often concerned with expanding their social circles further.

The final group is what we call Family Relationalists. The respondents in this category believe that family provides a central source of meaning in their life. Gerald, an Asian male attending a state research university offers an example:

> My life is mostly based around my family. I want to make money, not for myself, but for my parents. They gave up everything for me,

so I want to like do the same thing when I like pretty much make whatever I can to give to them. That's pretty much my meaning.

For many of the Family Relationalists, particularly the males, family tends to be first on a list that includes other things, often accomplishments or goals that make life meaningful. In this respect, they spoke in a manner similar to Individual Achievers. For example, Spencer, an Ivy League student lists among his priorities, "I think family definitely comes first. And then I really pride myself in my work, so that probably gives me meaning, and I love sports too." Esther, a female student spoke in a similar way,

> So, I would definitely say family and friends, and knowing that there's something out there for me to pursue, knowing that I always feel like I need a goal, an end goal to just like keep going, and there's always something I want to accomplish, so that's really what I want to live for, in a way.

In this regard, as opposed to the pure Individual Achievers, Relationalists see family, friends, or serving others as the first priority. Achievement still has an important place, and, in some respects, family is sometimes almost treated as an achievement. Quinn, a liberal arts college student, even recalls the importance of his father in this lesson:

> Sure, I mean, your family is always important. As someone who doesn't have an extensive religious background, I would put family first. And then family, friends, and obviously, I mean, you do certainly have that will to succeed and drive to deliver, and that's certainly something that I think has been instilled in me specifically. And it's certainly something that I picked up from my father, I would say. I'm sure he picked it up from his father; it's something that I hope to continue.

Although Quinn is nonreligious, a disproportionate number of Family Relationists in our 110 Targeted Qual interviews identify with the LDS and Orthodox Jewish tradition. The rationale for finding meaning in family life may not always explicitly stated as religious, but sometimes religion can be directly referenced. For example, a Jewish Relationalist combines the two:

> I would definitely say my family and my religion. They kind of, they also actually go together because my parents have very strong, religious backgrounds, and so I think this is very strongly rooted in

me. It's just something that I always associate as kind of the meaning for me, and the purpose and everything for me. Yeah. Something that I want in my own family, I guess I can say too, when I get older.

In this case, and in most cases, no particular theological belief is used to justify the Relationalist finding meaning through relationships.

The Transcendents

When we introduced Cody, the music and psychology major who attended a public research university in chapter 2, he spoke effusively about his family life. The oldest of four kids, he also shared how his family background made college difficult for reasons we rarely heard from college students. "Like my family is all really extremely close. I guess that's been one of the harder things about being in college. Like good, because I've grown personally, but hard in that like my family's really close." While this might appear to make him a candidate to be a Family Relationalist, as noted later in the chapter his family's shared Christian faith profoundly influenced his meaning. Consequently, for Cody,

> Meaning for me is my faith. My Christian faith is where I find meaning. Some people would kind of take that as like, "Oh you need to spread the gospel and love others," and I think those are true, but I think that like meaning in my life is learning more of who God is and how he loves me and how I can be closer in a relationship with him.

In this respect, Cody's view of meaning includes relationships, but his faith is what primarily shapes his views about the meaning and importance of relationships.

> And then these other things kind of naturally come out of that, or sprout out of that. But, meaning is learning more, to me, learning more of who God is and like how he loves me and different ways that he shows that.

Cody provides an example of the group we label the Transcendents. These students are those that find meaning in a larger being or concept to which one relates or adopts. Specifically, we use this label to describe three types of individuals: those who find meaning in a divine being (e.g., God or Christ), a spiritual community or entity (e.g., "religion" or "church"), or an ideal to which they hope to change the world (e.g., a vision of the good society).

The first two types we categorize as Religious Transcendents, although a subtle distinction existed between two groups within this category. The first group is almost always Christians, and they specifically talk about finding their meaning through God (e.g., "I would say like first and foremost my relationship with God.") or Jesus (e.g., "I would say what gives my life meaning is my relationship with Jesus."). If they discuss making a difference in people's lives or serving them, it is done within the context of the relationship with God or Christ. As one student notes,

> Okay, well, I'm a follower of Jesus Christ and I would say that the articulation of my life's purpose, at least what I want it and what I hope that it is, is to be a disciple maker who serves others and someone who walks with God and teaches others how to walk with God.

The vast majority of these Christian Transcendents, perhaps not surprisingly, can be found at the faith-based institutions, such as the Baptist, Catholic, and evangelical universities. Like Cody and the student quoted above, the majority of the Christian Transcendents also mention the importance of human relationships, but they see these relationships as secondary to their relationship with God. Mike provides one example:

> I would say, like, first and foremost my relationship with God, but then also my relationships with others. . . . for me I'm just, like, very relational, so I just love like interacting with people, and if I can make a difference, like, in people's lives, then that's what makes it worth it for me.

Mike could be considered a Religious Transcendent first, a General Relationalist second, and what we later will identify as a Change Transcendent third. Similarly, this next student is a Religious Transcendent first and then a Family Relationalist next:

> God. Yeah. Just knowing that He loves me. God gives me the reason to live and I just want to grow in [my relationship] him. And then the next thing would be family, I think. Yeah, just family and God.

As with the student above, these students often describe this relationship with God using the language of traditional Christian virtues such as "faith," "love," and "hope." One student summarized his outlook on meaning by drawing on the virtue of hope, "What makes life worth living for me is that I know there's a hope after life. And also the relationships that I've found, my relationship with God that makes life worth living. I feel so blessed."

Another group of Religious Transcendents discusses the importance of faith, religion, or church in nonrelational terms that do not specifically mention God or other divine beings. The following responses provide some helpful examples:

- Religion: "[What] gives me meaning obviously would be that my religion. I'd say that's a big part of me."

- Faith: "I'd say my faith is a big part of it [meaning]"

- Church: "Well honestly, I would say that the church of Jesus Christ of Latter Day Saints. I would say without that, life would seem utterly, you know, meaningless, because it would just feel like I'm floundering, you know? Kind of searching for what is the point of existence, you know? And that definitely does give life meaning."

In our interviews, four-fifths of the Religious Transcendents who focused mostly on religion, faith, or their religious community came from the Mormon and Jewish universities. This is in contrast to the group of Religious Transcendents who speak primarily about a relationship with God. The Protestants, particularly the evangelicals, tend to talk about transcendence in relational ways. The Mormon and Jewish Religious Transcendents discuss religion by making reference to a particular community or institution and not a personal relationship with God. A comment by one Jewish student illustrates this point, "Religion, from the perspective of an Orthodox Jew, it's kind of like the way that you live I guess rather than just beliefs. It's a lifestyle." In this respect, their experience of the sacred is mediated through these rituals or institutions instead of relationally.

The second major group of Transcendents is the Moral Change Transcendents. These individuals speak about changing the world or people's lives so that it or they conform to some larger vision of the good life. These students want to "make the world a better place" and to "make a difference in people's lives." "Make" or "change" are the words that dominate their answers. Cheryl, an atheist attending a Lutheran college exemplifies this outlook: "I would like to try to make the world a better place for animals and just the world a better place in general." As an atheist, she explains her outlook this way:

I think it's very important to take care of the earth because this is the only one that we have and the future generations will live on this earth . . . I don't consider myself Christian, and I don't really believe in an afterlife. I want to do everything that I can in this world to live because I don't think there is anything else. This is my only life. I'm not living for another life. This is it.

While Moral Change Transcendents could be either religious or nonreligious, the distinctive aspect of their outlook is that their meaning in life comes from a vision of a better world that moves them to seek social and moral transformation.

Some Differences

While we think it is important to be careful about drawing too much from our nonrepresentative sample, we still think it represents a roughly accurate range of types among American college students. While we think it preliminary to generalize, we did find it of interest that Self-Achievers are disproportionately male, and nonreligious, agnostic, or atheist. In this respect, the Self-Achievers appear to reinforce certain masculine stereotypes: task-oriented, interested in adventure and risk-taking, and focused on accomplishing things more than relationships with people, a very different outlook from the second group. Relationalists are disproportionately female, and Transcendents, not surprisingly, were disproportionately religious.

The Limited Helpfulness of Meaning Talk?

Some time ago, the *New York Times* columnist David Brooks wrote a column titled, "The Problem with Meaning."[24] Brooks's problem had nothing to do with conversations about colleges abandoning meaning or the search for a meaningful life. Instead, Brooks expressed a different frustration, "It has to be said, as commonly used today, the word is flabby and vacuous, the product of a culture that has grown inarticulate about inner life." Brooks's claim would appear to be reinforced by certain scholars in positive psychology who contend that purpose is a better subject of focus because it "has a special developmental role not captured by the more inclusive, diffuse, and pluralistic concept of meaning."[25] In particular, they noted that purpose can be thought of as a driver of action, and this role makes it vitally important for healthy or positive youth development.

The particular reason Brooks found the use of *meaning* vacuous, though, was that he perceived the users of the word primarily saw it as reflective of their own emotional state instead of larger moral frameworks, "The ultimate authority of meaningful is the warm tingling we get when we feel significant and meaningful. Meaningfulness tries to replace moral systems with the emotional corona that surrounds acts of charity."

Since what is meaningful is tied to emotion, Brooks suggested its use produces numerous problems: (1) "it is contentless and irreducible"; (2) "it's subjective and relativistic . . . Who is any of us to judge another's emotion"; (3)

"it is useless. There are no criteria to determine what kind of meaningfulness is higher"; and (4) "it's fleeting. When the sensations of meaningful go away then the cause that once aroused them gets dropped, too."[26] We believe it is helpful to compare Brooks's musings with the empirical realities we encountered, since the danger of a column such as Brooks's is that its generalizations may begin to apply to the upcoming generation even though they do not reflect the subtle realities of how students actually speak.

In our own targeted examination, the understanding and use of meaning is slightly more complex. Brooks's description applies to certain kinds of Self-Achievers and Relationalists. These students, such as Chelsea, quoted at the beginning of this chapter, or Jacob the Achiever, clearly determine what might make life meaningful by the emotions they experienced when engaging in some particular activity. Brooke, the Service Relationalist whose story was recounted in chapter 4, provides an example of how meaning can be equated with certain subjective emotional states. In response to a question about what makes her life meaningful, she shares,

> I don't think about it [meaning] too often, but I would say when I do, I'll have that weird inner tingly feeling and stuff where if I'm interacting with another person. You make a connection with the person, you realize you could help a person, and just like that, I'm like "Oh, that's what it's all about and stuff."

Monica, a General Relationalist from a liberal arts college articulates a similar outlook:

> I feel like I'm happiest when I am laughing with my friends and even if it can be, you know, we're not doing an activity or being successful at something and it's not like we're laughing because we just won something, it's just like that feeling of being in that moment that I think gives me meaning.

We would note, however, that emotional language does not always predominate among each meaning type. In fact, the majority of the Self-Achievers and Relationalists do not directly tie what they indicate makes life meaningful to their emotions. Julie provides an example when using the term *value.*

> I guess what makes my life worth living would be other people, everything that I do is oriented for either helping people or connecting with people in some way. So I value the time I spend at the

> soup kitchen or like volunteering for others, and in addition I value
> the time that I spend just interacting with others and communicating
> with others and having conversations at the dinner table and stuff
> like that. All the interactions with other people is what adds meaning
> to my life. Without those communicative interactions, there wouldn't
> be any meaning, I guess.

For Relationalists such as Julie, as well as Self-Achievers, there is little direct appeal to what Brooks calls "moral systems." For many of these students what makes life meaningful certainly comes across as subjective and relativistic. Brooks's comments accurately describe how these students treat meaning as something more akin to a personal value that is a subjective preference.

In contrast though, one finds Transcendents and a few Relationalists and Self-Achievers appealing to larger beliefs systems or what Brooks calls a "moral system" for meaning. It should be noted that the appeals are often not to "moral systems" as Brooks describes them. The appeals are to identities linked to particular moral traditions. For instance, in the following case, the student appeals to a broader transcendent identity beyond-the-self that shapes his moral outlook:

> Being a child of God, that's very much like a family connection. . . . I'm
> a child of God, now I'll go eat breakfast, I should probably not just
> eat cereal, I should eat fruit or something like that. . . . Okay, being
> a child of God, I think, "Okay, I'm on this earth, I've got skills and
> things to do," . . . I definitely feel like God made me and God made
> me be an artist, and then underneath that, like going to college to
> become a better artist, and then being healthy, you know, keeping
> your mind strong and clear, also good for being an artist . . . because
> I wouldn't just want to be an artist to be an artist.

The identity appeal for Transcendents functions as shorthand for a larger moral or religious metanarrative that provides the student a sense of self. It locates them in a moral world. This finding reflects what Charles Taylor argues in *The Sources of the Self: The Making of Modern Identity*—"Selfhood and the good, or in another way selfhood and morality, turn out to be inextricably intertwined themes."[27] The reason why these themes are important, he contends, is due to the fact that, "To know who you are is to be oriented in moral space, a space in which questions arise about what is good or bad, what is worth doing and what is not, what has meaning and importance for you and what is trivial and secondary."[28]

In the case of Self-Achievers and Relationalists who do not use emotions or value language, identities related to career and family are the identity sources from which motivating factors are drawn. Isaac, the Jewish student who can actually be considered to be in all three categories, describes what makes his life meaningful using this combination of identity and motivation.

> It's my friends, my family, my activities, my work. I'm in ROTC, so I'm currently a cadet. I'm waiting for my commission into the United States Army as a lieutenant. You know that gives me drive. That's definitely a big part of my identity. What gives me meaning obviously would be my religion; I'd say that's a big part of me.

Consequently, the divide in students' language about meaning exists between those who derive meaning using their emotions, those who derive meaning from personal values, and those who appeal to identities that connect them to larger moral traditions.

Making Sense of Meaning Talk

When considering theories that might make sense of our diverse findings, we believe it is important to recognize that exploring what makes life meaningful for students is slightly different than another prominent focus in higher education literature on "meaning-making," although there is some overlap. The scholar who has contributed the most to the conversation about "meaning-making" in higher education and beyond is Marcia B. Baxter Magolda.[29] Based on longitudinal interviews with eighty young adults starting in college, Magolda has formulated a theory about how students can and should proceed to what she calls "self-authorship," which is the "capacity to internally define a coherent belief system and identity that coordinates mutual relations with others."[30] Self-authorship, for Magolda, is "a way of making meaning of the world and oneself."[31] Magolda's focus emphasizes both the process of building knowledge and conceptual frameworks in general, as well as developing what might be considered an overall philosophy of life.

In the first part of our interviews, though, we uncovered what might be considered the specific bases of meaning or what we are calling "meaning ingredients." These are students' fundamental sources of meaning. While we will later discuss the process of how students identify these sources of meaning and develop them, we first think it is important to identify these essential ingredients. Interestingly, Magolda discusses searching for meaning in three areas similar to our three types: (1) career contexts; (2) relationship contexts; and (3) belief contexts.[32] Yet, as the labels indicate, Magolda labels these three things as contexts for a struggle that results in a turn from external sources of meaning to self-authored sources. In fact, Magolda often tends to highlight only certain ingredients that supply the self-authored meaning. For instance, in the career context Magolda (2001) focuses on one or two fundamental sources of meaning—"career satisfaction and personal happiness."[33] In her interpretation, college students' dissatisfaction moves them from external formulas about how to derive meaning to self-authored sources of meaning. The dissatisfaction occurs when happiness is not achieved or when early sources of happiness, such as a job or relationship, fail to provide happiness.[34]

We think this interpretation of students' experiences does not quite capture what we found. Career, relationships, and beliefs are not just *contexts* in which the struggle between external and internal sources of meaning occur. They are the actual *sources* of meaning. Granted, they could be sources of meaning that students derive under the influence of others and have not embraced for themselves, but they are still the basic substance providing meaning.

Furthermore, while accomplishments, happiness, experiences, and creativity can be self-authored to a degree, what we call "beyond-the-self" sources of meaning also stem from partnerships with other external realities. Certainly, we agree with Magolda that one can move from feeling like these things are forced on oneself (e.g., a parental chosen spouse or religion) to choosing them for one's own. When it comes to this common developmental journey, we find Magolda's evidence of this process convincing. Yet, to fully understand how students derive meaning, we must recognize that one cannot self-author a spouse or children, God, or friends. In other words, finding meaning from these sources may require not only meaning making and self-authorship but also meaning *discovery* and *co*authorship. As Sharon Daloz Parks states, "one of the distortions of many psychological, developmental, economic, and religious models is a focus on the individual that obscures the power of the social context in shaping personal reality."[35] Or as another scholar has put it, how we create (we would add "and discover") the meaning of life is "a collective project."[36]

For this and other reasons, we find the theoretical framework provided by Gary T. Reker and Paul T. P. Wong the most helpful when seeking to make sense of how college students think about meaning (see fig. 5.1).[37] Still, we will note that there are some things that emerge from our findings that do not quite fit this model. As a result, we will propose a few modifications to this theoretical framework in light of our findings.

Reker and Wong's framework helps explain our findings in a number of ways. First, their model recognizes that meaning is something that students both create and discover. While students come to adopt certain meanings for themselves, most consider family, relationships, friends, God, and moral convictions realities they discover and share with others.

Second, Reker and Wong's distinction between situational and global meaning makes sense of the difference we find above between the different ways of thinking about meaning.[38] Reker and Wong use the term *global meaning* to

Figure 5.1. Reker and Wong Theory of Meaning

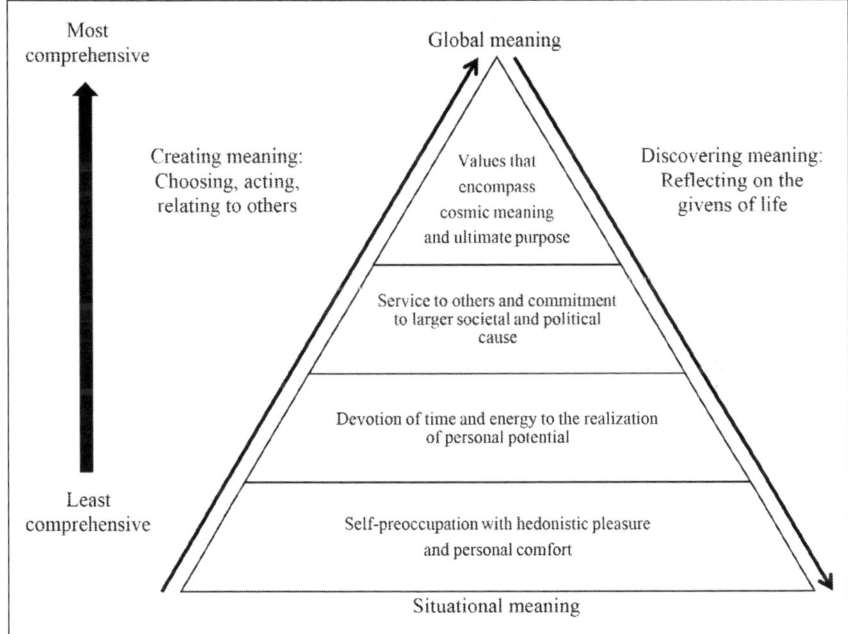

Republished with permission of Routledge, from Gary T. Reker and Paul T. P. Wong, "Personal Meaning in Life and Psychological Adaptation in the Later Years," in Wong, Paul T. P., ed., *The Quest for Meaning: Theories, Research and Applications*, rev. ed. (New York: Routledge, 2012), 437; permission conveyed through Copyright Clearance Center, Inc.

refer to "the existential belief that life has purpose and coherence whereby the individual attempts to understand how life events fit into a larger context."[39] In other words, those who focus on global meaning tend to think in terms of larger worldviews, identities, or belief systems that provide overall cognitive maps for how to make sense of life, similar to the student, Jason, quoted at the beginning of this chapter. Yet, although nearly all the students we interviewed were able to articulate an answer to a question about what gives life meaning, this does not necessarily mean that all students find global meaning. The concept of situational meaning helps make sense of the students who focus on deriving meaning from emotional states or subjective preferences. Situational meaning refers to "the attachment of personal significance to specific experiences in life whereby the individual tries to make sense of that experience."[40] In these cases, such as Malik and Chelsea, the student quoted at the beginning of the chapter, the students derive meaning from particular emotional or life experiences that then give them some direction. Most Self-Achievers and Relationalists answer questions about meaning by focusing on "situational meaning" instead of "global meaning."[41] Joshua provided a clear example of someone who uses situational meaning. As opposed to the Individual Achievers who focus on "situational meaning," the Transcendents, as well as a few Relationalists and Self-Achievers, approach the matter of meaning as one concerned with "global meaning."[42] Students such as Cody possess the existential belief that life has a broader coherence and use a transcendent worldview to identify and make sense of life.

Similar to our approach, Reker and Wong also set forth a typology of substantive answers to the question of meaning. They divide the types of meaning into four types:

1. Self-preoccupation with hedonistic pleasure and personal comfort

2. Devotion of time and energy to the realization of personal potential

3. Service to others and commitment to a larger societal and political cause

4. Values that encompass cosmic meaning and ultimate purpose

The various levels correspond to some degree to the types we discovered. The first two levels of meaning correspond to what we have labeled the Individual Achievers. We should note that virtually all of the students we interviewed from this category would be focused on the second level, where they give "devotion of time and energy to the realization of personal potential."[43] Although Wong claims, "Many people believe that money is the answer [to the question of life's meaning]; that is why money remains the most powerful motivator in a consumer society,"[44] we did not find money to be a primary source of meaning for college students. In fact, materialistic answers are often the only answers where students cast negative judgments. Several students mentioned, in a negative manner, that they perceive many of their fellow students to be motivated by money. This does not mean money never motivated the students we interviewed (it almost certainly did for some of them); it simply means that such a motivation is widely considered, to varying degree, to be a deviant or secondary motivation (e.g., I want to make money to help my parents). Yet, as we shall see in chapter 10, many students do think about material goods when describing future goals. We also wonder if it might have to do with the social class of students we interviewed. While one student notes,

> I feel like especially if I went somewhere that was more poor [sic],
> I would definitely like the good life; [it] wouldn't necessarily be

anything to do with money. It would be more like being with family and being happy with what you have and not being consumed with greed or envy or anything like that.

We found the opposite to be true. Students who speak about making money (particularly for their parents) tend to come from backgrounds with less material wealth.

Service Relationalists and the Change the World Transcendents fit within the category of those devoted to "service to others and commitment to a larger societal and political cause." Finally, the God and Religious Transcendents may be those who are considered to be devoted to "values that encompass cosmic meaning and ultimate purpose."[45] We should note, however, that it is unclear where Family or General Relationalists fit in Reker and Wong's model, since finding meaning in one's family can be related to service, but it can also be connected to personal comfort.

Reker and Wong's theory also makes sense of our findings in another way. Reker and Wong differentiate the categories using depth and "comprehensive" language. They place a preoccupation with the pleasure and comfort of one's self at the "shallow" or "least comprehensive" end of their hierarchy. In contrast, those that embrace "values that encompass cosmic meaning and ultimate purpose" are "at the deep end" in that they will be better able "to integrate the contradictions, conflicts, and absurdities of life by rising above them and viewing them in the context of a more comprehensive horizon."[46] In other words, their meaning frameworks are both more extensive and comprehensive.

Conclusion

Most college students are not lacking meaning. Almost all students already have at least provisional answers to the question of what makes their life meaningful. Moreover, the vast majority claim they are not primarily concerned with what scholars identify as the least comprehensive forms of meaning, "self-preoccupation with hedonistic pleasure and personal comfort."[47] They maintain that they are attempting to fulfill their potential through personal achievements, relationships with others, or living for a transcendent purpose or being. In this respect, they have developed maps that they believe can provide them understanding and direction in life.

If what we found is true in general, college faculty and student personnel may need to consider focusing less on helping students make or discover meaning and more on helping students think in more profound and critical ways about the range of ways students currently discover and construct their sources of meaning. In this respect, students do not need help finding meaning in college. They need help making sense of their present ways of finding and making meaning and learning to think critically about those approaches in light of other approaches to both discovering and creating meaning. In other words, the same thing claimed about adolescents in chapter 2 is also likely true of college students. Whether college students' sources of meaning will move from being relatively straightforward to being more complex and mature will depend on other important influences in their lives they encounter during college. Chapters 8 and 9 will address what influences these might be and how students perceive these influences. Before addressing these influences, however, we want to address the other important concept—purpose—in the next two chapters.

Chapter 6

———

The Diverse Purposes of College Students

I always felt like my purpose was to help people.

—Jessica, regional state university student

I'd say the purpose of my life . . . everything I do is to achieve that purpose
of being happy eternally.

—Terry, Mormon university student

I know that I want to get a good job, I want to be successful; eventually I'd
like to have kids that are good kids, model citizens.

– Angie, flagship state university student

Jennifer, a Buddhist student at a liberal arts college, grew up going to international schools throughout Southeast Asia in Vietnam, Hong Kong, and Thailand. A child of Vietnamese immigrants, she currently finds inspiration to study from her uneducated mother who did not speak English when she came to America. Jennifer recounted her mother's journey,

> But within a year she . . . worked in the daytime, went to school
> in the night and really worked hard. [She] went from not knowing
> how to even read and write in Vietnamese to speaking in English
> and writing in English.

Her father also worked long hours at night, and the sacrifices of her parents are what drive her today. "That pushes you to work really hard and become like them."

The hard work that she saw her parents demonstrate to reach their goals clearly influences what Jennifer claims gives her own life meaning, "I think what gives life meaning is your goals and what you want to achieve and how hard you're willing to work for that." While Jennifer first talks about these matters using Self-Achiever language, she also adds another language when she talks about the motivation behind her purpose. She indicates that she sees her purpose as pursuing a career as a doctor. Moreover, "it's not because it's for the money. It's for helping people." She also describes her purpose in much more specific terms, "Yeah, I would eventually like to work for Doctors without Borders, and I want to volunteer for the Peace Corps and just go to different third-world countries and help people out. That is my final goal in life." She recognizes though, similar to her parent's experience, that reaching that final goal takes more than merely identifying it, "There's all these steps leading up to that, you know . . . very, very long tedious steps."

Trinity, a first-year student at a public research university, recounts a much different kind of influence from her parents.

> None of my parents grew up with a lot of money; especially whenever my parents got divorced, my mom went through a really hard time with having me and my sister and just not having a lot of resources. After she married my step-dad and had my brother, my brother was very sick for many years and so we have just been America poor [versus poor in a non-Western context].

As a consequence, Trinity's parents envisioned her going to college as a way to help solve this problem: "Go to college and get a degree so I can make money." Their own financial story shaped and still shapes their hopes and dreams for their daughter. "They want me to not have to worry about stress, financial anything."

The problem for Trinity is that she derives her meaning from something different. "Well I'm a follower of Christ; I love Jesus with my whole heart." She sees what gives her life meaning as "bringing glory to God and doing that in everything that I do, whether it be my career, my friendships, or not just bringing others to Christ, but also living my life out in His name and for His glory." Her purpose, Trinity believes, is derived from this meaning, although it

> might be more specific, I feel my purpose, the reason why I changed my major from audiology to social work was because I very much feel called to the orphanages and foster care system and adoption and that kind of thing. I really feel like that's where God's leading me on my path and that's where I will ultimately lead out my purpose and His plan.

The change of major, though, has created difficulty with her parents,

> I mean, audiologists make plenty of money, so my parents were very like, "Oh you'll be great at that. That'll be a great way to go." Then

over the winter break when I told them, "Hey, I actually wanna do [social work]." . . . My real dad didn't really care, but my mom and my step-dad were both very upset, my mom especially. She was just so upset and just telling me, "You're not gonna make any money. You're gonna be poor. You're gonna go through what I went through, blah, blah, blah." And so that was hard sticking to my guns.

What helped Trinity stick to her guns were her ultimate views about purpose. "Being Christian I don't have those views. I don't see money as a necessity or a really important asset, like I have to have a lot of money."

For Peyton, a regional university student, money has not been a problem growing up or in college.

> My dad owns a small business . . . he's a successful businessman, and my mom is a loving mom and a good wife . . . my parents always pushed us to make sure that we went to college and that we strived to be the best. With four kids they paid 100 percent for all four of our college tuitions.

Although Peyton was pushed to go to college, he admits that when it came to matters of meaning and purpose, "They never really pushed us. They just kind of let us do our own thing in that aspect."

When it comes to meaning, then, Peyton has carved his own way by focusing primarily on self-achievement instead of anything transcendent. "I don't have a religious reason for living . . . I set goals for myself . . . you know where do I see myself in five years and that's what I strive to live for, to get to that point in five years." As indicated by his five-year goals, he believes he should "try to not get too far ahead of myself." Once he achieves the goals, he would then reevaluate "where I want to see myself down the road and that gives me something to look forward to."

When it comes to purpose, Peyton is a bit more unsure. "I don't know what my purpose per se in life is yet," but he does have some provisional self-achievement goals derived from common cultural scripts.

> I want to be happy, I want to have a family, you know, so it's, like I said, that's what I'm striving for. I'm trying to get a degree so I can get a good job. Just do the typical thing, you know, buy a house. Do what everyone is supposed to do.

For Peyton, it would appear that Jefferson's famous pursuit of happiness involved doing "what everyone is supposed to do."

"What are the types of purpose that inspire young people today?"[1] A prominent group of scholars researching purpose claim that this is the first and most important question that needs to be addressed when examining purpose. We can learn the general types of purposes students pursue by listening to Jennifer, Trinity, and Peyton. As their examples indicate, students talk about purpose using very similar categories as meaning. Many will draw on and use language related to the Self-Achiever, Relationalist, and Transcendent types developed earlier. Yet, there is one important difference in the way that students talk about purpose. Unlike meaning, a significant percentage of students, such as Peyton, admit that they do not have a purpose. These next two chapters discuss the nature of students' search for purpose, with this chapter focusing on understanding those students who claim to have found some kind of purpose and the next chapter examining those students who admit to still searching for a purpose.

This chapter concentrates in particular on two issues. First, it examines how students talk about their self-identified purposes using both the 110 Focused Qual and the 75 National Qual interview samples. Interestingly, students demonstrate the same purposes as they do sources of meaning. However, their sources of meaning and purpose may not be the same. Second, we report the results of a quantitative survey we created based on our interviews that was administrated by Gallup® to provide a national picture of how college students think about purpose. In particular, we examine the general support for certain purposes and the factors correlated with certain purposes. In general, we find race, religion/nonreligion, and perceived income-class play important roles. Finally, we end by exploring the question of what we believe the role of colleges *should* be in shaping students' understanding of purpose given our findings, as well as recent scholarship within positive psychology on "beyond-the-self" purpose development in young adults.

Differentiating Meaning and Purpose

How do students think about purpose differently than meaning? While there are a variety of subtle differences, Matt, a Catholic student at a private Baptist university provides an illustration of the key difference we found:

> I think the meaning of life should be the same for everyone. We are here to serve God, and we're here to learn about ourselves and figure out what's right and wrong, like figure it out for ourselves, of course with other people's help . . . but as far as finding a purpose in life, I think that we all have a different purpose. Of course, I think that's

pretty assumed by most people that we all do different things. We all have different jobs. So I think that finding a purpose and finding meaning in life are two completely different things.

Matt's differentiation is also one that other scholars have noticed. As discussed earlier, three scholars in the field of positive psychology have focused on differentiating meaning from purpose. In making the case for this differentiation, William Damon, Jenni Menon, and Kendall Cotton Bronk offer a unique definition of purpose. In their formulation, "purpose is a stable and generalized intention to accomplish something that is at once meaningful to the self and of consequence to the world beyond-the-self."[2] They set forth three rationales for this definition. First, they emphasize that while purpose is a goal, it is a unique kind of goal: "It is more stable and far-reaching than low-level goals such as 'to get to the movie on time' or 'to find a parking place in town today.'"[3] Second, they note that while purpose comprises an aspect of one's search for meaning, they claimed, "It also has an external component, the desire to make a difference in the world, to contribute to matters larger than the self."[4] Third, they point out that while meaning may or may not be focused on a defined end, "purpose is *always* directed at an accomplishment towards which one can make progress."[5] Since offering this definition, numerous authors have used it or a similar formulation in a variety of studies.[6]

One important basis for their distinction between meaning and purpose is their claim that it reflects common-language usage.[7] Based on our research, we can confirm that, at least in one prominent way, it clearly does. Three-fourths of students we interviewed, like Matt, either articulate or affirm that meaning is something broader, often universal, and purpose is something unique or more particular to an individual. The following student provides an example of this pattern:

> I guess when I hear "finding your purpose in life" it's sort of like "What are you here to do?" and it's sort of more specific than finding your meaning. Finding your meaning to me sounds a little bit like finding your universal truth and why you're here.

As the above quote reveals, one way students distinguish the two concepts involves identifying what one finds meaningful as the prized aspects of reality on which one focuses to prioritize one's affections and attention (e.g., helping others, loving God). These students then differentiate "purpose" as the individual goal, often derived from the meaningful set of realities that prompts one to action. One student stipulates that purpose is, "You know more of an action." In this sense, it usually relates to one's vocation in life, and it involves some kind of personal engagement. For example, David articulates this important distinction:

> So, I think there is a difference in the sense that the meaning of life is more the overall sense of what one is supposed to live his or her life [for], and the purpose of life is what you're supposed to do in that lifetime. So, I guess an example would be the meaning of life is to help people, and the purpose of life is to do this action, or to become a psychologist or something like that.

Again, David's description finds some resonance with the map analogy used earlier. While there are a variety of general human realities and actions related to those realities one could place on one's meaning map (e.g., creating things, experiencing nature, etc.), the above student placed "serving others" in the map legend. He then identifies a specific destination among the various roads related to "helping people" and chose "become a psychologist." Evetta, the first-year student profiled in chapter 4 also makes this common distinction:

> I think of them as different because somebody's purpose is what they should do while they are here, or what they can do, and I think that's definitely different than the meaning of life. 'Cause the meaning of life can be, I don't know, I feel it can be more similar towards people, but our purposes are different.

Overall, for the majority of students making this distinction, the various sources for meaning in life can be shared, much like a common map. Purpose, though, is related to one's particular gifting, vocation, or calling. It is the unique final destination that each person must find.

The importance of recognizing this distinction emerges when discussing what motivates students. While one might expect that students who describe their meaning according to Relationalist, Transcendent, or Self-Achiever categories would do the same for purpose, this is not always the case. Sometimes, a student's source of meaning might be described according to one category, but their purpose may be described in another category. Jennifer provides an example. With regard to meaning, Jennifer claims, "I think what gives life meaning is just, you know, your goals and what you want to achieve and how hard you're willing to work for that." This would appear to make her a Self-Achiever. Yet, when asked about her purpose, as indicated from the rationale for hoping to work with Doctors without Borders, her motivation stems from wanting to help people. Dakota, a student from a Lutheran liberal arts college provides another example. She describes what gives her meaning solely in terms of individual achievement, a job as "the director of the wellness center here on campus." She also does the same thing with purpose. "I would say I'm not totally sure, but I want to be a counselor eventually, or a therapist." Yet, her motivation for this purpose is grounded in the Service Relationalist understanding of meaning discussed earlier:

> I worked on a crisis phone line in high school for teens, and that gave me a lot of sense of purpose, and so I definitely want to do something along those lines, because I really like feeling like I'm helping people and that's just really rewarding.

These types of nuances are important to keep in mind in order to understand how the way that students discuss purpose differs from how they discuss meaning.

We should also note one other thing about how students discuss purpose. The scholarly definition of purpose used above contains what might be considered a normative or operational definition. This definition specifies that what may be understood as self-focused purposes are not really purposes. In other words, if one wants to find a particular career, become happy, or achieve a certain level of material wealth, these do not qualify as purposes. While we believe that this operational definition of purpose can be helpful, in our interviews we sought to find out how students understand the concept of purpose without defining it for them. After all, as Hill, Burrow, O'Dell, and Thornton recently observed, "it is as yet uncertain whether adolescents think of purpose in ways similar to researchers"[8]—the same could be said of college students. We wondered if they might actually use the terms differently and thus have different understandings of different kinds of purpose.

The Purpose Ingredients of College Students

According to our 185 qualitative interviews, if you ask college students about their purpose, you will likely receive one or more answers from a list of twelve. They identify at least eleven unique types of purposes while the twelfth group of responses consisted of those who claimed they did not currently have a purpose. These eleven purposes and illustrative quotes from the interviews are listed below, and they are placed within the general meaning categories established earlier.

Self-Achievers

1. Career (e.g., "Well, I know I want to be a nurse. I'm in nursing school and I know I probably want to get a postgrad degree in nursing").

2. Happiness (e.g., "I mean ultimately I just want to be happy").

3. Creative accomplishments (e.g., "Making things. That's kind of broad, but I'm a studio art major, so I like to create interesting things").

4. Experiences (e.g., "Learning new things, seeing new places").

5. Material goods or money (e.g., "I would like to make a lot of money and not have to worry about making car payments or worrying about insurance or when I buy a house-mortgages, and just, you know, being financially secure. I think that's a big purpose for me").

Relationalists

6. Service and/or Love (e.g., "I always felt like my purpose was to help people").

7. Family (e.g., "Have a family, kids, grandkids").

8. Friends (e.g., "I'd have to say family and friends").

Transcendents

9. God or religion (e.g., "My biggest purpose is to love God and bring glory to Him").

10. Change the world for good (e.g., "I want to use my knowledge and ability to try and better life for somebody else").

11. Civic involvement (e.g., "I want to serve others through leadership roles").

As the listed quotes indicate, some students focus on only one purpose. Many students, however, combine these purposes in a wide variety of ways. In fact, one way to make sense of how students speak about these purposes is to think of them as *ingredients* for the good life. In some cases, students combine only two of the ingredients: "My purpose is to excel in my career and somehow use that career to help other people." Indeed, this kind of combination is common when students understand their purpose as the motivation for their career: "The main point that I have behind my career choice is that I want to work in aerospace, specifically with space flight because I feel that I want to help humanity get into space and push out the boundaries more."

Some students even add together three or more different purpose ingredients. Certain ingredients are especially prone to combinations such as friends, happiness, material goods, and family. Indeed, not one respondent that we interviewed listed friends as the sole purpose, although this student comes close:

> Making my friends happy. . . . in my brother's graduating class, the valedictorian, I barely remember his speech. I barely remember anything, but this has stuck with me. If you can't be happy yourself, the best thing to do is make other people happy. . . . So I try to make my friends as happy as possible.

As in this case, the primary ingredient of happiness is often combined with other things. "My friends and my family and just being around happy, uplifting atmospheres, so that's what gives my life meaning."

Also, as the above quotes indicate, a general desire (e.g., a desire to help humanity, a desire to be happy) usually serves as the primary purpose ingredient and the prime motivator. In some cases, students themselves order the ingredients under one overarching ingredient as in this case, "Overall, for me, it's God and through Him I can be happy, I have meaning in my life and—I mean then there's also my family and my friends. But the utmost thing would be God." In this example, God provides a common ordering purpose. Similarly, happiness often serves as an overarching purpose: "Having a family, a nice family, a good job, nice cars, [and a] nice house. Just really being accomplished . . . Having those things would make me happy." It should be noted, however, that not all students prioritize their list of purpose ingredients or even can came up with a purpose (as the next chapter will explain). Moreover, some students talk about purpose using two types of purpose languages. Grace, a student from a regional university describes her purpose this way. "I feel like I have this plan: graduate college, get a job, have a family, that kind of thing. So I feel like that's my purpose, to make those goals." This response makes her sound like a Self-Achiever, but then she adds a Transcendent caveat, "but also, you know, like praising God. Like purpose-driven life kind of thing. I don't know. I've never really thought about it." Grace's use of two languages about purpose is not an isolated case. Of course, adults also use this approach. For example, when answering the question, "What is the purpose of life?" Warren

Buffett described it in partially relational terms, but also primarily as a personal achievement: "*The purpose of life is to be loved by as many people as possible among those you want to have love you.*"[9]

Similar to meaning, very few students articulate their purpose primarily in terms of achieving material possessions. Usually, those mentioning material possessions include other purposes as well, such as the following student: "To own my own house, have kids, [and] get married, like everyone else. Be well off." As in this case, quite often family proves to be a purpose listed along with other purposes: "I definitely want to be married, and like I said, the graphic design thing, I'm dying to go into that. I can't wait to graduate and just enjoy life, that's very important right now." Similarly, as one religious student articulated his purpose, "I would definitely say my family and my religion . . . they also actually go together because my parents resonate with very strong religious backgrounds, and so I think this is very strongly rooted in me."

In general, our findings share some similarities with other scholarly lists, but some differences also are apparent in light of the approach that we took. For example, Bronk identified six common life purposes that individuals identify: religion, family, career, political and/or civic activities, and artistic pursuits.[10] While an examination of our student interviews confirmed the presence of these purposes, it also revealed additional items Bronk did not identify. One reason for this difference is that Bronk relied on the "beyond-the-self" definition of purpose noted above. As can be seen from our interviews though, most of the Self-Achiever purposes would not qualify as purposes using this definition, even though students clearly understand and answer questions as if it is.

Our method, particularly the way we cluster the responses, shares more similarities with approaches that do not seek to limit the concept of purpose to beyond-the-self purposes. For example, Moran found in a study of adolescents that only one in ten youth defined purpose using the "beyond-the-self" definition specified by Damon et al.[11] Instead, her understanding of purpose fit into four types of cultures that they label as the "Supported, Strivers, Givers, and Disciples." In her words,

> The Supported focused on reasons and meaning for what they could gain from others and were confident in tandem with support received. Strivers aimed for primarily standard career success goals but felt uncertain. Givers felt certain about their aims to help others. Disciples, who tended to provide the most complex definitions, felt certain about their faith-focused purpose to serve God.[12]

In this case, the Disciples would be one type of what we call Transcendent, the Givers would be one type of Relationalist, and the Strivers and Supported would be two types of Self-Achievers.

Understanding College Students' Life Purpose:
A National Survey

Using the eleven ingredients and the three general categories of ingredients as a guide, we undertook a national survey of college students that approached issues of purpose in a different way than previous surveys of college students regarding meaning and purpose.[13] Our questions focused on the degree to which college students supported forms of the eleven types of purpose ingredients we identified. We created one additional ingredient for this second part of the survey, since we noticed that students rarely talked about making money and tended to talk more about being comfortable. We wanted to see how this division would play out in a quantitative survey. With the "experiences," we broke the possible responses into two parts: (1) experience life to the fullest; (2) discover new things about the world. We found respondents often distinguished between experiences sought out of pleasure or curiosity. We should note that we did not make the purpose categories exclusive, so that students could affirm any or all of the purpose ingredients in some way.

Overall, we drew data from a nationally representative sample of 2,503 college students in both private and public institutions of higher education.[14] As indicated by figure 6.1, students tended to strongly identify with a broad

Figure 6.1. Percent of students who strongly agree or strongly disagree with various purposes (N = 2,503)

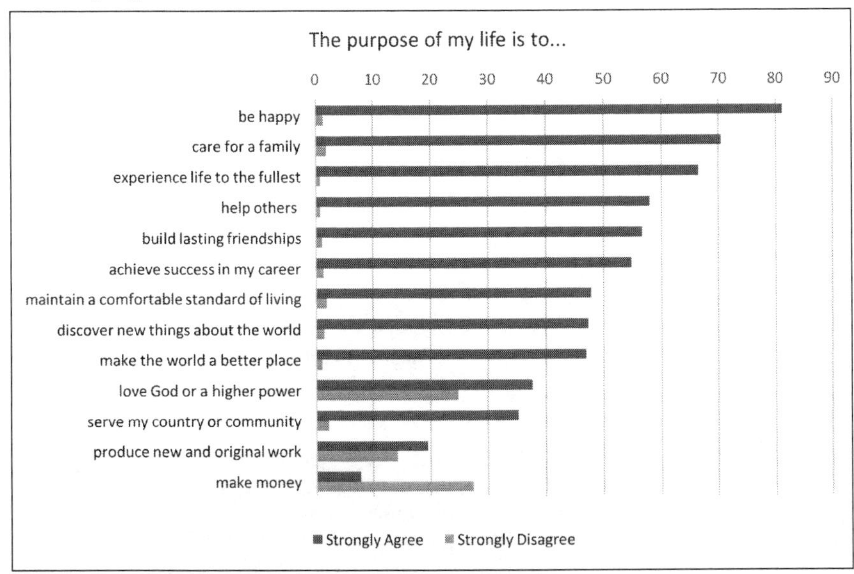

Source: National Survey of College Students about Purpose, 2014.

range of purpose ingredients, although we found they were less likely to identify with certain Self-Achievement and Transcendent purposes. The most important purpose for most students, by some margin, was to "be happy," with over four-fifths strongly agreeing that this is one of their purposes. Over 50 percent of college students strongly agreed with three Self-Achievement-oriented purposes and three Relationalist purposes. Interestingly, not one transcendent purpose was strongly agreed on by over half the students.

Moreover, the transcendent purpose, "love God or a higher power" was the second highest category with which students strongly disagreed as a purpose (24.8 percent), finishing just below making money (27.4 percent). In other words, around one quarter of students were strongly opposed to seeing making money or loving God as their purpose. In fact, when we consider total agreement or disagreement (fig. 6.2), over half of students disagree with the idea that their purpose is to make money, and over a third disagree with the statement that their purpose is to love God or a higher power. Judging from the survey, college students are first and foremost Self-Achievers and then secondarily Relationalists. Yet, they are particular kinds of Self-Achievers. They are less interested in money or creating new things and most supportive of being happy and experiencing

Figure 6.2. Percent of students who strongly agree/agree or strongly disagree/disagree with various purposes (*N* = 2,503)

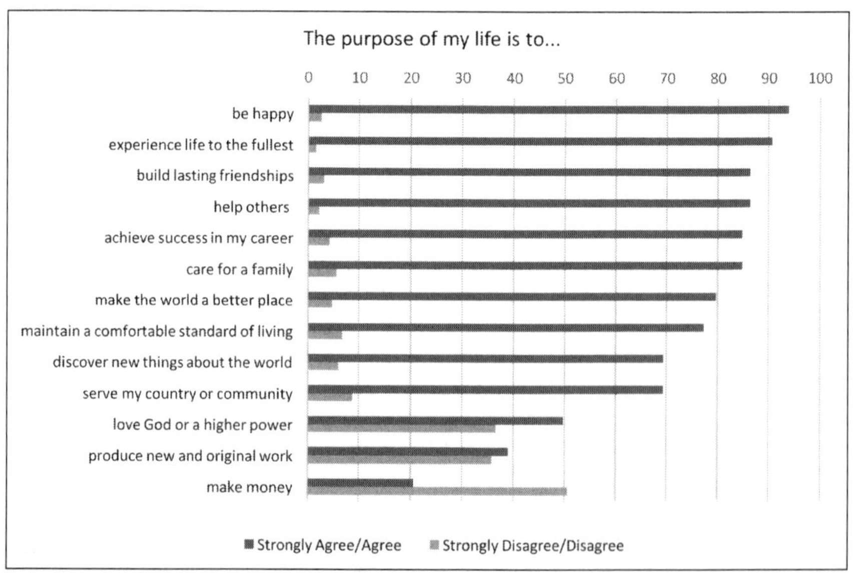

Source: National Survey of College Students about Purpose, 2014.

life to the fullest. They are also Relationalists when it comes to their support for helping others, friends, and family. What they appear to be the least supportive of are Transcendent purposes such as loving God, serving one's country or community, or making the world a better place.

In order to learn about the possible individual factors that may influence students' support for a purpose, with help from a colleague,[15] we conducted a logistic regression to produce results for a total of thirteen different purpose ingredients to which respondents *strongly agreed*. Overall, we examined whether religion, race, gender, political affiliation, income, type of institution, and college major were significant predictors of any of the purpose ingredients. The next three tables show the results of this analysis.

Race proves to be one of the most consistent factors (table 6.1). In every purpose ingredient category, White students are less likely to indicate support for particular purposes than Black and Hispanic students. This finding is consistent with Ryff et al.'s finding that highly educated African Americans report higher purpose scores than highly educated Whites.[16]

This finding is true for a wide variety of purposes whether they were Self-Oriented, Relationalist, or Transcendent. The reason why this might be the case, we believe, deserves further study, although Bronk's hypothesis may prove true if one considers the college environment similar to the workplace: "Educa-

Table 6.1. Significant Racial Correlates of Purpose ($N = 2,503$)

The purpose of my life is to . . .	Postively Correlated	Negatively Correlated
be happy	Black; Hispanic	White
experience life to the fullest	Hispanic; Other	White
achieve success in my career	Black; Hispanic; Other	White
produce new and original work	Black; Hispanic	White
make money	Black; Hispanic; Asian	White
maintain a comfortable standard . . .	Black; Hispanic; Other	White
discover new things about the world	Black; Hispanic	White
help others	Black; Other	White
care for a family	Black; Hispanic	White
build lasting friendships	White	
make the world a better place	Black; Other	White
love God or a higher power	Black; Hispanic	White; Asian
serve my country or community	Black	White

Source: National Survey of College Students about Purpose, 2014.

Note: Variables listed are significant at the $p < .05$ level.

tional attainment may serve as an important signal of status attainment, especially among ethnic minorities, and it can lead to increased opportunities in the workplace that may facilitate the pursuit of purpose, especially career-oriented and familial-support purposes."[17] Our findings would indicate that, for African-American and Hispanic students, being in college leads to greater support for purpose in general, while for students from other races it leads to support for certain particular purposes. Though we do not have a noncollege sample to see if this finding only applies to those who are currently students.

Unlike race, whose influence is quite consistent across all purposes, religion proves to be a very important factor in *distinguishing* between certain purposes (tables 6.2 and 6.3). First, not indicating a religious identity proves to be positively correlated with four kinds of purposes (experience life to the fullest, produce new and original work, make the world a better place, and serve my country or community). In contrast, being a Mainline Protestant, Catholic, or evangelical is negatively correlated with particular purposes (Mainline Protestant: experience life to the fullest and help others; Catholic: discover new things about the world and make the world a better place; evangelical: serve my country or community). Identifying as Catholic is positively correlated with the purpose of building lasting friendships.

Interestingly, how students view religion is either positively or negatively correlated with almost every purpose. In other words, whether one views religion as important or unimportant profoundly shapes how one views particular pur-

Table 6.2. Significant Religious Correlates with Purpose—Religious Identity (*N* = 2,503)

The purpose of my life is to . . .	Postively Correlated	Negatively Correlated
be happy		
experience life to the fullest	no religious ID	Mainline Protestant
achieve success in my career		
produce new and original work	no religious ID	
make money		
maintain a comfortable standard . . .		
discover new things about the world	other religious ID	Catholic
help others		Mainline Protestant
care for a family		
build lasting friendships	Catholic	
make the world a better place	no religious ID	Catholic
love God or a higher power		Catholic
serve my country or community	no religious ID	Evangelical

Source: National Survey of College Students about Purpose, 2014.

Note: Variables listed are significant at the *p* < .05 level.

Table 6.3. Significant Religious Correlates with Purpose—Importance of Religion and Religious Service Attendance ($N = 2,503$)

The purpose of my life is to . . .	Postively Correlated	Negatively Correlated
be happy		imp of religion; service attend
experience life to the fullest	imp of religion	
achieve success in my career	imp of religion	
produce new and original work		imp of religion; service attend
make money		service attend
maintain a comfortable standard . . .		service attend
discover new things about the world		imp of religion; service attend
help others	imp of religion; service attend	
care for a family	imp of religion; service attend	
build lasting friendships	imp of religion; service attend	
make the world a better place	imp of religion; service attend	
love God or a higher power	imp of religion; service attend	
serve my country or community	imp of religion; service attend	

Source: National Survey of College Students about Purpose, 2014.

Note: Variables listed are significant at the $p < .05$ level.

poses. We find it fascinating that viewing religion as important leads to a positive correlation with all the Relationalist and Transcendent purposes (help others, care for a family, build lasting friendships, make the world a better place, love God or a higher power, and serving one's country or community) as well as two self-achiever purposes (experience life to the fullest and achieve success in my career). In contrast, it is negatively correlated with three self-achiever purposes (be happy, produce new and original work, discover new things about the world).

The same divide also exists for those who are more likely to attend religious services. In fact, it is even more pronounced. Attending religious services is positively correlated with all of the Relationalist and Transcendent purposes (help others, care for a family, build lasting friendships, make the world a better place, love God or a higher power, and serving one's country or community). In contrast, it is negatively correlated with five Self-Achiever purposes (be happy, produce new and original work, make money, maintain a comfortable standard of living, and discover new things about the world). Those who do think religion is important and those who do not attend religious services frequently clearly approach purpose differently, particularly with regard to Self-Achievement purposes.

Finally, certain particular individual characteristics are correlated with particular purposes. Interestingly, gender makes no difference. What clearly makes a difference is the self-reported socioeconomic status of the student (see table 6.4). Believing that one's family financial situation is "above average" is consistently (with one exception) associated with less agreement with any of the purposes.

Political affiliation and major also proves to be an important factor (see table 6.5). Self-identified Republicans are more likely to support making money, caring for a family, loving God or a higher power, and serving one's country or community. They are also less likely to support producing new and original work and discovering new things about the world. In contrast, Democrats are more likely to support maintaining a comfortable standard of living and are less likely to support loving God or a higher power. Independents often appear to be the opposite of Republicans on most purposes, although they also contrast with Democrats in one case (maintaining a comfortable standard of living). They are more likely to support producing new and original work and discovering new things about the world, but they are less likely to support making money, maintaining a comfortable standard of living, caring for a family, loving God or a higher power, and serving their country or community.

Finally, a students' major can also be correlated with support for particular purpose types (see table 6.6). Perhaps most surprising is that business majors

Table 6.4. Significant College and Demographic Correlates of Purpose—Perception of Family income ($N = 2{,}503$)

The purpose of my life is to . . .	Postively Correlated	Negatively Correlated
be happy		Income
experience life to the fullest		Income
achieve success in my career		Income
produce new and original work		Income
make money		Income
maintain a comfortable standard . . .		Income
discover new things about the world		Income
help others		Income
care for a family		Income
build lasting friendships		
make the world a better place		Income
love God or a higher power		Income
serve my country or community		Income

Source: National Survey of College Students about Purpose, 2014.

Note: Variables listed are significant at the $p < .05$ level.

Table 6.5. Significant College and Demographic Correlates of Purpose—Political ID (N = 2,503)

The purpose of my life is to . . .	Postively Correlated	Negatively Correlated
be happy		
experience life to the fullest		
achieve success in my career		
produce new and original work	Independent	Republican
make money	Republican	Independent
maintain a comfortable standard . . .	Democrat	Independent; other party
discover new things about the world	Independent	Republican
help others		
care for a family	Republican	Independent
build lasting friendships		
make the world a better place		
love God or a higher power	Republican	Democrat; Independent
serve my country or community	Republican	Independent

Source: National Survey of College Students about Purpose, 2014.

Note: Variables listed are significant at the $p < .05$ level.

Table 6.6. Significant College and Demographic Correlates of Purpose—Major (N = 2,503)

The purpose of my life is to . . .	Postively Correlated	Negatively Correlated
be happy	Non-STEM major	
experience life to the fullest		Health and science major
achieve success in my career		
produce new and original work		
make money		Education major
maintain a comfortable standard . . .		
discover new things about the world		
help others		
care for a family	Business major	
build lasting friendships	Humanities major	
make the world a better place		
love God or a higher power	Business major	STEM major
serve my country or community		

Source: National Survey of College Students about Purpose, 2014.

Note: Variables listed are significant at the $p < .05$ level.

are more likely to support a Relationalist (care for a family) and Transcendent (love God or a higher power) purpose. Humanities majors are more interested in building lasting friendships. Education majors, not surprisingly, are less interested in making money. Health and science majors are also less likely to support the purpose of experiencing life to the fullest. Our measures of institutional type—public four year, private four year, and public two year—were not significantly correlated with any of the measures of purpose.

Overall, these findings reveal that when talking about developing a purpose, students exhibit a whole range of interests regarding what kind of purpose they want and hope to develop. Certainly, higher education leaders and administrators should be aware of this diversity and recognize the unique needs of various student types. In particular, we think it is clear that upper-income students will need particular support when it comes to developing a purpose. Another question we think is important that emerges from these findings concerns whether higher-education leaders need to think about trying to shape students' purposes in particular ways.

Should Cultivating Beyond-the-Self Purposes Be a Developmental Goal?

Overall, the fact that students support a variety of purposes is certainly not surprising. Moreover, the finding that students tend to focus on more individualistic or self-oriented purposes shares similarities to what others have found by studying the styles of moral reasoning among emerging adults.[18] Personal happiness and moral individualism are the dominant frameworks young emerging adults use to make sense of ethical choices, instead of philosophical or religious moral traditions that might encourage beyond-the-self sorts of purposes.

Should the university be helping students develop what we call Relationalist and Transcendent purposes? Christian Smith has argued that colleges and universities as a whole have failed to address young emerging adults' individualism and shallow thinking about moral issues.[19] Should they seek to address these issues when it comes to purpose?

Early student development theorists in this area tended to present a narrow approach to the role the university should play. For instance, Arthur Chickering's influential *Education and Identity*, first published in 1969 and later revised in 1993 with Linda Reisser, focused on how students develop their own life purposes, which involved integrating three practical areas: (1) vocational plans and aspirations, (2) personal interests, and (3) interpersonal and family interests.[20] As this list reveals, most of Chickering and Reisser's emphasis centered on matters of what we would identify as self-achievement purposes with interpersonal and family interests addressing one part of a Relationalist orientation. The whole range of Transcendent purposes, as well as certain Relationalist purposes, were not addressed. In addition, William Perry's work, first published in 1968 and also issued again in the 1990s, also set forth a theory of moral development that reinforced the ambiguity regarding the role of the university in students' purpose development. Perry suggested that the role of the university is to expand and complicate the students' conceptual map of the world and the variety of intellectual and ethical roads one can take in life.[21] According to this approach, students need to understand the complex range of purposes that exist and then learn how to critically analyze their own purposes in light of the range of options. Although Perry indicated that educators should leave it to the individual student to parse and weigh the relative value of different commitments, he also claimed, "it is no longer tenable for an educator to take the position that what a person does with his intellectual skills is a moral rather than intellectual problem and therefore none of the scholar's business."[22] What the teacher could offer was an experience of common community and modeling one's own "making of meaning," "daring to take risks," and "courage in committing."[23] The educator was not suggesting that particular moral ends were better than others. Ultimately, following Perry's theory might help students develop a more complex map about life's meaning and purpose, provide a community of support, and provide an educational model of someone who has chosen a meaning or purpose, but, like the values clarification movement that developed during the same time period, adult interference with choosing which purpose road is best was understood as dangerously authoritarian.

According to positive psychology purpose scholars, however, psychologically healthy students need to move beyond formulating limited goals, particularly self-achievement oriented goals, and think about how to formulate life aims that go beyond-the-self. For instance, one recent study examined whether different purpose orientations, which the authors identified as creative, financial, personal recognition, and prosocial, predicted personal well-being over the short and long term.[24] We have labeled the first three as Self-Achievement-oriented purposes. They found "at middle adulthood, only the prosocial purpose orientation was predictive of greater generativity, personal growth, and integrity," which they suggest points "to the benefits of having goals focused on helping others rather than helping oneself."[25] Other scholars have found, as we have mentioned earlier, that developing a purpose is a critical aspect of positive youth development, flourishing, and thriving.[26] Finding and having purpose contributes to happiness, positive affect, hope, resiliency, better school performance, and life satisfaction.[27] These findings would apply no matter how diverse the students or institution or no matter the students' particular worldview.

The question then emerges, based on this kind of research, should colleges and universities attempt to shape students' general and specific understandings of their purpose? It would appear that this kind of normative vision could apply with a pluralistic system of universities. The next question though is what kind of moral and scientific appeals will universities make to encourage this development, and what kind of programming and initiatives will they create to accomplish it? In the next chapter, we explore some of these issues through the lens of those students who report having no life purpose. We will also return more fully to this normative question of what we believe colleges and universities *ought* to do in the conclusion of this book, as we consider how some of our findings might be addressed by administrators, student life professionals, and faculty in chapters 8 and 9.

Chapter 7

Is Purposelessness a Problem?

I don't feel like I lack purpose, but I also couldn't tell you what my purpose was, if that makes sense. I don't feel like I'm lost. I don't feel like I'm wandering. And I don't feel like I'm angry or, you know, purposeless. I'm not raging against this like meaningless existence, but I'm mostly trying to keep my eyes open as I move through the world and am waiting for the appropriate time to really know what my purpose is because I don't think I've found it yet.

—Jamie, senior private university student

"I think it's something I'm looking for." Emilee a senior French literature major at an Ivy League university shares when asked her about her purpose. Interestingly, she says that she only recently entered this questing phase. When younger, she actually had a sense of purpose. As the daughter of African immigrants, she had a certain kind of mentality impressed on her by her parents,

So my closest friends, we're like a group of girls and we're all children of immigrants and we're all pushed to do like pre-med or be engineers, and that's what kind of grouped us together . . . to do really well in school so you can go to a big college.

This experience shaped her understanding of what makes her life meaningful. She describes this perspective by sharing a comment we already used to describe Self-Achievers in chapter 5, "I guess my studies give me satisfaction. And my ambition, like what I want to achieve in the future. It really stresses me out, but it like gives me satisfaction." Yet, when it comes to purpose, she shares dissatisfaction with this achievement narrative:

I was taught that my purpose, as a child, should be to do well in school, so the goal was always to do well in school so I can get into this school, and then do well in that school so I can get into this school. But I found that that's kind of like empty, because I can only go to so many schools and I'm like, "What am I going to do with my life after?" Am I supposed to like make more money than my parents afterwards?

She realizes that part of this outlook she absorbed from her immigrant parents. Yet, she no longer finds the rationale for this narrative that her parents offered convincing:

> My parents were always like, "Oh, we're working very hard and we're sacrificing a lot so you guys can be comfortable." I'm comfortable now, but you know . . . what's the point? I don't see making a lot of money as a purpose in life, you know? Because getting a good education was always to make a better income, to live a more comfortable life, but then I find that that's kind of, not boring, but it's not fulfilling. So then what's the point in that?

As a result, even though Emilee is nearing the end of her college career, she realizes that achieving the American Dream so she can live comfortably is not the end she wants to guide her purpose.

The reason Emilee gives for her disillusionment stems from her own observations while attending an Ivy League university.

> I had that do well, make a lot of money mentality, but then I see people who do that and I don't see them necessarily having the happiness that I think I would like to have in my life . . .

What will replace this old narrative is currently unclear.

As we indicated in chapter 5, we rarely interviewed a student who could not list something or someone that made life meaningful. When asking students about life purpose though, a different story emerges. Mike, a Baptist research university student, made this distinction in his interview:

> It depends on if you're talking about the meaning or purpose of life. As far as the meaning of life goes, I don't really have questions. Um, but as far as purpose goes, I have questions about what is the right thing for me to do with my life, what I should do, [and] what God wants me to do.

Like Mike, almost every college student does not appear to lack for meaning, but a certain percentage lack a purpose.

When one considers the adult population as a whole, purposelessness appears to be a rather rare phenomenon in America. National surveys of all Americans by Gallup® have found that only 6 percent of Americans claim to be without purpose.[1] Young people, perhaps not surprisingly, are different. Although the actual percentage of adolescents, or young emerging adults, who lack purpose depends on how one defines purpose and purposelessness. One national survey focusing on young emerging adults (18–23) found that about a quarter "lack clear goals or directions."[2] Those using the dominant definition of purpose used in the field of positive psychology described in the last chapter ("a stable and generalized intention to accomplish something that is at the same time meaningful to the self and consequential for the world beyond-the-self"[3]) have found even more uncertainty. One study of twelve- to twenty-six-year-olds determined that only 20 percent claimed to have found "something meaningful to dedicate themselves to, who have sustained this interest over a period of time, and who express a clear sense of what they are trying to accomplish in the world and why."[4] On the other end are those who clearly express that they do not have a purpose. The study cited above found 25 percent of twelve- to twenty-six-year-olds in this category. The rest had identified a possible purpose and had not acted upon it (25 percent identified as dreamers), and another 31 percent, identified as dabblers, had actively engaged in pursuing potential purposes but had not settled on a specific purpose or purposes.[5]

This chapter will explore the nature of these purposeless students by drawing on our own qualitative sample in which 35 percent of the 185 students interviewed told us they lacked a purpose in life. We start by overviewing the current scholarly discussion that hinges on whether purposelessness in college students is a problem or a natural stage of development. We then turn to unpacking two sets of languages college students use to articulate their purposelessness. The existence of different languages, we maintain, explains why a divide exists in the scholarship about purpose. It also helps us understand why solutions to the problem of purposelessness will vary according to the students themselves.

The Problem of Purposelessness?

Is purposelessness a problem for college students? It depends on the scholars you ask. In fact, assumptions about the nature of the search for purpose often shape the research questions being asked in the field. One group of scholars, such as William Perry, Alexander and Helen Astin, and Jeffrey Arnett, have focused on approaching the period of searching for purpose in college as a developmental stage.

Indeed, there is much about Emilee's story that would fit a transitional approach set forth by one of the early scholars of college student development cited in the last chapter, William Perry.[6] Influenced by Piaget, Perry relied on interviews with students at Harvard University to outline a theory that showed how students' intellectual reasoning moved from simple dualism, to complex dualism, to relativism, and, finally, to commitment in relativism.[7] The role of the university in this scheme is to expand and complicate the students' conceptual map of the world and the variety of intellectual roads one can take in life. It should also encourage students to understand how complicated a life map is and how courageous it is to take the road of commitment instead of the road of escape or to retreat back down the simple dualistic road they had been traveling.[8] Emilee's self-description would appear to fit within Perry's framework. She previously had a very simplistic and self-focused understanding of her life purpose. She even speaks about how college has helped move her from a former dualistic or "black-and-white" view of the world to something more complex. Or as one other student put it, "I did not necessarily expect the gray areas to come. I'm still a pretty strict black-and-white person, but there are some areas that I'm becoming gray on now, that I did not expect."

More recently, *spiritual quest* is a term used by Astin, Astin, and Lindholm to describe this process of searching for meaning and purpose.[9] They claim that the

> spiritual quest represents the "seeking" in us that can lead to a better understanding of who we are, why we are here, and how we can live a meaningful life—the "big" questions we all confront, often for the first time as young adults.[10]

Those engaged in a spiritual quest, according to their measure, are not those who are settled in their views about meaning and purpose. Instead, they are more likely to be "seeking," "conflicted," or "doubting" regarding their beliefs than those scoring lower on their measurement. In addition, high-scoring first-year students on this measure are 41 percent more likely than low scorers to claim that "finding my purpose in life" is an "essential" or "very important" reason to attend college.[11] In Astin, Astin, and Lindholm's research paradigm, the Searchers are going through a life phase, and the process of questing is generally understood as something that is mostly positive. In fact, one gets the impression that those who are settled about meaning and purpose and not questing are the ones about which we should be concerned.

A similar outlook has been expressed by the scholar who helped coin the term to describe this life period, *emerging adulthood*.[12] Jeffrey Arnett developed the term to describe the emerging reality that the transition to adulthood is now taking much longer since the timing of transition events such as leaving home, finishing school, finding work, getting married, and having children has extended later into the twenties and early thirties for many young people. The result is the decline in the dominance of a particular, default pathway to adulthood. This eighteen- to twenty-nine age group, which he labeled emerging adults, does not construct pathways from scratch, but they select from a multitude of competing narratives that define adulthood and negotiate various routes to reach it. Arnett points out that this extended development allows for a greater chance to develop one's overall future purpose and life goals. He notes five particular characteristics of it:

1. It is the age of *identity explorations*, of trying out various possibilities, especially in love and work.

2. It is the age of *instability*.

3. It is the most *self-focused* age of life.

4. It is the age of *feeling in-between*, in transition, neither adolescent nor adult.

5. It is the age of *possibilities*, when hopes flourish, when people have an unparalleled opportunity to transform their lives.[13]

Certainly, many of these descriptions appear to capture Emilee's reflections about her own identity and purpose. Arnett does not view these qualities as negative, even the self-focused and unstable qualities. He maintains, "To say that emerging adulthood is a self-focused time is not meant pejoratively. There is nothing wrong about being self-focused during emerging adulthood; it is normal, healthy, and temporary."[14] Of the instability regarding their purpose and direction, he notes,

> Emerging adults know they are supposed to have a Plan with a capital *P*, that is, some kind of idea about the route they will be taking from adolescence to adulthood, and most of them come up with one. However, for almost all of them, their Plan is subject to numerous revisions during the emerging adult years.[15]

For Arnett, these plan revisions are not gut-wrenching ordeals about which other adults should be worried. Instead, they are largely matters of recalculating one's future life map.

> [T]hey enter college and find themselves unable to focus on their studies, and their grades sink accordingly—time to revise the Plan. . . . Or

> they move in with a boyfriend or girlfriend and start to think of the Plan as founded on their future together, only to discover that they have no future together—time to revise the Plan.[16]

Again, for Arnett, not having found a purpose is not a problem, as long as one is still questing.

It is interesting to compare the positive view of the theorists above with certain psychologists and sociologists who are not quite so optimistic. William Damon admits that he is more concerned than Arnett about what the development of a new emerging adulthood phase might mean for emerging adults' purpose development and notes, "I would argue that [Arnett's] optimism is appropriate for only a minor portion of the youth population. For the rest, increased attention on our part is a more appropriate response."[17] Psychological research has found that both youth and adults who lack a life purpose report more psychological problems.[18] Scholars such as Damon would likely argue that Emilee's problem is that she has self-focused goals and has never really developed a key aspect of purpose, "a stable and generalized intention to accomplish something that is at the same time meaningful to the self and consequential for the world beyond-the-self."[19]

The sociologist Christian Smith raises a similar concern.[20] Smith describes the young emerging adults he surveyed as more typically lost, as opposed to questing. What exactly is the difference? It pertains to whether one believes there is a moral order to find and one has some idea of how to find this moral order. Smith largely faults emerging adults' lack of moral compass, moral individualism, and the sizable minority who believe in moral relativism for their disorientation.[21] They appear stuck in relativism, and he concludes that many emerging adults "need some better moral maps and better-equipped guides to show them the way around."[22] In other words, emerging adults are not simply on a journey to some destination. They are, as the title of Smith's book indicates, *Lost in Transition* because they do not have a general conceptual map of various moral, philosophical, and religious traditions that can help guide them toward a purpose or a larger understanding of the good life. The result is similar to what David Brooks bemoaned about the use of meaning language—students largely resort to using the self-focused language of emotions and personal preferences to talk about purpose instead of making references to larger moral traditions. Indeed, despite being a senior, Emilee appears to be mired in relativism and not yet committed to a larger purpose. If anything, she is abandoning the language of purpose associated with a larger moral tradition.

To understand whether this lack of purpose deserves our concern, or is simply a transitional phase that will soon be left behind, we think it helps to dig deeper into the lives of college students who admit to being without purpose.

The Nature of Purposelessness

What characterizes the purposeless student? The simple answer, as this student demonstrates, is that they admit to not having an answer to the purpose question:

> I'd say my purpose is definitely something I'm still trying to figure out. I was never one of those people who knew exactly what they wanted to do with their lives, kind of taking it one step at a time, which is different from my personality 'cause I like to plan out everything. That's been something I think I've really tried to identify while being in college. It's my third year now and I wouldn't say I necessarily have a definitive purpose.

Beyond the obvious, though, we propose that purposeless students may have two other characteristics. First, students without purpose appear to have fewer sources of meaning. We thought it noteworthy that purposeless students had an average of 1.3 sources of meaning versus 2.4 of those with purpose. Moreover, an inordinate number of purposeless had singular sources of meaning (40 of the 54 purposeless). For instance, one student simply stated that his source of meaning was to "be happy," while another claimed it was "to make my parents proud." Yet, when asked about purpose both admitted that they were "still trying to figure that out." Moreover, all but five of the purposeless with more than one source of meaning derived meaning from the combination of "family and friends." For example, when asked about sources of meaning, this student shared, "I'd have to say family and friends. Just being there for them." When asked about purpose, he told us that he's "still trying to figure that out." Overall, a lack of purpose was clearly associated with limited sources of meaning.

Second, students with certain kinds of Self-Achiever or Relationalist sources of meaning were the primary participants who had not yet discovered a purpose. Those who found meaning in family (16), accomplishment (12), or happiness (9) were the most common types to lack purpose. In this respect, those without purpose appear to fit most closely Smith's description. They largely lacked a language by which to talk about meaning or purpose in ways that moved beyond-the-self. The only beyond-the-self language they had related to family.

We also found that not all purposeless students are alike. We found that a key difference existed between students whose purposelessness stemmed from whether or not they see this as pervasive in their life or only applying to one area of their life, particularly their career. Consider Jayla, a regional university student. When talking to us, she makes a distinction between what she considers a pervasive purpose in life and what she considers a more specific purpose:

> I guess it just depends on what aspect of my life I'm talking about, because I feel like I know my purpose as far as, like, what God wants me to do as far as like in ministry and stuff like that, because I work with kids, and that's something I really feel like is my purpose to work with like young teens and stuff like that.

When it came to her primary purpose in life and what she wanted to do to fulfill that purpose, she has clear direction. Yet, she also notes,

> But when it comes to career and stuff, I am in between. I really like working in the office over there so I was thinking about getting into, my parents don't like it, but I wouldn't mind being an executive assistant somewhere because I really like helping and serving people. But at the same time, I've been thinking about getting my master's in editing. To go into like magazine editing. So I don't, I don't really know as far as that goes yet.

Jayla's quote represents the two aspects of purpose that the purposeless students discuss. Some of them refer to confusion about their career purpose, but others admit that they have more confusion about a wider life purpose.

Career Questers

For some students, the question about purpose primarily relates to their future career or calling. We label them the Career Questers. Kelly, a student at a regional university provides an example of the former. She actually responds to our question by claiming, "I do feel like I have a sense of purpose." Yet, the feeling of a sense of purpose did not translate into actually knowing or identifying her purpose. Consequently, she said, "I do also feel like I'm still searching for exactly where it is." For Kelly, her search for purpose mainly has to do with what she wants to do in life, as she says, "I think maybe I just want to do like a variety of things. . . . I don't know, I can't decide." She continues, "I originally wanted to be a homicide detective, but it's so hard for women to be cops in general, and then to rise through the ranks to be detectives." With that in mind, she notes, "Now I'm thinking I should just be a lawyer because it will be so much easier for me to get into it. But I don't know which one I want to choose." Kelly equates her lack of certainty about purpose with her inability to identify her future career. Interestingly, how she talks about purpose is much different than the ways she finds life meaningful, which is through her family relationships with her mother and brother.

Career Questers such as Kelly may actually affirm or believe that some kind of purpose exists for them, but they simply believe they have not yet determined their major or figured out how their major will lead to a particular type of work. Kaitlyn, a student from a private Baptist university in the South, articulates that she found meaning through her religious beliefs, but purpose for her is more specific than meaning:

> Meaning is definitely following Christ. I know that I'm here to live on this earth to share the gospel and live the gospel. And I think purpose kind of comes into that with, 'cause, for me personally, when I think of purpose, I think of occupation, like job, what I'm doing with my life, where I'm serving, what I'm doing.

Her religious beliefs also lead her to the view that she does actually have a future job or calling; however, she also notes one thing about that calling:

> Yes. I think I definitely know that I have a purpose; I think I'm still figuring out what it is. When I think of purpose I think of occupations and so I'm an education major, and I want to teach at least for a little while. But I'm not completely set that that's my purpose. I'm not sure my purpose is being a teacher yet.

Although she is concerned about not finding this purpose, she does have a strategy for ultimately finding this purpose that relies on her heart's desires:

> I really like thinking about purpose and those questions are important to me. But I think, as of now, I'm still figuring it out. I think I know what I'm passionate about and what just sets my heart on fire. So I feel like I'm following that to find my purpose.

Although Kaitlyn equates purpose with one's career, she does not equate it to her major. Despite majoring in education, she appears surprisingly open to seeing her purpose as something else.

Overall, one might consider the Career Questers' way of talking about purpose as actually relating more to what is often defined as a vocation. What exactly a vocation is, though, is subject to considerable discussion and can be understood in multiple ways in the current scholarly conversation.[23] Students tend to speak according to the two definitions found in the *Oxford English Dictionary*. Some, such as Kelly, simply understand their purpose as related to "One's ordinary occupation, business, or profession," while others such as Jayla and Kaitlyn understand it as "the particular function or station to which a person is called by God; a mode of life or sphere of action regarded as so determined."[24]

Defined in either way, this sort of vocational quest is quite normal and necessary in college.[25] One Catholic female from a liberal arts college made this point when reflecting about college and purpose:

> I think college is when you're trying to make all these decisions about what you're going to major in and if you're going to go to grad school, 'cause these all determine what you're going to be doing with the rest of your life. So I think this is a question I've been struggling with a lot recently—what is my purpose?

Another student even noted that she had some of the general human virtues that she thought she would need for her wider approach to life, but she lacked the specific job skills that college can provide,

> I think I have the sentimental things down in life. Like, you know, the caring, the giving, all that jazz, but I feel like I still haven't developed the skills I need to, to determine what I want for a career or job or like real long-term goals. So I'm still figuring that out.

If these students perceive themselves as currently struggling in this area, it relates more to the failure to settle on a particular major, career calling, or vocation. Mary, a student from our national survey related:

> This may be a little silly, but I expected to go to college and take some classes I had a little bit of interest in and for my life to kind of fall into place after that. That I would take one or two classes under a specific major and realize that that was where I needed to be and have a career plan in mind simply because of those two classes. So that was something I expected that has not really happened yet. But I know it has happened for some students that I've spoken with.

The question for Career Questers is whether they will continue with their uncertainty about purpose once they find a major or settle on a future occupation.

General Questers

Emilee represents a second group of Purposeless students we call the General Questers. These students perceive their purpose as extending beyond their career or vocation, and they also cannot quite decide about purpose in multiple areas of their lives. Brooke, the fourth-year student whose story we related in chapter 4, represents this group, as does a student we call Joey. Joey admits regarding purpose, "I would say it's something I'm trying to figure out." The reason for his confusion relates to the fact that he recognizes, "I'm going to be many different things," but he has not figured out what those different things will be. General Questers such as Joey see themselves as swimming in a sea of choices in which they have not yet located their direction.

Emilee herself was wrestling with multiple overarching narratives by which she was trying to make sense of life. While we noted above that she currently rejects the "immigrant American Dream narrative" that she believes her parents tried to pass along to her, she also has not found a replacement. One possible alternative she recognizes is the Christian faith she learned from her mother. She used to go to church every Sunday. "I think I grew up taking the Bible seriously, and the idea of like heaven and hell seriously, and the idea that you have to be a good person for good things to happen to you." For her, Christianity has less to do with salvation and more to do with a belief that explains the good and bad consequences in life. She observes, however, "That's changed a lot." She no longer believes Christianity offers a satisfactory explanation for the consequences good and bad people experience: "I find that the world was so black and white. Just because you're a good person doesn't mean that things will happen to you and vice versa." Consistent with William Perry's theory of ethical and intellectual development, Emilee sees herself as moving beyond a simple dualistic perspective and now she finds herself swimming in a sea of choices.

Consequently, it is not surprising that another weakness she finds with her "God will reward Christians who do good" theology stems from the religious diversity she has experienced in college, "I saw that like it's really unfair to think that your religion is the only [true] religion in the whole world." The sense of unfairness emerges from her new belief about the goodness of different religious outlooks.

> That's my biggest problem with Christianity, it's not that it's exclusive, it's just that if you believe in a different religion and you're like a good person, let's say that you follow everything that Jesus said you should do, but you don't say you don't believe in Jesus, you say you believe in Allah or say you believe in Buddha, then you're still lost.

She concludes, "I don't agree with that."

She still believes that she has certain Christian habits. "Like if I curse, I'm always completely like, 'God forgive me' . . . If I want something really badly, I just like instinctively like pray for it . . . if I'm in a bad situation, I find myself praying to God." However, she notes that she has now abandoned some of the doctrinal parts. "I don't believe in heaven and hell . . . Yeah, belief in God, in one God, I believe in that. I think that's it." In reality, the religion, in which she now appears to trust is that of self-reliance, although she cannot quite give up her Christian identity. "I think that's up to me individually to figure out, but I don't really know, like I can't not call myself a Christian. . . . I'll not call myself a Christian, and then I'm like what am I doing? Like either I am or I'm not." Part of Emilee's struggle is that she realizes she faces a dualistic choice regarding her Christian identity.

Currently, she believes Christianity is not something that will help her grow. "I think it's constrained me. Because there are certain things I feel like I can't consider because they're off limits, and then . . . I feel like I can't really consider everything because of that." Yet, she admits that in some ways Christianity, or at least Theism, is still so ingrained in her that she cannot contemplate purpose and meaning apart from it. "I can't consider life with meaning if you don't believe in God. But maybe it is possible, but I just feel like I can't find that . . . It's just, I am just incapable." She actually longs for the ability to step away from her belief in God. "I wish I would be able to, at least get out of this perspective, and if I decide that I prefer this perspective, that's fine, but I can't step out of the belief in God." Emilee struggles because she realizes that she cannot take the objective observer perspective of modernism. As a result, she cannot abandon her identity as a Theist. Yet, she also longs to be able to step away from her identity and analyze it, because she still holds the modernist belief that one cannot truly evaluate something without separating oneself from it.

Interestingly, institutional or individual identity does not seem to correlate with whether students will be General Questers. We found General Questers such as Emilee on every type of campus where we interviewed and among various genders and ethnic groups. We should note, moreover, that these General Questers were not monolithic in their outlook regarding the concept of purpose and how they thought about it. For example, they were not all struggling with their religious faith as Emilee. We actually found three different types.

The first group of General Questers consists of those who simply affirm that some kind of purpose exists for them. These are the General Religious Questers. This outlook is represented by Allison, a senior at a Baptist university. When discussing meaning, she fits both our Transcendent and Relationalist categories.

> I would say like first and foremost my relationship with God, but then also my relationships with others. I'm just like very relational, so I just love like interacting with people, and if I can make a difference like in people's lives, then that's what makes it worth it for me.

Despite having a clear sense of what gives life meaning, when asked about purpose, Allison admits, "I would say it's something that I'm still figuring out," although she does add, "I feel like I have a purpose." This outlook is similar to Jamie, the student quoted at the beginning, or the student who claimed, "I do feel like I have a sense of purpose. I do also feel like I'm still searching for exactly where it is."

For most of these students, this confidence in a larger purpose comes from their religious identity. Ryan, a Catholic at a regional university, exemplifies this outlook. Although he's "still trying to figure it [purpose] out," he sees himself as "spiritual in that I feel like everyone's life has a purpose, and you're put here for a reason." This confidence does not provide him with easy answers since he confesses,

> I'm not totally set on what I want to do with my life so that's part of it too I think. If you want your occupation to have a part in that you can, as far as if you feel like you're helping people or doing something meaningful with your occupation. . . . And I plan on doing something that I love, something I feel like that I'm passionate about.

This confidence is not unusual among students with religious identities. A Baptist student shares, "I mean I think that we all have a purpose in life which we are destined to find as we grow. God kind of gives us our purpose and it takes us time to find it." Another Catholic student from a regional university notes:

> I'm very much spiritual in that way as far as I feel like everyone's life has a purpose and you, you're put here for a reason whether people figure that out right off the bat or later on down the line. I'm not totally set on what I want to do with my life.

This religious confidence that a purpose exists appears consistent with general surveys. For instance, one survey of emerging adults found that the nonreligious report having the least purpose in life, while the most religious emerging adults report having the most purpose.[26]

The second group of General Questers also show a confidence that they will find purpose in the future. We call them General Secular Questers since most students have identified various nonreligious types of passions and possible purposes that are important to how they conceptualize their future. Graham's comments provide a helpful example. "I mean one of the biggest issues that I care about is climate change and energy policy and hopefully being able to realize some conservation and climate control measures. Hmm. I still feel like I'm trying to figure it out." While Graham identifies one particular passion, other students may describe how they are actively making a decision among different options. A first-year student at a liberal arts college describes his choice between what we label the Transcendent Change option and the Family Relationalist approach:

> I haven't figured out what my purpose in life is in general. I'm really interested in social activism, I'm into Slam Poetry, and so a lot of my Slam Poetry deals with social critique on how I see the world and things that I want to inspire in the youth to like help them think about their world in a more critical manner. And so I really want to reach a level in my life where I can inspire other people to reach their full potential. But my main purpose . . . I really focus on the closest people in my life—so the closest people in my life are probably my family. And so I really want to help them in any way I possibly can; whether that's financially or just helping them reach their full potential.

These students have not yet made their choice from a menu of purposes they are considering or from the general cultural script from which they are drawing. In some cases, the students discuss the issue in ways that indicate they are deciding between types of purposes within what we would call one purpose category. For example, Charles largely talks about his efforts to find purpose by emphasizing Achievement, particularly creative or academic achievement.

> Purpose is definitely something I'm trying to figure out. . . . I know there are things I like to do and things I want to do in the future and I'm decently good at them. To be interesting and to become more interesting and educated and just to create interesting things for the other people.

Others within this group would go so far as to say that they could identify some provisional purposes. Sienna, a Catholic student who attends a Catholic university provides an example. Upon speaking about her purpose, she tells one of us, "I feel like I'm still searching for that one thing I'm very passionate about, and would like to work in and concentrate my efforts into." Yet, she would also claim to have provisional purposes: "I think for the moment it's my family and my faith . . . God and my Catholic identity is something that's still very important to me. So I think for right now it'd be those two." She then adds, "and also just friends, there are groups of friends that I think I'm very close to, not that they give me so much purpose, but it's definitely a fulfilling part of my life right now." Still, she also reiterates that she considers herself a searcher, even using this language, but clarifying that the searching primarily pertains to specific dimension of her life and must fit into her Transcendent approach to meaning.

> I'm still searching, but I think in the end I'm gonna do something that matters and that makes a difference. I really think that somehow things are going to align, and I'm going to find it. With all my different interests, like taking random classes or just random interests that I have, I think it's going to all align.

Overall, this group shares some characteristics with what Damon describes as the dreamers, those who have identified a purpose but have not taken the steps to get there.[27]

Again, like the first group of students, this second group of General Secular Questers does not doubt that they ultimately have a purpose. Moreover, they do not express anxiety or fear about finding their purpose. They see themselves as recognizing and identifying purpose options. In this respect, the students appear not to think of their lack of purpose as a major problem about which they expressed deep anxiety. They reflect the "it's a stage" mentality of the first group of researchers cited above.

One group of General Questers, however, does not fit this category. We call them the Doubting Questers. These are the students who express doubt about the concept of having a purpose. Nathaniel, a public university student, exemplifies this outlook,

> I'd say it's something I'm still figuring out because—I'm not sure. The sense of purpose is a thing that I think—I don't necessarily agree with the concept because I just don't think anybody is truly like necessary or anything. I think that if I accomplish things that help other people, that's great. But I also don't think that I can make a large difference in the world and I feel that way about most people.

The basis for Nathaniel's doubts about the concept of purpose, as with almost all students in this category, relates to his lack of religious belief. He notes, "I would say, if anything, I'm an atheist. Religion doesn't play a large part in my life." For Nathaniel, this outlook leads to his view that life is "a joke" as well as to a certain pessimism about his own accomplishments in this life and the next life: "I essentially don't know what I can accomplish in my life, and I don't think there's anything after it." Leonard, a private university student who calls himself spiritual but not religious observes in a similar way.

> It's definitely something I'm trying to figure out. I have ideas, but I'm also not entirely sold on the each person has a purpose type idea. I know there are things I like to do and things I want to do in the future, and I'm decently good at them.

For these students, they resist the concept or language of purpose and prefer to talk about future goals and their own role in the creation of these goals.

In some cases, the talk about future goals appears to be similar to purpose language. The main difference concerns the metaphysical assumptions associated with the concept of purpose. Anne's story provides a deeper understanding of this "doubting the concept of purpose" outlook and its consequences for how she approaches her purpose in general. When asked whether she has a purpose in life she admits, "I would like to think that I have a purpose." Yet, she went on to admit, "I don't know." Anne considers herself agnostic about purpose—at least in any larger metaphysical sense. She associates purpose talk with religion and consequently is not sure if purpose is something one can discover. She does, however, have what she herself terms "a bucket list." "I definitely, you know, want to complete the things on that. I want to travel a lot. I wanna like get a good job so that I can support a family. You know, things like that." What she resists is a belief that her life might be part of some kind of larger story. "I wasn't born and then I'm meant to do this. I don't believe that kind of a thing." Instead, she understands her purpose as something she creates for herself.

Thus, while she would not say she has a particular life purpose, the way she talks about upcoming life goals is similar to those undecided about choosing from the purpose menu. She places a strong emphasis on her friendships, which make it seem like she is appropriating the Relationalist approach. However, when she brings up friendships it is always in the context of her own drive to succeed, which makes her sound like an Individual Achiever:

> I think that I've made good choices as far as the friends that I've made. And I think that all of them contribute a certain part to my personality and all of them are good for something for me. I know that might sound selfish, like I'm just collecting friends! But like, no, no, like I mean I'm very loyal to my friends.

Yet, even when she tries to backtrack and discuss her friends in less self-oriented ways, she basically praises her friends for what they do for her. "I'm very loyal to my friends, and I think that, I think that they're the ones that are always there to build me up, so I think that means a lot to me."

When asked what makes life worth living for her, she also uses Individual Achiever language:

> I would like to do great things hopefully one day. . . . I really want
> to work in publishing. . . . I think if I can just spread literature
> everywhere. I know that it's like dying, but I don't care, I just like
> want to, want to bring it back.

Her heroic and noble achievement would be to help save the publishing industry. When she becomes more specific about this individual achievement, however, she again makes a Relationalist turn. She sees herself one day starting her own nonprofit: ". . . something with child illiteracy, and I really just want to push for that because reading should always be important. I have a drive to help children, or even adults, that can't read. I think that's important." She also perceives this emphasis on relationships and service in her current boyfriend. "He's just so giving to everyone. I mean we're all poor college kids, but 'Take less, give more' is his motto. He just wants to spread niceties and do everything for everyone he possibly can." She herself would like to be more like him: "That's what I want to do, even though sometimes it's hard and you're selfish." She uses saint- or hero-like language to describe him: "Anything is possible with him, so that makes me inspired to be that way . . . it makes me want to do things. [I'm] just like, 'Okay, let's go get married and take on the world.'" Ultimately, she views him as an ally in her effort to achieve great things in life. "We both have big dreams and accomplishing them together is really exciting, so I'm looking forward to that after graduation." In some respects, Anne appears to be on the road to developing an others-focused purpose, although she even recognizes that she is a bit focused on self-oriented goals. Yet, she also acknowledges the moral superiority of being others focused, particularly through the model of her boyfriend.

Overall, this last group may prove to be the most challenging one to engage with talk about purpose and vocation. In his study of purpose and vocation programs at private colleges and universities, Tim Clydesdale observed that discussions about purpose and vocation resonated with students because the "concepts of purpose and vocation impart a meta-narrative that infuses the arc of one's life with meaning and provides a base for constructive engagement with the world."[28] While we also observed this reality among two types of Purposeless students, we would add that this infusion occurred with a certain understanding of purpose—one that was either others-oriented or transcendently oriented. Among students who doubt a larger purpose even exists, such a discussion will likely prove more challenging.

Conclusion

So should we view purposelessness as a stage or a cause for concern? We believe the answer depends on the type of purposeless student, although in general we think purposeless is a potential problem if it is not addressed (no matter what the type).

Career Questers certainly see themselves at a stage in life through which they will pass. Still, one might argue that for these students their conceptions of purpose are rather shallow and, in fact, do not fit with a more robust definition of purpose, such as that offered by Damon. Perhaps these students need help in thinking in deeper and more sophisticated ways about purpose. Certainly, the equation of one's purpose with one's career is a very narrow and possibly self-focused idea of purpose that does not fit with Damon's other-oriented conception of the idea. In addition, those focused only on self-oriented goals have not developed the other-oriented focus that many scholars suggest is needed for a true purpose.

Most General Questers also betray little angst about their situation, and perhaps there is less reason to worry about them. Our finding that virtually every student already has at least one source of meaning indicates that some building blocks for purpose already exist in their lives. Still, the fact that purposeless students have fewer sources of meaning from which to draw does raise questions about their ability to build on their sources of meaning to find a purpose. In this respect, we do believe Damon and Smith raise some important concerns. We contend these students likely need greater exposure to historical traditions and ways of thinking about meaning and purpose, as well as particular contextual types of support for purpose development, so they can find more extensive and durable forms of meaning from which they can then develop a purpose.

Further, there are some General Questers who may face additional challenges. The Doubting Questers believe that no grand purpose for life exists and, therefore, focus most of their energy on creating goals for themselves. We suspect that these students may balk at the idea of receiving support from their college or university in the area of life purpose. These students will likely need to be approached differently if universities aggressively seek to help all students develop purpose.

Overall, in light of the possible need for students to obtain more mature and complex views about meaning as well as a deeper understanding of purpose, and perhaps better critical thinking skills regarding purpose, we will explore in the next few chapters how the university experience helps and does not help students with their purpose. We find it interesting that Emilee, who is a senior, experienced largely one type of help in college. Experiences with diversity in college caused her prior conceptions of purpose to be thrown into doubt. It was actually her experience at college that helped undermine this particular understanding of Christianity. For the first time, she experienced extensive religious diversity. In other words, as Perry's theory predicts, college had complicated her outlook. It also, as Magolda's theory of self-authorship would affirm, has given her a critical perspective of her parents' traditions of thinking about meaning and purpose. Yet, while the university experience has helped to undermine her former commitments, it has not helped her find new ones. Does this lack of help demonstrate a possible failure of the university system or at least the Ivy League university that Emilee attended? Does the contemporary postmodern university fail to move students toward more sophisticated forms of commitment? William Perry thought the university should help students make commitments within a sea of complex choices, although he never addressed how the university should help students parse and weigh the relative value of different commitments.[29] The university may provide students with a more complex map about life's meaning and encourage them to take a journey, but like the values clarification movement that developed during the same time period as Perry's theory, the student may bear the burden alone of choosing which destination is best without significant help from mentors. In the next two chapters, we explore the degree to which students' experiences at a variety of different colleges and universities influence their development of meaning and purpose.

Part III

Questing in the University

Chapter 8

Encountering Purpose in the Classroom

I thought college would be more about finding friends and stuff and learning about my classes, my major, and myself—I never felt that it was necessary for it to give meaning to my life.

—Nathaniel, public university student

Scholars don't take ideals too seriously; academics remain pretty much in the de-divinization business, which is the business of deflating or attacking ideals . . . Few believe that reading the best that has been thought and said can give a young person something to live for and teach him or her how to live.

—Mark Edmundson, professor, University of Virginia[1]

"I think they're ultimately almost unanswerable questions." Albert, a sophomore computer science major at an Ivy League university, shares this conclusion during a fall day off-campus. The "unanswerable questions" to which he refers concern the meaning and purpose of life. While one might conclude that the hopeless nature of this outlook would lead Albert to abandon the quest for answers, the key word in his answer is "almost." He clarifies what he means: "They might not be answered in the sense that you can answer a math question," but "maybe you can get close to finding answers." He admits he is not close to these answers himself, though.

Albert acknowledges that being at the university has led him to start thinking about larger questions of meaning and purpose. Yet, he does not necessarily attribute this exploration to the university environment itself. "I think part of it, most of it," he says, "is me growing up—transforming from a child into an adult. [I'm asking] what kind of man do I want to be?, and when you're a kid you don't really have to think about those questions." He also attributes this new exploration to a change in his life stage, to "looking after yourself and being independent, and making your own decisions about your life instead of letting a parent make decisions for you." In contrast, "when you're a kid, it's mostly that parents are trying to mold your character, if you will, but when you're an adult you have to do that yourself and figure out what you want to do."

Interestingly, Albert does not perceive higher education as playing a significant role in his search. He does, however, understand higher education as having a dual purpose. First, there is the "very practical, just learn the materials so you can get a job" part. Second, "there's also the liberal arts aspect" that teaches you "to think deeply about all sorts of issues," including issues such as life's meaning and purpose. But this second part of college does not engage him. He sees the required liberal arts portion, "as more something to get through, to jump through the hoops." He fondly paraphrases Mark Twain, "Don't let your schooling get in the way of your education" as his inspiration for this perspective. He finds his general education classes informative but not transformative. Speaking about a required general education philosophy course, Albert claims,

> It's interesting, but it wasn't really about morality or [the] purpose of man. It's more like Ivory Tower academic kind of philosophy, you know. "How do you know this cup exists?" That sort of stuff. It was definitely interesting. But as far as shaping my life, I wouldn't say it was helpful. But it was still interesting in the way that, you know, you might watch a science documentary and say, "Oh that's interesting," but you wouldn't change the way you live your life.

He experiences the same clinical distance from professors as well and certainly does not see them as someone to talk to about the meaning of life. He even admits, "I guess I've never really wanted to talk to professors about anything besides academics, but I definitely do think they're available, and I suppose if you wanted to talk. Hmm, I don't really interact with my professors very much outside of class."

A clear Self-Achiever, he largely lists individual-oriented achievements and interests when asked about what gives his life meaning. "I really like traveling, that's one thing, just exploring . . . just to get the sense of exploring and going to places you're not familiar with, really excites me." He also adds, "And I really like learning, usually I'm a very curious person." His love of learning relates primarily to his major field of study. "Before, computers were just this mysterious black box. Now I can sort of understand why it does the things it does, and it's just really interesting to me." He does note that family relationships and friends are important to him as well, but they are not the primary sources of his meaning.

When thinking about his purpose, he tends to speak in terms of his future job, experiences, and income:

> I have a few different ideas. I've thought about graduate school, I've thought about getting a job in hardware design or something of the like. Guess I'd like to see myself do a lot of traveling . . . I think I'd definitely want to have high income, not, but only to a point, I mean. After you know $80,000 a year, I think money would not be terribly helpful, but you do need to travel.

He does not mention any family plans or relationships among his future goals.

Perhaps it is no surprise, then, that he shares at the interview something he thinks is important to understanding his worldview. "Um, I've become, do you know what libertarians are? That's what I identify as now." It is at this point that he mentions for the first time an intellectual inspiration on his perspective about meaning or purpose. "There was a book I read by John Stossel that really influenced me." Beyond this book, which he read on his own outside of class, he does not believe that the world of academia or his professors influenced his search for meaning or purpose.

In many ways, Albert's story (like Andrea's in our introduction) would appear to reinforce the claim made by Anthony Kronman that professors' preoccupation with the research ideal is responsible for the universities' lack of interest in meaning (interestingly, all three come from Ivy League institutions). Still, Albert's story also demonstrates something Kronman may have missed. Part of the reason that some colleges and universities have given up in this area may also have something to do with the students themselves. If Albert and the student quoted at the beginning of the chapter are any indication, perhaps students do not expect, or even want, the university to help them in this area.

If this is true, this change may prove vitally important to the development of purpose. Sharon Daloz Parks has argued that the period of early college life is a key time when young adults need mentors or coaches and self-chosen ideologically oriented communities that can guide them along their journey toward meaning and purpose.[2] Certainly, scholars find this true of the adolescent search for meaning.[3] Parks departs from Perry who at times seemed to place an inordinate emphasis on students making their journey alone and sometimes interpreted efforts to look for or expect adult assistance as signs of retreat from development (although to be fair Perry did encourage educator modeling of commitment).[4] What also sets Parks apart is that she does not believe just any mentor or any type of ideologically oriented community will do. She notes, "The good mentor simply recognizes that the young adult is still dependent in substantial ways upon authority outside the self, while at the same time, the mentor is a champion of the competence and potential the young life represents."[5]

Parks maintains that the role of the university is to provide direct mentors and mentoring communities that assist young people in this process.[6] Instead of buying into the old modern ideal that separates the objective from the subjective, facts from values, Parks suggests that higher education does and should serve "the young adult as his or her primary community of imagination, within which every professor is potentially a spiritual guide and every syllabus a confession of faith."[7] According to Parks, "The mentoring professor, therefore, must convene and mediate among multiple perspectives, composing a trustworthy community of imagination—a community of confirmation and contradiction."[8]

Although Albert did not encounter this type of environment, do other students experience these kinds of mentors and communities? The next two chapters explore possible answers to this question by examining how the students we interviewed perceived the influence of the college experience on their quest for meaning and purpose. This particular chapter will cover the influence of course work and faculty, and will explore these themes in greater depth by looking at two particular aspects of students' college experiences. First, we examine student expectations and perceptions. How do students think college should and does influence their search for meaning and purpose? Second, we investigate the principal way that colleges have traditionally been thought to influence students' lives: the wisdom and formation propagated through classes, course readings, and professors. We explore through national surveys and our interviews whether students identify these influences and perceive such influences as actually making a difference in helping them answer these important questions.

Expectations

Do students expect colleges and universities to deal with issues of purpose and meaning? One of the most well-known higher-education surveys touches on a possible answer. As described earlier, the Higher Education Research Institute has asked first-year students, to "Please indicate the importance to you personally of each of the following," with "developing a meaningful philosophy of life" being one of the options (a slightly different goal than purpose).[9] In 1967, 79.1 percent of college students surveyed considered it essential or very important for college to help them develop a meaningful philosophy of life. By 2015 the percentage had dropped to 46.5 percent.[10] In contrast, "being well off financially had risen during that time from 44.1 percent to 81.9 percent.[11]

Among the students we interviewed, we found a general divide between two types of students that reflected these dual goals. We label the two types of students the Instrumentalists and the Holistics, a type of distinction that other scholars have also noted.[12] The Instrumentalists tend to understand the role of their university in relationship to their purpose in one of two ways. The first type, Happiness Instrumentalists, conceptualize their purpose in terms of happiness, and they find the university may not necessarily contribute to their happiness. An example of this mind-set comes from Paxton, a community college student, who conceptualizes his purpose as the dominant one we found in our national survey: "to be happy—wherever that comes from. For me, this comes from having friends and having time to relax, not spending all day doing things that aren't a lot of fun." Paxton links college to those things "that aren't a lot of fun," and not surprisingly, he does not find much engagement with his classes or faculty members. Albert, the student that was profiled at the beginning of this chapter, provides an example of the second Instrumentalist type, the Achiever Instrumentalist. These students perceive the university as providing a credential or perhaps a skill that will help them achieve their vision of career success or some other form of personal success.

The Holistic students enter the university with expectations of finding a certain set of supports that they can then use to develop their personal sense of purpose (including, but not limited to, classes, friends, professors, families, or mentors). Hannah provides an example of this type.

> Yeah, I definitely came into college thinking, okay, right now I have absolutely no idea what I want to do with the rest of my life—what kind of career I want to build, what kind of family life I might want to build, and I expected college to give me some answers.

It is interesting, though, where she expected to find help while in college. In classes, she anticipated one type of answer. "I kind of expected to find a field in academia where I excelled and really comprehended all the material that was presented." When it comes to life wisdom beyond her professional field, she expected insight from a different source, "just learning from friends, like what plans they have." She would say in the latter case she has not been disappointed. "My friends in college, I think, are smarter than my friends from high school. But just like knowing what they have planned, how they're preparing for their lives, has definitely given me more perspective." Holistics tend to have Relationalist or Transcendent purposes. Like Hannah, Holistics also expect college to help them think about issues of purpose, particularly as it relates to a future job, but many also anticipate that higher education may influence their larger views about meaning. In their view, classes help with one's career, and college life as a whole helps with the development of purpose or meaning. Interestingly, students—even those looking for help with thinking about big questions—do not expect to find anything beyond career help from faculty or the classes. They look instead to their friends or other experiences to inform their views about life's meaning. One student simply said he did not expect help from "education specifically, but maybe the experiences that I've gone through while being at college."

It appears that a slightly higher percentage of Instrumentalists attend public institutions. HERI data indicates that while 51.2 percent of first-year students at private universities (which includes religious universities) deem it essential or important to develop a meaningful philosophy of life; only 44.6 percent of public university first-year students and 41.9 percent of public four-year college first years share this view.[13] While these differences are small, they are statistically significant. These different goals of first-year students indicate that while the university environment may play a role in whether students encounter issues of meaning and purpose, some students enter public and private institutions with different aspirations. Not surprisingly then, in both of our interview samples, a greater percentage of the public research university students entered the university as Instrumentalists. When asked whether they thought college would help with developing a purpose in life, they admitted, "I wouldn't say I expected it to," or, "I was kind of just like, 'I'm going to go to school, have a good time, hopefully get good enough grades, and I'll get a job afterwards.'" Another student shared, "I don't think that I necessarily did. I expected it to kind of be more or less like high school where I just kinda come and start my group, make some friends, get my degree, and leave and find a job." For a small percentage, the nature of an institution shapes students' initial expectations in that they do not expect to wrestle with what might be considered the larger philosophical questions of meaning and purpose.

Yet, these institutions also change some students. In the most recent HERI senior survey, 58.8 percent of seniors considered it essential or very important to develop a meaningful philosophy of life, while only 50.7 percent of this same senior class answered this way when they were first-year students.[14] In addition, the percentage that indicated being well-off financially was essential or very important dropped from 67.2 percent of first-year students to 59.9 percent of seniors.[15] Both student goals were among the eight of twenty-one goals that saw a six-percentage point change. Similarly, in our 110 Targeted Qual sample, 10 percent of our participants claimed to have experienced a conversion while attending their college or university.[16] Although these students admitted they did not expect college or the university to help them with purpose and meaning, they realize at the time of our interviews that it now did. Eight of the twelve students who indicated a change came from two institutions—the secular liberal arts college and the public research university. As one first-year student admitted, "I'd say it definitely has [shaped meaning and purpose], but when I first came here I wasn't looking for that—definitely wasn't looking for meaning and purpose when I first came here." Another neuroscience major noted, "Now I expect that of my college education, but I think when I was coming here I didn't necessarily. I just thought of it as getting the schoolwork done." The remaining part of this chapter explores what aspect of the university engaged students in conversations about meaning and purpose.

Meaning and Purpose in Their Course Work

Adrianna, whose childhood story we recounted in chapter 2, is one of the students who experienced a meaning and purpose conversion in college. A Latino student at a secular liberal arts college, she admits that when it came to attending college, "I didn't expect anything . . . for giving me meaning in life." However, she notes,

> Now, reflecting back, from classes from sociology or anthropology or math or English classes, the courses gave me meaning in life. Like introducing me to literature that I wouldn't have picked up on if I saw it in the library, and those books have really given me meaning in life.

She cites one book in particular, "Americo Paredes's book, *George Washington Gómez.*"

> I read that my sophomore year and that has changed my life, my meaning in life. The character, the protagonist in the book, I can relate to, because his name was George Washington Gómez, and Gómez was his Mexican side and George Washington was his American side. He lived on the border of Texas and the United States, and he didn't know what to relate to, so he was dealing with double consciousness, and identities and boundaries. It's something that I've gone through. Like in high school, when I had to choose to have friends or not to choose friends or who to mingle with. So I really related to George Washington Gómez.

Specifically, she connected to his existential identity struggle because at every level he was divided—even his name was divided. She notes, "His family would call him Guálinto instead of George Washington." She was able to draw connections to this example and her own story:

> So for me, my persona is different here at [her college] 'cause I'm surrounded by so many Whites. I can say that I can't really speak Spanish or anything, so I have to act a different way than when I am at home, where I am surrounded by Spanish speakers, by my mom.

And that's how George acted when he was with different cultures. At the end it's really disappointing. He ended up betraying his own culture. And so, for me, it made meaning. I'm not going to betray either of my cultures. I'm going to take advantage of both of them. So that gave me meaning as to what I identify as my ethnicity or identity.

In this respect, Adrianna clearly differs from Albert, who found his course work disconnected from questions of meaning and purpose.

Adrianna's affirmation that matters of meaning and purpose were addressed in the classroom is actually typical among both sets of the college students we interviewed. We found that over three-fourths of the students in our 110 student database and over half in our 75 student national interviews report discussing the meaning or purpose of life in the classroom. This is corroborated in the CSBV data. Fully 72 percent of college students report that faculty members have at least occasionally encouraged explorations of questions of meaning and purpose in the classroom.

However, similar to college expectations, the experience of exploration about these matters in courses differs substantially by college type. Thirty-five percent of students at public institutions in the CSBV survey data report that faculty never encouraged this type of exploration, while only 4 percent of students at evangelical colleges reported the same. Likewise, only 14 percent of students at public institutions say this type of classroom exploration occurred frequently, while over half (52 percent) of students at evangelical colleges say their professors frequently bring up the topic. Other institutions tended to fall in between; although, public institutions, where a majority of students are enrolled, are noticeably distinct from all private institutions in this regard. We believe these findings cast some doubt on Kronman's claim that "our" universities have given up on this topic. "Our" universities may have only given up on meaning if one considers the "our" to be a certain group of public universities.

- "Um, if you count the Book of Mormon, yeah. But, that's pretty much it, my other classes not so much."

- "I mean, in Christian scriptures we have books of the Bible to read and those conversations came after that, but I can't think of any specific articles right now that address that."

- "In my Judaic studies, actually, we did. We talked about meaning and, of course, the answer, or meaning in life, or purpose in life, is to learn Torah. [That] is what was extolled to me by my rabbi. So yeah, we have talked about it one time."

Similar to Jacob's story recounted in chapter 4, the students know that religion relates to existential questions, but they often just give cursory answers that appear to indicate little engagement with the course material.

In contrast, students tend to elaborate on wrestling with these matters in great texts and Western civilization courses as well as certain kinds of history, psychology, leadership, ecology, or sociology courses. In particular, the students talk about three types of course types that have an influence on them.

1. A Liberal Arts Education in Meaning and Purpose

One group of students describes what might be said to be a liberal arts education about meaning and purpose. At three institutions in particular: the Lutheran college, the Baptist research university, and the secular liberal arts college, students mentioned the importance of great texts or Western civilization courses for addressing these questions. Kathryn, a student at a secular liberal arts college, simply recalled that this type of course reminded her that searching for meaning and purpose has been a continual quest:

> We did a Civilization of the West, History of Western culture with a big Greek part. Those books, I don't think they changed my mind so much as just showed me that people years and years ago wondered the exact same thing that we do now. Which is kind of funny because society seems like it has come so far, but really human thought still wonders the same questions.

For other students though, these courses did more than merely connect students to historical traditions of thinking about meaning and purpose. It also encouraged the students to reconsider their options and deepen their own thinking. Julie, a student at the Baptist university, recounted:

> I mean for my great text course last semester that was the title of the course, What Is the Real Meaning of Life? . . . We read Beowulf and Thomas Aquinas, and then I took another great text before that, and that was Augustine and some of the great church fathers, so they weren't all religious texts, but they were all like really old, famous books. And I guess that more than anything, we've really talked about different views on what the meaning of life is and what all these different people are saying . . . They've challenged me to really think. A lot of these classes are not saying things that are word for word what I've been taught before or what I believed before, so that has really forced me to challenge my beliefs and really decide why I believe what I believe.

Madeline, another student from the Lutheran college, shared how a similar set of courses focused on great texts and big questions helped her think about purpose:

> One of the classes that I've taken is a very philosophical. It explores: What is human nature? What is knowledge? Looking at the great works of Western culture and seeing how they influenced how we view things today. I think that has helped me continually reevaluate and rediscover why I think there's purpose in life.

Both Julie and Madeline could be said to be poster students for what the important outcomes of a liberal arts course about meaning and purpose might accomplish.

In these types of courses, students would often be able to cite a specific book or author that influenced them. For instance, a book that came up a few times at these three schools was Boethius's *Consolation of Philosophy*. This student at a Baptist university found the perspective both familiar due to its Christian background but also challenging due to its different outlook.

> Last semester we were reading old literature, so nobody was really like from a Christian perspective, but Boethius was a Christian and so he sort of draws a lot from Plato and Aristotle in his writing, and you can tell that, so you get that whole like philosophic side to it. But he ties in with the Christian perspective, and I think that's pretty interesting. One thing he says is that happiness is the ultimate good, and so from a Christian perspective we know to be pretty doubtful about that. Why would you consider happiness to be the ultimate good? But he sort of makes an argument for it and explains it from a Christian perspective.

Boethius did more than challenge Christian students though. Malik, a Muslim student at the secular liberal arts college also found this particular work stimulating. The students were asked to write an essay that examined Boethius's meaning of life in comparison to their own approach, "So I wrote my essay saying that the consolation of philosophy wasn't enough for Boethius because he needed a higher consolation from theology. And so I argued for that point." Malik found this assignment helpful in that it forced him to wrestle with his own approach to life's meaning:

> It really helped me understand myself and what consoles me as an individual. Because like, is it philosophy? Is it theology? Is it family?

> Like, what really helps me as an individual to understand my place in life? *Interviewer: What did you conclude?* I found that it's mainly my family and my own personal beliefs that console me. I feel, I'm really interested in Stoicism, and so I found that working on yourself and trying to develop yourself into a noble and virtuous upstanding man is the best path you can take in life, because if you take that path upon yourself and you implement those policies or ideas in your daily life, then it impacts the people that surround you. And it impacts your family, and it impacts them in positive ways rather than taking away from them by being a negative person and just being hedonistic or pleasure-seeking.

Kronman, who recommends the reading of classic texts for addressing issues of meaning and purpose in college, would certainly not be surprised at its effectiveness.[18] Yet, he appears to misunderstand or mischaracterize this approach. He considers the study of great texts as something undertaken in the secular humanist tradition. In reality, a great texts curriculum that considered issues of life's meaning and purpose was embraced at both religious and secular campuses. In addition, Kronman did not mention some additional approaches that students noted as instrumental in helping them think about meaning and purpose.

2. Exposure to Diverse Cultures and Perspectives

Other students who spoke of their class experience in the humanities tended to highlight one of the common outcomes expected from a university education—their eye-opening exposure to diversity and wide-ranging social problems. Julie, a neuroscience major at a secular liberal arts college, discussed this process in classes outside of her major, "that have expanded my awareness of the world and what's important." In particular, she noted the

> sociology classes that I've taken that have just blown my mind with like what's the reality that I don't necessary see in my own day-to-day life that's occurring around . . . like the facts and figures that I've been exposed to that show the inequalities in our society.

She believes what she learned "has affirmed that meaning of helping others and the meaning of life being a people-oriented meaning, rather than a self-oriented meaning." Peyton, a student from a regional state university, shared how his classes definitely broadened how I see people. Even though [his university] isn't that diverse, the classes that I've taken, and the professors that have taught them, they've expanded my horizon from [the perspective of] white males. I've kind of seen the other side of things and some classes they expose you to, just because this is a way you're going about your life, that's not how other people do it.

Chandler, a student at a Catholic research university recounted a similar experience, "[In] history classes, you're always studying these different cultures, so you're gaining new perspectives, how people have thought about certain philosophies, how they've thought about other cultures. Every class opens your eyes to something new." This type of experience again would be something that is usually expected of the college experience, but it is important to realize that these students connected multicultural conversations not simply to understanding others but also to understanding and thinking about various life purposes and meanings.

3. Vocational Transformation

Amber, a student at the Baptist research university, was one of the students who experienced a conversion to the view that college should be about more than obtaining a credential. What helped with her conversion was a particular course she took her first year. "The whole course was based around: What is vocation? And what's the point of a higher education?" The professor would likely have been proud of the results,

> I think that really helped shape the rest of my college career, because I came in thinking, "This is so I can have an education so it will lead to a better career for me." And entering that class it was, "That's not the case. Higher education is more than that, and if you only focus on a career you'll be miserable. Because you're not getting what the true underlying purpose of a college experience is meant to be."

This whole course changed Amber from an Instrumentalist to a Holistic. Amber was not alone in finding the conversation about vocation to stimulate her thinking about her larger purpose. A third group of students experienced life-changing discussions about meaning and purpose in courses that talked about vocation or first-year seminar courses that discussed purpose. These courses were often associated with funding the university received from the Lily Foundation to sponsor the exploration of vocation and purpose. As has been recounted in a recent work evaluating such programs, they proved quite successful.[19]

Since the concepts of "vocation" or "calling" are rooted in religious history, it is perhaps not surprising that we found students at the Baptist, Catholic, and Mormon research universities and the Lutheran college most engaged by these course discussions.[20] Chelsea, a student at the Lutheran college noted,

> My roommate and I both took a class called Psychology [number omitted] at the same time but in different sections last year, and then suddenly the actual words meaning, purpose, [and] vocation came into our literal vocabularies because we read a couple books related to vocational discernment and things like that.

Erica, a Baptist student also talked about "a servant leadership course in my sophomore year of college where we did discuss it to an extent: What is your purpose? What is your calling? What is the purpose and calling of human being?" Ruby, a student at a Catholic university, mentioned a discernment class aimed at helping seniors decide where they are called that was instrumental in helping her contemplate her life purpose.

> It was all about trying to help you personally find your place in the world, and it talks about these bigger questions of purpose. The readings we'd have to do talked about finding joy in your life and where are you being called.

As a result of the course, Ruby would say her thinking about purpose changed. She is now applying for teaching programs like Teach for America, ACE, and Pace. Moreover, "the way I approach teaching is that I really want that relationship. So it's more of the teacher-student relationship and just having that impact on a life." Whether in a specific general education course or within their majors, students noted learning how to think about their vocation in ways that include a larger moral or religious element that related to matters of purpose or meaning.[21]

The courses that introduced and expanded students' understanding of vocation extended beyond the humanities. Tom, a business student at a Mormon university, found that many of his classes touched on meaning and purpose in some way. For instance, he shared,

> I took a game theory economics class, and it was all about evolutionary economics, and most of the discussions we had in class, 30 minutes were spent talking about what it meant in our personal lives, and 30 minutes were talking about what it meant for corporations

and businesses. I mean the class had a conversation for a full class period about the meaning of life and the purpose of life and how it ties into what we're studying.

All of this emphasis on purpose changed his whole outlook toward business,

I guess before I kind of thought as a cold, hard business man. You do everything to optimize your revenue, make the most money. . . . Here we hear about ethics and I think [his university] is known for being a very ethical business school. We hear about treating people right. I think that's really shaped the way I think about "How do you deal with problems in an organization?" It all comes down to people and how you treat them right, which I guess would be understanding their meaning and purpose in life, which I would believe to be similar to mine, and treating them so they can fulfill that purpose.

In this regard, Tom's professional major engaged him in a discussion about more than being a good professional. Tom's transformative story was not the only one among business majors. Marianna, a business student from a Catholic university, noted about one of her finance professors who dealt with investing:

He said it like almost every class or every other—every week . . . he was like, "The end goal is the money that you make off of these investments [is] to give it back, [to] do good." So he really harped on that, and I feel like in all our business classes . . . I feel like once you're here with the whole Catholic identity, that it does translate into doing good for others. You know the motto of the business school is "Ask more of business," so it means, like, it's not just business. It's asking more of it, like what can you do with this business degree? What can business do for other people in the community?

Sienna, another business student at the Catholic university, simply says she had learned through a particular class, "You can do a high-quality kind of business that's aimed at uplifting people."

The insertion of language about "vocation" or "calling" also occurred in professionally oriented classes beyond business. Emily, a student at the Mormon university, talked with passion about her interior design class.

I love just going to class, just to see what she would say. You know she'd bring it so we would talk about, you know, designing your home and how you want it to feel and—and I think that kind of goes along with your purpose in life . . . she'd be like, "You know what? You guys are all going to be wives and mothers and this is something we've got to do as women. Think about how you're going to be able to help your family. Think about your calling in life." And so I liked how she would bring your purpose in life as a woman into class, and that was something I hadn't even thought about.

Beyond talking about one's particular major as a vocation or calling, we also interviewed some students who simply understood their purpose as primarily involving their future career or job, and who certainly saw classes as having an important role to play, especially in either affirming their choice or confirming their desire to change majors and careers. In these cases, the curricular experience simply provided confirmation regarding a particular choice of career or major.

Reasons for Not Encountering Meaning and Purpose in the Classroom

The minority of students who did not recall encountering meaning and purpose in classes and/or course readings either attended a secular institution (which was the case of Albert) or were science or professional majors (which was also the case with Albert). As one nonreligious student at a religious college related, "No, I'm a community health major, and we just talk about health." *Every one of those who claimed not to have addressed meaning or purpose in their curricular experience fit one of those two categories.*

The importance of major confirms what Astin, Astin, and Lindholm found about the influence of college about students' spiritual questing, a term they equate with the search for meaning and purpose in life.[22] They discovered that selected academic courses of study played an important role. Students from the health professions, fine arts, or humanities had greater inclinations to explore matters of meaning and purpose than those in business, computer science, or the physical sciences.[23] Not surprisingly, we encountered only four occasions when students talked about meaning or purpose in the context of science and health classes, and three of these four were at religious institutions. Furthermore, it was largely through general education religious requirements that science majors encountered these discussions as these two students from a Baptist research university illustrate.

- "I did my freshman year when I was in religion classes but definitely not in science classes at all. I don't think that conversation ever really came up. . . ."

- "In religion class we talked [about meaning and purpose], but besides that I'm in science classes and they don't really."

As these examples suggest, STEM majors without a general education curriculum that addresses these questions may be unlikely to wrestle with issues of meaning and purpose within the college curriculum.

Tracking Faculty Influence on Meaning and Purpose Using National Survey Data

If the negative effects of the research ideal on faculty's willingness to engage questions regarding the meaning and purpose of life are to be seen, one would expect to find them most in faculty discussions with students. In general Astin, Astin, and Lindholm found, "Across all different types of campuses, most students (62 percent) report that their professors 'never' encourage discussions of religious/spiritual matters, and only 20 percent report that their professors 'frequently' encourage exploration of meaning and purpose."[24] They also discovered that interactions with faculty play an important role in influencing students' search for meaning and purpose. For instance, students who report that faculty encouraged them to examine issues of meaning and purpose showed an 8 percent higher increase in their Spiritual Quest scale than those with professors who they indicated were "not at all" interested in encouraging exploration of these matters.[25]

Our own analysis of the College Students' Beliefs and Values Survey (CSBV) sought to dig deeper into the influence of professors as well as institutions. The survey contains 14,527 student responses at two points in time: first as incoming first-year students, and second, as spring semester juniors. Students were sampled from 136 colleges and universities classified as public (N = 2,517), nonreligious private (N = 3,215), evangelical (N = 3,238), Catholic (N = 3,352), and other religious (N = 2,205).[26] As we did in chapter 3, with the National Study of Youth and Religion, we present the results of our multivariate statistical analysis graphically to make them easier to digest.

The most relevant question in the CSBV, for our purposes, asked students how often they engage in a search for meaning or purpose in life. Students could answer "not at all," "to some extent," or "to a great extent." They were asked this question both as incoming first-year students and as spring semester juniors. One important limit of this approach is that *measuring whether a student is seeking meaning and purpose is different than measuring whether they currently have meaning and purpose or whether they have discussions about meaning and purpose.* Some students may not be searching for meaning and purpose because they consider themselves already to have found meaning and purpose.

We classified those who were searching "to a great extent" as active searchers. Active searchers made up a little more than 20 percent of all students as incoming first-year students, and a little less than 22 percent of all students by the end of their junior year. In other words, actively searching for meaning and purpose only budges a little over the course of two and one half years of college.

But this is not the same at all types of schools. Figure 8.1 shows the percent change in active seekers by institutional type. Students at evangelical colleges lead the way, with an increase of around 7 percent between first- and third-year students. Catholic colleges are next with an increase of more than

Figure 8.1. Percent change in actively searching for meaning/purpose in life by institutional type, weighted ($N = 13,271$)

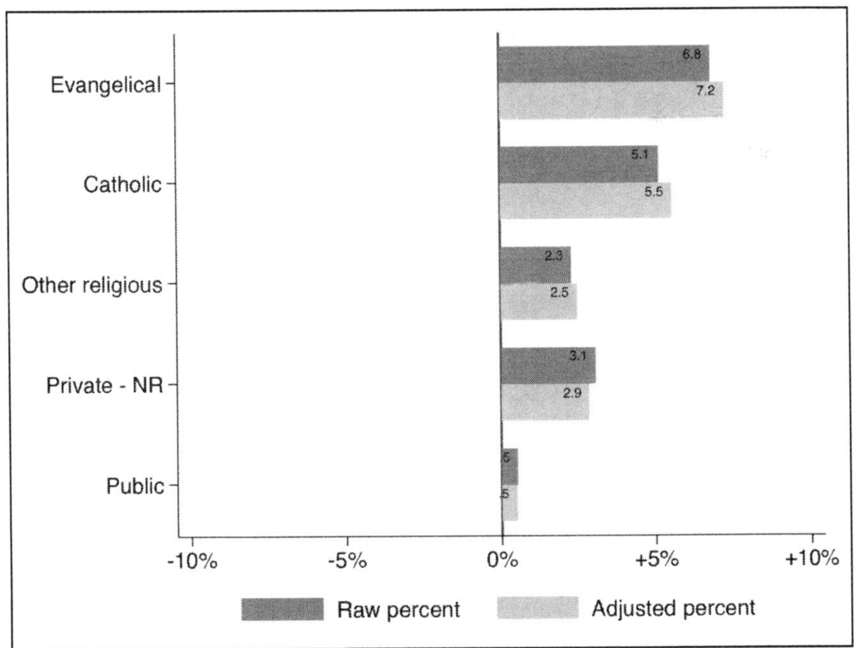

Source: College Students' Beliefs and Values Survey, 2004–2007.

Note: Adjusted percent controls for age, sex, race, parents' income, parents' educational attainment, citizenship status, family structure, high school GPA, and high school type.

5 percent. Other religious and nonreligious private institutions hover around 2 to 3 percent, and students at public universities show very little change in this measure (about half a percent). To ensure that the institutional differences are not due to the different types of students that attend these institutions, we also ran models that control for demographic characteristics such as age, race, gender, household socioeconomic status (household income and parents' educational attainment), citizenship, and family structure. We also control for high school GPA and the type of high school the student attended.[27] The percentages that are adjusted for these factors appear to show very little difference with the unadjusted figures.

In this chapter we also were interested in student-professor interaction. The CSBV includes some relevant measures. Figure 8.2 looks at the same measure of purpose change over time, but this time separating this out by the number of hours during a typical week that students report talking to faculty outside

Figure 8.2. Percent change in actively searching for meaning/purpose in life by weekly time spent talking to faculty outside of class, weighted (*N* = 13,191)

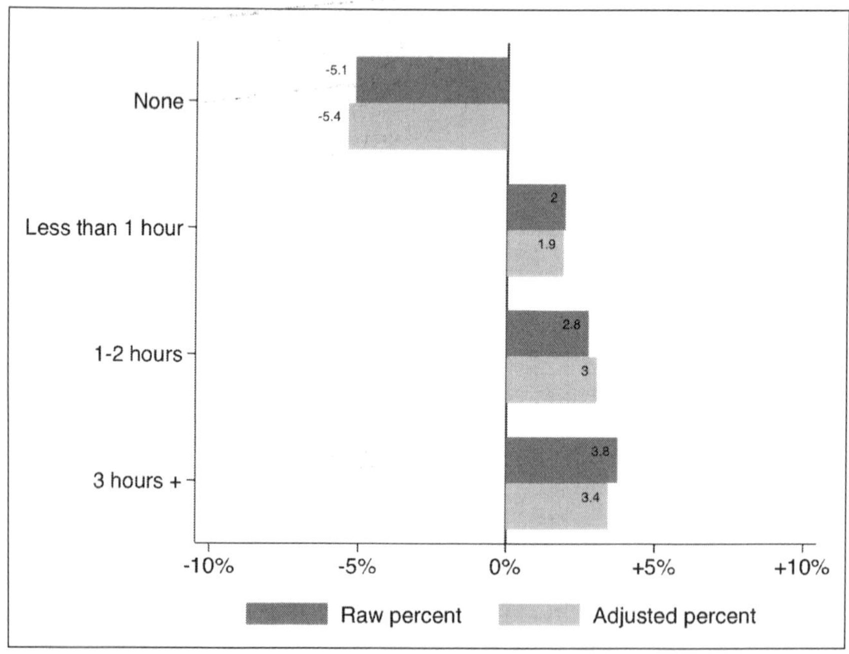

Source: College Students' Beliefs and Values Survey, 2004–2007.

Note: Adjusted percent controls for age, sex, race, parents' income, parents' educational attainment, citizenship status, family structure, high school GPA, and high school type.

of class. The most noticeable gap is between those who talk to their professors at least a little (even less than one hour per week) and those who never talk to their professors outside of class. The latter group drops in active purpose seeking by more than 5 percent, while the other students all show positive gains in seeking meaning and purpose in life (from around 2 to nearly 4 percent).

The next figure (fig. 8.3) uses a measure that asks students to recall how often faculty at their institution encouraged exploring questions of meaning and purpose. The big gap is between those who say their faculty do this "frequently"—who show a 10 percent gain in active seekers, and those who say their faculty do this less than frequently—who show no discernable gains. The group only makes up around 20 percent of the total student population (although this differs quite a bit by institutional type—53 percent of students at evangelical colleges say faculty do this frequently, while only 14 percent of students at public universities say the same). We should take a moment to caution against

Figure 8.3. Percent change in actively searching for meaning/purpose in life by student report of how often faculty encourage them to ask questions of meaning and purpose, weighted (N = 13,180)

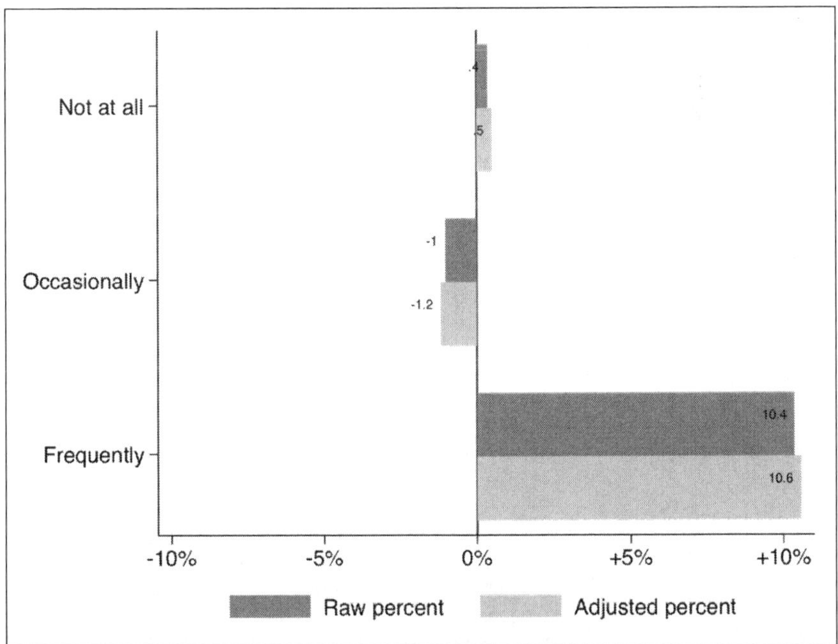

Source: College Students' Beliefs and Values Survey, 2004–2007.

Note: Adjusted percent controls for age, sex, race, parents' income, parents' educational attainment, citizenship status, family structure, high school GPA, and high school type.

a straightforward causal interpretation here as well. It is important to remember that it is the very same students reporting on both themselves and faculty. If students begin to work harder on developing a sense of purpose in life, they may be more sensitive to campus opportunities to help them do this, including those efforts by faculty. It's difficult to estimate the true degree of this without some independent measure of faculty engagement with these issues.

And, we happen to have such a measure. Faculty were given a separate survey. One of the questions asked faculty to indicate how important it was to them to facilitate a search for meaning and purpose among undergraduates. Unfortunately, we are unable to link up faculty responses with students' responses directly, but we are able to take institutional-level mean responses to this question. In other words, we know, for each student, what the average faculty response to this question was at their institution. Institutions near the bottom (10th percentile) tended to have faculty mean-level answers near "somewhat important." Institutions near the top (90th percentile) tended to have faculty mean-level answers near "very important." As figure 8.4 shows, there is *some* difference between these institu-

Figure 8.4. Percent change in actively searching for meaning/purpose in life by institutional mean-level faculty response to importance of facilitating student search for meaning and purpose, weighted (*N* = 10,867)

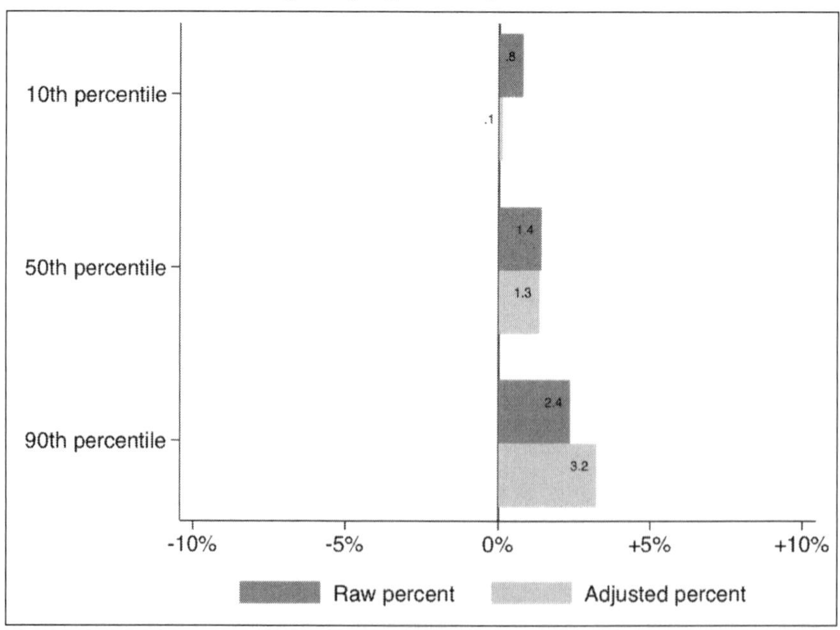

Source: College Students' Beliefs and Values Survey, 2004–2007.

Note: Adjusted percent controls for age, sex, race, parents' income, parents' educational attainment, citizenship status, family structure, high school GPA, and high school type.

tions—with those near the bottom showing no gain in active purpose seekers and those near the top showing a 2–3 percent gain—but these are not big differences. Nor is the measure of faculty institutional means statistically significant at the normal levels that social scientists use ($p < .05$). Since these are institutional-level differences, we are missing all of the intra-institutional variation in faculty influence. We think it is likely that the true influence from faculty attempts to facilitate purpose fall somewhere in between the institutional effects we see in this figure and the student reports in the previous figure.

Finally, it is worth revisiting the institutional-type effects from figure 8.1. To what extent is the Catholic and evangelical college successful in moving the needle (a bit more) on the search for meaning and purpose due to differences in student-faculty interaction? We ran the same models as before, but this time we included the two student-reported variables we examined in tables 8.2 and 8.3 as controls in the adjusted model (in addition to the regular controls).[28] The results, in figure 8.5, suggest that nearly half of the advantage for evangelical

Figure 8.5. Percent change in actively searching for meaning/purpose in life by institutional type, including additional controls for student-faculty interaction, weighted ($N = 13,101$)

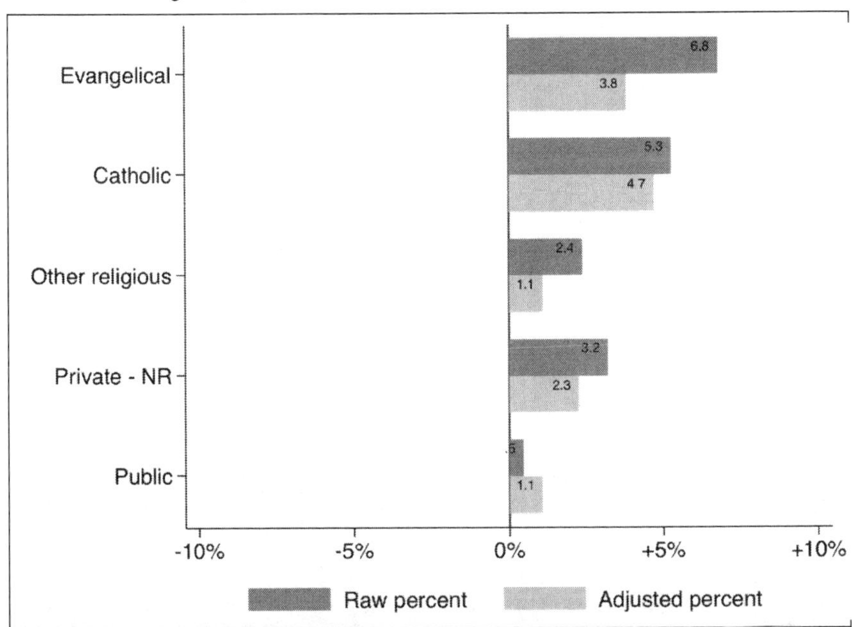

Source: College Students' Beliefs and Values Survey, 2004–2007.

Note: Adjusted percent controls for student-faculty time outside of class and student report of faculty encouragement to search for meaning and purpose in life, age, sex, race, parents' income, parents' educational attainment, citizenship status, family structure, high school GPA, and high school type.

colleges comes from how students perceive their interactions to be with faculty. The reduction at Catholic colleges is far less, indicating that it is primarily something else at these institutions that accounts for the uptick they see in students actively searching for meaning and purpose in life.

How Students View Faculty: Digging Deeper

In our interviews with students, we found further evidence of what the quantitative data reveals as well as deeper insight into the why behind it. For instance, we found the experiences of Kimberly, Ryan, Grace, Jayla, Sid, and Kelly at a regional state university and Susan, Marsha, Bill, Tim, Karen, and Paul at an evangelical institution were completely different when it comes to faculty relationships. At the regional state university, students reported that personal topics in general, much less the meaning of life, were not broached with faculty outside of class. As Kimberly, a senior, shared,

> I've never had a professor with whom I would talk about these types of things. . . . I feel like there's sometimes a line with some professors. They don't want to talk about these things. It's like it never really comes up.

For most students from this college there really was not much to share when asked about whether they've had conversations with faculty regarding these areas:

- "Ryan: Um, I don't think I experienced any of that."

- "Grace: Not that I can think of off the top of my head."

- "Jayla: No, no, it's just like "come, talk to me about your paper" or something and that's really it."

- "Sid: No."

- "Kelly: No."

Much like Troy whose story we recounted in chapter 4, these students had no significant interaction with faculty about issues of meaning and purpose.

The responses to students from the evangelical institution offer a striking contrast to this experience. They talked at much greater length about the personal nature of their relationships with professors and their ability to talk with professors about issues of meaning and purpose as well as other areas beyond academic concerns.

- Susan: "There's a professor, and he's really great. I'll just be sitting down and he'll come and talk, and you just start talking . . . it's a linguistics class, so pretty much about language, and yeah, it's really great. Or just about what's going on in my life."

- Marsha: "Like last semester my theology teacher . . . the first faith he came to was Mormonism because that was the first faith he'd ever really known. And so me being super-interested in Mormonism and my friends, I just wanted to talk more about that with him and hear more about his experience, and so I just went to his office hours and we talked about Mormons for an hour and it was great . . . I know a lot of students are mentored by our professors. They're very interested in students' lives. Most classes, you fill out a sheet about yourself, and prayer requests, and a picture of yourself, so the teacher can get to know who you are and get to know your name, and be intentional in their relationship with you."

- Bill: "Uh-huh, definitely. I went into my New Testament history and literature professor. He has office hours you can sign up to go into; I signed up and I didn't even go in there and ask him a question about the class, I just said, 'Hey, I want to talk to you for an hour and get to know you, because, I respect you, and I'd just like to know more about you and stuff' . . . a lot of the professors here really want to pour into the students."

- Karen: "Absolutely yeah. I actually went to an event at a professor's house. They're very open to the students and speaking to them about anything, not even academic-wise. . . . they're very open to including us. They don't see us as academic people. They see us, maybe almost as mentors to us, not only in the academic realm, but maybe [a] more personal feel. Because they understand that we're away from our families and so they're willing to be that kind of support team."

As this comparison reveals, when it comes to personal conversations with faculty, we found a dramatic difference among students at different institutions.

In our interviews at ten different campuses, the kind of holistic care the students at the evangelical institution experienced was not the norm. The experience of the students from the regional university proved to be the norm. One student at a Baptist research university even declared, "I don't know any adults in college. Isn't that the downfall of college? It's that it structurally cuts you off from real adults. Um, that's kind of true. I don't interact with any real adults."

Overall, the vast majority of students we interviewed had rarely talked to a faculty member about these matters.

It should be noted that, as Albert's story above indicates, and as Andrea's introductory story reveals, sometimes, it's a two-way street. Maria, a student at an Ivy League university shared,

> I mean there are some professors who are just so cool so, I guess, but it's not like I would be like, "Your lecture today was so cool; we should talk about this at lunch." I don't think I would do that. *Interviewer: You don't feel comfortable in that sort of, there's a boundary there that would be crossed?* Student: I mean it's not a boundary, I just would rather not.

Would this change if a professor took the initiative? Leslie, a student at the same Catholic university shared this example that leads one to doubt it would.

> One of my professors really emphasized that, "I have all these lunch credits that I can literally just use to go and sit, eat, talk with you guys." But I'm not interested in talking about his subject so . . . He's a really interesting guy, and it would be interesting to go and have a meal with him; but, at the same time I wouldn't know what to talk about. He's the only one that has actually said anything like that too, though.

The assumption that students want to learn from professors about life as a whole appears far from the norm. The general pattern would appear to be that students are not interested in talking to a professor about life as a whole. They appear to have absorbed Max Weber's famous claim that out of one hundred professors, ninety-nine "do not and should not claim to be football coaches in the field of life."[29]

Even among the minority of college students who did claim to talk to professors about these issues, most equated purpose or meaning with a job and recalled talking to professors about their future professional plans. For example, a psychology student shared about a professor who "was just really helpful in giving me advice about following things that I'm passionate about and not focusing so much on applications and grad school and jobs and money and stuff like that, but really just doing what will make me happy."

The exceptions to this trend were those students who attended four faith-based institutions, the Baptist, Catholic, evangelical, and Jewish institutions. These findings could perhaps provide a partial explanation for why Baptist or Catholic students show the most increase in scores of what Astin, Astin, and Lindholm identify as spiritual questing (or the search for meaning and purpose) in college.[30] At three of four of these institutions, however, only a minority of students claimed to have experienced these kinds of conversations, often citing one specific professor or a certain class of professors (e.g., rabbis). As one student from a Baptist university shared, "I've had a few conversations with my education professors about that, just like why we're teaching and the purpose and meaning of life and finding meaning. But I definitely think they were kind of rare." In most of these cases, it involved one particular professor as with this student.

> I have a professor friend here that I'm really close to, so I like talking to her about these things. I've known her since freshman year. She does groups, kind of get-togethers for talking about spiritual things, so I have a really close group of friends from there. She's more like my special director, and so that's why I feel very comfortable talking to her about these things.

As can be seen from this quote, the issue of trust loomed large in the reason for the lack of or presence of these conversations.

The major exception among our sample was the evangelical institution. As the above examples indicate, students at this campus as a whole talk about faculty in general as not only being open to but also initiating personal conversations about life in general or the purpose or meaning of life in particular. The question is why? Again, the reason for this difference, we contend, can be ascertained just by looking at the quotes above from the students at the evangelical university. Since students share the same worldview as the faculty, students at the university trust that they can go to them to talk not only about course work, but also about their core beliefs about the meaning and purpose of life. In this regard, we wonder if Kronman mistakes one of the important factors for the decline in faculty discussions with students about the meaning and purpose of life. While diversity likely helps stimulate discussion and learning, it also means fewer students will perceive a shared worldview with professors. Without a shared worldview, they may not trust professors and certainly do not appear to want to talk to professors about anything beyond the subject matter of their class.

Making Sense of It All

Have universities given up on the meaning of life when it comes to the formal curriculum? We think Kronman perhaps too quickly concluded that they have. From our interviews and the quantitative data we examined, we think that the answer to this question will likely prove more nuanced among institutions and students.

First, we need to recognize that part of the issue pertains to students' expectations. The students we call Instrumentalists are much less likely to be interested in exploring issues of meaning and purpose and college. In their mind, college is primarily a means to enhance their personal happiness or achievements. In contrast, the group of students we called the Holistics, are much more inclined to want to explore these matters. Interestingly, they are also those who already have Relationalist or Transcendent sources of meaning or purpose that go beyond-the-self.

Second, when it comes to the curriculum, we found more reason for hope than Kronman might indicate. Most of the students we interviewed expected these discussions and experienced them in the curriculum, although at different levels. In this regard, Albert, our student described in the introduction, proves to be the exception. If an institution requires religion courses, offers great texts, exposes students to multicultural issues, or integrates faith, ethics, and thinking about vocation, then students will likely find curricular discussions of meaning and purpose. Indeed, these courses appear to provide the best context for thinking about purpose. Based on these findings, Kronman's claim that the tradition of secular humanism that emphasizes great texts is the answer to helping colleges once again address issues of meaning and purpose is empirically not accurate. There are a variety of traditions that emphasize great texts, and there are more curricular ways to address meaning and purpose than the great texts approach (although this approach is certainly an important and influential one).

We also found it striking that students tend to have two basic responses to discussions about meaning and purpose in the curriculum. Some experienced them in the way you might "experience" Pythagorean's Theorem. It was brought up, they "learned" about it, and then moved on. This seemed particularly true for those who encountered it in religion courses. Other students deeply reflected on and wrestled with these issues when they were brought up, especially when they encountered the topic through less familiar texts, topics, or approaches. This reaction took place for students with classes in the humanities, social sciences, or other professional courses. Only in rare instances, however, did students majoring in STEM fields report encountering matters of purpose and meaning. We consider this last matter a particular challenge.

Third, we also found that institutions make a big difference. Religious institutions are more likely to require religion classes or great texts classes where these kinds of discussions are fostered. Furthermore, we found that students at secular institutions were less likely to report having these discussions in class. This finding also extended to professors' discussions with students outside of class. It would appear from general surveys and our own interviews that, apart from the rare exception, a greater percentage of professors at state institutions have given up building relationships through which they talk to students personally about these issues. In this respect, our findings were, for the most part, consistent with the broader findings from Astin, Astin, and Lindholm.[31] Professors at religious institutions are less inclined to give up, but even in these cases, we found in the quantitative and qualitative data that only students at evangelical universities indicated consistent faculty involvement in their lives in a holistic way. Few students, it would appear, experience the kind of faculty mentoring that Parks suggests students need.[32]

The difference between evangelical and public institutions, we would propose, pertains to the lack of commonality among students and faculty that builds the necessary trust for such conversations. If institutions of higher education were to embrace Parks's admonition, they would need to encourage faculty mentors to identify student groups with whom they share much in common and would be willing to help them develop thoughts about all of life and not merely a particular vocation. This approach recognizes that building a life does not happen in the abstract. Adults become experts in a particular vision of the good life associated with a particular community and with particular ways of thinking, talking, and acting about the various spheres of life. Such particular expertise and experience, as another scholar has noted, creates a problem for inclusiveness that is only overcome at particularly focused institutions or communities.[33]

Overall then, students' experiences with professors and the classroom appears to be a mixed bag when it comes to its influence on how students think about meaning and purpose. While there are certainly areas of strength, there is still room for improvement, and we will make some suggestions for such improvement in the conclusion. Still, as we will see in the next chapter, the role of the curricular dimension may be of secondary importance when it comes to developing students' purpose. Students' experience of meaning and purpose through faculty or the formal curriculum proved to be less important than the co-curricular. As one student related, "Yeah, I've learned a lot in the class, but I feel like I've grown more as a person, as a student, outside of the classroom." Indeed, as the next chapter demonstrates, friends, clubs, sports, roommates, romantic relationships—all of these, are where the real issues of life come up.

Chapter 9

Looking for Purpose Outside of Class

(with Jessica Robinson)

I think having a person of the same sex that's older than you, that believes in many similar things that you do, that can help you. I think that can shape a lot, and I think a lot of my thought process reflects a lot of the conversations we've had about dating, about school, about grades, and I think that [this person has] been incredibly influential in my life, and I worry that college students who only hang out with people their own age. It gets really scary because we all think similarly.

—Jasmine, public university student

"I mean because purpose is such a broad question and everyone has their own answer, you can never come up with the right answer, because there is no right answer." Kelsey, a senior biology major at a public research university, offers this hypothesis about why she has not taken a class that has addressed the purpose of life. Although a STEM major, she also participates in the liberal arts honors program at her university. The purpose of the program, she says, is "to make you well rounded in all different types of subjects out there." Yet, despite having taken a set of classes that historically explore big questions, she claims she has not taken a class where they discussed the meaning or purpose of life. She does note, "Maybe in philosophy class, we talked about it a little bit," but she could not remember if they actually did.

As Kelsey's quote reveals, she appears to believe that academic classes are meant to focus on providing the right answer and not meant to cover questions to which various people might offer multiple answers. Regarding questions about the meaning or purpose of life, Kelsey tells us the following:

> Because most of this stuff is done like outside on your own, I don't
> think there's ever gonna be a class that directs what [one's] life's
> purpose is to by the end of the semester [and] have you answer that
> question. Because even then the purpose and meaning changes with
> time. You might think this is your purpose or this is your meaning,
> but six months [later] you will find out it's not this but it's another
> way. It's always changing, so there's no way to learn about it and
> this is the final answer, because then you're still living life so it's still
> changing constantly.

Kelsey's answer reflects her own outlook regarding meaning and purpose as well as perhaps a certain Eastern perspective toward the issue.[1] With regard to college, she takes both the Self-Achiever approach to meaning and purpose described in chapters 5 and 6, and the Instrumentalist approach described in the last chapter. "My purpose is obvious, like you have to get a good GPA, because that's gonna help you get the job that you want, or go to med school or grad school or whatever other, you know, paths that you choose to take." Yet, when asking about her own meaning or purpose, beyond this provisional purpose, she expresses that she considers herself undecided at this point and admits, "I don't think I know that a hundred percent right now."

In some ways, Kelsey answers this question in a way that might be considered an extended exposition about her philosophy of life that sounds a bit like a mixture of Aristotle and John Stuart Mill:

> So obviously anything you kinda do in life is so you can be happy,
> like everything is a means to an end. The end is hopefully going
> to be like your happiness. If it's not directly you're hoping that by
> doing this, this is going to make someone close to you happy, which
> is therefore going to make you happy. So like everything boils down
> to your happiness.

As the survey questions from chapter 6 reveal, Kelsey's ultimate goal of happiness is the most common one for college students. She situates most every activity in relation to this final end of personal happiness.

> Anything you do is [for] personal satisfaction or the feeling of getting
> fulfillment in like what you're doing or feeling happy. Like being with
> the people you're being around, feeling happy that you're making
> your parents proud of you, or like, you know, you're still praying to
> God, or you're still doing all the duties you have to do with life, like
> keeping up with school and all of your organizational responsibilities,

> while at the same time still having time to yourself. Like everything
> you do is so you can be happy in the end.

Since Kelsey basically sees her end as being happy, the means to become happy, which she sees as the purpose parts of life, will change depending on what brings her happiness.

In light of this outlook, the co-curricular experience has shaped Kelsey's own approach to her quest for purpose, which has continually informed her views about what brings her happiness. Since she was raised by immigrant Indian parents in a somewhat conservative Hindu family, her initial outlook regarding what would bring her happiness involved a certain kind of lifestyle:

> When I went into college everything I believed was pretty steadfast. I knew that I didn't want to date someone who was not Indian. I knew that I didn't want to be physical with anyone else who's not my boyfriend. I knew I didn't wanna drink, didn't wanna smoke . . . I didn't think any of that was gonna change.

For Kelsey, some of these things did stay the same, but some of them have now changed for her. The place where she wrestled with all of these matters, however, involved the co-curricular dimension of college life and not the curricular.

The most important place where she grappled with what would bring her happiness concerned conversations with a roommate of close to three years that she also identifies as a mentor. The roommate is a slightly older family friend from her home city, although they were not necessarily close when they began rooming together: "At first I was super-intimidated by her and stuff, and I didn't even know how we would be able to live together, but now we've become like really close friends." This relationship proved particularly important during her senior year when she started to question some of her core moral beliefs, particularly,

> Why do I think it's wrong to do it before marriage . . . like marriage is just a sheet of paper, it's just a contract, like a certificate that two people sign. It doesn't mean anything if you feel that close to the person that you're with and they love you and you love them, isn't that the same thing?

Kelsey realized, "I had been living my whole life thinking that I don't want to do that until I get married, but I didn't have a good enough reason as to why I thought before marriage is wrong." Kelsey then notes that her roommate was also asking the same questions. "For a long time she also believed the same thing, and eventually like she came to the conclusion: "It's okay to do it before marriage if you love the person, and they love you." These conversations with her roommate made a big difference in shaping Kelsey's perspective, "So she talked to me about a lot of these issues and concerns I had, 'cause everyone basically goes through the same boat and all that stuff, so she was the person who talked to me about all that." These talks led Kelsey to ask a series of questions:

> Why does marriage have a higher like sanctity than relationships do? Or what happens if I get married, and then I choose to do it for the first time with the person I'm married to, then two years later we divorce? You don't plan on divorcing when you get married, and so all that time has gone to waste because we're not married anymore.

She then concludes, "Who decided like marriage is the best time? It was probably society . . . they're trying to prevent unwanted pregnancies or prevent people from getting hurt, so they think marriage is like the best threshold or something." In the end, "society" proved a rather malleable form of moral authority, especially in light of what, in Kelsey's mind, were outdated reasons for waiting to have sex before marriage. Ultimately, she changed her views about sex before marriage.

Kelsey also shares about other conversations regarding her overall life meaning, purpose, and vision of the good life as it related to her original convictions coming into college, particularly drinking. She is a member of a Hindu group on campus. "We have meetings every week and every week the two officers present a topic." One of the recent topics they discussed was alcohol and substance abuse. The students present the topic by researching the topic.

> So they talked about, whoever was presenting, they talked about how in the past alcohol and different drugs were used in a lot of religious ceremonies. They were used to get psychological highs, which were like meant to expose you to a different level, get you to another level so you could experience God in a different way.

According to Kelsey, the researchers then noted, "But now alcohol and drugs are looked down upon, so there's like a shift in time. So the question, whether using alcohol and drugs nowadays, is that okay or not? If you use it in moderation is that okay?" She continues to uphold her old views about alcohol and drugs. "I don't drink alcohol, I don't wanna smoke, . . . and people are always, 'You're a senior and you still don't drink and you're twenty-one?' And I was like, 'Yeah I feel like I don't need to.' "

Interestingly, Kelsey admits that the actual source of the research relies quite substantially on secular academic sources and only tangentially on any Hindu sacred texts. She notes,

I haven't personally read any of the texts, I mean they're all huge books and really old, but at this age, I don't think anyone's actually read the text themselves . . . I don't think that many college kids, at least, actually read the texts in Hinduism.

Despite the fact that the Hindu Student Association does not delve into Hinduism's sacred texts, it still provides a place for discussions about topics related to the good life, and in Kelsey's case, the questions she's considering regarding the happy life.

The Importance of the Co-Curricular

While professors may like to believe that most learning occurs in the classroom, we know that for most students, a substantial amount of learning during college occurs in the co-curricular dimension of college.[2] Not surprisingly, students are often quick to note this fact as these three quotes from students attest:

- "For me personally, I get more out of like the social things I know, like my club and I work at the writing center. Like, I get more out of that than I do out of some of my classes."

- "I've learned a lot in class, but I feel like I've grown more as a person, as a student, outside of the classroom. I do feel like that is a huge part. I feel like that's almost like fifty-one percent of the college's experience. It is—you do develop a lot as a person."

- "I'm probably learning more about myself through the social."

Learning in the moral dimension of students' lives, which includes matters of meaning and purpose, proves no different. In fact, historically for many institutions, when moral education was removed from the curriculum in the early twentieth century, the administratively run co-curricular dimension of universities emerged to take up the endeavor.[3] Administrators at this time began to hope that social clubs, living arrangements, and even athletics could be harnessed to accomplish the task of moral formation.

Whether the co-curricular still influences students developing conceptions of meaning and purpose is subject to some questioning. While some scholars, such as Kronman, focus on the lack of attention to meaning in the curriculum, other scholars have also noted that the co-curricular world also neglects issues of meaning and purpose.[4] In our research, we wanted to learn if this claim was the reality for the students we interviewed, and, if not, exactly where in the co-curricular world students encounter discussions about meaning and purpose.

We also wanted to see if the particular identity of the university and its associated ethos made a difference. Overall, in our 110 Targeted Qual interviews we discovered that despite the distinct variety of institutional types where we interviewed students, student experiences discussing meaning and purpose share a great deal of commonality.

In general, students describe co-curricular influences on their purpose development that fit into two categories (both exemplified in Kelsey's story): (1) organizational influences and (2) conversations about meaning and purpose with adult mentors or peers. We should note that these influences are not necessarily exclusive. Indeed, students sometimes speak about how these influences work together, promoting a holistic sense of development, while other students chose to emphasize one over the other. This corroborates what we find in our quantitative survey findings. As best as we can tell, institutional mission and ethos *do* make a difference in encouraging some students to pursue serious reflection on meaning and purpose, but a good deal of this comes through informal conversations with peers and mentors.

Organizational Influences

We should first note that although students may be able to identify ways the formal curriculum addresses matters of meaning and purpose, students rarely refer to particular university-sponsored co-curricular programs that might address purpose as part of larger religious or philosophical goals. For example, at religious institutions, required religious worship services or other kinds of religious programming are rarely mentioned as important for purpose development.

Only in a few cases did students cite a specific program set up to address purpose or vocation. Often it came about by an indirect choice. Ruby, a student at a Catholic university, provides an example of a student who experienced one of these programs. She shared the following with one of us:

> I think I didn't have that sense that I had a purpose in life until I came to college and started exploring more deeply different avenues of myself and taking classes and getting into programs . . . where we act as a mentor in faith for high school students in the summer, and so just exploring my own faith and God's involvement in my life that has made me feel like I have a purpose. Whereas before when I was younger I was like, "Oh, um, if I study hard I can be a doctor," whereas now I'm like, "Maybe I'm not meant to be a doctor, maybe [with] my skill set I'm called to be something else, to do . . . something for someone."

The primary development of her purpose, she noted, "comes from the religious activities that I've chosen to be a part of. With [name omitted], it was a program I applied to, and that's where we explored the concept of vocation." This unique co-curricular program in particular provided something important for her.

> I have a whole new vocabulary, like *discerning* and *vocation* and stuff like that, so that's how I approach it now that I'm looking for things to do after college. Just contemplating what my gifts are and what does this mean about what my vocation is.

Whether in the curriculum or the co-curricular, as Tim Clydesdale has reported, specific programs exploring purpose and vocation appear to be quite effective in influencing students.[5] However, we found little evidence of such programs when we interviewed typical students on these campuses. This could be because of the limited exposure most students have to this type of programming. Choose a student at random from the crowd, and it is highly unlikely he or she will have participated in a program to help develop a sense of purpose and vocation in life.

In general, when asked about co-curricular influences, students tend to refer to other parts of the co-curricular arena. They usually mention involvement with particular kinds of co-curricular organizations, the majority of which were largely student-run, with the primary exception being athletic teams.

Student Groups. If you want to discover where students have discussions about meaning and purpose or perceive themselves as developing purpose, you need to visit their student groups. While the groups likely have a social function, the ones where purpose discussions take place are likely to be clubs directed at a broader social or transcendent purpose (e.g., Model United Nations, Glee Club, social justice organizations, religious student groups, etc.). The students we interviewed describe their participation in these types of organizations as fostering a process of self-discovery that leads them to greater clarity of purpose. Miranda, a student from a state university, provides an example. She identifies a student philanthropy organization that raises money for a Children's Hospital and the university's Alumni Chapter as the two social contexts where she has discovered her purpose. She tells us, "I love both [of these organizations] because I think they have, especially the alumni organization, helped me come up with meaning and purpose." She connects her work at the Medical Center to an ability to "know that, my purpose on this earth is to help others," while she believed her work in the alumni group helped her "develop what I'm supposed to do while I'm on this earth," which involves connecting to the community.

Quinn, a business major at a secular liberal arts college, identifies his involvement with the student investment club with his discovery of the importance of including "giving back" in his overall conception of purpose and the good life. He admits it even played a role in his conversion from Self-Achiever purposes to a more Relationalist purpose:

> I think I've certainly understood that giving back's important—maybe something I didn't completely understand earlier . . . Investment Club is a way of giving back for me. I have this knowledge and if I'm able to give this knowledge to others so in the future when they have a portfolio, they're not getting taken advantage of by their adviser, getting hit by high fees or investing in things they shouldn't. And I really hope that that's giving back.

Quinn connects this sense of "giving back" to his purpose, understanding that he should not live for himself, but should give back to others. He concludes by saying, "I hope that sharing my knowledge with others is how I can give back in the future."

Religious groups were cited equally by students at both secular and religious campuses as providing a context for these discussions. Similar to the story of Kelsey at the beginning of the chapter, these groups provide a like-minded group of supportive others as well as a means to have conversations about purpose, often using resources like sacred or popular religious writings to stimulate this type of conversation. Brock, a public, state university student, described this type of religious involvement: "We've got a small group thing on Monday nights where we discuss passages of scripture. We also discuss what's going on in each other's lives." He understands that it is that context which allows topics like purpose and meaning to come up because, "a lot of times when the Bible or conversation address topics like, 'you shouldn't be this way.'" He concluded by explaining, "It kind of comes back to how it intertwines with life purpose."

Moreover, this encounter with religious groups' discussions about purpose extends to experiences with religious groups with which one did not identify. For instance, Jennifer, a secular liberal arts student, noted that her roommate brought her to a Christian group mainly for college students.

> I'm Buddhist by the way, so I'm very foreign to this. I would go with her just to see how it is. But they would play music and then you have the pastor talking about, you know, going over scriptures in the Bible; and I guess that's like my tiniest window into the meaning of life and what you do.

For her, it was an education. "I'm not that religious, but you see where people get their faith and hope and stuff." Interestingly, she juxtaposed this experience with going to local Buddhist groups where "they would have some discussions, but mainly it was just meditating." In contrast, she noted the Christian group would have talks about how "the purpose of life is to find God and be with him."

Not all experiences with ideologically-oriented student groups may support conversations about purpose. For example, Albert, an Ivy League student, introduced in the last chapter, noted that he did find support for deeper kinds of conversations among a co-curricular group of secular humanists at his university. "It's just nice to have a forum to talk about, you know, difficulties with switching from a religious to a nonreligious background," he said. Ironically, while Kronman believes the tradition of secular humanism provides an answer to helping students discuss life purpose, Albert did not find answers in the secular humanist club on campus.[6] He admitted, "I wouldn't say we talked about like the meaning of life, really." Instead, they'll have conversations about questions such as "Is America a Christian nation?" or they might have meetings to discuss a certain argument for the existence of God. He also observed that the group is completely student run and that he himself lacks any adult mentors when it comes to matters of life meaning. Albert's experience was similar to the other nontheistic students who mentioned secular clubs.

Since most student groups that foster purpose discussions and development have some purpose beyond socialization, whether or not Greek organizations foster this kind of discussion likely depends on whether they emphasize a service component. A few of our students saw fraternities and sororities as functioning to help them understand their passion in a more meaningful manner. As Andres, a state university student, shared:

> The main thing that we work on is service for the community and so giving back, it has shown me different ways of giving back. There is of course the community service, going out and helping people, but there's also giving back within [our university] community . . . so I think the fraternity has also helped me realize my purpose in life is to help people. That's my overall purpose in life, to help people and to help my family, [and] to help in general.

As illustrated in the example above, these students identified moments of service as times when they discovered particular passions that would become their purpose, such as helping others and serving the larger community. Again, we should note that the influence of these groups was not always positive. In some cases, a Greek organization might contribute to the problem. Mike, a Baptist university student, explained, "I really don't feel like I have much free time. I spend most of my time keeping up with my classwork and my [Greek] organization. I don't get much time to think about things like that." Busyness has been identified in other studies as something that impedes this exploration.[7]

Overall though, students consistently identified clubs and organizations that involve a community of like-minded peers who are engaged in a common external mission as the most conducive to exploring meaning and purpose. Often, they discovered passions they did not realize they had, and as a result, their understanding of personal purpose expanded or was transformed.

Athletics. Beyond voluntary student groups, our respondents spoke about only one other type of university-sponsored group as a context for discussions about purpose: athletic teams. The reason, we surmise, is that athletic teams have some of the characteristics of the student organizations mentioned above. Usually, the discussions about purpose occurred as a result of relationships between older and younger students on the team, the older students fulfilling the role of mentor for the younger students. Edward, a secular, private, liberal arts university student, commented, "Some of the juniors and seniors on the [cross-country] team, when I was a freshman, got me thinking about those kinds of questions." He observed that some of them shared his views and others had different views. He explained:

> We would end up getting into these conversations and everybody else in the café leaves and there's like two or three or four people still talking about [our purposes] . . . or out on long runs, we had these conversations about meaning and purpose. I can definitely think of those guys that sort of got me thinking about these questions.

Emily, a private, religious university student, explained her participation on the athletic team as developing her purpose in the following way, "One of my really close friends on the soccer team, we talked about the meaning of life or kind of what we're doing or where we're going, when we're not practicing." While Emily separates between "field-time" and "off-time," she attributes the team to putting her in touch with others who share a similar sense of purpose and desire to talk about where they are headed in the future. Still, another private, liberal arts university student named Spencer attributes this type of conversation to "only things that come up when you're doing athletics." As he said, "There's things, certain things that in athletics, only through athletics you can understand, like perseverance, commitment, and passion." Spencer connects the cultivation of certain virtues to a larger understanding of his purpose, which he sees as, "trying to figure out what I'm going to do next." Without the qualities Spencer mentioned above, "I wouldn't be able to dream about how I'm going to impact the world and what I'm going to do." Overall, the consistent community and development of common athletic-related virtues appears to provide a unique type of environment that stimulates conversations about purpose. Although these groups were not student-run, they share in common the mission focus and voluntary nature, which set the context for the possibility of moral formation.

Individual Relational Influences

Conversations about meaning and purpose require not just time but also a significant degree of trust and intimacy. As we noted in the chapter on students' adolescent experiences, students often reported not broaching issues of meaning and purpose with even their most trusted high school friends. This issue of trust and intimacy also proves to be a key reason students avoid talking with professors about the subject. The place where students are able to build this trust proves to be informal, individual relationships developed outside of a class context.

Indeed, virtually every student interviewed spoke about particular relationships developed in college where they enjoyed these conversations. Yet, we found that the nature of these conversations tended to come in two different forms. A divide existed between those students who experienced conversation and mentorship with faculty and other older mentors (upper class students, college staff or off-campus adults) and those who experienced these conversations with roommates and friends.

Older Mentors. In *The Heart of Higher Education*, coauthor Arthur Zajonc tells of his personal journey toward finding purpose in higher education. Along the way, he noted, "Had I not found a mentor, I would have left the university."[8] If most students were like Zajonc, our guess is that the universities would be much emptier. If our interviews are any indication, most students lack a mentor. Moreover, they may not even care. Ruby, a student at a Catholic university, recounted the common refrain we heard from most students regarding their professors,

> I don't really go to office hours or talk with my professors, but I feel like they're all really good people, like I would be able to have relationships with them. I just have conflicts with work, and the other activities I was involved with that I felt like I didn't have time to go to their office hours, but within the class I felt very comfortable approaching them if I had like a quick question.

As explored in the last chapter, while students respected faculty, most could not see ever seeking them out to talk about the larger issues of life.

In all, over half the students we interviewed could not name an adult mentor with whom they talk about issues of meaning and purpose. While we noted earlier that some students were quite satisfied living in the college world without input from older adults, some students expressed sadness or simply a lack of awareness to this part of their environment. Two students from a liberal arts college share a similar experience:

- "I don't have a lot of adults in my life here actually. That's interesting, I hadn't thought about that. No, there are very few adults in my life here."

- "I haven't really developed any meaningful adult relationships in my time here."

One student at the Ivy League shares that the basic message she received was "Here's the options, figure it out." She, herself, found this type of approach problematic, since she recognizes she needs help with relationships in general, including adult relationships, "I've had problems making friends, especially that of adults. Like, I'm not sure how to speak to them. . . . So I don't necessarily have close mentors. I can ask anyone a question. But I don't have that sort of guidance." The secular colleges contained most of the students without mentors, with the regional state university being particularly noteworthy for the disconnect between students and faculty. This last finding would appear to raise questions about Kronman's claim that the research ideal is the major factor to blame for the failure to address meaning.[9] Even at less research-intensive institutions, students lacked adult mentors.

The reason for this finding, we believe, relates to what we found out about adult mentors beyond faculty who discuss larger questions of meaning and purpose. Among those students who mention older mentors, the mentoring occurs in either a co-curricular dimension or in religious contexts outside the university. Allison, a student at a Baptist university, illustrates the typical mentoring scenario we found when asking students if they had mentors with whom they discussed matters of meaning and purpose. She said:

Definitely my small group leaders at church and my hall director that I've worked with for three years. Um, no real like professors or anything like that, but mostly just people at church or at work. . . . They've just been like a good support for me, I think, if I've ever gone through anything or talked to anyone where I'm kind of like questioning or wondering, like I'm pretty comfortable going to them to ask questions or just kind of process what I've been going through.

In light of the importance of trust that we described earlier, it should be no surprise that religious affiliation plays an important role in students finding mentors. Indeed, almost one-fifth of the students we interviewed named a pastor, rabbi, imam, a small religious group leader, or other religious individual as a mentor. For instance, Jasmine, a student at a public research university, speaks of one of the Christian group leaders of their student group on campus:

> I think, I could call her at, which I have, at two o'clock in the morning, and just be like, I need someone to talk to right now, if you're awake can I please come over. I live alone, so sometimes in college it gets lonely. I think her outlook on life and I think having someone older than you that's gone through something, or that's already graduated and is in a completely different stage in their life is encouraging, because I felt like sometimes as a college student I get so bogged down and, oh my gosh if I don't pass this test, if I don't get through tomorrow, the end of the world's basically gonna happen. To see someone that's gone through something very similar or someone that hasn't gone through that but has gone through other things that have led her to the thought process she has now is really encouraging for me, especially through her.

One of the distinctive features of the group who found mentoring within religious contexts was that they experience relational and programmatic encouragement to actually seek out older adults. A Mormon female student noted, "We have home teachers here, so they come over once a month and we discuss kind of topics of, like, life, you know, meaning and purpose, that they're definitely involved." This programmatic setup created a mentoring relationship among students. The home teachers,

> they would visit whatever girls they're assigned to, and they kind of become their friend, get to know them, see what they're struggling with, and then they kind of work on like the deeper issues of each other's lives, you kind of bring each other up, and then so you have this set of girls watching over you.

Another student from the evangelical university described a similar culture:

> I got involved in my church. They're really huge on discipleship, and I get that from my community here—people in my community group and [my] youth pastor . . . But they definitely do emphasize saying to the older men, "Hey, disciple these guys" or like, if we're

the single guys, they say to us and the married couples, like, "team up, talk to each other and figure out these questions of life and marriage and having a family."

The importance of religious communities for these discussions also extended to secular campuses. Mary, a first-year student at a public research university, shared:

Yeah, like kind of the structure of my Bible study is, it's run by people who've already graduated so most of them are like mid- to late-twenties—it's really cool because it's their job to spend time with us, to come pick us up and take us out to eat or get together at their houses and they're just like very welcoming and they're willing to just take time out of their day to sit down with you and just talk about whatever, so I would definitely include them.

In an environment where students do not trust going to faculty with their big questions and few other older adults are available, religion proved to be a major avenue for the provision of trusted older adult mentors.

Beyond religious contexts, the rest of the mentors identified by college students tended to be spread evenly among various types of co-curricular university staff such as resident assistants (6), campus group sponsors (6), and campus work supervisors (6). In these cases, mentorship did not occur through intentional efforts of the students; instead, the students happened into the relationships through the consistent contact with the mentors that occurred in a living, club, or work setting. Heather, a student at a Baptist university, observed,

One of our sponsors for the organization I'm a part of, he's someone who's just like a good friend to all of us and is always willing to talk about life and things that we're going through, so I've talked with him a lot about that kind of stuff.

In secular institutions, students mention finding these kinds of staff mentors only if the conversation focused on career. For instance, Dennis, a public university student, explained that his purpose was directly linked to finding a career that he loves, "Doing what you love for a career is very critical to my idea of purpose, and I have a career advisor who I've met with since the beginning of my sophomore year." In meeting with her about two or three times a month, he says that the "outward purpose of the meetings is very practical and utilitarian. We're making my resume look as good as it can to find a job." He continued by describing the effect of these meetings:

Having a job that I love is very important to finding my meaning in life. That seemingly practical purpose of the conversation lends itself to deep, philosophical discussions of why I want to do what I want to do for a career.

Dennis concluded by explaining, "Being able to feel a genuine connection and being able to open my heart and soul to her has been a big impact on my purpose."

If the conversation involved more than a student's future career, the religious institutional identity of the university as a whole (and not a particular kind of religious institution) mattered the most. For example, Kaitlyn, a student from a private Baptist university, shared:

> My two residence hall directors have been huge mentors that I've talked about purpose with. They are very encouraging and they encourage me to strive after what I'm passionate about. And they really challenge me to think: where do you think God wants you to be? They've always just really challenged me and really guided me.

Connecting these conversations to her sense of purpose, Kaitlyn explained:

> I am an RA, and that's really helped me understand that I see my purpose as helping people get closer to God. I'm really passionate about this and I've seen my hall directors do that for me.

In turn, Kaitlyn understood that "my conversations with my residents have been transformational for me, as well."

Marianna, a student at a Catholic research university, reflected on her relationship with one of her campus priests, explaining, "They understand what's going on, they live with these people who are our age, so I feel like they're really, really easy to talk to." She continued by describing a specific incidence, in which her sense of purpose was challenged:

> I went to my priest because I didn't know if I wanted to do something in business, but I saw all the business students applying for internships. I thought I wanted to do this poverty studies wing. He was someone nice to be able to talk it through with me. I would say things like, "I love leading a small group and talking about faith with people, and how to bring that into your everyday life," and he'd say, "Maybe that means something to you." He'd also say things like, "What kind of job can you do that takes that, and you can use that to create a career."

Again, we would note the importance of trust and a common worldview in facilitating these kinds of conversations. In a higher-education world that constantly espouses the importance of diversity, something should perhaps be said on behalf of commonality (which in reality is what many student groups and multicultural centers provide for minority groups). In these cases, students felt much more comfortable talking with those with similar beliefs about the big questions in life.

We should also note one thing we almost did not find. We only found one student who had a mentoring relationship with an adult that was not a relative, a university employee, or a religious leader. This student from the Lutheran liberal arts college, Chelsea, volunteered with a student club once a week at a retirement center. Through that experience, she established a relationship with someone she describes as "one of my closest friends." She noted that "I've had these conversations with her," but she explained that it was only because of her own outlook, "just because I value the input of people who are older than me because they've seen more of life than I have and they can often point out mistakes that I'm making." Chelsea's experience appeared to be quite unusual among students, many of whom, apart from interaction with professors, remain cut off from the world of older adults.

Roommates and Friends. Ruby's story also provides an example of what we found with students when it came to peers. While she did not talk with professors, she noted, "I think where I found the most mentoring was in our little dorm group where I felt free to ask questions about stuff I was exploring in my life. It was an RA that led it." Fellow students and nonadult mentors proved to be the most formative relational influence for students in this area. In fact, Ruby claimed, "I guess having someone to mentor me is not something I usually seek. I enjoy just crashing in someone's room and just talking." The same would be true for most of the students we interviewed. The vast majority of participants in the 110 student study (94) mentioned participation in intentional conversations with peers about their sense of purpose. This experience proved consistent no matter what the institutional type. For instance, Sabrina, a student at a Jewish research university, described her relationship with her roommate as one that provided both support and challenge in this area: "We talk about purpose a lot, too . . . at the end [of our conversation] we don't agree on [purpose], but we're still fine." She continued by saying, "One of my favorite things about this school is how many different people are here—everyone talks about purpose, but everyone has so many different ideas about it. Look at me and my roommate!" If colleges move to single occupancy dorm rooms, students would miss quite a bit of development in this area because they often talk about these matters with roommates.

These types of conversations about purpose mainly revolved around the future, religion, and developmental struggles. One-third of our students recalled specific conversations about the future that focused on purpose. These conversations focused either on a general discussion about the future, as Katie, a public regional university student, shared: "My friends and I, we definitely talk about our futures a lot and like our plans of studying and what we hope to accomplish here," or students mention specific conversations about their future career plans and how those relate to a developing sense of purpose. Matt, a regional research university student, commented on his friendship with a fellow student in his major, as he explains:

> My major [speech communications and public relations] is a good field to get into because I can really use it for almost any aspect of life, and [my friend who has this same major] has influenced me in this. I would say she's had an impact on my purpose because she's just one of those people that lives out this major and really wants to see it become something.

By having these encouraging conversations with his friend, Matt explained that his purpose has "become more real" to him, and concluded by saying, "It's just like I've been able to pursue it better."

Finally, students also reported meaningful conversations with peers about the purpose of college itself. Mark, a student at the same university as Matt, explained, "My freshman year, I was doing a lot of questioning like why I was at my institution, why I made that decision, if I wanted to stay." Speaking of his friendships, he noted, "I've talked a lot about my purpose with them, and what I'm involved in here, and if I even want to stay, has all factored into that." For students like Mark, having a group of friends to discuss the current purpose of the university with has been helpful to understand a larger sense of purpose, even if it is, as yet, unrealized.

Another quarter of the students mentioned specific conversations with friends or roommates about religion and how a certain set of religious beliefs affects one's sense of purpose. Understandably, more of these conversations came from students at the faith-based institutions and marked one of the distinctives of these campuses; at two of the secular campuses, none of the students we interviewed mentioned these types of conversations. Nathan, a religious university student, explained, "We'll just be doing our homework and suddenly someone's like, 'You know . . . if God is . . . ,' and just, like, goes off on something, and we'll talk about it for a little while." He comments about the effect of these conversations on his sense of purpose, which he understands to be honoring God, and notes, "the discussions that we've had about religion helped me to understand my own purpose better." Madeline, a private, regional university student, repeated Nathan's thoughts in a similar manner: "My roommate is very wonderful at talking about purpose and life, and we've had some good discussions about it." She saw her purpose in religious terms and believed that getting involved in church is part of her purpose. Through conversations with her roommate, she had seen that

> Some students encourage people to go to chapel every Sunday and be more involved in the church, but every weekend they go out partying until four in the morning and have premarital sex. When they tell people not to, and when their actions don't follow what they're telling people to do, I think it's confusing to people that aren't set in their purpose.

Madeline concluded, "These are the types of conversations that I have with her. I want to find out what it means to live in a purpose-driven manner."

A sixth of the students also spoke specifically about a growing discovery of purpose in the midst of sharing difficulties with roommates and friends. David, a student at a religious university, explained his sense of purpose as "wanting to help people" and connected his conversations with his friends to this developing sense of purpose. He noted:

> Having conversations with some of the friends I've made here who have been going through harder times or friends who've been stressed out, by being able to be there for them and speaking to them has really been wonderful. Then, seeing afterwards how they feel better and seeing how a weight has been lifted off their shoulders by talking to me has definitely, *definitely* affirmed my belief of like what I want to do and how I want to help people.

David connected his experience of "being a good friend" to a larger sense of purpose of helping others and "being there" for them. Similarly, Alisson, a Baptist university student, explained her current purpose in life as "being there" for people she cares about, especially when they are going through hard times. Exemplifying this point, she described her current relationship with her roommate, "this past semester—my roommate has been going through difficult stuff relationally with her boyfriend, and going through a faith crisis." She continued, "A lot of times we are randomly getting ready for the day or are having nothing to do, so we just kind of start talking about, amidst the pain, and stuff like that, like what is the purpose of life. . . ." She concluded by stating that she found it important for her to practice, "affirming each other and encouraging each other in our life purpose—even though it's hard."

Overall, the relational influences in the co-curricular dimension of students' lives functioned in a similar, yet distinct way from the organizational influences. While the organizational influences helped students voluntarily connect with a group of interested others around a common purpose, the social influences provided sounding boards for their ideas and helped them develop an initial language to articulate their purpose.

Interestingly, among the few students who reported a failure to engage with others regarding their meaning and purpose, the core problem appeared to be a perceived lack of personal fit within the relational culture of the school. James, a private faith-based university student, explained this effect in the following manner: "I have noticed that, at least here at [my university], it seems more like high school 2.0 where it's very clique-y." He continued, "Community is talked a lot about, but my experience of community has something that was very different." James commented that he expected his university to provide an "intentional community where people do life together, but it might just be harder here." James concluded, "It's big, and I guess I feel small in how big my university is." He understood his purpose as "serving God," but was confused because, "You know, the world is so big." He asked somewhat dejectedly, "How can God care about each one of us when there are so many people out there?"

Leslie, a religious, research university student, echoed James's sentiments. "I thought that a lot more students were going to be involved in the campus and there was going to be more unity in the school." She explained, "It really isn't like that. A lot of students know people from back home, and I'm just sitting there while people around me talk about people from their high schools." She commented on not being able to participate in those conversations, and concluded by saying, "I'm ready to move on from high school. I'm really wondering if my purpose is to be at this *specific* school, or if I shouldn't be somewhere else."

Interestingly, four of the twelve students who mentioned this issue were from the Ivy League institution. Emilee, one of the Ivy League students, commented, "I think my views on purpose feel different to the ideas other people hold to, so sometimes I wonder if I'm not getting it." She explained that this caused her to question her own sense of purpose, as she related, "I ask myself if I should just stick with what I believe in or go with what they want?" These questions frustrate her and cause her to ask herself, "What's the point of all this?"

> I wish I had sought out schools that like fit me as a person, just because I'm accepted officially here, doesn't mean I'm accepted by the social realm, or automatically accepted into like the academic realm. I feel like almost every moment is like another hurdle where I had to prove something. It's really distracting from me finding out my overall purpose.

These organizational and social barriers do not necessarily cause students to disengage from purpose development, but they do contribute to a feeling of purpose*less*ness and act as discouragers from this overall quest.

Social Media. Since college students spend much of their time communicating through social media, one of the questions we asked our 110 Focused Qual group concerned the degree to which they explore or discuss matters of purpose through social media. We found the topic produced a variety of opinions about social media usage as a forum for discussions about big questions. Students could be divided into four types: (1) the non-purpose users, (2) the bystanders, (3); the active participants, and (4) and those who saw a problem or limit with using social media for big question discussions.

The largest group of students simply did not use social media for these matters. They used it for casual socializing, sharing pictures, talking about parties, doing homework, catching up on the latest gossip, keeping up with family, checking the news, and more. In contrast, when it came to meaning and purpose, as one student put it, "I don't use that as a way to get moral guidance." Social media, for these students, was a bit too public. As Troy, an atheist student said, "I just don't feel like it's necessary for other people to know that type of stuff. Like, if you talk to them personally . . . you don't need to broadcast it. I don't post any, any religious, antireligious things, or atheist things."

The second group was best described by one student who said she was "like a bystander reading information." Another student put the same concept into economic language, "I'm more of a consumer." One student even described it in less flattering biological terms, "I'm kind of like a parasite on Facebook; I just watch everybody else and don't really post anything myself." The bystanders (which we prefer to call them) did not actively participate in debates about meaning and purpose through social media, but they might use social media to read about others' active engagement with issues of meaning and purpose. For example, one student shared, "I'll follow different people on Twitter that I think talk about subjects that I find important." The bystander attitude also influenced the degree of authority this group would place in what they observed. Brock, the self-described "consumer" mentioned above, observed:

> Generally what I read in blogs or Facebook, for the most part I don't give [them] much authority. So if I disagree with it, then I don't feel like it's coming from a reliable source 'cause I don't know this person, or if I do agree with it, that doesn't necessarily give credence to my own beliefs, because once again I don't know them. I have no rapport. I have no, you know, history. . . . It sounds bad, but why should I respect that opinion. . . . ?

Interestingly, the fact that he did not know some of the sources personally contributed to his skepticism.

The third group we labeled Active Users. Composed of about one-sixth of the students, they deeply engaged in such conversations and could be shaped by them in profound ways. As Tyson, a public research university student told one of us, "There's actually a lot of serious philosophical debates that go on there, besides the funny pictures of dogs." The actual source and nature of the discussion varied. One student named Ray noted, "Even before coming here I used to have intellectual discussions on Facebook, and people used to mock me for that. I mean, of course, in a very friendly manner, but there were some people who used to really mock me and tease me because of that." Another student referred to a particular website

> Have you heard of "Good," the website? It's like good.org, and it's just like a collection of good things going on in the world, like, innovative entrepreneur type of things, so they have a lot, anything from any study of prosthetics that are coming out, how to cultivate more green farming, more sustainability, and like soybean planting.

The student behaved almost as a salesperson for the site. "It is more like just sharing it and just saying, like, 'Hey look at this, I think it's cool, you should look at it too,' but then that's how I found how to have a good conversation with people, because I'll be like, 'Oh I saw that, like, what do you think about it?' Or maybe they'll write 'I can agree with this.'" Still another student mentioned, "Well I'm a Tumblr fan and my blog is on Tumblr." She told us about how someone can type in tag words and then whatever a blogger has written with that label is automatically retrieved. She herself typed in a word associated with one of the sources of meaning and purpose, "Usually the word I type in the most is happy, just because I like to see what's making other people happy, and that usually, like, brightens my day." She did note that you have to be discerning about the responses. "Some are questionable, like of course there are people putting stuff up about like drugs and whatnot, then people like put pictures of food, or they just like go on a rant about their day or take a nice picture of something."

The influence of this kind of engagement turned out to be quite profound for a student named Chase we will profile in chapter 11. He recounted,

> I think that a lot of my kind of loss of faith was precipitated by looking on the internet for things; I mean I was reading about science obviously, but you know you find yourself, there's no shortage of religious debate on the Internet for one thing . . . The use of the Internet, the fact there were so many different viewpoints and so many people strongly defending their viewpoints in ways I was unable to do really kind of pushed me in that direction. So it wasn't as if I was necessarily looking for reasons to lose my faith or anything, it was just, you know, as you begin to ask questions and seek answers, the answers you were given just called forth a hundred more questions

and because the Internet just gave you access, instant access to the answers to those questions and information about beliefs, and history, and, religion and all these things, I think that had a profound impact on the way I thought about religion.

Yet, while Chase found his former religious worldview undermined by the Internet, he said he did not necessarily see it as a source for a new worldview. He claimed, "I wouldn't seek the answers to like 'what's the meaning of life?'" through Google. Those are questions that I think about and I contemplate myself, but I don't expect some stranger on the Internet to have an answer for me." Ironically, he did find that viewing the plethora of answers from strangers to other religious questions undermined his former religious faith.

Finally, the smallest group of students consisted of the critics. These students saw a problem with using social media for serious discussions, particularly about the big questions of life. As one student told us, "Facebook is not the place for intellectual debates." Another noted, "The Internet, I don't really use as a medium for . . . voicing my own opinion. I mean, on all levels would rather do that in person." The last student, Erin, learned her lesson the hard way. "No, I sent an e-mail to my headmaster saying, 'Fuck off.' I thought it was his son. We were all brand new to the school—it was really uncomfortable. But he was very nice about it." The lesson has ramifications that continue to this day. "I do not put anything in a text message, I don't put anything in an e-mail, you know, . . . I've grown up being very careful about that ever since—it was a great lesson. I thank him often."

Another student named Max shunned social media as a source for conversations less from a bad experience in the past and more about his own critique of the sources,

> I mean Facebook and some of those other social media sites and a lot of the stuff on the Internet really is the polar opposite of what the good life is. There is a lot of bad stuff out there that you see. People engaging in and news stories about and a lot of negativity for like a lot of things.

Max admitted that one could find some good in social media.

> There are always these like little gems of, you know, occasionally a Facebook post will consist of inspiring story about, I don't know, a young boy or a dog or something, or a you'll see some of your old friends from high school who are now engaged and that's inspiring, and you're happy for them.

Still, he himself had concluded that social media was not a helpful source of inspiration or discussion about the good life.

Tracking the Influence of the
Co-Curricular in National Survey Data

Just as we did in the previous chapter with student-faculty measures, we now turn to explore how a limited number of co-curricular measures influence the search for meaning and purpose using the College Students' Religious Beliefs and Values survey.[10] Again, as noted in the last chapter with regard to the CSBV data, measuring whether a student is seeking meaning and purpose is different from measuring whether they currently have meaning and purpose or whether they experience discussions about meaning and purpose. The data contain measures of participation in a campus religious organization, the frequency with which faculty act as spiritual models for students, and the frequency with which students discuss matters of religion and spirituality with their friends.[11] All of these measures were asked during the spring semester of students' junior year in college.

The impact of the first measure—a simple "yes/no" response to whether or not the student had participated in a campus religious organization—can be found in figure 9.1. About 20 percent of all students report attending a campus religious organization at one point during their college career (although this ranges from 16 percent at public institutions to 43 percent at evangelical colleges). As we expected from our interviews, this measure is associated with

Figure 9.1. Percent change in actively searching for meaning/purpose in life by participation in campus religious organization, weighted (*N* = 13,271)

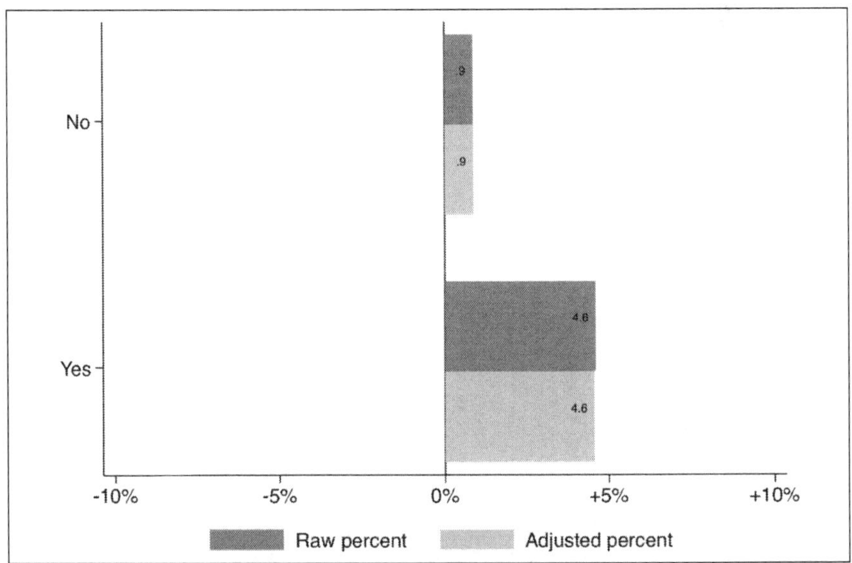

Source: College Students' Beliefs and Values Survey, 2004–2007.

Note: Adjusted percent controls for age, sex, race, parents' income, parents' educational attainment, citizenship status, family structure, high school GPA, and high school type.

a slight uptick in actively searching for meaning and purpose in life among students (4.6 percent increase for those who participate, 0.9 percent for those who do not). But the differences are relatively small, and they do not reach the standard levels of statistical significance in our models ($p < .05$). We also know very little about what *type* of religious organization the students are participating in and how *active* the students are in these organizations. If we had additional measures we might be able to parse out some of these differences.

Our next measure—how often students report their faculty members acting as spiritual models for them—connects to the adult mentoring we explored in our interviews. Unfortunately there were no additional measures of adult mentorship outside of the faculty-student relationship available to us in the survey data. Consistent with our interviews, most students in the survey report that faculty never act in this way (72 percent), and only about one in twenty report that their faculty members "frequently" provide this sort of mentorship. There are substantial institutional differences here though—with evangelical colleges being a noticeable outlier again. At evangelical colleges, half of the students say their faculty members do this "frequently," and only 7 percent claim they never do this. By comparison, only 2 percent of public university students claim their faculty do this "frequently," and 82 percent say they never act as spiritual models. Does this sort of modeling influence the student search for meaning and purpose in life? Figure 9.2. tells us

Figure 9.2. Percent change in actively searching for meaning/purpose in life by frequency of faculty acting as spiritual models, weighted ($N = 13{,}163$)

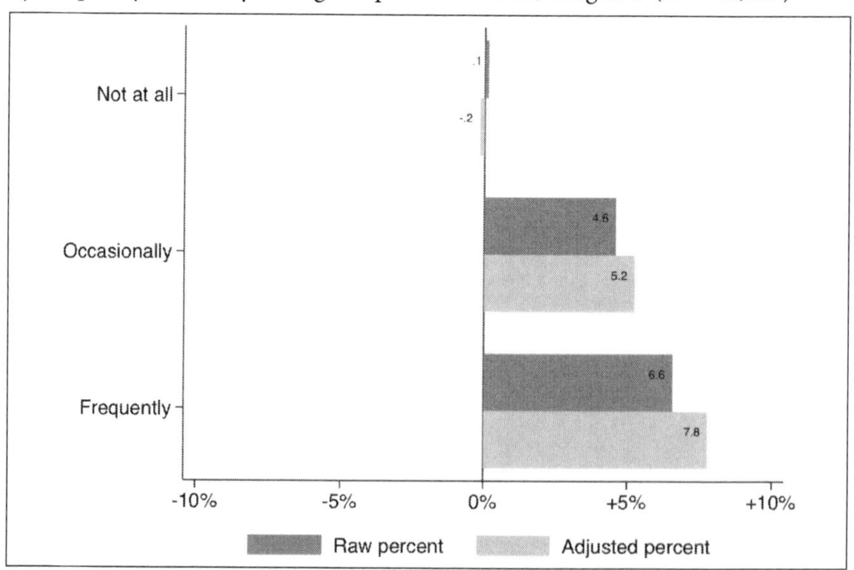

Source: College Students' Beliefs and Values Survey, 2004–2007.

Note: Adjusted percent controls for age, sex, race, parents' income, parents' educational attainment, citizenship status, family structure, high school GPA, and high school type.

that it does. The main difference here is between the large "not at all" group and everyone else. The 28 percent that say that faculty do this at least "occasionally" are more likely to take up actively searching for meaning and purpose in life according to our models.

The last variable measures informal student relationships. How often do students report discussing religion or spirituality with friends? Around 20 percent say they do this frequently. The majority says they do this occasionally (63 percent), and about 17 percent say they never engage in these kinds of conversations with their friends. Again, there are institutional differences, with at least twice the proportion of students at evangelical colleges (65 percent) frequently engaging their friends this way compared to any other type of institution. And, as figure 9.3 reveals, this is where the major impact on actively searching comes from. Those that frequently discuss religion and spirituality with their friends show an increase of nearly 9 percent for actively seeking meaning/purpose between their first and third years of college.

We want to reiterate the caution we extended in the previous chapter. These figures do not necessarily tell us about causal direction. Students who become interested in thinking about meaning and purpose in life may very well begin to bring these types of topics up with their friends in conversations. It is nearly impossible to convincingly demonstrate that one is reliably

Figure 9.3. Percent change in actively searching for meaning/purpose in life by frequency of religious/spiritual discussions with friends, weighted ($N = 13,245$)

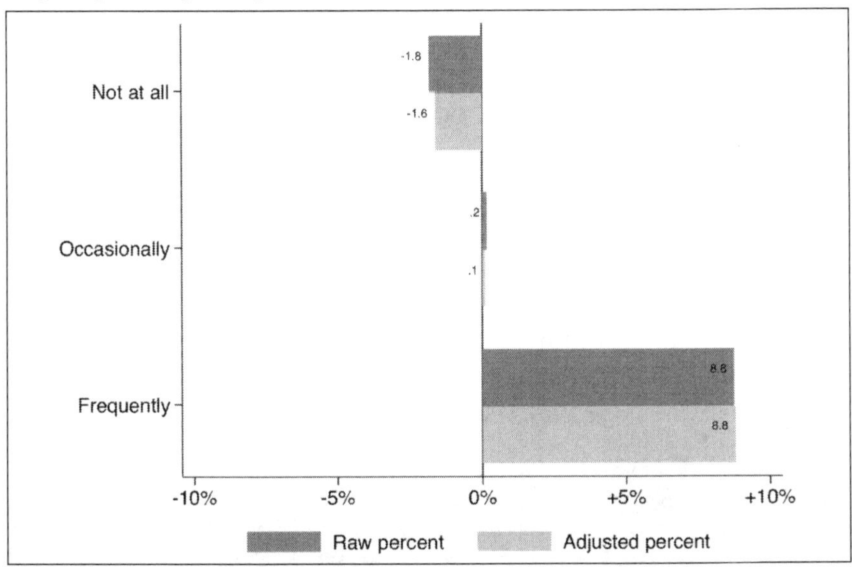

Source: College Students' Beliefs and Values Survey, 2004–2007.

Note: Adjusted percent controls for age, sex, race, parents' income, parents' educational attainment, citizenship status, family structure, high school GPA, and high school type.

causing the other. Still, as the CSBV data show, they *do* tend to come packaged together.

Evangelical colleges, quite consistently, were outliers on many of these measures. More participated in campus religious organizations, more students reported that their professors acted as spiritual models, and more report frequently talking to their friends about religion and spirituality. Catholic colleges and universities, although having somewhat higher values on a few of these measures, were not substantially different from other private institutions. Public universities consistently scored lowest on all of these measures. How much, then, do these co-curricular factors explain institutional-level differences in students actively searching for meaning and purpose? As we did in the previous chapter with other measures, we ran models that controlled for these co-curricular factors (along with the standard demographic controls) to see if they explain the "gap" between different types of institutions. The results, in figure 9.4, tell us that these three co-curricular factors explain most of the evangelical college

Figure 9.4. Percent change in actively searching for meaning/purpose in life by institutional type, including additional controls for co-curricular activity, weighted (*N* = 13,138)

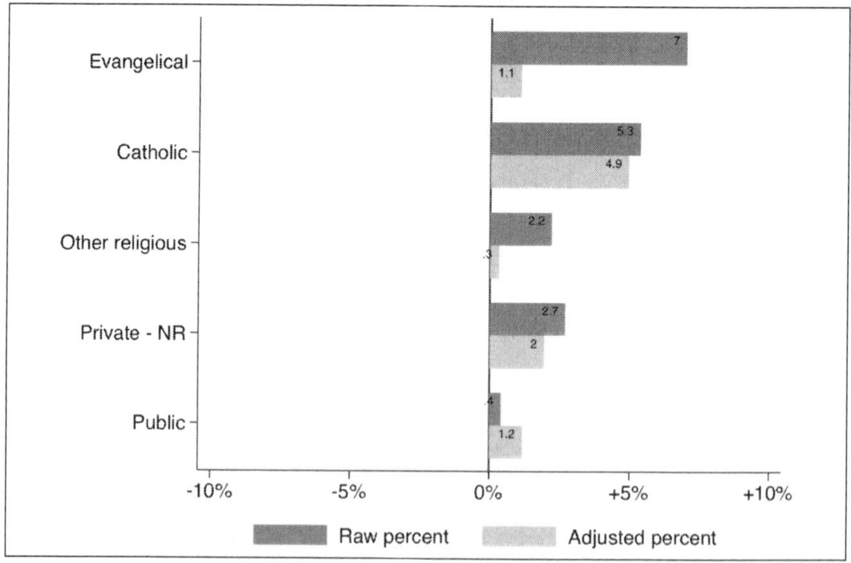

Source: College Students' Beliefs and Values Survey, 2004–2007.

Note: Adjusted percent controls for participation in a campus religious organization, frequency of professors acting as spiritual models, frequency of discussing religion/spirituality with friends, age, sex, race, parents' income, parents' educational attainment, citizenship status, family structure, high school GPA, and high school type.

gap but little of the Catholic college gap. The 7 percentage point increase in active seekers at evangelical schools goes down to 1.1 percent once these three factors are controlled for. Catholic institutions only drop slightly from 5.3 to 4.9 percent. This tells us that, between the factors in this chapter and the previous chapter, we've largely been able to account for why evangelical colleges successfully increase in their students a desire to actively seek out meaning and purpose in life. On the other hand, we haven't been very successful in explaining the same for Catholic colleges.

Conclusion

Parks' claims that the ideal co-curricular environment would be a "mentoring community" in which students would be engaged in intentional conversations about purpose.[12] In our interviews, students' experiences of how the co-curricular world mentors and supports their search for purpose, however, proved uneven. When it comes to discussions with professors outside the classroom, unless the students share a somewhat similar worldview (e.g., the evangelical institutions), there is reluctance and even resistance to talking about these matters with professors outside of class. The idea that students would gladly engage in these matters if only professors addressed them (but they are too busy with research or constricted by narrow cultural expectations such as political correctness), we found, is not necessarily true.

Overall, older adults with whom they have intimate conversations about these matters become scarcer during the college years. Indeed, less than half have adult mentors with whom they discuss these matters. Most of these trusted mentors are acquired in religious settings or with the staff of a university where they develop more intimate relationships and experiences. The institutional context, as our CSBV survey analysis shows, appears to play the most difference when discussing relationships with university faculty and staff. In light of the fact that it is largely students at the evangelical university who find support for holistic development, we wonder whether the claim that religious institutions provide holistic student development may need to be modified slightly.[13] We suspect that while such support is found among staff, it is largely found among faculty at smaller religious liberal arts colleges or universities where publishing pressures are limited and mission and administrative support exists for holistic forms of faculty care that include addressing questions of purpose with students outside of class. Another recent study has also supported this claim.[14]

Yet, when it comes to peer discussions, an important change still does take place in college, which is not that surprising. Whereas before students talked with their parents about purpose and meaning, and maybe a select high school teacher or youth group leader, college is the first time for many that they begin to talk about issues of meaning and purpose beyond these trusted relationships. Still, they primarily only engage in these discussions in trusted venues with their peers.

In many cases, these discussions occur in the midst of student organizations. When students voluntarily engage with like-minded others in mission-focused and morally formative organizations, they experience the greatest degree of purpose discovery and development. Evidence for this finding emerges from students at a variety of institutional types. This finding fits with Astin et al.'s claim that the degree with which a student is involved in their environment, *in a meaningful manner*, affects the students' development of meaning and purpose.[15] In an earlier study, Astin maintained, "the amount of student learning and personal development associated with any educational program is directly proportional to the quality and quantity of student involvement to that program."[16] The findings in this study highlight both the *qualitative* and *voluntary* dimension of Astin's theory.[17] The qualitative dimension is especially important as those who are more involved in the environment, literally "busier," did not necessarily have an automatically deeper connection to the development of their purpose. With an ever-increasing focus of simply "getting our students involved," higher-education leaders may need to help students involve themselves in ways that allow for maximum development of meaning and purpose, rather than maximum time spent "being involved."

Students experience the most purpose development when they converse with friends and roommates about their futures, their worldviews, and their developmental struggles. These findings reflect the developmental process that Baxter-Magolda describes as a major piece of student purpose development: "the capacity to internally define a coherent belief system and identity that coordinates engagement in mutual relations with the larger world."[18] Relational encounters help students define their beliefs and identities through clarifying conversations that shine a light on their larger purpose.

Overall, if a university, including its staff and professors, wishes to help students toward a deeper understanding of meaning and purpose, this study provides some helpful insights into how to provide that support.[19] The most obvious implications for practice are quite straightforward. If universities want to help students develop purpose in the co-curricular, they should support a robust array of mission-driven, morally-formative student groups, opportunities for adult mentoring from faculty and staff, and space for deep conversations with roommates and friends. One of the worst things to do would be to fail to give students roommates and allow students to isolate themselves. Indeed, recent research consistently links social connectedness with a series of important prosocial and positive outcomes that often focus on service to others.[20]

Conversely, isolation tends to be correlated with self-absorbed and narcissistic behavior that can lead to depression, abuse of alcohol or drugs, or other self-destructive behavior.[21]

Our study also confirms the necessary impact of peers in a student's development of purpose, as the vast majority of students cite specific conversations with peers that helped to define their purpose in a deeper manner. Student affairs professionals would do well to keep this "mentoring community" in mind, carving out intentional space for these conversations to occur, and giving students permission to have these conversations freely and openly. Indeed, it is largely in the groups and relationships that students create that they experience purpose development. In fact, students rarely mention top-down, co-curricular programming as an influence on their purpose development, except in the context of personal advising types of relationships.

As the previous two chapters revealed, one of the places that students find trusted mentors, peers, and discussions about meaning and purpose is in a religious context. Moreover, as chapter 6 revealed, religious (or nonreligious) identity, belief, and behavior all play a crucial role in determining whether students support certain purposes or not. Thus, the next two chapters attempt to explore the role that both religious and nonreligious identity, beliefs, and actions play in students' development of meaning and purpose.

Part IV

The Heart, Hope, and Soul of Purpose

Chapter 10

Purpose with Soul

The Religious

As a religious person there's got to be meaning.
There's got to be purpose.

—Jacob, student at a Jewish university

Why is there purpose if there is nothing that created us? If we're just a product of years of evolution, and we're the highest type of human in history, what gives us purpose? Do we have a purpose just because we're humans and we're the smartest? Like, we're the best species, therefore we have purpose?

Paul, an African-American student at an evangelical university, voices these questions to one of us when explaining his outlook toward purpose. Although Paul shares that he went through an earlier agnostic phase, he now describes himself as a Christian. Part of the reason is that he believes the nontheistic point of view fails to provide satisfactory answers to the questions he's raising.

Paul attributes part of the agnostic phase to some events during adolescence. His parents divorced when he was "late-middle-schoolish," leaving him and his mother quite impoverished. "I was definitely angry. . . . divorces are messy, and so for some time I couldn't talk to one parent, like, just even legally." The result was that during middle school "there was a period of time where I didn't believe in God or didn't think we could know, kind of like [an] agnostic view." Later, though, he found the theistic viewpoint "made the most sense to me."

As noted by the quote above, one of the reasons for his theistic view has to do with the fact that theism provides answers to the question of purpose. Another has to do with morality. "It doesn't seem logical to me. If I didn't believe there was a God, or even like something that created everything, there's no standard of right or wrong." Interestingly, at the end of the interview, Paul wants to make sure he was understood correctly regarding nontheists, "I do think they can be happy, and I think they can definitely live good, moral lives." He now just finds their answers to questions about purpose and "why be good?" unsatisfactory.

Paul actually credits the divorce with forcing him to think through his own worldview. "That was difficult, but I think it like formed the way that I think and especially my faith. I think that's the time when it grew the most. I can take it as my own rather than my parents." In fact, he saw himself having to come to his own beliefs earlier in life than many of his peers. "I feel like that was an independent time. My good friend and I had like our like concrete viewpoints, and the rest of our friends were like, 'Wait, we shouldn't disbelieve what our parents think . . .'"

This does not mean that Paul does not attribute any of his beliefs to his parents. In fact, he attributes a key shift in his own beliefs regarding Christianity to his mother's own faith journey from when she "kind of transitioned from Lutheran to just kind of like no religion, like no faith, and then to Christianity." He says he used to believe "that God is to provide for what I need and what I want, you know? More like a personal life satisfaction, like 'I'll have a good job' kind of thing." Now, he claims that he views "the bigger picture," which specifically includes "helping others." He claims his mother communicated the following example: "My purpose in prayer shouldn't be, 'Oh let me have a comfortable life and a good husband and be able to travel, and happy kids,' you know?"

He would suggest that this change in outlook was set in motion particularly by his mother's example and how she handled living in poverty.

> We struggled financially, and it was like a lot of [my] hopes [were] like, "Okay this year, God will relieve me. We'll have financial stability and be able to have this." But the way my mom prayed about it was that so we could bless others too. I don't think I really caught onto that until [later]. It was our lifestyle to live paycheck to paycheck [and] to understand, to see we were still happy. My mom does a lot of nonprofit work, and even just personally choosing to help the community, and see how we're so happy to be able to help. We had enough to eat and we had a place to live, and that kind of life transformed [my faith] from like a personal, just my own satisfaction, to helping others.

One of the effects of poverty on Paul's older three siblings was that not one was able to attend college. Paul, himself, became the first one in his family to attend college.

Paul's expression of his faith clearly fits within the evangelical university he attends. He summarizes his beliefs as the following:

> I understand that God created the world, created us and the universe and that there's like a gap between us and God because of sin . . . nothing we can do, like our own works or our good deeds, could get us back into relationship with God, and that He sent His son, Christ, to pay for our sins and that, like, that God is just and that sins have a penalty. The penalty is death, and that Christ took on our penalty and the wrath has been put on him, and he died and he rose again.

Despite this worldview alignment with the evangelical university, Paul did not originally want to a go to a Christian school. Having attended a public high school in another region of the country where he was good friends with Muslims, agnostics, and atheists, he initially thought he wanted a school that might challenge his beliefs. At one point, he says he thought, "I'm gonna go look for the most liberal school I can find." Yet, in the end, "once it came like down to the wire . . . I really, I felt like [his university] was the environment I should put myself in, even if it was gonna be people who think similarly." At times he wishes he would have gone to a different university,

> where I was uncomfortable and have to be like confronted with different opinions, and be able to like defend mine and really think of good arguments and be able to listen to what they have to say, like really listen to them, like I really like those kinds of discussions.

Yet, he also appreciates the strengths that being at an evangelical university offers:

> I'm grateful to be here because I can fully understand my faith and what the history behind it is, and where it comes from . . . I can clarify a lot of things I had questions about. . . . I can talk to the theologians who helped produce that kind of stuff and they can ask me questions to help me understand what I'm thinking too so I can process things.

One of those things includes matters of meaning and purpose. Not surprisingly, he identifies with the Transcendent approach. "I would say probably my faith gives life meaning for me." When explaining this perspective, he points to the way that it situates his life in a larger story:

> [I] understand that my life isn't an independent thing in history, like
> I go from when I was born to when I die and that's how, whatever
> story happened, happened. That it's kind of woven into a bigger pic-
> ture of the plan that God has for His children and for His people. I
> think that's what like gives my life meaning. I can understand [that]
> day-to-day my interaction with people counts. The way I treat people
> means something.

Paul admits he does not necessarily relish experiencing challenging parts of this story. "I don't enjoy the fact, thinking about when I go through something diffi-cult that it has a purpose, that a purpose can come out of it, even though it might not be good or planned for that to happen." Even with the tragic consequences of his parent's divorce, he took this outlook. "I knew God had His hand over their lives, and what about me and my siblings? We can do something in the world, too." Specifically, Paul believes his purpose involves a particular calling. "I really want to teach English around the Middle East. . . . I really love their culture, and I'm learning Arabic and it's close to my home, my parents' home country." Paul's parents, he notes, are actually recent immigrants from northeast Africa.

Since Paul finds both his meaning and purpose shaped by his particular religious worldview, he understands himself as different from many of his others peers. He ruminates,

> When I compare to my friends in high school who had talked about
> [these] things, my outcome and my goal isn't materialistic or fame or
> something superficial that's not going to satisfy you, but something
> that glorifies God. I don't know. It just seems like a backwards way of
> thinking when you compare it to the world, of not being so obsessed
> with like my personal gain, but just doing good.

At the evangelical university, Paul is one of those students, like the students described in chapter 8, who appreciates the role of his professors in helping him think through his purpose and his faith in general. He finds the professors embracing difficult discussions.

> They throw different ideas at us. They give us something to really
> think about, and there's not a straight answer to it right away. I think
> they do a good job of giving dignity and validity to other worldviews
> or other perspectives.

He gave an example of one professor who challenges evangelical students on issues such as environmental stewardship.

> In the class the professor was like really pushing toward that, and I
> was just like, "Yeah, I'm glad you're saying this," but the consensus
> in the classroom is that like, maybe it's not that important, maybe
> we should just disregard it, and I did not even know that existed
> within a Christian community.

He not only appreciates the fact that the professor pushes the students to examine their beliefs in various areas, but he also senses a freedom to explore a variety of issues, including what he believes about meaning and purpose. Moreover, he receives encouragement from professors to undertake this exploration,

> They genuinely want to hear our opinions. They normally want us
> to ask questions . . . and they're not going to think we're crazy if
> we're not believing [their views] just because they said it, you know,
> but they want us to pick at it and find a fallacy if there is one in it.

What Paul also appreciates is that this concern with students' development extends beyond their intellectual views in the classroom. He shares how one professor asked for prayer requests at the end of an assignment. He thought, "That's crazy," but he saw it as crazy in a good way, "he's not limiting it to just the content of the class and like, don't give me any other junk of your life, you know, so that was really amazing . . . They care for us holistically." Being able to question and wrestle with life's big questions with professors who care about him as a person meant a lot.

Paul expresses a bit more mixed opinion regarding his experience with his fellow students. He had experienced a significant amount of ideological diversity in high school and still keeps in touch with his Muslim, agnostic, and atheist friends. Yet, he finds some resistance among some students to what he considers some ideas from outside,

> like talking about gay marriage or stuff like that. . . . in high school,
> my friends bring up good points and that I still think about them,
> and so I bring it up here, and they . . . don't want me to bring that
> up because it gives a good light to this idea you know, and I think
> we should discuss those.

Paul also reveals though that

> there's a really good population [of students] here . . . I think it's
> kind of like any other environment you go to, kind of have to seek
> out people who want to really pick at their brains, and they want

to like pick your brains and then you get to the depth of an issue, not just like a superficial answer we all know.

Overall, despite some weak spots, Paul appreciates how his university experience at the evangelical university shapes multiple dimensions of his exploration of big life questions including meaning and purpose.

The Difference that Religion Makes

We know that religious identity, especially the nature and quality of a person's religious commitment, makes an important difference in his or her understanding of purpose.[1] Religious identity, belief (e.g., believing in God), and practices (e.g., praying and regularly reading the Bible) have all been shown to be positively correlated with higher degrees of purpose.[2] As noted earlier, a positive relationship between religion and some form of purpose has been found for adolescents, college students, emerging adults, and adults.[3] For example, Christian Smith found that "the most religious [emerging adults] . . . appear to have the most purpose in life, while the least [religious emerging adults] have the least purpose."[4] Similarly, Stephen Cranney discovered that "those who indicate that they are confident in God's existence report a higher sense of purpose compared to nonbelievers, believers in a higher power, and those who believe but occasionally doubt."[5] In addition, scholars have identified that being spiritual or religious correlates with a greater sense of purpose on certain purpose scales.[6] While this correlation exists when individuals simply identify as religious or spiritual, scholars have also found that the depth of religious belief also increases the way in which a person's religious beliefs relates to his or her understanding of purpose.[7] David Myers has also suggested that the purpose provided by a religious belief system may explain why religious respondents score higher on measures of happiness.[8]

The obvious follow-up question to all these studies is: Why do religious students have greater purpose? In a recent study of the correlation between religion and purpose, Cranney noted that, "ultimately the why behind this relationship is unknown."[9] Scholars lack of understanding of the role that particular religious or theological beliefs play is perhaps not surprising. Peterson and Seligman have attested that the field of spirituality, religiousness, faith, and purpose studies would "benefit from more substantive attention to the role of theology in shaping core beliefs, attitudes, behaviors, and psychological as well as physical health outcomes experienced by religious individuals."[10] Do particular theological or metaphysical beliefs shape students' views of purpose, and if so, in what way? For example, Paul's meaning and purpose were shaped less by certain beliefs that might be associated with a particular denomination, or even Evangelical Christianity, and more by general theistic beliefs relating to God's ultimate control of the universe and a faith that his own life somehow finds meaning in this larger narrative. Is this often the case?

Scholars appear to be a bit divided on this matter, although the reason is likely that they approach the issue focusing on whether a person claims to have a substantive purpose or whether they indicate they are questing for purpose. Christian Smith found that a particular religious identity (e.g., Baptist, Hindu, etc.) made less difference than the general level of religious commitment. He identified four types of religious: the devoted, the regulars, the sporadic, and the disengaged. The differences pertained to religious service attendance, participation in other activities (prayer, reading of sacred texts), feeling of closeness to God, and the importance of faith. Smith did not offer any particular theory about why this might be the case.

In contrast, Astin, Astin, and Lindholm did find that specific religious identity mattered, although they measured students' quest for purpose. They identified Hindus and Mormons as placing a high priority on the *quest* for purpose. Other groups, such as Baptists and Catholics, demonstrated significant growth in what they labeled quest inclinations (i.e., the search for meaning and purpose) during college. Yet, they noted that how students' religious faiths may influence the development of purpose needed further study.[11]

One of the objectives of our study was to explore the role of religious identity, background, and belief in college students' purpose formation. To do so we analyzed past survey data, and we also undertook our own national study. To begin we analyzed the College Students' Beliefs and Values (CSBV) survey[12] to corroborate the connection other scholars have made between religion and *purpose seeking*. Using the same measure of purpose seeking we used in the past two chapters, we found that religious first-years—as measured by belief, identity, and practice—are consistently more likely to report actively seeking out meaning and purpose in life than the nonreligious. Figure 10.1 on page 246 displays the results for one measure of religion: a scale of religious commitment.

This composite measure taps into the "internal" components of religion (as opposed to external behaviors such as church attendance and prayer).[13] Students who score high on this measure rate their own religiousness as high, try to follow religious teachings in everyday life, find religion to be helpful to them personally, and claim they gain strength by trusting in a higher power. When divided into five equal sized groups (quintiles) from low to high, first years who score low (in the first quintile) are approximately half as likely to report actively seeking meaning and purpose in life as the average student (10 percent

Figure 10.1. Percent actively searching for meaning/purpose in life as incoming freshman by religious commitment, weighted (N = 13,210)

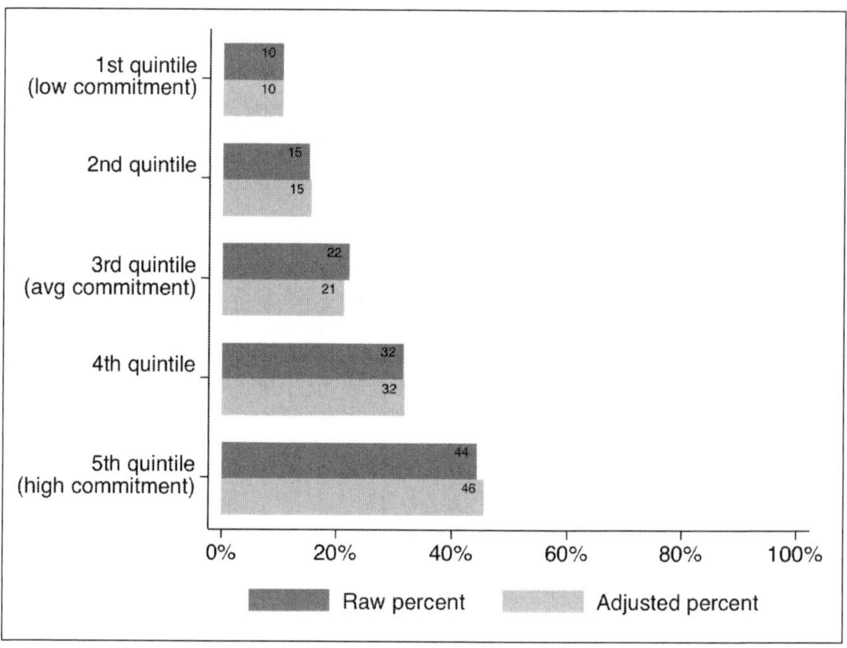

Source: College Students' Beliefs and Values Survey, 2004

Note: Adjusted percent controls for age, sex, race, parents' income, parents' educational attainment, citizenship status, family structure, high school GPA, and high school type.

versus 20 percent). Students who score high on this measure (5th quintile) are more than twice as likely to report actively seeking meaning and purpose (44 percent versus 20 percent).

Other measures of religion show similar patterns, although many are not as dramatic (these additional measures are not shown to conserve space). Only 9 percent of those who do not believe in God are active seekers, versus 22 percent who believe in God. Eleven percent of students who say they do not feel loved by God are active seekers compared to 26 percent who say they frequently feel God's love. Twelve percent of those who never pray are active seekers compared to 31 percent of those who pray daily. The list could go on—the religious, by and large, tend to come to college more actively seeking meaning and purpose in life. The survey, by itself, makes it difficult to parse the precise reasons for this connection between religion and purpose seeking, but we were able to draw out these connections through our student interviews.

Before turning to the interviews, we present one additional analysis using survey data. Since the CSVB survey, as we described previously, can only help us identify whether a student is seeking purpose and meaning, in our Gallup® Quant survey we sought to look at the relationship between support for certain types of substantive purposes and religion. Our own results from chapter 6 revealed that certain kinds of religious identity, belief, and behavior appeared to be positively correlated with certain purposes, particularly Relationalist and Transcendent purposes. To test this theory further, we separated the different purpose ingredients into the three purpose types. We then analyzed whether three types of religious variables, identity, belief, and behavior, demonstrated a relationship to the broad classifications of purpose we identified in chapters 5 and 6—students with Transcendent, Relationalist, and Self-Achiever purposes.

Based on their self-reported responses of denominational affiliation, we divided students into Catholic, Mainline Protestant, evangelical, Nonreligious, and Other. Not surprisingly, students who identified as Catholics, mainline Protestants, and Evangelicals were more likely to report *transcendent-focused purpose in life*, whereas students who were nonreligious were less likely to report *transcendent-focused purpose in life* than students who fall in the "Other" category of religions (see appendix C, tables C5–C7).

Interestingly, students who were Evangelical Christians were more likely to support *relationalist-focused purposes in life*, whereas students who identified as Nonreligious were less likely to support *relationalist-focused purposes in life* than students who identified with the "Other" category of religions. Finally, students who self-identified as Catholics and evangelical were more likely to support *self-achievement-focused purposes in life* than students who identified with the "Other" category of religions. In sum, whatever category of purpose, self-identified evangelicals were more likely to have it, whereas the nonreligious were less likely to have relationalist or transcendent-focused purposes.

When asked to indicate whether religion was important or fairly important, we found students who indicated religion was important or fairly important in their lives were also more likely to support all three types of purposes (Self-Achiever, Relationalist, and Transcendent) than students who do not report that religion is important.

Finally, when asked about attendance at religious services, we found the most varied response. More frequent attendance at religious services was significantly and negatively related to supporting Self-Achiever purposes. Stated differently, increasing religious service attendance was associated with decreasing self-achiever purposes. Moreover, students who attended religious services several times a month or several times a week were significantly more likely to support transcendent-focused purpose in life.

Overall, when it comes to purpose, if a student self-identifies as evangelical, identifies religion as important or fairly important, and attends religious services regularly, the student will be more likely to support transcendent purposes. Evangelicals who also see religion as important will be more likely to support relationalist focused purposes. In contrast, we found a nonreligious person who does not view religion as important and who does not attend religious services regularly will be less likely to support purpose in general, whatever the type. Clearly, religious identity, belief, and activity support particular purposes. Moreover, particular identities and religious habits appear to play an important role in the support for particular types of purposes.

Still, the question remains about how these identities, beliefs, or actions support purpose. Some studies of both religion and spirituality have offered possible answers to this question. For instance, one study by Mariano and Damon of the development of adolescent purpose led them to propose five distinctive contributions of religious faith/spirituality to purpose development.

1. It guides young people toward an intention to contribute (purpose), which, in turn, leads to contribution.

2. It invests young people's goals with value and meaning, which in turn, contributes to these goals becoming inspiring purposes.

3. It supports young people's intentions to develop character (moral/purpose), which, in turn, supports character development.

4. It provides the young person with a community of shared purpose, which, in turn, reinforces his or her own purpose.

5. It creates a bond between a coherent purpose and spirituality/religious faith, moral goals, and personal goals in the young person's life.[14]

Interestingly, one could find all five of these elements in Paul's story. For instance, the spiritual example of Paul's mother led him to focus on the importance of others and not using religion as something for his own good. In addition, Paul found in his Christian university a community of shared purpose, and he found Christianity helped him form a bond between his religious and moral beliefs and his personal goals. Indeed, this last quality was a major reason why students experienced conversations about purpose within student religious groups. Yet, the five elements listed above focus more on the sociological or psychological support that religion provides and do not explore the importance of particular theological beliefs in this process. Our qualitative data, however, helps to address this matter.

The Role of Substantive Religious Beliefs

One of the reasons we interviewed a variety of students at a diverse array of institutions in our interview set of 110 interviews is that we wanted to understand how a particular religious identity of a student or the religious ethos of a campus might make an important difference in how students understand and develop purpose. Table 10.1 gives some idea of our students' complex religious and philosophical identities and subidentities.

We should emphasize that the labels listed are those chosen by students. For example, while most scholars would divide between Reformed, Conservative, and Orthodox Judaism, our categories are derived from how students identified themselves. Some simply said "Jewish" or identified using a particular term "Modern Orthodox." We also included this kind of self-identification label when dividing the Catholics. Two respondents added "nonpracticing."

What we found about the influence of this identity in our qualitative interviews actually surprised us. Despite the variety of religious or nonreligious identities used by students and the variety of religious and nonreligious institutions where we interviewed students, when it came to how students talk about the intersection of their religious or philosophical identity and issues of purpose, the

Table 10.1. Self-Reported Religious or Nonreligious Identity of Students ($N = 110$)

Non-Catholic Christian	45	Catholic	15
Christian	15	Catholic	13
Nondenominational	8	Nonpracticing	2
"Follower of Christ"	4	Jewish	11
Evangelical Covenant	2	Jewish	6
Lutheran (ELCA)	2	Modern Orthodox	3
Pentecostal	2	Orthodox	1
Adventist	1	Traditional	1
Anglican	1	LDS (Mormon)	9
Baptist	1	Nonreligious	20
Christian Reformed	1	Nothing in particular	7
Episcopalian	1	Agnostic	7
Evangelical	1	Atheist	6
"I love Jesus"	1	Other Faiths	10
Lutheran	1	Buddhist	4
Lutheran–Missouri	1	Muslim	2
Mennonite Brethren	1	Unitarian	2
Presbyterian	1	Hindu	1
Reformed	1	Unification Church	1

major difference regarding how one's worldview influences his or her personal view of purpose, we discovered, is a simple one. The key divide exists between nontheists and theists. The rest of this chapter explores the specific ways that theists think about purpose, while the next chapter will explore the distinctive way nontheists approach the issue of purpose.

Religion, Purpose, and Theism

"Extra-senioritis." That's what Ryan claims to have as a fifth-year psychology major. Ryan's educational journey was extended since he switched majors a few times and attended a research university his first year and then transferred to a regional university for his next four years. He recalls that the state research university "turned out to be a little bit bigger than I thought it would be. I knew how big it was, but the largeness of the school kind of worked against me." He articulates his disorientation using geographic language. "It's kind of a weird concept, but I felt like I didn't have a place, so I didn't really know what to do with my time, which was new to me."

When it comes to meaning, Ryan does exhibit some basic orientation. When asked what gives his life meaning, Ryan answers, "I think relationships at the end of the day are most important to me . . . Friends, family members, just being close with people, sharing yourself with people. Not necessarily a romantic relationship, but just friendship-wise." He even interprets the value of the sport he's involved in through this lens:

> I am a runner and that's a huge part of life right now. It probably won't be forever. But, just camaraderie and being on the team I think is something that's really important to me too. Knowing that I'm a small part of something bigger.

The concept of being part of a group with a larger purpose proves to be very important to him; the lack of these types of relationships is what led him to transfer. As he recalls, "That's something that I missed my freshman year. I didn't really feel like I was part of something special." In particular, he identifies missing being part of a group of friends who are united in pursuing a particular purpose.

> I didn't really have a club that I could do. And I actually tried the running club, but it wasn't as meaningful to me as I thought it would be, so I think that's definitely a huge thing for me is being on a team and being a part of something.

While what gives life meaning was clear for Ryan, he was not so sure about his life purpose, even in his fifth year. "I think I'm still trying to figure it out." Admittedly, he believes some of his indecisiveness stems from his lack of a clear career path. "I'm not totally set on what I want to do with my life so that's part of it too I think." He says he wants to choose an occupation where "you feel like you're helping people or doing something meaningful." Ryan's standard for what that occupation might be related to is "doing something that I love. I feel like that I'm passionate about."

Ryan expected college to help him with his purpose. It did not, however, turn out quite as he planned. He admits, "When I got to [his university], my freshman year, I didn't really feel like I had much direction." Unfortunately, now in his fifth year, he still feels a bit lost. Perhaps he wonders if he hoped for too much from college.

> I think that, (pauses) I don't know, I, maybe I expected too much out of it because right now, I don't feel like I'm completely set on what I want to do. But I feel like, after my four or five years in college, I think I felt that I would be more settled or have a clear picture of what I want to do.

When asked if he had any major experiences that really shaped or disrupted his journey toward finding a purpose in life during college, he does cite one very important one. "I came out of the closet." That decision, he notes, was more of a process,

> There was that one, that instance where you kind of admit it to yourself, but it's always something that you think about, someone growing up, I mean, who is gay, I think, for the most part, it's not just one day you wake up and you're changed. It's something that's always been in the back of your mind. So, in that sense, I wouldn't say that it was a huge change. Like this day is the day that it happened, but it is a change to be able to be comfortable and say that to other people.

Despite Ryan's feelings of transition in areas of his life and sense of uncertainty about his purpose right now, he still holds a confidence that he will find a purpose. The reason, he claims, is due to his spiritual beliefs. "I'm very much spiritual in that way, as far as I feel like everyone's life has a purpose and you, you're put here for a reason." This belief stems from the influence of his Catholic upbringing. "My dad's very religious. He goes to church every weekend." Yet,

Ryan did not experience his upbringing as forced, perhaps because his parents' commitment was uneven. "My mom doesn't go as much anymore. And my dad, eventually, I think it was right around maybe thirteen or fourteen, stopped making us go, and said, you know, you can go if you want to." In addition, like many college students, Ryan's commitment has waned, "And I went for a little while. I went here and there throughout high school until I graduated and then since I've been here, I haven't really gone or found a church." Ryan even remarks when asked about his religious/worldview identity, "I was a Catholic." Yet, he also still embraces this identity to some degree. When pressed further about his religious/nonreligious identity he admits, "I don't say that, you know, I have no religion or have gone away from the church, so I think I would go with that [identifying as Catholic], with it being the most familiar one to me."

In addition, despite his lack of church attendance, Ryan would actually claim his religious beliefs have strengthened in college. Growing up,

> I went, and I believed, because I was told to believe, but I didn't really think critically about it. And I think now that I've gotten older I've thought more critically about it. I always believed in God, but now I do believe in God. I do believe that there is a higher power that dictates what happens to us.

He actually perceives his college experience as helping him own these religious beliefs, "I've kind of been able to think about and hear other people's opinions too. Because I didn't hear many other opinions [before]." He has not been convinced by the nontheistic option, although he admits that when it comes to his own beliefs,

> It's just I haven't acted on that, which whether that makes me a bad Christian or not, I mean, that's not what I'm really thinking about when I'm answering this question. I think my beliefs have stayed pretty much solid.

All of this means that Ryan still has a confidence that he will find his own purpose. Indeed, Ryan attributes his assurance to this outlook. "I think part of the reason that I have faith, that I'm kind of on the right path or that I'm going to end up where you want to end up, is because of my belief in God. And that there's a plan for you." He realizes:

> I think that although sometimes it might not be clear, you know . . . Even though you might not know why you're in that place or on that part of the path that you're on; it's still ultimately

a path that's leading toward the end goal or the end what you're supposed to do.

Not only does his belief in God provide confidence, this conviction provides an emotional comfort with having a certain kind of humility about the ability to control life and make it turn out right.

> I think that thinking about the meaning and purpose of life, I'm kind of comforted that I have my religion and faith and belief and a purpose and a path that, because I think to a certain extent, I have control, but I also think I don't have control in some aspects . . . some things happen to you that you might not choose or pick, and I think I have complete comfort in the fact that it's all on the path toward what you're supposed to do. You can rest assured that even though things might not look so great right now, that they will work out in the end.

Finding God's Plan and Direction

As Ryan's story illustrates, the dominant characteristic of theistic students is that they affirm the idea that meaning or purpose is something that they also discover and not merely something they create. Sabrina, a Jewish student made this connection between purpose, action, and her religious tradition. "Your purpose is more like a mission or like an action. It's a Jewish belief and it's definitely something that I believe, that like everyone in this world has some kind of purpose and some kind of mission." In other words, God has a plan for the world that also includes a plan for the individual lives of students.

As a result of this belief, theistic students view their religious tradition as providing a larger external story, map, or image through which they made sense of their lives. The following students used road or direction metaphors similar to the map metaphor we have used at times throughout this book:

- "Your purpose in life is supposed to be directed toward God's higher purpose and so I like to think that hopefully I'm heading down that road, and I'm making choices that aren't just good for me but are good for like the plan that God has for my life and how that affects other people." (Nondenominational Christian)

- "I think God has a purpose for all of us. And I think that gives life meaning, searching for that purpose gives life a direction." (Jewish)

- "Just knowing that He has a plan for you, that's what helps. Just knowing that He has a plan for you, and He has a purpose for you, and if you have faith and you believe, you will go through what God has planned for you. Just knowing that God will direct you to that place, it's comforting. Everything we know that happens in your life, it's because God is directing you through situations and He's like speaking through you, to you." (Pentecostal)

Whereas the nontheists we will examine in the next chapter contend that the belief that God provides general direction and guidance is constraining, these theists see it as both freeing and comforting. A student named Julie summarized this perceived advantage of her Christian outlook while also describing the burden she believed a nontheist outlook would impose,

It's given me a very clear, "This is what I'm meant to do," and that's sort of the outline, and then I color in between the lines. I think someone who didn't have that, it would be a lot more confusing and intimidating to try to come up with the whole image and the colors in between.

Since these students share a story or a larger picture that provides the basic outlines within which to find their personal purpose, they then find it easier to determine a specific course of action or specific purpose within that context.

The articulated or assumed basis for the theist's view rests on the belief that God designed us. Therefore, if God designed us, we fulfill our *telos* or end by following His plans and purposes. This student articulated the outlook that appears to be assumed by other college students who trust God's story, map, or picture:

I believe that we are created in the image of God, and that he has designed us for his glory and his purpose, and he didn't need to create us. He didn't need us but he made us for his joy and his glory. And so I think that, it's not confining it's more free, if anything. There's direction and purpose in living to a higher calling and living for a higher purpose.

As this student noted, the conception that following this plan or direction is somehow constraining does not apply for these students because they believe they are fulfilling their original design. If one fulfills one's designed purpose, the end result is fulfillment. Within this understanding, the supposed constraints of religion actually lead to human flourishing and not suffocating restrictions. As one Native American evangelical student joked about the limitations of her religious outlook, "I mean I can't be a porn star," but she certainly does not see such a restriction as something that limited her human flourishing. This view about the importance of God's plan is something that we observed with Protestant, Mormon, and Jewish students (but not by Catholic students).[15]

Supplies and Motivates Virtues or Resists Vices

The second important element that theistic students believe their worldview adds to their understanding of meaning and purpose concerns particular virtues or vices. They have confidence that their worldview supplies or helps motivate particular virtues or helps them resist particular vices. Jason, a student at an evangelical university believed that his religious tradition supplies particular virtues while also claiming that the freedom the nontheists claim is a false freedom because they lack the particular virtue his religious tradition supplies.

> I do think it gives me hope . . . There is something that separates us from God, even if we try to look around that or go around in some way that, just denying that it's there, doesn't mean it's not there. That there are these things that separate us from God and through Christianity, through hope in Christ, we're given a way to do away with that, and to be in a relationship with God again, and so I feel like people who aren't Christians don't have that hope to be in a relationship with God.

Emily, a Mormon student articulated the relationship between the idea that God has a plan and the way that her religious tradition supports a particular virtue that leads to her emotional well-being.

> I feel like that's what brings me a lot of peace in my life. I honestly don't know where I would be, without this religion in my life. I wouldn't feel so calm and secure and comforted. Everything's part of the plan. Everything's going to work out as long as I'm doing my best and trying to do what Heavenly Father wants me to do. So I think if I didn't have this religion, I would be in a lot of confusion and not knowing what was going on, and I think it would be very hard.

Emily's sense of peace from the plan her religion supplies, we will see in the next chapter, contrasts with the uneasiness some of the nontheists observed in their lives regarding purpose.

Some theists also believe their religious worldview motivates or inspires them to achieve other virtues. As one Catholic student noted, "That's why you look to the Saints because it gives you examples of how to be holy." Another Catholic described how the tradition heightens his ability to love and serve others:

> You have a purpose in life and it's not for yourself, it's for others, like what are you doing for others, and it could be something super-small, or it can be something huge, and I feel like Catholic faith really enhances it.

What motivates this particular student toward a purposeful life of virtue is the larger religious narrative in which he believes.

Interestingly, while some theistic students see their religion as motivating or contributing to certain virtues, others also perceive religion as helping them battle some negative aspects of their selves, particularly selfishness. Evangelical or nondenominational Protestants in particular identified this option. Evetta, the African-American Pentecostal student whose story was summarized in chapter 4, touched on this point when she explained:

> If I wasn't a Christian, the way I would view life and the meaning behind it would be totally different. Like I wouldn't be living my life for God, I would be living my life for myself and so the intent behind everything would be changed.

Her worldview transformed her motivations, which echoes the value identified earlier of living in a larger, grander story,

> I wouldn't be helping somebody else because it's what God wants me to do or it's because what I think the Bible tells me to do; but I would be doing it because, maybe because I think I'm trying to be a good person, or they look like they need help. And I think those are all really good reasons, but it would be different than the reasons I have now. Like, those can also be my reasons, but like I also have a bigger reason behind it.

For Evetta, her religious outlook added additional dimensions and thus additional reasons for her actions. She saw the former approach as focused on the self, while her theistic approach as focused on God and others:

> Do I want to better myself? But that's not just my reason. I want to better myself so that I can be more in tune to God so that I can

be a good example for my sisters so that they want to follow God.

Others saw it helping them resist the lures of a hedonistic lifestyle. Jenny, a nondenominational Christian described it this way,

> I mean I could go out and be crazy on the weekends if I really wanted to, you know, I could go out and party and get wasted but I mean, I choose not to do those kind of things because Jesus plays a role in my life.

Overall, students from a variety of religious traditions identified connections between virtue or resisting vice and their beliefs (5 Catholic, 12 Christian-Protestant-nondenominational, 4 Jewish, 2 Mormon, 1 Buddhist). We found it interesting that only Protestant Christian students focused on the role of their worldview in helping them resist vice (8 students).

Provides Identity, a Foundation, and a Story

Another way that religion supports purpose development has to do with something not identified by Mariano and Damon, although another scholar has included it.[16] At least one student who identified as evangelical, Catholic, Mormon, or Muslim also described his or her religion as something that proves central to understanding self-identity and, therefore, proves central to thinking about meaning and purpose. As one Mormon student described it,

> Oh I think my meaning and purpose is defined by my religion and by my religious identity. I think if I didn't, if I wasn't religious I would feel that I had no purpose or identity in life, if that makes sense. So I think that every—all of my beliefs about identity, religious meaning, and purpose in life come from my religion.

As opposed to constraining them, these students describe religion as an essential part of who they are. Indeed, they cannot see themselves as being who they are without their religious identity. They can no more think of discarding their religious identity than any other essential part of the self. Angie, a Catholic from a public research university described it in this way:

> I know that part of my meaning is Catholicism. That's how I would describe myself. I can't describe myself without it. I'm really glad for that. I know it definitely has influenced my college life, my entire life

and just knowing that that's a core part of who I am. Being in church, a lot of times you reflect on things. My mind is always wondering, goes a thousand miles a minute, so while being in the actual Mass, I often think about why did this happen? Or what am I supposed to do about this? What is God asking me to do in this situation?

As this student illustrates, religious identity is so central to self-understanding, that thinking within a religious framework seems second nature.

These primary ways of connecting religion and purpose, of course, do not exhaust all the possible connections. Additional smaller groups of students spoke to us about how their religious identity and worldview provides eternal significance or reward, offers a relationship with God, and/or supplies a foundation for their moral beliefs. Julie, a Catholic neuroscience major at a secular liberal arts college claims that she saw no other persuasive option by which to make sense of life experiences:

If I didn't believe in God or an afterlife, I would be lost as to what the meaning or purpose of life is—that's the only way that I can validate what we do here, and it's the only way that I can understand the deaths of the people who are twenty years old, just like me, that I've experienced just recently. The only way that I can understand those deaths and that I can give meaning to their lives is if there's a God or there is some sort of, something else out there other than us—something more important than us.

Similar to Paul at the beginning of the chapter, the nontheistic option proved unpersuasive to Julie as she tried to make sense of tragic events she has experienced. Erica, a Christian sociology major at a Baptist university, found the thought of eternal significance both compelling and a major shaping influence on her purpose:

I can remember—before I accepted Jesus to be my Savior and understood what that meant—going to a funeral and just thinking about how life was, "Okay, you grow, you get married, you have kids, you work your whole life, and then you die. And that's it." And then when I got old enough to understand what heaven and what eternity meant . . . I understand this isn't it. That my purpose extends beyond my eighty years on this planet, that it goes beyond that and there are lasting effects from the things that I do and the way that I fulfill my purpose in loving others and bringing them to the Lord, that that's a lasting thing, that purpose is such a lasting thing.

Brian, a Protestant at a Catholic university found the divine relational aspect of his faith compelling. Most importantly, he believed God is not a distant, uncaring being. God desires his flourishing.

> I think it gives a purpose in life in that there's someone, something that wants the best for you. And having those beliefs is important to seeing that even on the worst of days there's something better out there for you and not to get discouraged to the point that you're ready to give up or throw in the towel in that sense.

For theists, far from being a lonely, uncaring, and unjust place ruled by random force, the universe has the potential to be a place of love, connection, and justice due to belief in a God who represents these qualities.

The Contribution of Religious Community and Institution

Julie, a sophomore at a Baptist university, claims she has taken a wandering road toward discovering her purpose, which she understands as largely career related.

> I started when I was five, and I told my dad I was going to be a banker just like him. And then I was going to be an artist, then a musician, then a . . . I mean I've been, [there are] so many things that I want to be.

She came into the university undecided and briefly became a journalism major. "I've never been content to not know what's going on. I read the news every day diligently and I have for years, and I was thinking that journalism would be obvious. I like the news so much."

Then, the past summer, she came to a different conclusion about the direction and calling in life.

> I've always been really engaging myself in the world around me, [and] I realized the job of a journalist is really as an onlooker and someone who's kind of looking in from the outside and, in some ways, even finding what's going wrong, so really a negative sort of viewpoint. But then I realized that I really want to be the one on the inside, the one who's doing something and making change. So that sort of led me to international studies, that really I hadn't even known that was an option necessarily before I came into college, and just started exploring more.

While this sort of growth in self-understanding and change of major would be considered fairly typical college student experiences, Julie also encountered something different at her university that changed her perspective.

The office of spiritual life at her university recently put on a conference the semester before our interview. The conference helped her think about her future vocation in light of her Christian beliefs. "It was very cool for me because the theme of the week was how God can use your gifts, and before that I had really not seen how my career plans could fit into God's plan for me." During that week, Julie had come to a more specific realization regarding her own gifts, passions, and major:

> I really see myself as somebody who can bring justice in the world and safety to people who desire justice, and this is new. I mean it's something I really just have kind of come on in the last year or so, but just a real passion for, you know, bringing a better life to people, and bringing better quality of life.

The speakers at this conference enabled her to see this new passion in a whole new light.

> You know, what one of the speakers really communicated was that doing research into the peoples of the world can—which is what I wanted to do, do research and analysis on international affairs—that gives people who want to help them such a clear picture of how to do that. Because if people don't know what the needs are, then they don't know how to help them. And if they don't know how to help them, then they just come in and start slapping a Band-Aid on everything they see and no lasting change is enacted. And that, for me, was sort of a "Wow, okay, so this is a way that I can actually be using what I want to do for God," you know, and making a real difference in the world with what I want to do. So that's a long answer.

For Julie, the conference helped her see a convergence between what she perceived as her own desires and gifting and God's purposes in her life. Julie's example illustrates what we also found about religious community among students. As Mariano and Damon note and our findings from the co-curricular chapter confirm, religion can supply a young person with a community of shared purpose that can reinforce the student's own purpose.[17] We would merely add that religious students like Julie discovered that religious communities, and the institutions supported by religious communities, also give particular types of support to fostering conversations about purpose.

Particular practices prove to be important for theistic communities and faith-based universities in sustaining conversations about purpose. For instance, one area where particular religious identity makes a difference concerns personal reading connected to matters of meaning and purpose. The Astins and Lindholm found that practices such as "reading sacred texts, reading other material on spirituality and religion, and discussing religion" were positive influences on students' quest development.[18] We found that only two types of students mention being engaged in this kind of activity: Protestant evangelical/nondenominational students and Jewish students. The Protestants tended to talk about reading the Bible and a whole range of popular Christian literature (*Heaven Is for Real, Love Does, Mere Christianity, Blue Like Jazz, Kingdom Calling, A Thousand Gifts,* etc.). The Jewish students referred to specific books by particular rabbis within the Orthodox Jewish tradition. Both of these groups of students read books on their own to explore the importance of their religious tradition in their life in greater detail.

In addition, required religion classes in faith-based universities, as chapter 8 described, also supported conversations about meaning and purpose. An institutionally sponsored chaplain's office with particular programing related to vocation, retreats meant to address life purpose and chapels also added to communal conversations about purpose. Overall, religious communities and institutions supported an intellectual conversation about purpose both through student meetings and conferences, where meaning is discussed, and through creating a tradition of informal learning where purpose is explored and discussed.

The Interaction between Religion, Purpose Seeking, and College

While understanding the role that theological beliefs and communal practice play in supporting purpose are important for understanding religious students, religious and secular colleges also play unique roles in supporting students' exploration of the soul of purpose. As explored earlier, religious students may come to a university seeking purpose, but it is important to distinguish between this initial level of seeking and subsequent changes in seeking during college. In chapters 8 and 9, we specifically looked at what factors were associated with *change* in active seeking because we were interested in the college experiences that are associated with drawing students toward active engagement with life purpose.

The religious identity, practice, and beliefs that students bring with them to college are *not* associated in any consistent way with change in purpose questing over time. We ran models using multiple measures of religion, and there was no consistent pattern where initial levels of religiousness predicted change in purpose questing over time. The vast majority of these were not statistically significant, even with our large sample. To be clear, high levels of religion are associated with purpose, but high levels of religion do not somehow set up students to become more receptive to *becoming* active purpose seekers during college. This means that students attending evangelical colleges (and to a lesser extent other faith-based colleges) are not somehow automatically primed to make *gains* in purpose seeking during college. The relative success these colleges have in causing students to take up contemplating life's meaning and purpose are due to the experiences these students have at college. In fact, when we control for incoming student religiousness, the success that evangelical colleges (and to a lesser extent Catholic institutions) show in creating an uptick in active seekers of meaning and purpose is even larger. Figure 10.2 shows this in the adjusted percentage bars. Once student religiousness background is taken into account,

Figure 10.2. Percent change in actively searching for meaning/purpose in life by institutional type, including additional controls for student religiousness as first years, weighted (*N* = 11,972)

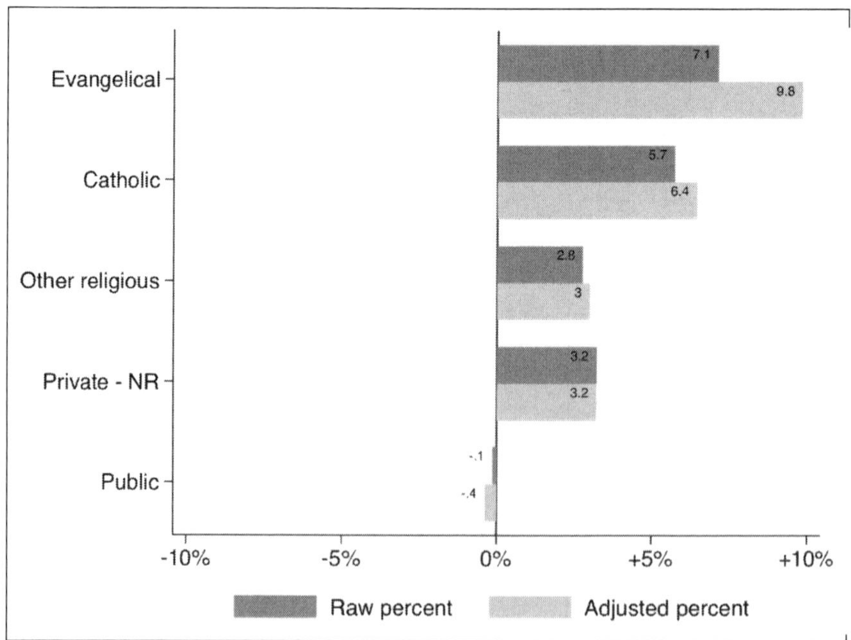

Note: Adjusted percent controls for religious tradition, church attendance, religious commitment, belief in God, frequency of prayer, age, sex, race, parents' income, parents' educational attainment, citizenship status, family structure, high school GPA, and high school type.

evangelical colleges are expected to create a 10 percent net gain in the number of students actively seeking meaning and purpose in life. If anything, all of those religious students make gains in purpose seeking *less* likely.

How do the religious experiences students have in college impact their propensity to search for meaning and purpose? In figure 10.3, we show the results of an analysis that asks students to assess whether interactions with faculty have weakened, strengthened, or had no effect on their religious beliefs. The vast majority (83 percent) reports there was no effect from faculty interactions on religious beliefs. Thirteen percent say their beliefs were strengthened, and 4 percent say they were weakened. The CSBV also include similar questions about the influence of other staff, peers, and course content. In each case, the majority reports that their religious beliefs were unchanged because of these interactions. The minority who report that their religious beliefs changed are much more likely to report that their beliefs were strengthened rather than weakened (the

Figure 10.3. Percent change in actively searching for meaning/purpose in life by how interactions with faculty have altered religious or spiritual beliefs, weighted (*N* = 13,139)

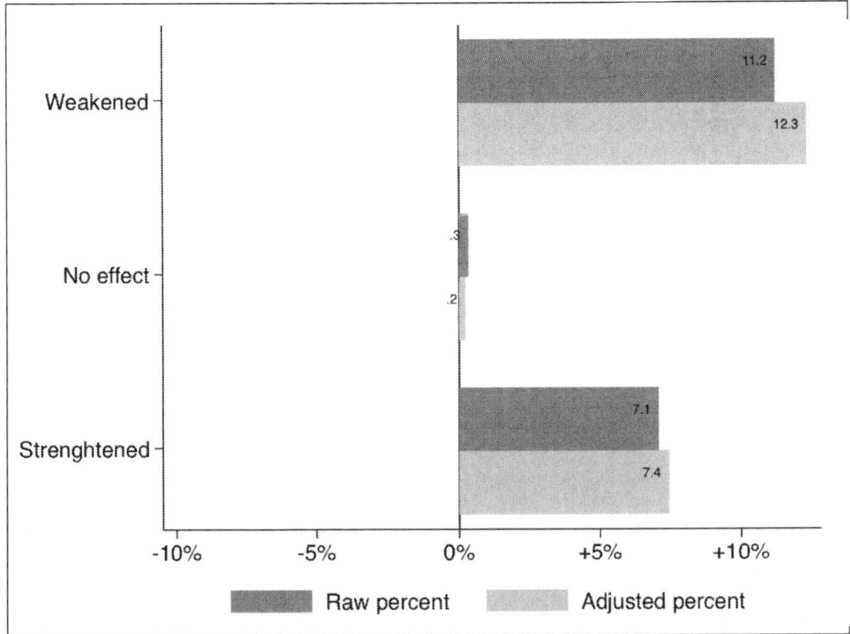

Source: College Students' Beliefs and Values Survey, 2004–2007.

Note: Adjusted percent controls for age, sex, race, parents' income, parents' educational attainment, citizenship status, family structure, high school GPA, and high school type.

former group is 3 to 5 times the size of the latter depending on the question). In none of these questions does the percent of students who say their faith was weakened go beyond 6 percent (it is important to remember that these data are weighted so that they approximate the real percentages for students nationally). The positive influences on religious beliefs range from 10 percent (interactions with campus staff) to 32 percent (interactions with peers). All of this is consistent with recent sociological literature that shows college having little influence overall on religious beliefs.[19]

Returning to figure 10.3, it is clear that religious change in college of any sort—whether a strengthening or weakening of religious beliefs—is associated with an increase in purpose seeking. Those whose faith was weakened show an increase of 11 percent while those whose faith was strengthened show an increase of 7 percent. This is true of all the measures we looked at. It does not matter whether faculty, college staff, course content, or friends initiated this change; in every case religious change was accompanied by an increase in actively seeking out meaning and purpose in life. In some ways, friends are the most important source of this change because nearly a third of all students claim friends have strengthened their religious beliefs in college. Within this group, we see a 7 percent increase in active purpose seeking (figure not shown).

Given the general positive relationship between religiousness and purpose seeking, perhaps it comes as a surprise that experiences that weaken faith (which admittedly are relatively uncommon) would be associated with an increase in purpose seeking. It is important to remember, however, that in order to have one's faith disturbed, there must first be some sense of coherence to the faith itself. These conflicts provide an opportunity to reconstruct or leave behind aspects of a religious or spiritual system. It would be unusual if such a process did not also involve a consideration of one's purpose in life. Figure 10.4 supports this point as well. Among those who say that they "frequently" experience conflicts between their faith and course content, we see an 11 percent increase in active meaning and purpose seeking. Again, this is not common; only one out of twenty students say they frequently experience this kind of conflict.

Last, we include another item that measures how frequently professors encourage discussion of religious and spiritual matters (fig. 10.5 on page 265). Consistent with everything we have seen up to this point, when students say professors do this frequently, they are also more likely to report becoming active seekers (9 percent increase). When it is occasional or not at all, there is very little influence on seeking behavior. This measure was part of the same battery of questions that asked how often professors encouraged exploring questions of meaning and purpose (one that we examined in figure 8.3). It is interesting to note that the influence on seeking behavior is remarkably similar whether faculty are encouraging this seeking behavior directly (fig. 8.3) or whether they

Figure 10.4. Percent change in actively searching for meaning/purpose in life by how often the student experiences a conflict between course work and religious beliefs, weighted ($N = 13,206$)

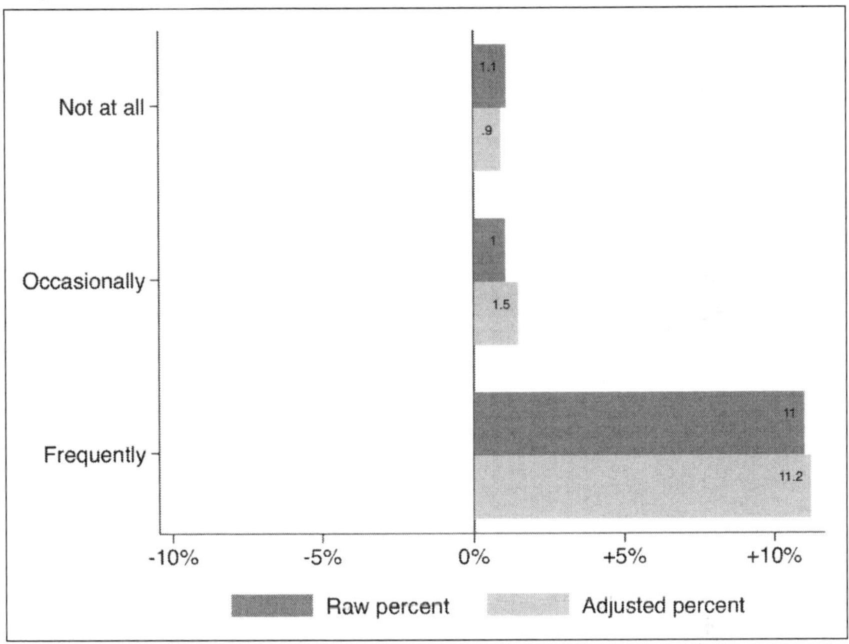

Source: College Students' Beliefs and Values Survey, 2004–2007.

Note: Adjusted percent controls for age, sex, race, parents' income, parents' educational attainment, citizenship status, family structure, high school GPA, and high school type.

are bringing up spiritual or religious matters (fig. 10.5 on page 266). This goes to show how wrapped up religion and spirituality is with questions of meaning and purpose for many college students.

As we did in the previous two chapters, we explore whether the factors we have explored in the CSBV data help explain the gap we have seen between different types of institutions. Figure 10.6 on page 267 includes a basic measure of this difference (the top bar) as well as a measure of the difference once standard controls and college religious experiences are controlled for (the bottom, "adjusted" percent change). The extra controls are the three variables we just examined in figs. 10.3 through 10.5. Similar to what we found in previous chapters, these measures explain much of the advantage we find in evangelical colleges but less of what we find in other institutions. If we simply removed the influence of the three variables measuring college religious experiences, then

Figure 10.5. Percent change in actively searching for meaning/purpose in life by how often the professors encourage discussions of religious and spiritual matters, weighted (N = 13,179)

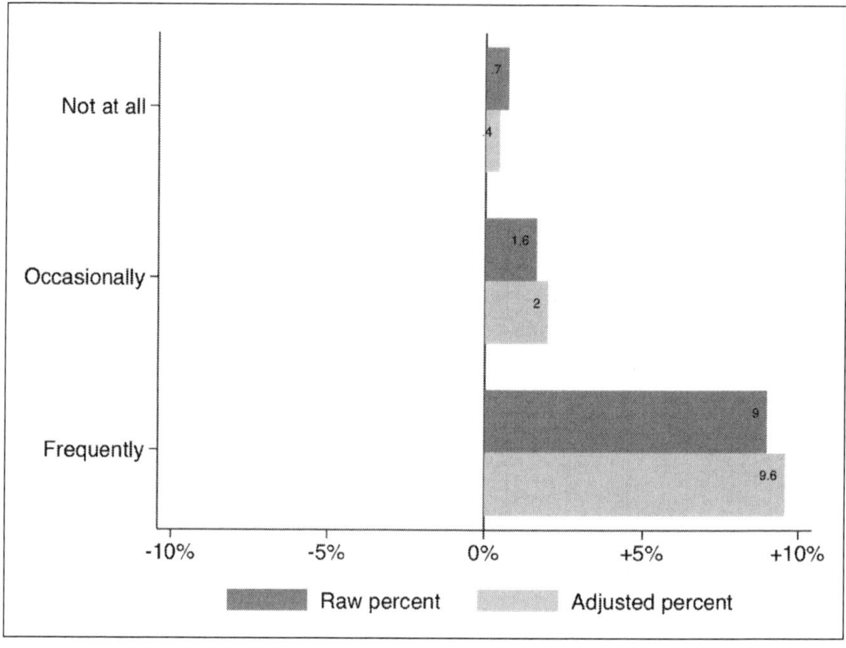

Source: College Students' Beliefs and Values Survey, 2004–2007.

Note: Adjusted percent controls for age, sex, race, parents' income, parents' educational attainment, citizenship status, family structure, high school GPA, and high school type.

evangelical colleges have roughly the same influence on purpose seeking as other private, nonreligious institutions (an increase of around 3 percent). Thus, it is these three extra factors, interactions with faculty, experience of conflict between course work and religious belief, and whether professors encourage discussions of religious and spiritual matters, that students disproportionately experience at evangelical colleges that make these institutions relatively more successful in encouraging students to seriously think about meaning and purpose in life.

Conclusion

Overall, our findings confirm previous research indicating that religious identity, belief, and behavior all correlate with the presence of purpose. In addition, our

Figure 10.6. Percent change in actively searching for meaning/purpose in life by institutional type, including additional controls for religious experiences at college, weighted (*N* = 13,027)

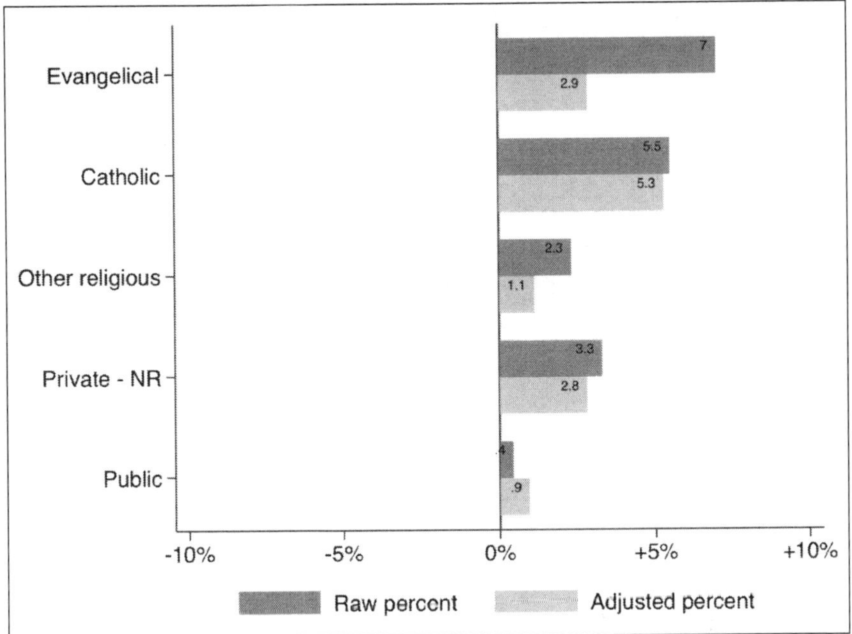

Source: College Students' Beliefs and Values Survey, 2004–2007.

Note: Adjusted percent controls for how interactions with faculty altered religious or spiritual beliefs, how often coursework conflicted with religious beliefs, how often faculty encouraged discussions of religion and spirituality, age, sex, race, parents' income, parents' educational attainment, citizenship status, family structure, high school GPA, and high school type.

qualitative findings indicate some possible reasons for why religious students often indicate having more purpose. For instance, Mariano and Damon note that spirituality or religion help students develop an intention to contribute to something beyond-the-self.[20] Our qualitative interviews indicate some ways this happens. Religion provides an identity that connects a student to a larger story or narrative, cause, and community beyond-the-self. Second, this narrative provides a larger cognitive plan that is bigger than oneself and is looked to for making sense of the world, particularly death. Third, this identity and larger story provide reason and motivation for resisting one's selfish desires that may conflict with this larger story and identity, and they help form the virtues necessary for living out this larger story.

Mariano and Damon also suggest that spirituality "invests young people's goals with value and meaning, which in turn, contributes to these goals becoming inspiring purposes."[21] We would propose that how it invests these goals with meaning is through connecting them to a larger story or narrative about life. While some may become a teacher or doctor because helping people feels good, religion appeals to something beyond one's self. It offers a cognitive explanation or story that gives meaning to a goal or life destination that goes beyond one's personal feelings or satisfaction.

Mariano and Damon also claim that spirituality "supports young people's intentions to develop character (moral/purpose) which, in turn, supports character development."[22] Our findings also support this point as attested by the students who see religion inspiring them to love and service, but they also add something additional. Religion provides substantive content that shapes the virtues that one then develops. For instance, the narrative linked to the afterlife supplies students not merely with an intention to develop a character quality of hope but also supplies a substantive reason to have hope. Without this religious reason, it is not clear that the students would have had this particular view of this specific virtue.

Finally, our findings reveal that the particular religious community or institution may add important elements. We already observed in chapter 8 how a common ethos at the evangelical university appears to build trust between faculty and students in a way that allows conversations about meaning and purpose. As this chapter notes, it allows for common efforts that address meaning and purpose from a shared worldview. Tim Clydesdale's recent book, *The Purposeful Graduate* that studied particular programming designed to enhance programming at many religious institutions, also reinforces this point.[23]

We believe these findings raise questions about approaches to helping students explore purpose that do not take the diverse religious lives of students into account, particularly the common view of theists that through God one discovers one's purpose. We are thinking in particular of the kind of approach outlined in the book, *Helping College Students Find Purpose: The Campus Guide to Meaning-Making*, by Robert J. Nash and Michele Murray.[24] Since Nash and Murray reject ontological realism, they appear most comfortable with students who privatize and personalize their religious beliefs, what today is often labeled spirituality.[25] They exalt one student as finding a "refuge of consolation and comfort."[26] Virtues such as "love, faith, hope, forgiveness and compassion" are "spiritual emotions."[27] They approve of approaches "highly correlated with such emotional states as joy, optimism, and hope than any other human belief system."[28] It also carries into their pedagogy. They talk about the importance of students sharing stories in a "nondoctrinal, mutually respectful manner."[29]

The problem with this approach is that it undermines the perspective of the students above and, in this respect, fails to accommodate religious and philosophical diversity. As seen above, theistic students do find emotional comfort in their religious outlook, but the substantive beliefs and narratives related to their worldview's understanding of reality are what help provide that emotional comfort. Underneath Nash and Murray's approach to avoid issues of belief is a noble desire to avoid quick-and-easy judgments about others' religious and philosophical views. They share about the need to learn empathy for the other view, to "learn to honor, not critique, those beliefs that give people's lives a special meaning."[30] Nash and Murray "try to avoid raising questions about the validity of the truth claims of various religious-spiritual points of views."[31]

The reality, though, is that the philosophical assumptions from which they start already critique and raise questions about alternative approaches to meaning and purpose. Overall, Nash and Murray's approach too heavily emphasizes the human aspect of creating without acknowledging the role that students perceive external reality may play in this creating process for theistic students. By rejecting ontological realism, their foundational framework does violence to religious and philosophical students who believe they did not create the divine being or beings with which they have relationships. We contend we need to think about approaches that might help and show justice to all students.

In contrast, Reker and Wong's model for understanding the nature of meaning, referenced in chapter 5, provides a more holistic model to think about purpose that can help educational leaders know how to help these students.[32] In their model, meaning is both created and discovered. We would maintain that students perceive the same dynamic with regard to purpose. These students see themselves as caught up in a larger drama with different characters instead of the writers of dramas unanchored from existing stories about reality. In contrast, as the next chapter reveals, nontheists take a much different approach to how they think about purpose.

Chapter 11

Finding Purpose in a Universe without One

The Nontheists

I'm kind of up in the air [about my purpose] because the thought of something as meant to be or you have a purpose, I don't know. That's an interesting concept in my mind, but I can't decide if that's something that actually exists. So, I don't know.

—Anne, self-described as "I'm just not religious at this point"

[S]ome people recognize that it was simply a childish mistake to assume that the universe *does* have an ultimate purpose, and that we can get on with our lives without having to continue making this mistake.

—Steve Stewart-Williams[1]

"As a child I just thought that meaning and purpose was in everything, and I was so happy to be where I was and to be doing the things I was doing." Kathryn, a sophomore majoring in environmental science at a secular liberal arts college was describing her former childhood beliefs. She recalls her thoughts about purpose. "[I] definitely questioned it more as I got older, because the idea of just every day is a perfect day and everything's wonderful, it doesn't stick with you. I think that was just me being a little kid." She now sees herself as grown out of this idealistic phase and into a grown, skeptical adult.

The questioning of her thinking about meaning and purpose emanates from her growing doubts about religion. She grew up in a partially religious family that provided an uneven religious experience. "I was raised Jewish, because my mom was Jewish. My dad wasn't . . . [although] he kind of participated in everything we did at home." She labels the particular Jewish tradition in which she was raised "Very Reformed," in that "the stuff geared toward teenagers and kids, was just trying to be as fun and interesting as possible." At first, she embraced the tradition fully,

> probably until about ninth grade I was really into Judaism, and I thought it was the best thing. And I loved going to synagogue and praying to God and having that idea of someone out there to help me and to talk to me whenever I wanted, and I would at services have these great long prayers and . . . get really excited about it and get really annoyed at my fellow students when they would be talking or something during services. I'd be that girl that was, "Shush, like, we're doing something important—this is really, really good." And I thought it was just so great.

Her growing knowledge of religious pluralism changed everything. Suddenly, she realized that Judaism "wasn't the only religion" and "wasn't believed to be true by everyone." She also "questioned aspects of it," but she "still thought that it was the best." In particular, she found herself attracted to the Jewish conception of God. "I thought that it should be true, because it was really, really great and it was just such a good idea to have that kind of God, like the kind of God described in Judaism—looking over people." This outlook extended into seventh grade,

> I remember that was when my Bat Mitzvah was, and so I remember just being really into learning the words of God and the Torah and really excited to be able to talk to the congregation . . . I was so determined to be Jewish and really believe it.

Early in high school, however, she experienced a slow transformation,

> I started questioning it. I'm not exactly sure why, maybe it was just getting older, in the process of realizing that the world has much more than the things that you see at first—you know, there's always problems on the other side of things that you don't realize.

Her mother did not react negatively to this questioning. In fact, Kathryn found her quite supportive. She recalls that sometimes she would go to her mom and say, " 'I think religion's stupid, and I don't think we should do it,' and she would totally be open with me about that." The exact source of the questions emanated from a couple different things, "learning about wars that were started from religion and worrying about all of the different disagreements that people have because of religion." She also reacted negatively to her realization that she did not have a choice in learning her initial religious tradition:

I think part of me is still in that phase of seeing that the consequences of religion and of being taught something kind of forcefully
and being taught this is right. This is what you should believe—that
idea still bothers me a bit.

In particular, she reacts to the proselytizing aspect of religion. "I don't want
someone to tell me what I should believe."

Her present journey leads to her confession, "I've become to . . . really
stop believing in God since then." Now she identifies herself as "somewhere
between atheist and agnostic, I guess, but not so much that I want to be antitheist." By not being antitheist, Kathryn means that she understands why people
might be religious.

I think that people who do believe in religion, it's great for them, and
I think they should continue doing that because it gives you some
kind of purpose. It gives you something to look toward. It may give
you hope, and so for some people, it's what they need.

She, however, takes a different, more pragmatic view, "But for me personally,
I don't think it's what I need anymore." In her understanding of religion, the
fundamental reason for accepting or believing in the tenets of a faith has less
to do with whether it was true and more to do with its pragmatic usefulness.

Still, she also does not believe it real in any way. She now interprets religion
as purely a social construction. "I see it as more of an institution that people put
up . . . they build up this religion because they need something to look to." She
often comes back to the theme that religion is something she has outgrown, "I
don't know, the idea of God just seems childish to me and a little naive." If anything, she seems to have converted to a form of pragmatism. She even confesses,

I think if something really, really bad was to happen, I might pray just
in case; you know, just the idea of maybe there's something up there
and . . . in a time when you really need it, you want it to be there.

However, right now she admits, "I don't really need it." It also no longer "works"
for her in the sense that she now sees the human construction involved in
religion,

It seems so human—the fact that it was . . . all the things were written by humans, all the ancient books were written by people, and
the way that it was constructed is so imperfect that it's obvious to
me that it's not divinely created; like religion isn't divinely created
because it's imperfect. So it must have been created by people.

For Kathryn, God and all the associated religious rituals are simply human projections. She wants her belief guided by something that is not humanly constructed.

> What I've been trying to do since then is look to something other than God and look to the power of humanity, or the power of nature, or the combined powers of humanity and nature, and see beauty and peace and spirituality that are not religiously related.

This outlook has deeply influenced her views of meaning and purpose. She sees her agnostic/atheistic approach as offering her a kind of freedom when it comes to her purpose, "because it's not like my opinions should be tied down to anything. They can really go in whatever direction I want; if I want to go to another religion, I could—which I don't think I will."

So what does she believe is her current source of meaning and purpose? Currently, she sees herself as divided. On the one hand, she concludes, "I've come to think that meaning and purpose are just . . . I mean I want to believe that it's from helping other people." She refers back to something she picked up when she still believed in Judaism. "I have this quote that I loved in seventh grade that was: 'What we do for ourselves dies with us, what we do for others in the world remains.'" This comment helps identify why Kathryn feels like she no longer needs God or religion to give her hope and some sense of a future. In helping others, she finds a possible source of lasting influence beyond her own life.

> So I always try to go back to that and think, you know, no matter how purposeless I feel as an individual, I can still make an impact on people around me, and I can still do something to help others and kind of leave a legacy in other people. And so that would be the purpose of my existence and maybe legacy on the world perhaps.

In particular, she connects this purpose with the environmental science major that she's undertaking. "Maybe I can go help the world be less polluted and then in the future things will grow better in some small way. Being able to make an impact on that would be meaningful."

Despite her convictions about purpose rooted in an others-focused approach that is grounded in a form of Relationalism and a Transcendent moral belief that she should try to make the world a better place by majoring in environmental science, Kathryn still has some doubts about her purpose. These doubts stem from her agnostic/atheistic outlook. After articulating her purpose, she admits,

> But then sometimes even that seems ridiculous because in the grand
> scheme of things, the human race doesn't even matter, so even if
> you make a great impact on one person's life, they're going to die,
> too; and then you will be forgotten, and there's not really a purpose.

As a result, her atheist/agnostic outlook still leaves her with misgivings about purpose:

> I guess that's what I go back and forth between really believing that
> being with other people and having an impact on the people around
> us is the meaning that we can have versus maybe we don't have that
> much of a meaning.

In light of this doubt, she wonders if she may return to religion, albeit on her own terms and for emotional and not intellectual reasons. "I think eventually I'll probably go back to Judaism just for the comfort of it and the tradition. I like being raised with a tradition, and so I would want to pass that on to my children, eventually." She indicates, though, that she likely won't embrace the substantive beliefs. "I don't know if I will go back to necessarily believing in God, and I think I believe more in the community it forms and the traditions that are made, rather than some divine being looking over us." Like a number of young emerging adults, Kathryn searches for meaning and purpose apart from historic moral or religious traditions of thought. While her current purpose was in some ways derived from her earlier religious experience, since she no longer is involved in that tradition, she has started to question the foundation of her purpose. Indeed, she still wonders if she does not need at least the communal support of the tradition and still desires to pass it along to her children.

As previous chapters have noted, theistic or religious students are more likely to identify having a purpose and have a greater sense of purpose than nontheists. While we described some of the ways that spirituality and religion contribute to students' sense of purpose in the last chapter, these findings also raise the question of how nontheists' beliefs influence their development and understanding of purpose. Why do nontheists as a group express less support for and sense of purpose in general?

We should be clear that our findings indicate that nontheists are clearly capable of supporting specific purposes, as Kathryn's example indicates, they just tend to indicate less certainty of and support for purpose in general, which Kathryn's doubts also illustrate. One could argue that this lower sense of purpose merely results from having one less ingredient to consider. As our findings from chapter 6 indicate, 37 percent of students strongly disagree or disagree that their purpose is to love God or a higher power. Many of these students are likely nontheists or those only loosely connected to a faith tradition, so the reduction of one purpose ingredient reduces the number of purpose options. Yet, as chapter 6 indicated, religious identity, belief, and service attendance were positively and negatively correlated with a whole variety of purposes. What these kind of quantitative surveys do not tell us is how nontheists reason about purpose.

Similar to the second part of the previous chapter, this chapter will use our qualitative interviews to explore the reasoning nontheists use to think about purpose and meaning to discover some possible reasons for the quantitative survey findings. We found plenty of examples. According to surveys of freshman, 21 percent of students either do not believe in God or are unsure about the existence of God.[2] The percentage of nontheists we found in both our qualitative samples was actually either the same percentage or higher (21 percent of the 110 Targeted Qual interviews and 41 percent of the 75 National Qual interviews). So, how did the nontheists we interviewed combine their beliefs about the world, which often includes a belief that there is no big "P" purpose in life with their search for individual purpose? What do those beliefs contribute, or how do they perhaps strengthen or pose a challenge to students finding a purpose in life? This chapter seeks to answer these questions.

Becoming a Nontheist and the Role of Higher Education

The nontheists we interviewed included students who identify as nonreligious/ nones, atheists, agnostics, cultural Jews, and all but one of the self-identified Buddhists. In our 110 Qual, we found more students who did not believe in God at the public institutions and two private liberal arts colleges. Among our other sample of seventy-five students, 83 percent were found at public institutions. It is not surprising that nontheists tend to be attracted to public institutions. Our interviews helpfully reminded us of the diversity among the nontheists. While these students share a lack of belief in a deity, they come to their nonbelief differently. Based on our sample, we suggest that they take at least three particular paths.

Students who are the first type of nontheist see themselves as becoming nonreligious during adolescence in opposition to their parents' religious beliefs. Kathryn fits this model as does Anne, the purposeless student discussed in chapter 6. Anne's nonreligious beliefs had early beginnings. Anne describes her mother as "deeply religious" and "definitely pushy" with her faith. In contrast, Anne says, "I'm not religious anymore. At all." In retrospect, she would not consider herself religious even as a child. But this nonreligious identity did not really cement until around age "thirteen or fourteen." "I just started questioning things," she recalls. "Just, like, why is all this bad stuff happening in the world."

Like being lost in a foreign city, she claims, "There are just all these things, and the signs don't make sense." Religion did not provide the map that made sense of this world. Consequently, when it came to church "at thirteen or fourteen, I was like, you know, 'Mom I don't want to go anymore.'" This is when Anne says the conflict really started. "So she works there [as an administrative assistant], so she's like 'You have to go, you're going with me.' And then I'm like 'No, I'm not.'" This was the reason for what she calls "teen aches." Her mother would ask her, "Why don't you believe this?" Anne interpreted the questioning as pressure and lamented, "They try to push their beliefs on you." Like Kathryn, she feels that her parents forced a certain kind of religious perspective on her.

College, for this first kind of nontheist, becomes a place of freedom for exploration while free from the restrictions of one's parents. Again, consider Anne's story. She shares how college provides the occasion for a clean identity break from the past. "It's an opportunity. No one knows you. You can just go and be completely someone else, reinvent yourself. It's just nice to be like, 'All right, here's the new me.'" Higher education in a public setting supplies the freedom she felt lacking in her family life. She perceives her college experience as largely affirming her new self and new worldview. In the midst of this freedom, she has chosen a new source of guidance for life. "I'm much more a believer in science. Not that I would say I don't have faith at all, but if there's a hard fact in front of me, I'm going to believe it. So, I think science is much more persuasive that way." Like Steven Stewart-Williams, the psychologist quoted at the beginning of the chapter, Anne thinks science provides a compelling narrative that can, at least in some respects, come to replace religion in her life.

Anne's experience at the regional college parallels Kathryn's experience at the secular liberal arts college in the support she finds from her institution in her new nonreligious worldview. In fact, Kathryn tells us, "I've taken a lot of science classes here, and the more science I take, the more impractical religion seems because science is more real." In particular, she talks about a class called the Science and Ethics of Genetics, where they discussed "how you could potentially twist genes to alter humanity and make super-babies, you know, that are ultra-smart and ultra-tall, and just ready to succeed." She concluded from the class:

> It makes you question religion too because there's the whole question of like, "Well, didn't God make the babies to be like that?" Why do we want to change them out of that if they're naturally like that, you know, if they've evolved that way?

Kathryn appears to believe that the fact that humans can play god with genes and that babies can be improved on, undermines a reason to believe in a larger God. Like Anne, Kathryn finds that science provides a counterpoint to faith and is the source of a worldview that appears to her as more rational than religion. In this regard, for these students, one part of the university serves to replace the role that religion played for their parents.

A second group of nontheists either grow up with nontheistic parents or with parents who do not encourage theistic belief and practice. Katie, a student at a liberal arts college, provides an example of a student who absorbed the nontheistic teaching of her parents. She notes, "Well, I wasn't brought up with a religious background at all really." Katie emphasizes though that her parents still provided a certain kind of moral teaching:

> Instead of going to church or going to temple or following a strict religion, my parents would actually get together with the parents of my neighbors and they would kind of put their heads together and think of ethics lesson to give us on the weekends. Like, maybe one theme would be respect for one weekend, and they would do like a short story or a little activity and just teach us about why respect, for instance, was important.

Although the lessons were largely moral, her parents' approach did have a spiritual element to it. According to Katie, her parents claimed, "that nature was like our religion." Thus, instead of attending church or temple, "we would go for hikes like every Sunday and just be together outside and appreciate that." So what exactly was the identity label of their beliefs? Katie confesses,

> We don't really, like, [my mom] doesn't identify with agnostic or even atheist, but I guess. . . . I kind of mentioned that they always said that nature was our religion, but they joke that we have our own religion of [Marshish]—'cause that's my last name.

This approach is similar to an approach to religion described in the book *Habits of the Heart* by an interviewee named Sheila, who called her religion Sheila-ism.[3] Yet, while the authors of this book talked about how this outlook reflected an individualistic mind-set, Katie's family "religion" of Marshish reflects not a purely individualistic religion, but a small-group approach to religion that is defined against institutional, organized religious faith.[4] Some authors identify this approach as characteristic of spirituality versus religion. Katie simply shares her parents' avoidance of theism as well as their allergy to organized religious communities and labels. Indeed, she admits, "I've come to appreciate the fact and how I was brought up having the view of being able to look from the outside instead of being a participant from the inside and being single-minded about something."

For this second group of students, similar to the first group, college often reinforces the worldview that they already have. In fact, Katie cannot identify a way that college has challenged her worldview or beliefs and admits that her worldview has "mostly remained consistent" throughout college.

We should note that not all of the students in this category grew up being raised by nontheists. Some just have theistic parents who never encourage theistic belief or practice. In addition, other students in this category may rebel against their parents' belief, but they retain the nontheism of their parents. Monica provides one such example. She believes she "grew up in a pretty normal high school with like [an] Astroturf football field." Her parents' religious background, however, was far from normal. When they were in college, they had converted from Judaism, which in her words "is like a real religion," to Buddhism. She quickly adds,

> not that Buddhism isn't, but Buddhism I still think of as more of a philosophy than a religion, because there's no god that you believe in. There's no higher power, it's all just kind of believing in yourself and thinking that you are your destiny and only you can create it.

Monica, however, no longer identifies with the Buddhism of her parents. In Baxter Magolda's language, she began to self-author her own religious identity. She pinpoints this separation and initial self-authorship as occurring when she received her driver's license and her own independence:

> I think that maybe when I started driving myself around and, this is a kind of cheesy metaphor, but like literally taking the wheel and realizing that I was no longer under their jurisdiction as much. Although, I still like have to answer to them in some ways, but I think just realizing that you're a person and not a daughter and that they're a person, not just a mother [or father], is really interesting to me.

Coming to understand herself as her own person then meant that she decided to separate herself from her parents' religious beliefs, an act which she attributed to teenage rebellion.

> And I think if I had come to Buddhism by myself, I might have felt the same way my father did when he was twenty coming to Buddhism by himself, "Oh, my god, this is this great new idea and I don't have to answer to anyone but me." But because my parents were the ones who were Buddhists, it's like that kid rebelling and like my friends no longer wanted to go to Hebrew School after they

were bar mitzvahed, like the pushing away of what you grew up with. I think I did that.

Monica herself no longer considers herself either spiritual or religious:

> I've never in my life prayed or, except for like little off-hand comments like "Thank God" or, you know, things that you do unconsciously, because they are part of our language and our rhetoric, but I don't actually believe in God.

Monica had a religious rebellion, just not a theistic one.

The third type of nonreligious student recounts growing up in a particular religious tradition that they still embrace when going to college, but they then undergo a conversion experience sometime during college. Brooke, whose story we recounted in chapter 4, provides an example of this kind of nontheist. Another example is Chase, a junior mathematics and chemistry major, who experienced this kind of conversion while attending his Lutheran liberal arts college. Upon entering college he would have called himself a "fairly zealous" Christian from a Methodist background, but at the time of our interview he calls himself "pretty strictly nonreligious." Chase does not give the impression that his move to being nonreligious was a rebellion against his parents. He believes he had and still has an open relationship with his parents and explains that he shared one particular quality with his dad:

> We both had a certain like discontentment with the church and what not, and we would talk openly about that, and we'd talk a lot about religion and all that kind of stuff. I always felt like I could speak with him frankly about that kind of thing.

Similar to the other three groups, college may still provide a space for exploration. For instance, Chase had grown up in a Methodist Church, "the average age of our church [members] was probably about sixty, and it was like the services were very dry." As a result, when he went to college he hoped to examine

> a more Pentecostal or charismatic sort of belief . . . away from the more conservative liturgical, sort of church I grew up in. I was convinced that I'd become more zealous about my faith and I would become kind of freer to explore the expressions of Christianity.

This exploration meant that when Chase came to campus he originally became involved with the Charismatic group on campus.

Yet, unlike the other two groups of students, some aspect of the college experience often challenges this group. For Chase, his curricular experience had a profound impact on his Christian life. He took a set of classes associated with a Great Books curriculum, and it challenged his worldview. As part of that curriculum,

> We read the Bible, pretty much in its entirety and that was a task I had undertaken myself before, but because we came at it from a more critical light, a more academic or scholarly light, and we learned about the context in which the Bible was written and the history of the Bible, you know, that begins to change your mind. That begins to call into question certain doctrines you might have held about the inspiration of scripture.

Chase admits he had not encountered more sophisticated and critical academic approaches to Scripture in the Church. As a result, these conversations were entirely new to him. Yet, while the critical discussion of the Bible played a key role in his deconversion experience, it identifies the communal nature of the discussion as the element that he found most challenging to his previous worldview. He did not perceive the challenge to his prior Christian faith in this discussion as coming from an authoritative professor; instead, it came from fellow questioning students.

> The fact that you were with people who had divergent views discussing this book for three hours a week, you know you got a lot of exposure to why other people think the way they do. When we got to the Bible, we had lots of people who didn't believe the Bible talking about why they didn't and that was very powerful and that was a very different experience for me to discuss the Bible with a group of people and not have everybody say, "Oh yes that's true" and "I accept it" and, you know, it was refreshing to have kind of a critical eye toward it. And it was refreshing to look at people who you disagree with and see that they're not, you know, terrible people or they're not, you know, so different from you.

This experience of interpretive diversity differed from what he encountered in the church.

> I feel like growing up in church, I was kind of given this expectation that people who didn't believe the same way that I did, who weren't Christian, were missing something in life, they were less joyful or

they were less moral, or anything like that. I've increasingly found out through this course or the sequence of courses that that simply was not the case.

As Chase notes, it was not the study of texts written by nonbelievers that led him to be nonreligious, it was the critical study of the Bible with those who did not believe it.

> What we read wasn't particularly shocking. We didn't spend ten weeks reading Nietzsche or anything. It was just the fact that every day you were forced to come in and to give your viewpoint and defend it while you heard other people do the same thing. I think it was a really kind of formative experience.

Chase is one of those one out of twenty students who frequently experienced conflicts between his faith and course content. Moreover, as explored in the last chapter, those whose faith was weakened in college show an increase in actively seeking out meaning and purpose in life. Chase illustrates one example of how this change can result in further purpose seeking.

Chase would also identify something else beyond the classroom as exposing him to diverse ideas. He admits that the Internet played an important role in his loss of faith. Like the classroom experience, it exposed him to a wide diversity of beliefs

> I think that a lot of my loss of faith was precipitated by looking on the Internet for things. . . . the fact there were so many different viewpoints and so many people strongly defending their viewpoints in ways I was unable to do really kind of pushed me in that direction. So it wasn't as if I was necessarily looking for reasons to lose my faith or anything, it was just as you begin to ask questions and seek answers, the answers you were given just called forth a hundred more questions and because the Internet just gave you access, instant access, to the answers to those questions and information about beliefs and history and religion and all these things. I think that had a profound impact on the way I thought about religion.

Once Chase lost his faith, he reevaluated more or less everything, "because everything you thought hinged upon this faith, this body of scripture, and that sort of thing."

For this third type of student, the challenges to their theistic belief at college might also come through co-curricular experiences. For instance, Dennis, a third-year student at a public university finds the most transformative experience he encountered was through the friendships he experienced that led him to come out as gay after his first year of college.

> I have some really close friends here, coming out was a big part of this, but being able to feel a genuine connection like opening up your heart and soul to people has been a big impact on meaning and life.

In particular, he identifies the key as his successful effort to start a group that has formal discussions each week that touched on big questions relating to his sexual identity,

> I don't wanna harp on it but being gay, we talk about that a whole lot and like finding love in your life and genuineness and kind of the impact of having people abandoning you when that happens and what's the true nature of friendship and acceptance and love.

Unlike Ryan from the last chapter, as Dennis grew in his understanding of his gay identity, he also abandoned his former religious identity.

> When I first got to college . . . I still went to Mass every week my freshman year, I still thought of myself as a Catholic, although I disagreed with a lot of the teachings. Although, I don't know if I disagreed with any of the fundamental teachings at that time.

What drove him away from the Church was what he experienced after coming out, "a hateful reaction from a lot of very religious people I knew that pushed me further and further away." As a result, he attended Mass less. Still, he admits not all the reaction was unsupportive,

> There was also a priest who I grew up with and he was my parent's priest and he was a very kind guy and I loved him a lot and he was really helpful to me when I came out and told me that he's going to try and help my parents come to terms with it.

Yet, "tragically last year, he was in his seventies but very healthy and robust, and he . . . died. So that was a big blow, and even as I was starting to not really care too much about religion . . ." Dennis confesses he still appreciates his religious upbringing and would not say he's particularly bitter about it. In many ways, he sees it as a helpful part of his liberal education. "Being raised Catholic certainly gave me a unique perspective in terms that I was always contrasting, even when I was growing up, the Catholic atmosphere of my schooling and the secular American cultural atmosphere." In this regard, he understands his Catholic upbringing as contributing to a type of diverse education.

Overall then, these college nontheists demonstrate at least three particular pathways to their views. Parents may have supported their nontheistic outlook or students rebelled against their parents' religion. Students may have started considering themselves nontheists in adolescence, or it may have emerged in college. Despite these differences, some similarities exist in their experiences. Few claim to have mentors that led them along this path. At the same time though, both curricular and co-curricular experiences are largely understood as encouraging the development of an already existing nontheistic outlook or their journey from theism to nontheism. Finally, students believe their increased skepticism is aided by what they perceive as a newfound freedom in college. This last reason also had important implications for how the nontheists approach issues of purpose.

The Freedom of the Nonreligious

"I can't remember in my mind any time actually going to church with my parents," Peyton, a senior marketing major from a regional university recalls. Although he was baptized as a baby, his parents, he noted, "never asked me to go [to church]. It was never forced upon me. So I was able to decide on my own what I wanted to do." While this might place Peyton in the second category described above, the reality is that he was more like Chase in that he experienced a conversion in college. In high school, he would have identified as a Christian, "just because that's what everybody else was doing, if that makes any sense." College proved an important time for him with regard to his religious/nonreligious identity:

> I've always had doubts, but maybe I didn't really put a whole lot of time into actually thinking about what those doubts were and what they mean. And now that I'm in college and I've really had the time to, I don't want to say sit down and stare at a wall, but I've had more time to think about these things that I've realized that those doubts do exist.

At the time of the interview Peyton described himself as an agnostic, an identity label that he only adopted in the last couple of years. The label change, he believed, was closer to his true identity.

The regional public university Peyton attends supported his identity change by offering nothing, or perhaps more specifically, it offered free space for thinking:

> I was in that vacuum where there was nothing there. I was able to
> think freely and determine on my own which direction I wanted to
> go. So the university atmosphere that I was in allowed me to think
> more freely I guess.

Similar to the students above, college provided an atmosphere of freedom away from the constraints of both home life and any previously existing familial faith commitments.

When identifying any actual prompts or causes for his identity transformation, Peyton primarily believes his willingness to identify as agnostic was prompted by his maturing into an adult. Peyton draws a comparison to sexual identity when discussing the role of maturity in his identity change.

> You see more people as they mature come out of the closet. Well,
> they've probably known they were gay for a while, but they didn't
> have that maturity to own up to what it is. And by no means, am
> I saying being agnostic is the same as coming out of the closet, but
> I think there's definitely a maturity level with going through college
> and realizing that "okay, I can own up to who I am and let the world
> know this is who I am."

Peyton is quick to add that the label change "doesn't prevent me from living a moral life. I don't think living a moral life goes hand-in-hand with religion."

For virtually all of the nontheists, the relationship between their worldview and purpose, and the advantage their worldview provides in this relationship, is quite simple. They love the freedom to create their own meaning and purpose. This embrace of freedom also entails rejecting any view that there is a universal or overall objective meaning or purpose to life. Or as Jamal, a secular liberal arts student stated, "You know, when people talk about the meaning of life, they try to impose some kind of ideal . . . there is no ideal to live up to."

Nonreligious students often defend their own freedom by denigrating what they saw as the dependent, constrained, or disempowering outlook of the religious believer. Monica provides an example of both the celebration of freedom and the disparagement of theistic constraint. She perceives her nonreligious outlook as providing her with tremendous creative freedom with regard to purpose and meaning. "I don't believe in a higher power, or I don't think anyone is making me do the things I do or that anyone has any plan for me. I think I am completely in charge of my own life." Monica contrasts her outlook regarding her life purpose to how she believes taking a theistic outlook would influence her perspective. "I wouldn't think as critically about my meaning and purpose, because I would think, 'Okay, I can rely on someone else for that. God has a purpose for me, and I'd just have to listen to God.'" She realizes that this outlook is perhaps a bit condescending, since she confesses, "I've always been so careful about saying these kinds of things, because I can really offend some people." She treats God as the imaginary friend of other students that perhaps one shouldn't criticize. "I realize that to many people God is their life, and they really believe and in their head it's real, so therefore, it is real for them. But it's never been real for me." In contrast to what she sees as the constraining nature of theism, Monica celebrates the freedom to be the author of her life's meaning and purpose.

> And I think that's important to me, knowing that my meaning and purpose in life has nothing to do with anyone else . . . that's all my decision and not like God has a plan for me and it will see itself out because it's His plan and not mine, so therefore it has to happen. I just have to wait and see. But I can't wait and see if, you know, it's my own plan.

Overall, the two aspects of Monica's outlook depicted above, the denigration of religious approaches and the exaltation of freedom, characterize virtually every nontheistic approach to how they think about meaning and purpose. Dennis, who is a former Catholic, claimed:

> I think religious people, although they would really like to think freely, I think the fear of Hell is a big obstacle to thinking freely a lot of the times. Belief in an absolute final word of God that can't be changed, I think that's an obstacle to thinking without any preconceived notions.

Brooke, the atheist from a Catholic university whose story was told in chapter 4, calls religious belief a "crutch." Anne, the nonreligious student at a regional university claims, "I don't want to be stereotypical here because I don't mean to do that. But I think it tends to be if you're religious then you kind of have this 'meant to be' mentality." Jeremiah, a nonreligious Jew from a secular liberal arts college, maintains, "I think religion can sometimes be—I don't want to say a cop-out, but an easy way to find purpose, because, I mean, the meaning of life is essentially spelled out in most religious doctrine." Chase, the atheist liberal arts student at a Lutheran college, declares of his earlier religious outlook:

> Whereas before I think morality was more simplistic because you had a book and you could look it up, you know, now you're taking

responsibility for more morality and you're being forced to question whether what you're doing is right.

For all of these nontheists, they believe their worldview is more mature, complex, and real than the theists.

Creating Their Own Story

Since these students renounced belief in any sort of god and associated religious doctrines, the nontheists now believe they are free to create their own story. As Tyson, a public research university student notes, "I've kind of made my own purpose, and I kind of like that, being able to control why I was here." Brooke professes, "I think I definitely feel more liberated and stuff." In some cases, the freedom was freedom from a particular religious belief. Albert, a student at an Ivy League school maintains,

> I would say, in the instance that there's no book to tell you what to do, there's no clear rules, but um, I'm definitely, I think, happier because I was always very afraid of hell when I was religious, and it's very disturbing.

Cheryl, an atheist from a Lutheran liberal arts college declares, she does not "look to one place to find where the meaning of life is because the meaning of life is all around us." All of this freedom though came at what nontheists admitted was a difficult price.

The Burden of No Religious Belief

Chase, the Lutheran liberal arts college student already referenced in this chapter, admits that when it comes to atheism and purpose, "It's kind of a mixed bag." The problem is that atheism does not provide what his former Christian belief provided. "When I was religious," he recalls, "I had kind of an overarching purpose in life. Which would be nice." He summarizes this prior purpose with a verse from the Bible.

> I looked at the purpose of my life in accordance with Micah 6[:8], "What does the Lord require of you, to act justly, love mercy, and walk humbly with your God," or something along those lines. And so there was this sense that you know regardless of where I was in

life, I would be living out my faith. That's what gave my life meaning. That's what gave me a sense of peace. That regardless of what I was going through, regardless of what situation I was in, there would be God looking out for me.

Chase's earlier sense of clear purpose and the peace that resulted echoes the students from the last chapter. Yet, while Chase still appreciates this overarching purpose and the accompanying peace, he also did not like the constraints of Christianity.

> . . . but with that being said, you know, it didn't leave me much freedom to explore different things, to think about different ideas, and so ultimately, I think that getting to a meaning or a sort of purpose now is somewhat easier.

He adds a caveat, "even though, as I've said previously, I don't really know what that meaning is, but it's because you get to create your own meaning."

He also points out something else that causes epistemological problems for him,

> There were issues of accessibility from the deity. I kept hearing that God had a purpose for me, but how do you get to that purpose? How do you understand what that purpose is? And what if you make the wrong choice? What if, you know, you do something that you think is a good idea, but God had a completely different plan for you?

In this regard, Chase hits on what theistic students see as the biggest benefit to their worldview. Theistic students understand themselves as cocreators with God. In contrast, Chase is unsure how to find what the will of God might be in his life. He has not experienced a sense of divine calling, and even if he did, he is not sure it would fit with his own plans. He finds abandoning a belief in God solved that problem.

> So it's somewhat easier to make decisions now because I don't second guess myself about these things, I don't have to go, "Are we sure this is what I want to do?" because now I can make decisions without feeling like maybe I just made the wrong decision and without feeling like I had to please somebody else with my decisions. Rather just to decide things for my life, to make decisions about where I go to school, or what I study, or what I do with my time and to not feel like I have to second guess my decisions.

Chase's observation points to a fundamental difference we find between theists and nontheists that is not necessarily addressed in theories about self-authorship and meaning-making. While theists see themselves as cocreators with God of their meaning and purpose, nontheists view themselves as individual artists. They relish and embrace the freedom. So, while the concept of "self-authorship" may describe some students well, many of the theists describe something more akin to the idea of "coauthoring" their lives as they try to align their purpose with God's will.

Nontheists recognize the aid this kind of coauthorship provides, but they also reject it. For example, despite Chase's manifesto of relief from the burdens of pleasing a deity, in the next breath he admits, "I mean it's harder too because you don't have those sorts of decisions kind of made for you. You don't have a Bible that is supposedly completely true and you can look to for what is guidance." Since his conversion to being nonreligious, at the time of the interview, he now identifies a different meaning in life, one that is largely associated with particular individual "activities that bring me happiness." He gives the example, "when I'm working in the lab and I'm working on my research that's a very fulfilling thing for me." In contrast to his former outlook:

> I don't know that I really have a grand overarching sort of statement of my life's meaning. I think it's just to be happy to live in a way that I can be proud to live morally, and to I guess bring happiness to others as well, something like that.

Yet, even this current outlook he holds provisionally. "I mean I'm not really sure because I don't really have like an overarching vision for my life."

Albert, the Ivy League student introduced in chapter 8, provides a similar example. He grew up in Minnesota, and his parents divorced when he was in fourth grade. His mother raised him in a Christian household. "When I was younger I always took religion a lot more seriously than my brothers and sisters . . . and thought a lot more about scripture and took it more seriously." He largely viewed his religion as a set of constraining moral rules. Still, this outlook had its benefits according to Albert. "I think life was a lot simpler for me, because it was just, 'Do this, don't do that, and you'll go to heaven and everything will be okay.'" In high school, however, Albert's life took a different direction. He became an atheist due to what he perceived as philosophical contradictions in Christianity. Yet, atheism did not always provide easy answers,

> I became an atheist, and it became a lot more ambiguous. What's right and wrong? What should I do with my life? Is there a morality and if so what it is? There's no book to tell you what to do. There are no clear rules.

Overall, while nontheists love their freedom, they also feel the burden of this freedom. Self-authorship of one's purpose proves difficult. As a result of this type of outlook, they may fluctuate between celebrating their freedom but also recognizing the problems and difficulties that freedom created. For instance, Darren notes,

> Religion generally provides some sort of starting point for that sort of discussion without religious view, I would just sort of start at nothing and just try to build it all by myself and through discussion with others, which I think can be both a detriment and an aid in trying to figure things out I guess.

Gregory, a self-identified Buddhist who said he follows a "religion of the self," claimed,

> I guess I personally feel very liberated that I sort of can control my own destiny . . . but then again I do have to find a purpose, right? I do have to find a philosophy that I feel comfortable living . . . So it doesn't make it that much easier . . .

Katie, a nonreligious student at a liberal arts college, admitted,

> Not having anything to identify with on a spiritual level at least, you kind of have to guide your own values and sometimes it's maybe difficult to remember exactly what you want to stick true to, like what your priorities are.

In general, these students see themselves as nobly taking the "road less traveled" or the hard road. They want to be artists who create their own story and draw their own maps. Yet, starting from a blank page proves challenging.

The reward to this challenge is the sense of authenticity and lack of alienation they describe. Jeremiah, a nonreligious, cultural Jew admits that his outlook

> probably made it harder for me to find the meaning of life, but I think it'll also give me a more, a truer meaning of life—like a definition of a meaning of life that better fits the way I feel, the things I believe, as opposed to some described doctrine.

It should be noted, though, that the nonreligious students do not say that they find life meaningless. They still affirm some kind of meaning; however, their meaning in life is one that they create themselves. They see themselves as artists who can create something individual and personal on the canvas of life.

Finding Secular Substitutes for Religious Scripts

Although these students enjoy their creative freedom, the reality is they must still choose new guiding scripts that already exist in the culture. The alternative scripts they pick fit into five categories. First, like Kathryn and Anne above, some students claim to find guidance through science or education. Chase provides a helpful example:

> My purpose is to kind of learn new things and appreciate new ideas and try to understand, you know, why people who I agree with, who I disagree with might believe the things that they do. And to kind of become cognizant of different ideas and to become kind of open to different ideas that are presented only if for a moment.

In many ways, Chase has become content to become a learner. At least that was his provisional purpose. He admits though, "That being said, I don't know if I've necessarily, you know, I haven't come to a grand overarching sense of purpose." Being nonreligious, for him, means that he now has only smaller provisional purposes, at least for the time being. His provisional purpose especially focuses on his scientific work.

> I now work in a research lab on campus doing chemistry research, and you know what we do is fairly theoretical, it isn't so applied but when you talk with the professor who runs this research, and for whom this is a passion, you not only see that this is a passion but that this is what she wants to do with the rest of her life, which is powerful in some ways because you recognize that you can get contentment from work and you really can find a lot of your purpose in your work, but also even though this is very theoretical work, she sees a grand sort of application to which she sees that this work, given time, will make life better for other people in either appreciable or nonappreciable ways.

Thus, while Chase does not view his professors as the catalyst behind his unbelief, the model this chemistry professor provides proves instrumental in shaping Chase's view of his ultimate vocation in life.

> That was something that I think was a revelation to me because, you know, I've wanted to be a chemist for a very long time, longer than I've probably, I mean, I don't know, like in fifth grade when my parents bought me a wall-size periodic table for Christmas, and I loved it. So it's been for a long time an indulgence of my own curiosity.

> I haven't really seen too much of a way that this could actually be applied in a way that could make people's lives better, and so this fact that like you could find very fulfilling work and you could find your meaning in your work and in the sense that it will help people, I think, has been something of a revelation to me.

This new "revelation" has nothing to do with religion. Interestingly, while a Christian, Chase did not see how his work as a chemist might fit into God's larger purposes, as his particular theological tradition understood them.

> Before I kind of saw work as a necessary thing to do in order to continue to basically live with the whole purpose of life was to serve God, so if you weren't called to kind of a full time indication of ministry then the work was a necessary distraction from whatever your personal ministry would be, and that the work was somehow lower than that higher calling. So the fact that, you know, you can find a lot of joy in your work and that you can find a lot of your purpose and a lot of your meaning in your work has been something that has been modeled by this professor but then some of it has been kind of a new idea.

Chase provides an extended version of the common nonbelieving students' comments about the role of their metaphysical views. Without the traditional moral maps and guides, often associated with theistic religions, these students feel a bit more disoriented. While they can turn to a common cultural script about science for help with some answers and a view about valid knowledge, science provides limited help in constructing a purpose. Consequently, others look to other cultural narratives.

The second source of purpose for nontheists is some kind of professional narrative. Interestingly, in Chase's case, science provides this new vocation, but its limits leave him drawing on standard cultural narratives or focusing on vocation or career-oriented understandings of purpose. College thus became a place to grow deeper in his career prospects and how to use his career. Anne provides another example of a Self-Achiever with a similar focus. When asked whether college is supposed to help her develop her identity in a particular direction—to help her with questions of life's meaning or purpose—she replies that it did. As she further articulates how this worked, it becomes clear that meaning and purpose for her are mostly about practically navigating the world of work. "All of the professors are really adamant about getting you prepared for life." Helping with meaning and purpose seems to her to be primarily about job preparation.

A third group of nontheists also face this challenge in a different way. They appeal to the third source of guidance for nontheists: their personal feelings. For instance, Monica derives both meaning and purpose from the happiness she feels from relationships with people. She even makes the case for why self-oriented accomplishments are not her basis for meaning.

> But that's something that is like "a moment" that just kind of lasts in and of itself; whereas being with people and friends can always just kind of build on each other and you always know I can see my friends tomorrow and the next day and the next day, and then the next day I can meet someone completely new and develop this completely different relationship with them.

While she identifies people as what gives her meaning, it would appear that what Monica is really chasing is happiness and the feelings associated with happiness. The quest appears to emerge when she speaks about how college has challenged her understanding of meaning and purpose. Interestingly, this challenge did not come from her class, but it instead came from her experience in the co-curricular dimension of college life. Before coming to college, she imagined college as a place where she would find a certain kind of relational happiness.

> I was so eager to get out of high school and start my college life that I built it up in my mind until like college, when you get there, everything gets better, like immediately. Like parties and friends and boyfriends and all this stuff and your life is just going to be like a 24/7 like happy, happy, happy.

The reality, however, is that college exposed her to a terrifying loneliness that she did not expect.

> If I was sitting inside on a Saturday, [I would think] "Why aren't I with people right now?" which comes back to my obsession with people. Sometimes I find it difficult to be alone, and because I know I'm on a campus with two thousand other students that are my age, I'm like, "If I'm alone, is there someone I could be with right now or something I could be doing instead of being by myself?" And I think I just had to learn to calm down and not care about being alone for ten minutes or more—hopefully more.

In the end, what she has been trying to learn is that her conception of what gives her meaning also proves to be a particular weakness in her life. "I learned that

I kind of have this social anxiety sometimes that I have to be with people to be happy." She claims, however, that she is learning something that is completely changing her understanding of her purpose.

> Now I realize that sometimes my friends will be like, "Come down!" and I'm like, "I'm reading and going to bed early so, no, I'll see you tomorrow." But I had to learn that, and I think that completely changed kind of what I originally envisioned my purpose to be—to be always surrounded by people.

In this sense, Monica's self-construction of her purpose is actually a remodeling of what she earlier envisioned. As a result, she is learning in college how to be content without being surrounded by the people and relationships that give her life meaning.

Interestingly, the one nontheist who identified as Buddhist noted the priority of this appeal to feelings when considering purpose even over and against his Buddhist religious identity. "It's not like, oh, because I'm Buddhist I'm doing good things, it's because you feel good doing it." In fact, when it came to his meaning and purpose, he said of his Buddhism, "I don't think it relates at all."

The fourth type of nontheist finds purpose through a political identity and narrative. For instance, Dennis whose deconversion was described earlier, identifies himself though a political label: "I'm a liberal." He particularly celebrates the ideal of autonomy that undergirds the belief system and his understanding of his purpose in life.

> Essential to my identity would be the belief that everyone should be empowered to be who they really are and to do what they really want to do, going back to both the career thing and being gay. I think everyone should have the right to take ownership of who they are and be proud of it and as long as you don't infringe on other people's happiness or other people's freedom, everyone should be able to pursue their own happiness and be free to do what they love, love the person that they love, do what they wanna do in life. I'd say that's the core essence of my idea about purpose of life.

In Dennis's case, the American celebration of individual freedom becomes something he uses to guide his own personal philosophy of life.

The final group of nontheists simply borrows from other general cultural narratives about the good life, in particular the notion of living the "American Dream." Peyton, the student introduced earlier claims to be agnostic about his purpose. This agnosticism has left him without a larger narrative to follow beyond a default cultural script.

> I don't know what my purpose per se in life is yet, but, you know, I want to be happy, I want to have a family, you know, so it's, like I said, that's what I'm striving for. I'm trying to get a degree so I can get a good job. Just do the typical thing, you know, buy a house. Do what everyone is supposed to do so . . .

Without a religious narrative, Peyton draws on a general story of American success, even without seriously questioning what it is that makes this narrative appealing or worth pursuing. Understandably, with this sort of basis, Peyton admits that he's not sure his agnosticism will survive testing.

> Personally, I haven't experienced any type of tragedy in my life. I haven't lost a close loved one. I haven't had any real reason for what I feel like a lot of people would turn to religion for. So I guess my viewpoints haven't really been tested. I haven't been put in a situation where I need comfort and I feel like religion provides a really strong level of comfort, and I don't know how I'm going to react whenever my mother passes away and everybody else is, you know, praying.

Petyon realizes that faith provides real comfort in life's tragedies. He is just not sure that his commitment to standard ideas of American success will be enough to sustain him through more serious personal tragedy.

As these examples illustrate, the challenge for nontheists involves constructing their own script after rejecting a religious narrative by which to make sense of their lives and to look for guidance, particularly moral guidance. These stories should make it clear that they face this challenge. Moreover, not all nontheists understand this task as simply a matter purpose-making.

Some nontheists even retreat from equating nontheism with the idea that we live in a purposeless universe, where each individual must simply construct one's own meaning. Christina, a Unitarian at a Lutheran liberal arts college, encountered a philosophical difference with her boyfriend that stemmed from two conflicting nontheistic views of purpose and the universe. While both are nontheists, she found a fundamental difference with him.

> So, this guy I was seeing, he was really interested in like existential things and like we would talk about things like this, and as we started getting closer this is how he explained his worldview. He said that "I don't think," this is bracketed, this is in quotes, this is not me. He

said that "I don't think that there's really any purpose for why we are here or that there's like a central redeeming facet of the human existence, and I don't really think we're here for any reason, and I don't think anything happens to us after we die."

Christina's summary of her boyfriend's views, in many ways, captures the outlook of most of the nontheists we interviewed. Interestingly, although nontheist herself, Christina has a different reaction.

> I was just like, "Damn, that's really bleak," and he's like, "No I don't think it is, I think it like lets us really like pursue what we love just because we love it and not for any other reason, and that we just have to be like really passionate about our own lives, and that it's kind of freeing."

Again, Christina's boyfriend, like most nontheists, sees being a nontheist as having one central advantage. It provides them with freedom. For Christina, though, it fails to provide certain emotional elements that she needs.

> And I was like, "I'm sorry I can't work within that, your worldview depresses me." And it was part of knowing this, and like he was nice and he still is nice, I mean we're not, you know, we don't even like talk anymore, but I think part of what made me realize that we were fundamentally incompatible was that we just had really different ideas of how the world worked. . . . I can't be with someone whose worldview depresses me, just kind of not going to work.

Part of Christina's outlook stems from the fact that she believes "we're here to care for one another." She still wants to believe in a larger purpose that transcends the individual. Perhaps not surprisingly, she now finds herself less hostile to religion and confesses,

> I've gone through kind of a spiritual rollercoaster with going to Catholic school for ten years and then high school, questioning that part of myself and deciding that it didn't really identify with what I agreed with, and then being really pissy at religion for a couple of years in high school which kind of happens to a lot of people, then realizing that maybe like organized religion and groups of people don't have to be a bad thing.

She sees herself in a more "in-between" place. She calls herself a Unitarian and admits that identity "doesn't really tell you a whole lot either." Her mother has asked her whether she has "something to like pray to when you're sad and stuff like that." She responded at the time, "I don't know if I think about it that way." For now, she has settled on a Relationalist view of the world in which she finds some kind of transcendence. In many ways, Christina appears to fit the description of "spiritual but not religious."

> I think that something that keeps me going and makes my life worth living is knowing that we're all part of this kind of interdependent web of everything that exists, and it's our responsibility, and it's our privilege, to care for the rest of it. When I talk to somebody, or when I have a meaningful experience with somebody, I feel like I glimpse a little bit of that . . . we're here for some reason.

For Christina, even without a belief in God, she still wants to believe in something—she calls it "consciousness that we're all made of" that still offers some kind of metapurpose. She is not quite ready to embrace what she sees as the hopelessness involved with viewing the world as without some larger purpose.

Conclusion

Overall, our qualitative interviews reveal a number of possible reasons for the religious/nonreligious distinction in having a purpose. Nonreligious individuals, almost without fail, tell us that a major advantage of their approach can be found in how it granted them a sense of freedom to pursue whatever ends they desire. Yet, they still face the challenge of choosing those ends without the help of historical religious traditions and the evaluative frameworks they provide. A number of nonreligious students wrestle with the challenges this freedom provides, as evidenced by the fact that a higher percentage of purposeless students come from the nontheistic group of students we interviewed. This perceived handicap may provide one reason why studies consistently find the nonreligious to be less likely to have a purpose. Even the nonreligious claim that their views create some challenges or difficulties for purpose development. Moreover, both Self-Achievers and Relationalists face this issue. Often, the struggle to find purpose extends to the moral realm and issues of ultimate meaning. While a few extend their views about the meaninglessness of the universe to all of life, most instead find their meaning and guidance for their personal purpose through some other significant cultural script associated with science, a professional vocation, feelings, liberalism, or the American Dream. Some even still believe a larger purpose exists in the universe, even if God or the individual is not its source.

These findings may indicate two challenges facing higher education. On the one hand, it is not clear how higher education helps nonreligious students explore or address some of these issues. In general, religious believers find more challenge to their worldview in their higher-education experience. This finding is consistent with observations by Astin, Astin, and Lindholm that college students, except those at evangelical colleges, demonstrate increases in their levels of religious skepticism during the college years.[5] We wonder if religious skeptics need a broader liberal arts education that includes stronger challenges to their views that may foster deeper discussion and exploration of the challenges of building a personal purpose in a universe without one.

On the other hand, these findings raise one caution about using "purpose" discussions as the "answer" to the how to explore big questions in a way that respects diversity. As explored earlier, past discussions of "faith development" have been considered to be too Christian focused,[6] and even spirituality language has been critiqued for having various limitations because it is not inclusive enough.[7] As this chapter reveals, even discussions about purpose, if students understand purpose to mean a metaphysical purpose, may contain the impression that it favors theistic over nontheistic perspectives. The reason is that many (but not all) nontheists think of purpose as something associated with the nature of God or the universe. If meaning and purpose discussions are to be inclusive of nontheists, they would need to acknowledge that not everyone thinks of purpose as something one discovers in the fabric of the universe. After all, one's understanding of purpose always relates to the larger metanarrative one holds about the universe as a whole. In particular, one important part of the narrative as it relates to purpose concerns how that story will end. As anyone knows, the ending of a story shapes how one fashions and thinks about purpose and the good life as a whole. The next chapter explores how students think about the ending to their stories, the good life, and purpose.

Chapter 12

How Does the Story End?

Purpose, the Good Life, and the Future

I'm pretty much your average all-American, white girl, I want 2.5 kids, a nice husband with a steady income, the American Dream I guess.

—Marsha, student at Evangelical University

I'm not going to be like, "I want my kid to be like this; I want my husband to be like this; and my house should be blue." . . . The American Dream doesn't mean as much as it used to. You can get it and then you'll lose it in a second anyways, so I feel like you can't sit there and be like, "I have the American Dream."

—Leslie, student at Catholic University

"Making movies. That is my dream, just to make movies." Tyson, a Chinese-American film major who attends a large public research university is talking the particular passion that animated his vision of the future. "That would be the good life; making movies for people to enjoy and living off of it—just devoting all my time to my work, that would be great." Tyson's five-year goals line up with this focused purpose. He basically wants to pour himself into moviemaking. "I feel it's my responsibility to make as many [movies] as I can before I go. I want to put as much of me into the world before I can no longer do so. I guess that's my purpose." Tyson exhibits the focus and creative desire found in the handful of Creative Achievers we encountered.

When asked if he would include anything else in his five-year vision of the good life, Tyson does not touch on marriage or kids, but he did mention other relationships. "To not lose touch with my friends . . . without them, I don't know, what else would my life would be? I don't know. There's nothing else. If it's just work, it's not going to matter. You have to have friends too." He also adds a few other items to round out his vision of the good life.

> Besides that, a nice house to live in, maybe a dog, for my parents to be proud of me. They're real supportive of me. I hope they will be, as long as I do well. If I don't do well, I can't blame them. That's about it.

Like most college students we interview, Tyson does not claim to want riches. Instead, he pinpoints a few material desires and an important familial one.

While Tyson appears to place his friendships before his work, his creative work always remains at the forefront of his long-term dreams. When asked to envision what he would like to accomplish or experience before the end of his life, Tyson once again discusses his creative work goals.

> I want to get out as many ideas as possible, because there are a lot of ideas in my head, and I'm worried that I won't be able to make all of them. It is a big world for a lot of artists, and I want to get them out. I want people to see what I see, because I think it's really cool, and hopefully other people will think it's cool, and I want to share it.

He again adds one more thing to round out his dreams, but it clearly remains secondary. "Other than that, I would say contribute to the world in some big way, you know, I think that's definitely something I want to do before I go, besides my work." He even has a philanthropic plan in mind. "If I become really rich, I could be some sort of benefactor for space exploration. I love space, it's really cool, that kind of stuff. Help further humanity."

While Tyson has a vision for beyond-this-world exploration, his dreams remain focused on this life. "I don't necessarily believe in the afterlife, I mean, being a man of science, it's really hard to wrap your head around the idea that an entity without a brain guiding its movements and stuff can exist." As a materialist, Tyson uses a straightforward, pragmatic argument against a belief in the afterlife.

> But personally, I feel like living with the idea that after death you're still alive, it keeps you from living your life to the fullest. So if I think of it as, "after I die there's nothing," then everything has to be before death, and so fit in everything you can before you die so you will have no regrets. So that's kind of what goes along with the idea of how I live my life, the purpose of life. Fit in as much as you can before you're dead and you won't have any regrets.

For Tyson, seeing death as the final point gives him the urgency to act, it energizes his need to *carpe diem*. A happy ending does not involve heaven. Life's happy ending would mean that he is able to squeeze all the creative projects out of his mind into this life.

Caleb, a White student at a Mormon university, provides a stark contrast to Tyson's vision. For Caleb, "purpose has a lot to do with family. You know, obviously my parents' family, but also starting my family." This sense of purpose leads Caleb to a vision of the future concerned primarily with finding a balance between family and work, rather than a life devoted primarily to his job:

> Five years I'll hopefully be done with dental school . . . I'd like to be married, perhaps have kids . . . I think having a work-life balance is very important. That's part of the reason that I want to go into dentistry, because I think you can manage that for yourself.

Moreover, when Caleb thinks of what he wants to accomplish by the end of his life, he does not look to a particular career or creative accomplishment like Tyson. Instead, he paints a vision of a certain kind of family life:

> I'm picturing myself as an eighty-five-year-old man, I guess, I want my kids' kids to be happy. I want my kids to find success in their lives, you know, socially, spiritually, economically. I want them to be successful. I think that's what every father wants for his children or any mother wants for her children . . . I would hope to leave some sort legacy.

Whereas Tyson focuses on his parents' view of his accomplishments, Caleb reflects on his own view of his children's accomplishments.

Part of Caleb's inspiration comes from the older models he's experienced in his own family and the legacy left by one of his own family members. This vision of the balanced and rich good life was handed down to him by earlier family members:

> I look at my grandfather, my dad's dad. He was born and raised and died right in [location omitted], and I look at him as being incredibly successful in what he perceived to be his meaning and purpose. He had a very happy family and [a] very successful marriage. He taught school and was a farmer, so obviously he was never very wealthy, but he had [what was] sufficient for his needs. He never wanted for anything.

Another part of Caleb's inspiration comes from his religious beliefs, which he believes his grandfather exemplified during his life:

> I think becoming a disciple of Jesus Christ and becoming somebody that aims to attain those attributes that Christ had of charity and love, and just service . . . for me, [my grandfather] embodied a lot of those characteristics. Accomplishing that would be a challenge, but a worthy goal, to leave behind a legacy like that.

Unlike Tyson, Caleb also sees his vision of the future guided and shaped by the continuing narrative told within his religious community about life beyond this world:

> Yeah, I do believe in the afterlife, and, as per Mormon theology, that's, again, coming back to family. We believe that families can be together, not just in this life, but the . . . marital bond can be eternal. And so I think knowing that obviously affects my meaning and purpose right now. I would like to be married. I think a large part of that is knowing that there is a life after this life, and that having that bond with a spouse is particularly important, that it's not just until death.

This belief in an afterlife shapes his motivation for acting and behaving the way he does on earth. It does not supply an urgency to experience no regrets. Instead, it provides a motivation for a certain kind of life, "Knowing that we will be judged for our works and for those things that we have done I think that obviously affects—at least for me that affects—the way that I act and the way that I treat others." Ultimately, Caleb's belief that the full human story includes God's judgment of one's life, serves as a primary motivation to engage in good works.

Purpose and Future Life Goals

While research shows that older adults need both to identify their future aims and the concrete steps to achieve the aim to feel life satisfaction, adolescents and emerging adults are different. They "need only to feel they have the will to reach their ultimate aim . . . in order to feel satisfied with their lives."[1] For young people, as many parents can attest, dreams and the perceived will to reach them prove more important than focusing on the realities required to attain them. We too found students quite capable of dreaming about the future. Unlike our question about purpose, not one of them lacked for answers regarding their future goals.

On its face, the relationship between one's purpose and future life goals would appear to overlap significantly. After all, one's conception of a satisfactory conclusion to life contains the final destination or goal of one's life journey. This reason is likely why one prominent group of scholars of purpose state, "Questions designed to survey purpose need to focus on issues of future orientation, goals, and guiding forces that direct a young person through life."[2] Just as scholars have at times combined the concepts of meaning and purpose, scholars have noted that researchers may also equate future life goals with purpose.[3]

Yet, a student's future life goals and his or her purpose are not exactly synonymous. Purpose, scholars argue, provides a central organizing principle for one's future goals, but it is not simply one's goals.[4] Thus, while overlap exists, future goals usually end up being more diverse and disparate than one's purpose or purposes. In light of these possibilities, Hill, Burrow, and Sumner suggest that we need empirical research that differentiates purpose from similar constructs "such as meaning in life and eudemonic well-being."[5] While chapters 5 and 6 pointed out the important differences and similarities between college students' views of meaning and purpose, this chapter focuses on the similarities as well as the differences between students' purpose and their future life goals. In light of the differences we find, we suggest that educators must realize that helping students align their purpose and their future goals will prove to be an important challenge.

To gain an understanding of the differences and similarities between matters of purpose and students' vision of their future good life, we first undertook an analysis of 230 interviews of eighteen to twenty-three-year-old emerging adults conducted for the National Study of Youth and Religion.[6] These are not interviews we conducted, and not all of the interviews are with college students, yet the content of the interviews is very useful for our present purposes. The interviewers for the NSYR interviews asked questions about both purpose and the good life. Table 12.1 on page 304 provides our analysis of the content of these young emerging adults' answers and the percentage of interviewees who identified certain purpose ingredients or future goals.

As can be seen from table 12.1, similar to meaning, every interviewee had future goals. Yet, not every interviewee mentioned what they defined as a purpose. Moreover, while almost all of the future goals of these young emerging adults often fit into the same categories we use to understand meaning and purpose ingredients, they sometimes included additional areas of emphasis. When it came to future goals, these young emerging adults were more likely to talk about wanting to achieve certain self-oriented goals such as acquiring certain material goods (e.g., house, cars), being able to engage in certain experiences (e.g., travel, skydive), achieving success, and living with no regrets. These future goals, in many ways, function more as parts of a "bucket list" that may or may not be linked to a young person's purpose.

Table 12.1. Percentage of Emerging Adults Mentioning Particular Purposes or Goals ($N = 230$)

	Purpose*	Future Goals*
Purposeless	32	0
Achievers		
Happiness	11	35
Material	2	26
New Experiences (e.g., Travel/Skydive)	0	19
Professional	20	17
Success Achievers	0	8
No Regrets	0	6
Relationalists		
Family Relationalists	13	47
Virtue Relationalists	12	12
Friend Relationalists	0	5
Transcendents		
Religious	8	5
Change/Contribute to the World	2	9

*The numbers in each column do not add up to one hundred, because some respondents listed more than one purpose or goal.

The college students we interviewed for our 110 Targeted Qual database were not that different from the young emerging adults interviewed for the NSYR project. One thing we did differently than the NSYR interviewers is that we asked two different questions about future goals—one related to five-year goals and another to end-of-life goals. Still, although we left the possible responses to our question wide open, students almost always responded from the same limited menu of items (see table 12.2). As would be expected, many of the ingredients to a student's five-year vision of the good life or their goals before death often line up with their stated purpose. Achievers mention their future career or graduate school, Relationalists want to get married and have a family, and Transcendents talk about a certain quality of relationship with God. Those without purpose perhaps were the most interesting in that they were the dominant ones who talked about wanting to be happy (they accounted for 8 of the 14 who identified happiness as a five-year goal). Hoping for happiness, in these cases, appears to serve as a substitute for specific goals or a specific purpose.

Table 12.2. Percentage Mentioning Certain Five-Year and Before You Die Goals ($N = 110$)

	Purpose	5 Year	Before I Die
Purposeless or No Goals	25	0	0
Achievement Purposes or Goals			
Achieve a particular educational or career status	39	94	36
Achieve happiness	12	13	6
Acquire certain experiences (e.g., skydiving)	7	0	16
Obtain certain possessions or level of income	5	28	10
Accomplish certain creative endeavors	4	6	0
Live in a certain geographic location	0	26	4
Travel to certain destinations	0	0	32
Live with no regrets	0	0	6
Relationalist Purposes or Goals			
Obtain a certain marital or romantic relationship status	0	52	13
Have a family	16	24	35
Have close friends/relationships	20	29	6
Serve others	27	17	8
Transcendent Purposes or Goals			
Experience a certain kind of relationship with God	25	17	16
Make a difference	8	0	29

These students' answers about future goals demonstrate some important points. The first concerns material possessions. The fact that a discussion of five-year goals results in over a fourth of students focusing on material things would appear to reveal a materialism that students would not admit when directly discussing meaning and purpose. We should note, however, that students rarely talk about mansions or stacks of money. Instead, they mention that they hope to be "financially independent from their parents," be able to have a "comfortable lifestyle," "loans paid off," "a particular standard of living [so] I can eat organic food," "a home," or "a home and a dog." Andrew, an African-American student from a public research university expresses this perspective:

> I just want to live in a decent house. I don't want a mansion or two houses. I don't want things like that. I just want something that I can live comfortably in, a nice car, maybe, not an extravagant car, just

> a nice car. I just want to be able to live comfortably without having
> to live paycheck to paycheck like my mother did.

The students we interviewed clearly do not embrace an "I want to get rich narrative." Indeed, Andrea's story in the introduction in which she talks about hoping to make lots of money, or Troy's goals described in chapter 4 of hoping to amass certain material goods, are exceptions. Almost all of the other respondents always qualify their money dreams as Andrew does. The good life for them, materially speaking, is not the rich life, but the comfortable life, one in which they would not have to worry about money. In fact, not one respondent describes his or her five-year goals *exclusively* in financial terms.

While some scholars have made a compelling case that aspects of consumerism and materialism deeply shape the lives of emerging adults today,[7] the vast majority of the students we interviewed seem to acknowledge that this is not (or should not be) part of their purpose in life. Materialism is slightly more likely to show up in their future goals, but if anything, students appear more, or at least just as, interested in career, relationships, and experiences. In fact, the "consumption" of experiences predominates the category of future goals in ways it did not for purpose. Geography and travel emerge as the second future goal that never figures prominently in student discussions of purpose. Students never mentioned these types of experiences as a primary purpose, and in most cases, these future goals relate to a job, family, travel or life experience goal. The most common geographic destinations they identify are cities, and not one student hoped to live in the country or rural area.

Beyond the slight shift in how students discuss material possessions, future goals increase what could be considered self-focused aims when compared to discussions of purpose. Corbin, a Catholic student at a Catholic university provides a helpful example of this distinction. He summarizes his own purpose with a statement from the Baltimore Catechism. "It says that the purpose of life is to, well, love and serve the Lord in this life so you can live with him forever in the next." Yet, when asked what he wants to experience before the end of his life though, he somewhat jokingly shares, "Um, I golf a lot. I'd like to get my handicap down to like a five." He quickly admits that this is not the answer one would expect. "I guess a better answer would be like, 'I want to save, like, five-thousand kids in Africa or something.' But I don't. I don't really think like that. I'm not particularly socially active." While Corbin's answer sounds disappointingly shallow, it appears that he once had change-the-world dreams, but he has already become disillusioned,

> I mean . . . I thought it would be cool when I was younger to go
> to Congress and be a lobbyist or be a congressman and really care

about pro-life and life issues and stuff like that. But I've become a little more cynical of the party establishment since I was in high school, a little less idealistic. So that's on the back burner.

Corbin's outlook is the more common one among our college students. When talking about what they want to accomplish before the end of life, as we have already noted, the answers tend to fall into conventional categories (e.g., career, marriage and family, travel, have experiences, accumulate stuff) with a substantial minority hoping to make a difference in the world, focus on a relationship with God, or serve others. Indeed, even more than wanting to change the world, these students want to see the world.

Not everyone focused more on material possessions or more on self-focused aims. As we analyzed the responses to future goals, we noticed that those who were more self-oriented tended to use a different language and framework to think about their future. These different constructions of future goals were closely related to their purpose type as well. This construction fit into one of two general types of patterns, what we call the Balanced and the Focused.

The Balanced

When asked what the good life would look like in five years Lauren, an Ivy League student, admits, "I don't know at this point," but she does offer some tentative ideas. "I could be teaching. I could also be in grad/medical school. Depending on how things work out." Ultimately, she wants to become a psychologist, and adds, "when I find myself a real adult, I want to be in California." She also hopes to get married, but she admits, "For obvious reasons I kind of dreaded marrying a guy." The obvious reasons pertain to two things she told us earlier. She claims that she was actually the cause of her parents' original marriage which ended in divorce. She says of her father, "I think he felt that her being pregnant with me (I was the first child they had) kind of dropped him into this loveless marriage. . . . So, just with that, he's kind of resented me since before I was born." Lauren also shares the resentment. The reason is that Lauren's difficulties with her dad were later compounded by the fact that when Lauren was in sixth grade, she wanted to live with her mother only, instead of a joint-custody arrangement.

> And that backlashed because then my dad took us to court because he didn't want to pay child support. The judge . . . decided that he would listen to my father's allegations of my mom brainwashing us, and we weren't allowed to talk to her for a month. That turned into

three months. The court procedures extended to three years because of my dad. So, he took the majority of the child custody for those three years, and we took child support for it. *Interviewer: So do you resent those three years that he did that?* Lauren: Yes.

Lauren's other reason for not wanting to marry a man is that she recently concluded she is a lesbian. This conclusion, of course, changed her whole view toward marriage. "But now that I've clarified who I would like to [marry], I'm definitely looking forward to it. You know, having a relationship, settling down, having my two and a half kids. Probably just two kids."

Lauren's future goals, if one thinks of common categories such as career, marriage, kids, and future living location prove quite common among the group we labeled the Balanced. The Balanced use what we would consider a conventional American Dream narrative to talk about their five-year vision of the good life. It involves mentioning some of the above listed goals, usually career, marriage, material possessions, and kids, in a way that makes clear that all of them would be part of the good life. Arthur, a student from regional university provides another example:

> I'd really enjoy working in a nice place. It doesn't really have to be like a big office or the general stereotype of like what a good job is. But, being able to be financially secure . . . And maybe starting a good family and then still having enough free time to do things that I'd enjoy. Like hobbies . . . I include service as one of my hobbies . . . So, being able to help the community, but still be solid and [about] my family.

As can be seen from Arthur's example, the Balanced do not focus on a specific career. Indeed, the vast majority of the Balanced tend to be Relationalists when it comes to purpose and meaning, so they are less focused on specific accomplishments and more on connecting with people and having a career enhance their particular relational interest. Dakota, from a liberal arts college, exhibits this outlook.

> I would say having a rewarding career or feeling like I'm helping other people and helping them to improve their life, whether that be like as a counselor or doing something else. I've also thought about maybe doing some teaching. I think that would be really neat, just because I really like teaching people things, and I find that validating. It's also just really interesting to see when they have that "aha" moment. I like that. And I would say having a strong group of friends

and family and also just doing some volunteering because that's definitely rewarding and having a balanced life as well like making sure I exercise, get enough sleep, all that kind of stuff.

The Relationalist drive of the Balanced also comes through in their dreams about marriage. Of the fifty-seven Self-Achievers we interviewed, only four cited marriage or a serious relationship in their five-year goals. In this respect, students demonstrate consistency regarding their future goals and how they discuss meaning in life. Almost all the other students who mentioned marriage or a serious relationship in their future goals were Relationalists, although some were also Transcendents.

Religious or nonreligious identity also appears to play a role in this outlook. One-third of the students who talked about marriage or a serious relationship in our 110 Targeted Qual group came from the Mormon or Jewish universities. Almost all the others had a religious background. Just as the religious we interviewed were more likely to think about marriage in five years, they were also the most likely to think about children. Of the twenty-six students who mentioned having children in five years, all of them were religious with the bulk (17) coming from the Catholic, evangelical, Jewish, and Mormon universities. The nonreligious never talked about kids, and three even specifically said they did not want kids. Instead, most of them focused on happiness with three-fourths of the students who mentioned happiness (9 of 12) coming from those with no religious affiliation.

The Balanced students rarely exhibit a "change-the-world mentality." Instead, they long for less transformation and more stability. Max, a Catholic student at a Lutheran liberal arts college provides a helpful example of the Balanced. His five-year goals include:

> Well, I think I would like to be happy . . . So I'll be working hard, trying to find a job, or have a job, starting out a job. You know by that time have somebody special that I can enjoy life with, and I can talk to about anything, just being in a good place physically, mentally, emotionally, having maintained relationships with my parents, my sister, other relatives and other close friends.

Max, like the usual Balanced, focuses less on changing people or the world and more on being a source of stability and goodness. When speaking of what he wants to accomplish before the end of his life he shares:

> I guess I would want to have been there for someone or for many people, in whatever context that might be. Taking care of my parents

> in their older age. If it's raising kids, it's teaching them well and passing on what I learned. If it's being a lawyer, it's helping people accomplish things, transactional law and stuff, helping people do things, make things happen. Knowing I was a great guy, a decent guy, that I was there when you needed him and kept you safe, protected you, made you happy.

Max mixes his service-oriented outlook with some personal desires in ways that reflect the relational mentality of the Balanced. In fact, like many of the Balanced, he even mentions "balance" as a goal.

> Then also I would just want to have fun too and that means having life balance, that means going on vacations, that means doing crazy things, fun things, that means not working too hard, that means laughing, that means being content with what you have and living within your means and just trying to see the most in every moment, I suppose, which is sometimes harder to do—take time to be intro-spective and stuff—especially here when you're busy so [busy], but yeah. Explore nature, travel, find someone, see things.

For the Balanced, like Max, they often cover a whole range of goals when describing their future. The next group did not.

The Focused

Trinity, a student at a public research university in the South describes a fairly cohesive life vision to one of us. Her purpose is quite clearly a Transcendent one:

> Well I'm a follower of Christ, I love Jesus with my whole heart and so I definitely see my purpose in life as to bring glory to God and doing that in everything that I do whether it be my career, my friendships, or not just bringing others to Christ, but also living my life out in His name and for His glory.

For her, this particularly applies to her career, which she believes is not simply a choice but a particular religious vocation,

> The reason why I changed my major from audiology to social work was because I very much feel called to the orphanages and foster care system and adoption and that kind of thing. I really feel like

that's where God's leading me on my path, and that's where I will ultimately lead out my purpose and His plan.

Five years from now, she envisions her life in light of this particular calling and dream. Living a good life would be on a mission for God in a foreign country ministering to people in need. "I would just love to be missioning somewhere, anywhere. Preferably with orphans, but I would love to, even if I was just a teacher in an orphanage somewhere." She even paints a picture of one possibility. "I would love to be sleeping on a roof in Haiti, washing my clothes on a washboard with, you know, cold water that has sat there all day, something like that." Her relationship with a boyfriend also figures into this plan, but it does not rise to the same level of importance. "I would love to have some kind of idea of marriage, if my boyfriend and I are still together." In fact, for her that relationship needed to fit around her central life calling. She maintains that any decision about marriage would have "to work around where I want to be."

Trinity represents a group who speak in a different way about how they envision the good life, particularly their five-year goals. We call them the Focused. The Focused, however, break into two very different types. The first type consists largely of Achievers and shares something in common with Bill Gates Jr. and Warren Buffet. Warren Buffett recalled discovering their shared characteristic at a dinner conversation where they first met. "Bill Gates, Sr. posed the question to the table: What factor did people feel was the most important in getting to where they'd gotten in life? And I said 'Focus.' And Bill [Gates Jr.] said the same thing."[8] The vast majority of these Focused Achievers conceive of five-year goals, first and foremost, in relation to a particular educational or career status. They also speak in a particular way about their careers that make it clear that they are focused exclusively or primarily on career goals. For instance, Malik, a Muslim student at a liberal arts college, shared this story when asked about his five-year goals:

> This is a big dream of mine. There's a rapper who's a big influence for me and his name is Jake Cole. He was an amazing student and he went to St. John's University in New York—specifically so that he could sign to Jay-Z's record label. And so he went to New York. He graduated with honors and he was the valedictorian of his university and for the year after college he was out working three jobs at the time. He was staying in run down apartments, and he was just recording every single day or trying to work and make his way up to the studio. And one day—he would like stand out at Jay-Z's studio every single day—and one day Jay-Z came by and he was like, "No, I'm not going to take that, and he just like brushed him off." And

> so Jake Cole, he just like kept working on himself, and eventually he stood in the rain again for like another two hours and he gave Jay-Z his CD and then he kept building on himself and after that he got signed to Rockefeller Studios with like one of the largest deals. And so, hearing him speak is really motivational to me, and so I think I might try to go to Columbia University [for an MBA] because they have a partnership with this school.

Even for some of those who mention other goals, it is quite clear that professional goals remain at the top of the list with other goals (geographic and relational) subject to them. Jeremiah, a liberal arts student focused on "having a job where I can feel secure and where I can advance to a point where I can build that job into a career. That's a pretty tall order—that's an ideal place I guess." While he did mention, "Hopefully I'll still be with my girlfriend," he added "we'll probably be in different parts of the United States, unfortunately, but hopefully I'll see her as often as I can." In this case, he exhibited more concern with advancing his career than living in the same geographic region as his girlfriend.

The second group of students is the Transcendently Focused. Jenny, a pre-dental major from a Baptist university provides an example that is similar to Trinity. She speaks about finding meaning from her relationship with God, particularly "Christ the Lord." The reason is that "He breathes life into us and so he gives me my meaning in life and he teaches me what to do and how to live, and so I mean that's pretty much it." From that meaning, she derives her particular vocational purpose or calling.

> I really think that God brought me to college and, just like a couple of years ago, he set my heart to do the missionary dentistry stuff and to have that as a goal. Whether or not that comes true, that may change. But right now, that's what I'm working for and that's what I feel like he's calling me to do.

Monetary things and goals "are not a huge aspect to me," she claims. What she hopes to accomplish in life pertains to her driving purpose.

> I've been on so many mission trips, and I've been on so many service organizations and stuff like that, and I work at the dentist office. If I could just put those together. I just want to experience a medical mission and experience saving somebody's life, because in other countries people die from [bad] dental hygiene. It's not just like, "Oh my tooth hurts" type thing. It's like, "Oh my tooth is going to kill." I would love to experience that before I die, just to be able to

use those tools that God's going to give me and be able to use that for him and save other people.

Indeed, Jenny does not mention other goals; instead, she focuses on pouring out her life and her gifts into serving and even saving others.

In light of this kind of Transcendent mission from God, if these students mention the various parts of life that the Balanced discuss, such as Trinity's reference to marriage, they tend to hold on loosely to other life goals in light of their one overarching focus. The students talking this way were virtually all Baptist or evangelical Christians (with almost half coming from the Baptist and evangelical universities). These two students provide examples of this perspective.

- "I think five years from now a good life to me would just be that I'm devoted to God and that I'm constantly learning. I feel like that would be a good life. This is always how I've been. I don't really think, 'Oh, a good life equals husband, children, and perfect job.' 'Cause I just, I don't know what God has in store. So I think a good life would be all those things, but I think as of now, where I'm thinking is that, as long as I'm striving after God that would be a pretty good life to me." (Kaitlyn, a Baptist university student)

- "Living the good life . . . I would say as long as I was doing what I was supposed to do, and I don't know exactly what that looks like, but just making sure that I'm still like submitting to God's will for my life and his practices and his commands and purposes. That would be the good life. I don't picture myself with a lot of money or anything like that, but as long as I stay true to who I was and who God created me to be, then that would be a good life for me. . . . I think I have things in my head that I would like to do—like I would like a family, I'd like to have a job—but I don't think that would be related to my meaning and purpose. I don't think I would have any more purpose if I had a family and a job in five years than I do now." (Allison, an evangelical university student)

For these students, their focus on their relationship with God meant that the other common purposes or goals students mention play only a secondary role in their future dreams.

While we found these kinds of Transcendently Focused students largely at religious institutions, they could also be found among evangelical college students at secular institutions. Jake, a Christian student at a secular liberal arts college shared a similar outlook.

> Living the good life . . . I mean, I guess I'm not really looking for like a wife and kids in five years or anything like. I mean, I wouldn't mind a job but I'm just not really sure where I'm going to be and where I want to be exactly. I mean, as long as I got what I need to survive and [am] still able to honor God, that's what I want to do with my life. I'm not looking for a big house or anything . . . Yeah, I guess living the good life for me is, if I can still ride a bike, if I can still go outside and play, and I have my daily needs taken care of, and I can still honor God—I mean, that's the perfect life for me.

Jake added a few more items to his good life in order to survive, but he still reduced it to a bare minimum based on his view of the centrality of God in his life. Likewise, Christina, at a public research university related,

> I don't know, I'm most fulfilled when I'm where the Lord wants me to be, and so if the good life to me would be, is like wherever God wants me to be, because if I'm married and have a kid and have a great job, but like God wants me to be like in [location omitted] teaching, then I'm not going to be fulfilled because I'm not going to be doing what I'm made to do. So I have no idea what that looks like, but just wherever God calls me and whatever he has for me.

The sense of surrender of life goals by the Christian students was one of the most noteworthy distinctions among interviewee responses. The good life for them was determined by their relationship with God and everything else was relative to this.

It is quite clear that students in the evangelical or Baptist cultures have been taught, and have chosen for themselves, a certain way of thinking about their future goals and then use a common narrative when discussing them that is countercultural. Indeed, we found only one student outside of these students, a Mormon, who speaks in a slightly similar way. Chris shared,

> That's one thing that I try not to think about the future too much. I try and plan for it, prepare for it, but these past couple of years have shown me that even the best-laid plans for the future are not going to come to fruition, you know? Time has a way of destroying those things.

Yet, even in this case, Chris used *time* instead of *God*, and speaks more with a voice of resignation than optimism. For all the other Transcendently Focused students, they were not focused on making meaning or purpose, they wanted to discover God's plan for their lives.

The Good Life and the Life to Come

When asked about his end of life goals, Joshua, a student at a Jewish university took what often prompts bucket list sort of responses and instead answers that what he wants placed on his tombstone is simply: " 'Joshua, he tried.' You know, something like that [*laughs*]." When asked whether he believes in an afterlife and if his views of the afterlife influence his overall understanding of his purpose, Joshua responds with logic more than conviction. "I guess I would have to believe in an afterlife. You know if you believe in God, how can you not believe in afterlife?" The reason for this staid response pertains to his particular attitude toward this type of difficult metaphysical questions, as follows:

> But, at the same time, it's not a fixation. I don't really think about it much. People argue, "Is it physical? Is it more spiritual? Is it like this? Do ants go to heaven? Do dogs go to heaven? Are aliens in heaven?" There are so many questions . . . I guess that's another thing I learned from my dad, is to not ask these abstract questions that you can't answer. To be practical. And, in that sense, it hasn't had much influence in terms of what I would see as meaning or purpose, just because who knows, right? It's way out there.

In addition, he also suggests, "Hell isn't a very big focus in Judaism," so he does not put much stock in the idea that "because God exists we should be afraid and, you know, live well."

What this means for his actual outlook on life is that while he gives lip service to a belief in heaven, he actually finds the idea of future rewards a bit infantile when it came to thinking about motivations for living the good life:

> So, I mean, the answer is yes, the belief in heaven would influence meaning and purpose because it is a life after life, but it hasn't influenced my meaning and purpose in any practical way. I guess the reward for living well doing the right thing is simply doing the right thing. That's a reward in and of itself. You don't have to go to heaven and get candy or something for it. Just the fact that it's good would suffice.

In many respects, although Joshua affirms the afterlife, he remains a practical agnostic when it came to the influence of the afterlife on his purpose. He believes it makes logical sense to believe in heaven since he believes in God, but it makes little difference in how he thinks about his future goals.

Caroline, a Mormon student at a Mormon university provides a striking contrast to Joshua. A high-achieving pre-med student, when asked about the end of her life, she speaks with a more Relationalist voice, "I would like to look back and be happy with all the relationships I've made." Not surprisingly, her vision of relational happiness extends into her vision of the afterlife. Indeed, Mormonism provides her a vision of the afterlife that fits well with her future relational longings.

> I kind of want to be the best person I can be because we believe in different kingdoms, so my goal is I want to be in the celestial one, you know. . . . In our church we believe there are certain ways and to get there, I don't know, be the best person you can be, but like we believe in eternal marriage, it's the only way you can get into the highest kingdom, so for me definitely finding someone to marry, that's a big part of this religion.

While Joshua's belief about the afterlife is discontinuous with his purpose and other life goals, Caroline sees her view of the afterlife as continuous and reinforcing of her ultimate longings. In this respect, Caroline and Joshua provide a study in contrasts when thinking about the future.

Both Caroline and Joshua, though, prove typical of young emerging adults in their belief in the afterlife. Surveys of early emerging adults (18–23) find that the vast majority believe in heaven, with only 16 percent expressing disbelief in its existence.[9] Of course, believing in heaven is one thing, but having it influence your purpose and meaning is another. After all, Joshua expressed belief in heaven.

Throughout our discussions, students occasionally brought up heaven or the afterlife as motivating or influencing factors regarding how they think about purpose, but it was not common, even though a large portion of our sample came from students at religious institutions. When the belief or nonbelief did come up, both could actually be used to motivate similar responses. For instance, the following two students provide a distinct contrast, although both maintain their views of the afterlife motivate them. Darren, a nonreligious student at the Lutheran liberal arts college, observes that "without any sort of possibility of an afterlife" he can become more focused on this life. He claims, he's "working to make my life be as good as I think I can make it . . ." Like Tyson in our opening story, Darren believes that the lack of belief in an afterlife can lead one to seize the day and live for the moment. In contrast, Jake, an evangelical student at a secular liberal arts college shares a completely different view.

> I don't know like how familiar you are with the Bible. I don't know where it says it, but like getting to heaven and hearing God say, "Well done my good and faithful servant." That's like the biggest thing that like freaks me out. Like, what am I doing in my life that's gonna be able to hear that? 'Cause I mean, you don't want to get to like the end of your life and think, "Oh, you didn't actually, I don't know, help people or you didn't actually make your life meaningful I guess" . . . I guess the entire purpose of my life [is] if I could get to heaven and hear that, that would be awesome.

While the outcome of a nonreligious or religious outlook may be the same for how one thinks about life (e.g., *carpe diem*), religious and nonreligious identity makes the most difference in whether and how students articulate a motivation for purpose that is related to what one thinks about the afterlife.

Most atheists, agnostic, or nonreligious students we interviewed did not believe in the afterlife, although it is interesting to note that only 38 percent of younger emerging adults (18–23) who identify as nonreligious deny the existence of heaven.[10] Leonard, who calls himself an existentialist, claims this lack of belief meant,

> I'm sort of focused entirely on the seventy or so years that I'm spending here on this planet and not—I'm very focused more on what I do, what other people do now instead of focusing on like [a] higher power defining my difference here or the idea that if I act and exist and am a certain way, then something else will happen later on.

If the nonreligious students we interviewed did affirm heaven, they would often admit like this student, "I don't think it really has a huge impact on the way I view the meaning of life, but I do sort of believe in it, and I'd like to believe that it exists." Similarly, a number of Jewish students, like Joseph, mentioned that they believe in the afterlife but acknowledged that it does not really influence their views about life purpose and meaning (e.g., "I do believe in it, but it really doesn't influence how I think about meaning and purpose.").

For those students who do identify an influence, the dominant impact they share pertains to the effect that the expectation of future rewards or punishments has on them. We found this among Mormons, Protestants, Catholics, Jews, and a Buddhist student. Terry, a Mormon student maintained:

> I think it affects everything I do. I believe that afterwards, we'll be judged according to what we have become and what we've done,

> but more what we've become because what we've done, if we repent, sometimes doesn't matter. Then we will be able to live with God or without God depending on how we've done, and my goal is to be with God forever. And that means that I have to do things every day: I have to change my actions. I can't just stay stagnant. I have to continue to improve because that's what he expects of me as a person—to always be driven to try to become what I can.

Although not apparent in Terry's answer, at times, a particular religious belief linked to a specific tradition occasionally emerged in these answers, but it really did not influence the basic outlook regarding rewards and punishment. A Buddhist student, Gerald, simply stated, "I need to be a better person in this life so I can be a person again in the next life." The importance of the particular tradition proved significant in the level of confidence and conviction a student might have about the importance of the afterlife. Isaac, a Jewish student gave this perspective, albeit in an ambivalent manner that proved typical of Jewish students.

> So, that depends on the day, I mean, because, yeah, there'll be times where I'm like, "Okay, I know there's an afterlife, and I know if I do whatever it is x, y, and z, God will frown upon it, and I probably won't get into heaven." And then other days it's like, "I don't know if there's really an afterlife. I don't know if God really cares, not even maybe." Okay, so maybe I believe that there's always an afterlife, but sometimes I think maybe my actions don't—some of my lesser actions won't impact whether or not I'll get into heaven. Um, so I mean, I'm not sure exactly.

For all of these students, the afterlife involved a type of judgment in which God, or the divine, will review one's good and bad actions and reward one accordingly.

Anything beyond this view, however, was only articulated by the group that proved the most convinced of the afterlife's existence and importance, the Evangelical Protestants.[11] These students shared that a belief in the afterlife provides them with peace, hope, and an eternal perspective that is related to a motivation for their particular purpose or meaning. One student contrasted her experience before being a Christian with her outlook afterward:

> I can remember—before I accepted Jesus to be my Savior and understood what that meant—going to a funeral and just thinking about how life was, like, "Okay, you grow, you get married, you have kids, you work your whole life, and then you die. And that's it." And

then when I got old enough to understand what heaven and what, eternity mean . . . I understand this isn't it. That my purpose extends beyond my eighty years on this planet, that it goes beyond that and, like, there are lasting effects from the things that I do and the way that I fulfill my purpose in loving others and bringing them to the Lord, that that's a lasting thing, that purpose is such a lasting thing.

The sense of living in a larger story that is not of their creation was once again a common theme we found among many evangelical students. As Cody, the student profiled in chapter 4 shared, "There's a song lyric that talks about this world is merely a subplot, and so that's kind of how I see it. That this world is merely a subplot to the bigger plot of the afterlife in heaven and living forever."

Conclusion

Understanding the different kinds of future goals and conceptions of students, we maintain, can prove helpful as educators think about the role their institutions can and should play in shaping students' lives. These empirical realities also raise important questions, perhaps the most important one being: How should higher education attempt to inform and shape the future goals and future conceptions of the good life? Moreover, to what degree should it seek to help students align their purpose and their future goals?

State institutions obviously cannot take stands about the afterlife or even particular views about the good life students should choose. After all, part of the being involved in a liberal democracy is that it gives citizens wide latitude to design and construct the good life. Still, one of the most obvious functions of higher education, even in state institutions, should be to educate students about the implications of their goals and conceptions of the good life. After all, through history and social science, we know the results of structuring one's life in certain ways. For instance, one study has found that those with goals focused on others-oriented aims actually predicted higher subjective well-being. In contrast, those with self-related aims are associated with lower future well-being.[12] In other words, a focus on self-oriented goals could prove detrimental to students' well-being.

Of course, as we have cited throughout this book, numerous scholars have made recommendations about how to approach this issue. Often, however, the recommendations are made without reference to empirical realities. In the conclusion, we examine some of the various recommendations in light of the empirical realities we outlined throughout this volume.

Conclusion

In college, in some way that I devoutly believed in but could not explain, I expected to become a person.

—Margaret Mead[1]

I also took this pre-medical class . . . one book was terrifying. The stories [of doctors] they put in there. The people had turned hard. They thought they were omnipotent in the book. . . . Their stories from college to becoming a specialist in their field talk about how they've changed throughout the whole thing. And that book terrifies me because they go from this average, nice, kind person, and they said, at the end of it, they could see themselves as something they never wanted to be.

—Edward, Lutheran liberal arts college student

I think if I would have skipped the whole college experience, I think it would have been much harder for me to figure out "how do I stay me in the world?"

—Amber, Baptist university student

One of us enjoys reading our students' obituaries. They provide moments of moral clarity in one's life as an educator. Perhaps we should note that the obituaries he reads are those from living students in his moral development class. He relishes this assignment because game-like discussions based on hypothetical ethical dilemmas recede into the background. The students show their hands and reveal who they want to be—their highest life aspirations and ideals. Their true understandings of meaning and purpose emerge.

When this occurs, students abandon bland, general discussions about life goals and paint lively pictures of who they aspire to be. They envision tremendous sacrifices, such as adopting five children, feeding and caring for the homeless in the local town or in foreign lands, and educating those that society ignores or forgets. They also want to be remembered for doing "normal activities" in virtuous ways, such as loving their sisters and brothers deeply, being faithful to God and their spouses, and caring for their neighbors. They talk about being loving wives, caring husbands, and encouraging moms and dads. They hope to raise kind and loving children. Focusing on the end of life appears to sharpen students' focus. They hope to become moral heroes and heroines.

Sitting down and talking with students, or collecting their views through quantitative surveys, produces a much more varied set of responses. In our interviews with students, we find their highest ideals and goals, but we also hear their struggles, doubts, and loneliness. Some are confident and have clear purposes, while others express hesitancy and lack clarity. Some can identify mentors who have had a profound influence on them, while others are at a loss to identify anyone in their life who provides moral guidance (and many are perfectly content not to have this). Some know what kind of person they want to become, while others are at sea. Some who know are not sure which road in life will lead them to their desired destination.

While this diversity reveals the complexity of students' quest for purpose, we also believe our findings reveal some important insights and themes into how a variety of students experience this development at a range of colleges and universities. While a few institutions, as Kronman claims, may be giving up on exploring life's meaning with students, we found little evidence that they all are. Only a small group of students shared hesitancy about exploring these matters in college or report receiving little institutional support or encouragement to do so. In contrast, many students report finding various forms of direct and indirect institutional support while deepening their current understanding of meaning and purpose or finding a particular purpose.

We do not believe this is surprising. Institutions likely recognize that such explorations are in their own self-interest and in the interest of students. For instance, Clydesdale found that higher-education programs that explore vocation and purpose increased retention and graduation rates.[2] As discussed in chapter 6, numerous studies find that students with a purpose in life demonstrate a range of characteristics associated with human flourishing. It would be strange for a university not to care whether their students are thriving and preparing themselves well for adult life. And, to varying extents, we found evidence of this in our interviews. Students reported encountering issues of meaning and purpose in various forms through faculty, friends, the classroom, and co-curricular activities. By our own assessment, many possess clarity about what gives their lives meaning and what their future holds, although for a significant proportion, finding a definitive purpose is elusive.

Therefore, the final question is: So what? What are the implications of these findings for how colleges and universities help students with the development of meaning and purpose? Should universities just continue to do what they are doing or is there more that could be done? We believe our findings provide guidance about how to create approaches to addressing meaning and purpose that are inclusive and holistic, while also respecting the diversity of students and purposes we encountered. In the following section we will discuss some of the suggestions already set forth in higher-education literature in light of what we found as well as present our own set of recommendations. We begin with the underlying philosophy that we believe should shape approaches to meaning and purpose in our diverse system of higher education.

Dealing with the Difficulties of Diversity in Purpose Education

As we argued in the introduction and in chapter 1, the incredible pluralism within America's universities does make discussions about meaning and purpose more complicated and messy, but we would also argue it makes them more necessary. Part of the messiness, we noted, stems from the fact that problems related to inclusion involve different levels of diversity that we explored in this book. Combine this diversity with the fact that, as George Marsden observes, "American university culture is still shaped by a powerful impulse toward homogeneity and uniformity,"[3] and educators face a number of challenges if they hope to help students develop purpose. In this conclusion, we will address how our research might inform the effectiveness of approaching the challenging issues of meaning and purpose in the diverse university environment.

Including All Students: Meaning and Purpose as an Inclusive Approach to Big Questions

As argued in the introduction, we believe one of the reasons for the increased attention to issues of meaning and purpose pertains to its potential inclusiveness. The language of faith or spiritual development is now considered problematic by a number of higher education scholars for reasons having to do with inclusivity and the difficulty of defining terms.[4] In fact, we agree that addressing "faith" or "spiritual" development outside of a particular faith or religious tradition raises too many issues about definitions and ends. Our own interviews with students also lead us to believe that colleges and universities should not uncritically conflate discussions of spirituality or religion with discussions of meaning and purpose. While we agree that student affairs should be aware of all these dimensions of human identity and culture, we think it would be more profitable to recognize that nontheistic students may not always embrace terms such as *spirituality, faith,* and *religion.* Students, however, have much less difficulty speaking about what gives their life meaning, their purpose, and their visions of the good life. Simply focusing on students' meaning and purpose development, while simultaneously acknowledging and educating students about the influence of different faith and philosophical traditions, provides the most inclusive approach to addressing big questions.[5] We should also note that, in light of our findings in chapter 6, there is evidence that conversations and attention to purpose would be supported by those with diverse worldviews. Ultimately, we would argue that instead of talking about interfaith dialogue, co-curricular leaders should encourage purpose and meaning or worldview dialogue.[6]

Are there dangers for discussions about meaning and purpose in a pluralistic context? Of course. There are two particular approaches that we believe educators should consider, but each has its own challenges. One approach may alienate nontheistic students, and the other may alienate theistic students.

On the one hand, purpose is a concept that needs to be recognized as having two kinds of meanings for students. Indeed, as our chapter 11 revealed, some nontheists may even have trouble talking about a big "P" purpose in life. For example, Anne, the student we profiled in chapter 7 and quoted at the top of chapter 11, claims she would like to think that she has a purpose, but she admits she is not sure such a concept exists. Anne considers herself to be an agnostic when it comes to any larger metaphysical purpose. In other words, nontheists may be less comfortable speaking about some kind of universal or metaphysical purpose that one discovers and will be more comfortable talking about the purposes that one constructs.

On the other hand, we also believe that certain approaches that overemphasize how meaning or purpose are constructed, and not discovered, can be problematic for theistic students. Even scholars make this mistake. For instance, in their book titled, *Helping College Students Find Purpose*, Robert Nash and Michele Murray contend that helping students with finding meaning and purpose must be primarily understood in light of the basic philosophies of existentialism and social constructivism guiding their outlook. Nash and Murray present an approach to addressing issues of meaning and purpose rooted in existentialism and postmodernism that also emphasizes the humanly constructed aspects of meaning making.[7] Interestingly, this aspect of the book appears to be largely shaped by Nash's overall philosophy rather than Murray's Catholicism, which they confess in their life narratives in a final chapter. As Nash sums up when sharing his own personal philosophy, "We made up all the philosophies, all the religions, all the politics, all the arts, and all of the sciences, every single last one of them. This is our glory as a human species."[8] The existential struggle for Nash, which he also suggests applies to students, is that, "We need to create a meaning in a life that has no intrinsic meaning."[9] According to Nash and Murray's approach, we must teach students that they have the capability, and perhaps the responsibility, to create their own story that involves inventing "new ways of seeing, understanding, and transforming our worlds."[10] Nash and Murray do not believe in realism, a view that that would include the belief that meaning and purpose are also things that one discovers. Instead, as they put it, "each of us is free to find meaning that is no longer grounded in a predetermined set of absolute metaphysical truths that are said to exist outside of us in some transcendent realm."[11]

Such an approach might be helpful for nontheistic students such as Anne, but the difficulty with using Nash and Murray's approach for other theistic students, however, is that its presuppositions undercut the perspective of communities associated with most major faith traditions and a number of major philosophical traditions, many of which were held by students we labeled Transcendents. It also fails to accommodate the religious and philosophical diversity of many of the students we interviewed, such as the Purposeless who still expressed religious confidence in a larger purpose. The comment of one popular theistic author perhaps captures the attitude of these theistic students. "We'd much rather be included in something grand than have to create the meaning of our lives."[12] Proposals for how to address purpose must take into consideration these theistic students. An inordinate focus on meaning-making and self-authorship that does not take into account the possibility of meaning discovery and the coauthorship of life with God or a Higher Power, we believe, would not do justice to the outlook of these students.

Including All Universities? The Diversity of Universities

We think our findings support the hypothesis that most colleges and universities engage in the development of meaning and purpose in students to various degrees. We should celebrate and continue to encourage this reality. After all, part of the job of *most* colleges and universities, we contend, is to provide a liberal arts education addressing the most pressing human questions by exposing students to the wide varieties of meanings and purposes. As Palmer and Zajonc suggest, colleges and universities should engage "students in the systematic exploration of the relationship between their studies of the 'objective' world and the purpose, meaning, limits and aspirations of their lives."[13]

We also contend, consistent with Perry's theory about intellectual and ethical development, that it should be the job of universities to encourage students to find sources of meaning and to help students discover and commit to a purpose or purposes. We should emphasize, though, that we believe universities should also be concerned about the qualitative nature of such commitments. First and most importantly, they need to be examined commitments. As we indicated, particularly in chapters 5 and 7, some of the students appeared to derive their sources of meaning and purpose based on emotional preferences and had not connected them to their identities and the larger moral traditions associated with those identities. They had not developed sophisticated ways of thinking about meaning and purpose and the various moral traditions that supported them. The university has failed if students emerge with merely shallow understandings of meaning and purpose. Second, the commitments must in some sense be authored by the students, although we would also caution again against using self-authorship language in this area too much. As indicated in chapters 5 and 10, a significant number of theistic students understand their meaning and purpose as being coauthored with God. For them, to self-author one's purpose apart from God or a faith-based tradition would be problematic.

The question emerges, however, about whether it is the university's role to form students' meaning and purpose in any direct way. Should they simply expose students, in a sophisticated way, to the variety "out there," or should they provide guidance that leads students to consider some views more than others? We believe the latter is necessary, although as our findings reveal, the extent of formation will, of course, depend on the university. We do not believe it is a public or secular university's job to form students' particular purposes, but we do believe, based on the findings from positive psychology cited in this volume, *that students should be educated about the benefits of having a "beyond-the-self-focused" purpose that contributes to human flourishing.* In other words, the university should see it as their responsibility to encourage students to move from focusing solely on self-oriented Achiever purposes to Relationalist and/or Transcendent purposes (noting that Transcendent does not simply mean religious or spiritual but also includes moral ideals). Of course, the degree to which universities will engage in such an effort will also depend on their particular missions. For instance, religious colleges and universities will likely emphasize the importance of Religiously Transcendent purposes, while pluralistic universities will likely focus more on the Relationalist purpose of serving (e.g., community service) and the transcendent purpose of changing the world (e.g., social justice). As our findings in chapter 6 revealed, we think it particularly important for two-year universities to take up this mission, given the disproportionate focus on self-achievement by students at these institutions, but we believe every college and university should engage in it.

Including All Areas of the University

In addition to thinking about the inclusion of all students and universities, we also believe that our findings reveal how we should be thinking about the inclusion of all elements of the university when addressing purpose. Parker Palmer and Arthur Zajonc provide some helpful guidance by suggesting that universities help engage the learner's whole self with the subject being studied. This approach involves what they label an "epistemology of love" as opposed to a way of knowing that seeks to disconnect oneself from that being studied. Such connections help us understand and challenge various worldviews and values. They also form us into a certain kind of person. As Palmer observes, "Every epistemology, or way of knowing, as implemented in a pedagogy, or way of teaching and learning, tends to become an ethic, or way of living."[14] An outgrowth of this view is that, as opposed to Kronman who primarily offers a particular sort of curriculum as the answer to addressing meaning and purpose in life, they argue that an integrative pedagogy can and should be used to address matters of meaning and purpose in all aspects of the curricular and co-curricular:

> By expanding our ontology to embrace the interconnectedness of reality and its multiple dimensions, by extending our epistemology to include contemplative, aesthetic, and moral knowing, by recognizing the ethical dimensions of our way of knowing, we can grow the exploration of purpose beyond the humanities to all aspects of curricular and co-curricular life.[15]

In other words, developing meaning and purpose should not be relegated to a particular part of the college experience but integrated into the whole. Or as Clydesdale maintains, "Colleges and universities must unequivocally prioritize students, faculty, and staff *as whole persons*."[16] Along with these authors, we too would argue that colleges and universities should consider the full range of curricular and co-curricular approaches. With these overarching perspectives in mind, we will offer our recommendations for how universities should address students' exploration and commitment to meaning and purpose in light of our findings.

Students' Diverse Experiences with Meaning and Purpose Questing and Finding

To reiterate, we believe three of the goals of colleges and universities should be to provide a liberal arts education regarding meaning and purpose, inspire students to find sources of meaning and a purpose or purposes, and to encourage students to consider and embrace beyond-the-self purposes. To achieve these goals, college and university educators need to better understand the developmental process toward reaching these goals and the role that they can play in the process. In addition to the increasing amount of scholarship devoted to these topics, we believe our findings add helpful insights.

First, university educators must recognize, as our findings from chapters 5, 6, and 12 reveal, that students have different understandings of meaning, purpose, and the good life. Each of these concepts needs to be approached differently, although we should recognize the relationship and overlap between the concepts. Students compose both meaning and purpose from a set of eleven common ingredients that fit three larger categories. While the basic substance of the responses provides support for treating meaning and purpose as "family" categories, our interviews provide evidence that meaning and purpose should be differentiated due to three distinctions. The first key difference has to do with a contrast between generality and specificity. For the majority of students, whether asked directly about the difference or simply asked separately about meaning and purpose, meaning was described as something that can, and perhaps should be, shared generally (maybe even by all people). Purpose, on the other hand, was something specific to the individual. As one of the students noted, one might find meaning in serving others, but the particular way one fulfilled those broad ideals was to specify particular, measurable purposes (e.g., "become a psychologist"). In other words, the difference between meaning and purpose for the majority of students was not so much a difference in kind but one of degree. The difference concerned the specificity of life goals (general, universal versus specific, personal). This should not be surprising because meaning is a broader and more general concept that students may view as being shared by many.

Second, students' descriptions reflected another common view about the nature of purpose mentioned by previous scholars. Students generally saw purpose as "directed at an accomplishment towards which one can make progress."[17] Purpose provided a specific goal that one could achieve in ways that meaning did not. As a result, purpose directed and motivated action in a distinctive manner that would not be the same for meaning.

The final difference between meaning and purpose that emerged is that every student had sources of meaning, but not every student had a clear, definitive purpose. Consequently, when it comes to acquiring meaning and purpose, students do not appear to need as much help finding sources of meaning, but they do need more help finding a purpose or purposes. Understanding these differences helps us understand why it may be more important for university educators to focus on the development of purpose more exclusively than that of meaning.

Despite this conclusion, our research findings lead us to raise two cautions about an inordinate focus on purpose alone. Our first caution relates to the way positive psychologists define purpose and how their definition relates to college students. For students, purpose may have to do with "the desire to make a difference in the world, to contribute to matters larger than the self,"[18] but it may also concern more self-oriented sources of focus. This does not mean a "beyond-the-self" definition of purpose is not useful for study. It is simply not the only "common language" of students. We simply think it may be more helpful to distinguish between "beyond-the-self" purposes and "self-oriented" purposes, rather than defining purpose to include only beyond-the-self purposes. Maintaining that self-oriented purposes are not really purposes distorts how college students talk about purpose.

This suggestion also relates to our second point. It would appear that finding meaning in certain singular sources may be more likely to leave students without purpose. In sum, *those who derive meaning from more ingredients, particularly certain "beyond-the-self" ingredients such as transcendent sources (whether religious or simply moral ideals) as well as those more focused on helping others (versus simply friends and family), will be more likely to have developed purpose.* In light of this finding, we suggest that university educators should prioritize purpose development while also placing an emphasis on helping students critically examine and develop multiple sources of *both* meaning *and* purpose with a particular emphasis on beyond-the-self forms of meaning and purpose. In other words, though students may not need help finding a source of meaning, they may need help thinking critically about their sources of meaning and perhaps considering other or additional sources of meaning. They need a liberal arts education about meaning and purpose.

To undertake this task, college and university educators need to understand the growth of meaning and purpose along a developmental spectrum. As chapter 2 revealed, some students will already have had significant mentoring and conversations in this area prior to college, while others have not even started to explore these matters. Indeed, for many students, they will come to college with much more extensive academic preparation than preparation to engage in conversations about meaning and purpose. *Colleges and universities could and perhaps should survey students before entering their institution about their sources of meaning and their purpose.* We believe it is likely that colleges and universities would find significant changes if they survey the same students again on exiting the university. Further scholarly work, we believe, also needs to take place to trace the meaning and purpose development stages of students in college similar to the extensive amount of developmental work undertaken among adolescents.[19]

Curricular and Co-curricular Initiatives—Cultivating Diverse Conversations

The dominant approach that scholars and practitioners propose to aid student development in this area involves what we would call the conversational model.[20] For instance, Clydesdale offers this good news for colleges and universities:

> When colleges and universities meaningfully engage their organizational histories to launch sustained conversations with students about questions of purpose, the result is a rise in overall campus

engagement and recalibration of post-college trajectories that set graduates on journeys of significance and impact.[21]

The conversation might be among great texts and authors,[22] other students,[23] "diverse peoples and cultures,"[24] or faculty.[25]

Certainly, our findings would support this approach. Students found curricular conversations that included great texts as well as courses that exposed them to diverse cultures and perspectives beneficial. In the co-curricular, students' thinking about purpose benefited tremendously from diverse roommate conversations and conversations among different types of students within various groups. These conversations enrich students' understanding of various ways of answering the question of what it means to be fully human. The discussions hopefully produce both understanding and empathy. Conversations help complicate the meaning map students have created and/or discovered and demonstrate the range of meaning and purpose options. While we believe our findings reinforce the effectiveness of a number of approaches already in place at certain universities, based on our research, we would suggest some particular approaches to strengthening these types of conversations in both the curriculum and the co-curricular.

Curricular Initiatives. In the classroom, it did not surprise us that students found most of the conversation about meaning and purpose to take place in what would be considered the liberal arts curriculum. As Warren Nord observed,

> The great virtue of a liberal arts education is that it situates students
> in thick moral, civic and religious traditions—traditions that make
> sense of our moral values and provide deep justifications for them
> (and give students ground on which to stand in confronting the
> materialism and often mindless individualism of popular culture and
> the relativism of so much of our intellectual life).[26]

Still, we think our research might help universities and colleges think about sharpening the conversation cultivated in the liberal arts. It was clear from our conversations, though, that while religion classes helped with this endeavor at faith-based institutions, they were not exactly places where students had extensive conversations about meaning and purpose. Furthermore, those kinds of courses are not always required or available at secular institutions. Overall, we found three other curricular approaches that helped cultivate meaning and purpose conversations.

To begin, first-year seminars that communicate to students that college is about more than obtaining a credential would likely help those students who come to college with an Instrumental approach. A number of students identified these courses as helping them shift from a view of higher education as a place for vocational training to a view of college as a place to also think about the big questions of life and the good life. Courses that exposed students to multicultural perspectives also proved particularly helpful. Although not many students mentioned these courses, we also believe, based on the few students who did mention these courses, that medical humanities courses or other courses targeted at STEM majors that focus on evaluating their vocation in light of larger moral, philosophical, and theological issues and narratives will be helpful. For instance, one of the few STEM majors who encountered finding purpose in the university makes this observation.

> I guess the books that I've read about medical ethics or bioethics, often the ones that strike me the most are where they really zoom in on one individual person and show you what's happened in this person's life, and how they've experienced injustice in the medical world. Those have really made me more passionate about wanting to solve those ethical injustices. And so that has, in turn, affected the meaning that I put on life, because it makes me feel that if these injustices are in place in society, then in order to have a meaningful life I have to be part of the solution too . . . I have to try to do whatever I can to solve those.

Finally, we believe that great texts courses or curriculum, such as those suggested by Kronman,[27] could help address one particular weakness we observed, others have noted, and Nord says we need.[28] Students often failed to think about their meaning and purpose in light of larger moral traditions and frameworks. Courses in the great texts helped expose some students we interviewed to these traditions. In cases where a great text set of readings or courses might not be possible, we believe students would benefit from a curricular Search for the Good Life course that does the following two things: (1) explores the different conceptions of the good life and (2) explores how one achieves excellence through organizing and prioritizing all of one's identities in the midst of moral conflicts—thus creating a meaningful and purposeful human life.[29] Such a course would fulfill the goal mentioned earlier of providing students with a liberal arts education about meaning and purpose.

Co-Curricular Initiatives. In the co-curricular, we would affirm the suggestions by other scholars that student life education would benefit from giving attention to religious/nonreligious identity and matters of life meaning and purpose.[30] Similar to the attention to matters of gender, racial, or sexual identity, student affairs professionals need to understand how students' religious or nonreligious identity influences their approach to issues of purpose, meaning, and the good life and how to enhance conversations with students outside of class about these matters. One group of scholars has even suggested, "If student affairs professionals are serious about working with students as they develop their spirituality and life purpose, then that function should be funded by the division and assigned to an individual or office to show it is valued."[31] Indeed, we wonder if career placement offices should be expanded to include at least one staff member who can take interested students through the practice of life mapping with students. In this process, students not only think about their future career, but they also learn to think their whole life story in light of various aspects of their whole human identity and not just their professional identity.[32]

In addition, certain other kinds of student activities may prove particularly helpful in developing conversations that might lead students to consider "beyond-the-self" purposes. For example, three different intervention studies have found that high school or college students who were involved in intentional discussions where they were given opportunities to reflect on and discuss their purpose were more likely to develop "beyond-the-self" purposes over time.[33] We think these discussions could be aided by conducting meaning and purpose discussions among different classifications of Achievers, Relationalists, and Transcendents in a similar manner as interreligious discussions.[34] We believe that such discussions would not be threatening. We assume that they would likely be productive in helping students think critically about the various meaning and purpose ingredients that guide their lives and their daily choices. Encouraging students to analyze their own meanings and purposes in light of the various sources may prove helpful in the articulation of one's purpose and overall vocation.

Supplementing the Conversational Approach. We would add two cautions and one limit of this conversational approach emphasis. The first and most important caution is that educators sometimes rush to encourage students to have conversations about their different identities and related beliefs when students themselves have not had the opportunity to deepen their own understanding of their identity and the story or historical moral tradition associated with it. When this happens, students end up exchanging shared personal experiences or emotional preferences (such as some students' views about meaning discussed in chapter 5) instead of deeper understandings about how one lives out one's life in light of a particular moral, philosophical, or religious tradition. Consequently, it becomes vitally important to offer students the opportunity to begin conversations about meaning and purpose by first understanding the history of their particular identity and moral tradition in the curriculum. A liberal arts education about these traditions situates students in thick moral, civic, and religious traditions, which helps them make sense of their identity, their place in the world, and the justifications for their meanings, purposes, and worldviews. In sum, we believe a curricular liberal arts education in meaning and purpose proves to be the vital first step.

Second, as chapters 2 and 8 revealed, when cultivating conversations about meaning and purpose, the matter of trust proves vitally important. Particularly cohesive friendships, communities, and universities will have an advantage here. As we found, students who had close friendships, mentors from religious communities, or trusted their professors, experienced more meaning and purpose conversations. We believe this element is one reason why we and other scholars have found certain faith-based institutions to be effective at fostering meaning and purpose discussions.[35] Public institutions will have to make special efforts to build communities of trust so that these conversations can take place. They may also need to help nurture these conversations by first nurturing smaller communities of trust with like-minded students on their campuses. Once those conversations are nurtured in those safe places, then conversations with a broader, more diverse group of individuals can take place.

Another possible limit of the conversational approach occurs when it remains only a conversation. Focusing on having conversations may mean we do not ask students to engage in practices beyond discourse that may prove transformative in helping students discover their purpose. What we found is that students often discovered their purpose and meaning by engaging in such practices. Rarely did this kind of transformative participatory experience occur in the classroom. In fact, one of the noteworthy things that we did *not* find, when asking students about the curricular life, were courses that encouraged students to examine their own practices and not merely their thinking. For the students we interviewed, the examined life meant critically analyzing different historical or contemporary ways of thinking or gaining a deeper or more holistic view of their calling or vocation. They did not tell stories of classes asking them to examine what they currently do. We found this example noteworthy in that it stood out as an exception from all the other examples students shared. Christina, a student at the Lutheran liberal arts college talks about one professor's assignment that clarified her life's meaning.

> We did this thing called a room inventory where you count everything in your room and you write down like everything that was in your room, and I was just like, holy crap, I have so much shit, this is ridiculous! I don't know why it's so important to me that I keep thinking about things and money and concerns like that when, really, we're going to be okay. I started thinking about myself and what is

> important to me and I, it was when I really realized that what is the most important to me in my life are people and not things. And I mean I . . . Okay and I knew that. I knew that the most important things in my life were people, not things, but I started really critiquing the way I live my life and what do I make time for and what don't I make time for. This is all shaped by this class, and I feel like it really significantly changed my life, and so I am taking another class from the same professor.

As Christina notes, this class and the assignment did not actually change what she understood as making life meaningful. It merely showed her how inconsistent her habits and practices were with her currently held ideals. Strikingly, no other students shared engaging practices in class that shaped their development of purpose.

Where students encountered these kinds of transformative experiences most were in overseas experiences or in voluntary co-curricular activities and student groups. Indeed, we would suggest that the limit of conversations is that they may not necessarily foster what Palmer and Zajonk call an "epistemology of love." Such an epistemology, we contend, is best cultivated by encouraging students, like anthropologists, to immerse themselves within particular communities of commitment that are seeking to live out a particular vision of the good life. After all, many of our students discovered their purpose within such groups—whether it was China Aid and working to help orphans, volunteering at a local hospital or call center help line, working at a camp for autistic children, or taking an overseas trip to a foreign country with a particular mission in mind. Others have noted that wider student experiences such as community service, study abroad, and participation in leadership can play this role.[36] For example, other empirical studies have found that volunteering in the community, engagement in the arts, and participation in faith-related activities preceded the development of "beyond-the-self" purposes.[37] This last finding may also explain why some scholars have found certain faith-based institutions effective at fostering meaning and purpose discussions.[38]

Unfortunately, these morally focused communities are sometimes depicted as binding entities from which students must free themselves to become fully human instead of organic elements of communal life that may nurture and feed developing concepts of meaning and purpose in productive ways. While Perry suggests commitment is the end stage of development, what he fails to note is that commitments require communities to sustain the ends to which commitment has been made.[39] Within such communities, one can discover new ways of being in the world that shape our views of meaning and purpose. These communities *enabled* students to expand and articulate their meaning and purpose in ways that would have been impossible in isolation. If student life personnel really want to nurture the exploration of meaning and purpose, they should be nurturing such communities of commitment on their campuses and encourage students to inhabit them. Furthermore, they would need to encourage adult mentors to help such communities articulate this vision. These adult mentors, as Parks observes, prove vital during this time of students' lives.[40]

The limit of this approach, particularly with certain philosophical or religious groups, is that these communities on campus do not always exhibit the best of these traditions or the historical richness of them. The local secular humanist, Muslim, Jewish, or Christian group might be weak, shallow, and lacking connection to the historic tradition from which it springs. This is where the curricular component should complement such student experience. We would suggest that the liberal education about the meaning and purpose of life mentioned above should provide students with a Great Lives and Communities segment that actually helps students look at such lives and communities as a whole. If we study the best experts when learning what it means to be a great historian, social worker, biologist, or philosopher, we should also study those exemplars, both individual and communal, that sought to put together a good life as a whole. These are indirect mentors and experts who can help nurture a true, good, and beautiful life.

The Important Role of Mentors and the Challenge of Diversity. Still, as our findings revealed, students also need direct living mentors as well. Sharon Parks is one of the scholars to argue most forcefully that young adults need mentors or coaches as well as self-chosen, ideologically oriented communities that can guide them along this journey.[41] In this regard, Parks appears to depart from Perry who at times seemed to place an inordinate emphasis on students making their journey alone, and even, at times, interpreted efforts to look for or expect adults to help as signs of retreat from development.[42] What also sets Parks apart is that she does not believe any mentor or any type of ideologically oriented community will do. She notes, "The good mentor simply recognizes that the young adult is still dependent in substantial ways upon authority outside the self, while at the same time, the mentor is a champion of the competence and potential the young life represents."[43]

Our findings suggest that the majority of students are missing these mentors. Yet, Parks maintains the role of the university is to provide direct mentors and mentoring communities that assist young people in this process. Instead of buying into the modern ideal that separates the objective from the subjective, facts from values, Parks argues that higher education does and should serve "the young adult as his or her primary community of imagination, within which every professor is potentially a spiritual guide and every syllabus a confession of faith."[44] According to Parks, "The mentoring professor, therefore, must convene and mediate among multiple perspectives, composing a trustworthy community of imagination—a community of confirmation and contradiction."[45] This practice would then be enhanced by exposing students to models or expert practitioners of various traditions of the good life. After all, they need coaches/mentors who can give them wisdom about living out a particular conception of the good life. Clydesdale's study of effective programs at colleges and universities reinforces this point. He found that students who experienced life-changing forms of purpose development often were involved in purposeful mentorship programs.[46]

Based on our research findings, *we would also encourage colleges and universities to consider setting up expanded "good life" mentoring opportunities for students.* What do we mean by "good life" mentoring? Similar to the way that colleges and universities have programs to help students find careers, they could help students engage in a process of mapping out what the good life would look like to them in the future. Moreover, just as colleges often seek to place students in internships where they are apprenticed in a particular vocation, they could also be matched with possible adults who would discuss more than how to be a good teacher, social worker, businessperson, or journalist.

The "expanded" approach adds two important parts. First, the pool of potential mentors on a campus should be considered beyond the professors. According to our interviews, students often find staff and older students more accessible and approachable mentors than their professors. Second, the matter of trust must be addressed. It would appear that some students are not that interested in having professors mentor them unless it involves their particular practice or career. They are not necessarily willing to trust them with their personal lives.

This leads to the other possible limitation of mentorship programs. If institutions of higher education were to embrace Parks's model, they would need to supply and support mentors who can focus on a diverse group of students and help them develop a realistic imagination about all of life and not merely a particular vocation. This type of realistic imagination recognizes that those who are the best practitioners, similar to those who are experts in any field, are those who demonstrate expertise with building a whole, purposeful life. In other words, this building does not happen in the abstract. These models are experts in a particular community with particular ways of thinking, talking, and acting about the various spheres of life.

Such particular expertise and experience creates a problem for inclusiveness that Parks cannot escape (and we believe she should not). This issue becomes even more complicated if students want to find mentors that help them develop purpose, but they are not yet sure which community of purpose they identify with. To address this issue, scholars of student life working in this area continue to push for universal language and solutions. For example, Jenny Small critiques Parks because her language demonstrates a connection to the Christian tradition (e.g., talk about "the hand of the Spirit" and the "Kingdom or Commonwealth of God").[47] Like many mainline Protestants throughout the history of higher education, Parks exhibits a desire to be inclusive while still hanging on to certain general components of Christianity or Christian language. While such a strategy may have worked in the past, a tacit liberal Protestant consensus can no longer hold together the modern, pluralistic university. Indeed, Clydesdale found that campuses that used "an Oprah-esque, ahistoric spirituality designed to appeal to everyone" often failed to meet the objectives they hoped for in their vocation and purpose programs.[48] What this means is that an embrace of diversity must also not be afraid of groups and universities that may not be diverse in certain ways.

Respecting the Need for Cohesive Centers of Meaning and Purpose. We believe that one of the reasons students do not necessarily trust professors as mentors is that they do not share a common worldview or basic perspective about the good life. The one group of universities where students sought professors as mentors and had rich interactions with them regarding life's meaning was the evangelical colleges. Our research reveals that, while students certainly need exposure to diversity and that such exposure enhances their development of purpose, they may also need and desire like-minded adult mentors they can trust. The problem is that on a diverse university campus, even one that might be private and have a faith perspective, students do not necessarily have these mentors. In other words, to some degree, intensive mentoring in issues of meaning and purpose will likely flourish more within institutions or groups with a shared moral and religious framework.

What this reveals, we believe, is the importance of freedom of association for like-minded groups within pluralistic settings. John Dewey wondered, in his classic work, *Democracy and Education*, "Is it possible for an educational system to be conducted by a national state and yet the full social ends of the educative process not be restricted, constrained, and corrupted?"[49] The concern behind this question involved the fact that a nation-state may use the apparatus of education for ideological reasons that suppress freedom. One answer to this danger within liberal democracies has been, as Stephen Carter notes,

> to nurture many different centers of meaning, including many different understandings of how to find meaning, so that the state will have competition. To do otherwise is to yield to the totalitarian impulse, the impulse that says everybody must abide by my ideology.[50]

We would suggest that this approach could be important when it comes to how both state and private universities can nurture purpose. As positive psychologists have noted, purpose is a virtue. Yet, as Alasdair MacIntyre has also argued, virtues require certain narrative shaped communities to be cultivated.[51] They require coherent communities of purpose.

A higher-education system can provide these communities in two ways. First, political and educational leaders can ensure that opportunities for a whole variety of private universities with different faith or nonfaith perspectives to emerge. American education is certainly unique in this regard compared to other nations around the world.[52] It supports the most religiously diverse higher-education system in the world. As a result, the students we interviewed at Baptist, Catholic, evangelical, Jewish, Lutheran, and Mormon institutions can find classes, mentors, and friends from which they can learn about the depths of that particular tradition and wrestle with its implications for life purpose. There were certain kinds of common conversations about a Jewish, Mormon, or Christian approach to purpose that cannot take place as easily at a secular campus. Moreover, as the evangelical college students indicate, a certain kind of trust from which faculty mentorship can occur also takes place in these institutions.

This commonality can also enhance the others-focused nature of purpose that scholars find so important. For example, Clydesdale discovered that at a cohesive Christian Reformed university where efforts were made to use Lily endowment money to enhance purpose conversations, "we observed a palpable other-directedness among student participants . . . In contrast to students on other campuses, who spoke chiefly of self-understandings and future endeavors."[53] Like our study, he also found significant faculty support for mentorship as well as mentorship groups at this religious college.[54] Perhaps not surprisingly, the institution was also committed to three of the things we have suggested:

> (1) Fostering campus-wide involvement in undergraduate mentoring, (2) expanding off campus contexts in which students "could experience and express their vocation," and (3) enlarging academic programs and curricula so students could consider the "important spiritual, moral, and political commitments that may necessarily accompany one's vocation."[55]

We would merely add that such programs should be holistic and make sure that a broad focus is given to purpose, so that the focus does not too easily descend to a preoccupation with vocation understood simply as one's career. In this process, students not only think about their future career, but they also learn to think about their whole life story in light of various categories in life.[56]

Recognizing the importance of diverse higher education institutions in our systems is important even for those who do not identify with their sponsoring group. In fact, Clydesdale notes, and we agree, that higher-education leaders should recognize that students can and do learn from particular models and particular traditions without themselves being part of that tradition. Clydesdale offers the following analogy:

> I would never subject myself, for example, to the extreme conditions and inherent dangers that wildlife photographers endure, but that does not make me uninterested in their stories or their photographs—they fascinate me, in fact. Similarly, participants in exploration programs [about purpose], students and educators alike, might share nothing in common with their campus denomination, yet could find the journeys narrated by denominational figures, with their theologically embedded insights about a life of meaning and purpose, to be quite generative.[57]

We would also add that students at public institutions also need the opportunity to experience diverse centers of meaning that include theologically-informed options.

Thus, the second way colleges and universities can support communities of purpose is through the type of student life they cultivate. On public or private secular university campuses, student associations can be understood as a key expression of these "many different centers of meaning," in the same way that larger civil society serves this purpose.[58] In fact, student organizations serve as the principal way that students can create and nurture their own form of civil society and their own visions of purpose. For instance, Cody, a Transcendent student at a public research university, mentions this point:

> . . . Coming in as a freshman . . . there's a bunch of wise upperclassmen that I really liked and could just tell that they were wise and had wrestled with things and were really well read in scripture and stuff. Just in the way they talked about things, like being in Bible studies with them and the way they would talk about scripture, I was excited, or, like, "Oh, I want to be like that, I want to talk with this kind of peace and calm and understanding oozing out of my words." So that's been awesome.

This point could prove true of any student with a whole variety of different student groups, such as Kelsey's story of her involvement with her Hindu student group or Chase's involvement with the secular humanist group. In this respect, student groups in liberal democratic[59] institutions should not merely be considered expressions of a university's particular mission. They serve a larger educational purpose. Educationally speaking, one way students become introduced to civil society is by learning to create it and sustain it themselves. This notion coheres with Dewey's view that education,

> must represent present life—life as real and vital to the [student] as that which he carries on in the home, in the neighborhood, or on the play-ground. I believe that education which does not occur through forms of life, forms that are worth living for their own sake, is always a poor substitute for the genuine reality and tends to cramp and to deaden.[60]

To accomplish this larger goal, student groups, as much as possible, should be governed by the same approach to associational freedom that governs groups outside of a campus. Treating student groups as extensions of civil society allows for the creation of diverse and even competing ideological groups to exist in ways that foreclose the possibility of ideological discrimination. Thus, if a person is excluded from one group based on certain ideological or ethical beliefs, other students can form an alternative group. The ability to form different kinds of student groups works for the whole diverse range of purposes students may wish to pursue on campus. These student groups also provide another place where students can encounter particular mentors they trust and who, hopefully, provide models of a purposeful and meaningful life.

A Final Note of Humility

Finally, in a conclusion filled with suggestions about how to make changes, we wish to recognize the ways that students' development of meaning and purpose always remains beyond our attempts to produce certain ends. We think it is helpful to be reminded of ways that such influences can also prove quite serendipitous. Clydesdale shared the story of one student so moved by a service learning program that the student withdrew from college during his final semester and accepted a full-time job doing relief work.[61] We also came across a story of a student who decided to withdraw from the university. The impetus for the decision came from a class not exactly designed to explore purpose. One student at an evangelical university shared how one seemingly random question from a statistics professor started him thinking about his whole college experience and life purpose differently:

This actually started with a statistics professor—I'm in business stats right now—and, it was a little one-point extra-credit question, because he's conducting a survey between his students here and his college students at community college. And it was a simple yes/no question. It said, "Do you feel like you're getting your money's worth at [this university]?" So I was like "Yeah, I'm going to do that for one point!" and I was about to circle yes, and then I thought, "No, I don't feel like I am, actually." I circled no. I turned it in. And so that, actually, was about two months ago, and that really sparked some interest and reflection in my own life.

So I started breaking down everything. Am I really happy with where I am right now? Am I comfortable paying $20,000 every four months for a piece of paper? From there I went, "Do I feel like I belong here at school?" No, I don't really. "Where do I feel like I belong?" When I came into college I was in ROTC, but I dropped out because I didn't get a scholarship. I was like, "Well, I'm not going to do it for free." So, that stopped.

But I feel like I need to go to the military, and if I don't do that I'm going to regret it later on in life. So, I got to that point: yes, I feel like I wanted to be in the military, and I brought it up with my girlfriend. She said, "I'm sorry, I don't really feel like I can be a future military wife." And I said, "Well, I respect that." My sister even said, "Yeah, I don't think I could do that, either." So we decided to part paths. It's not been easy at all.

This student noted that at the end of the semester he was dropping out of college to join the military. As many professors have experienced, one cannot always anticipate the paths that a simple question may open up or close in one's teaching or reading. Even a well-designed course or set of co-curricular programs addressing the meaning and purpose of life might have less influence than one offhand question in a statistics class that strikes a chord. Sometimes, despite all of our best-laid plans and purposes, we inspire others to take different roads in ways that we did not even anticipate.

Appendix A

Methods

This study used both qualitative and quantitative methods that drew on multiple data sources. The sections below describe the different methods and data sources.

The Major Qualitative Component:
110 Interviews at Ten Institutions

The major qualitative phase of the study began with in-depth, face-to-face interviews with 110 students from ten different colleges and universities. The purpose of the interviews was to explore students' views about meaning and purpose. In particular, we asked for their understanding of these terms; their own current views about them; and the possible influence of their family, friends, educational institutions, other adult mentors, and religious/nonreligious beliefs on the development of their views about meaning and purpose. We also explored their views about the future and their future goals. In general, we were guided by Damon et al.'s admonition, "Questions designed to survey purpose need to focus on issues of future orientation, goals, and guiding forces that direct a young person through life."[1]

These interviews were conducted between October 2012 and March 2013. They lasted between forty-five and ninety-five minutes and were digitally recorded. Interviewees received a thirty-dollar gift card for their participation. All interviews, except those at one institution, were conducted by the coauthors. In that case, graduate students conducted the interviews with guidance from the principal investigator.

We chose the ten different institutions where we interviewed students in order to achieve two types of diversity. First, we wanted to conduct interviews at a variety of faith-based and secular institutions to determine what role a particular type of religious tradition might play in shaping students' experiences. Therefore, the institutions included those with the following identities: Baptist,

Catholic, evangelical, Jewish, Latter-Day Saints, Lutheran, secular regional university, secular private research university, secular public research university, and secular liberal arts college. Second, we sought to achieve a range of institutional diversity. Consequently, we interviewed students at a variety of institutional types (e.g., a regional university, liberal arts colleges, and various levels of research universities). Overall, we suspected that claims that "our" universities have given up on helping students find meaning are too general and needed to be nuanced.[2]

After obtaining an institutional board review (IRB) approval from the primary investigator's institution, we contacted the appropriate person at each university and presented our request and IRB approval documentation. All the universities initially contacted agreed to participate, although the range of support they gave for obtaining subjects varied. On one end, two universities requested that students be interviewed off campus (although recruitment could occur through appropriate on-campus channels), while in two other cases, helped us recruit students through their normal institutional research channels. We used a variety of methods to obtain student participants. In all but two cases we used student newspaper advertisements, on-campus advertising, e-mail forums, or relational networks. Initial contacts and appointments were all made through e-mail.

In all of the cases we sought diverse representation regarding religion, classification, gender, and ethnicity (see table A.1). Students were from twenty different states and eight different countries. Interviewers obtained both verbal and written consent from the respondent to conduct the interview. In the written consent form interviewees were also provided with information about the study, the use of the interviews, and contact information for the principle investigators and each institution's Institutional Review Board. The location of the interviews varied according to the institutional requirements. In two cases, institutions requested that the interviews be conducted off campus. These interviews were conducted in public settings such as coffee shops or study rooms at local libraries. In all the other cases the institutions provided rooms where the interviews could take place or chose locations requested by the students.

We analyzed the specific interview questions related to purpose and future plans using grounded theory.[3] Grounded theory works in the opposite fashion of traditional research paradigms in that it requires that the researchers not form an initial hypothesis. Instead, we used the open coding and analysis of the data to form our categories and any subsequent frameworks or emerging theoretical constructs. In other words, in our qualitative samples, we were not specifically testing a particular theory or hypothesis. Instead, we wanted to discover the answer to the general question: how do college students experience and describe developing purpose and meaning in their lives? We do not believe it is possible to become an objective observer, but the grounded theory approach emphasizes

Table A.1. Demographic Characteristics of Qualitative Sample ($N = 110$)

Variable	Category	Frequency	Percentage
Ethnicity	White	74	67.3
	Asian American	7	6.4
	Hispanic	7	6.4
	African American	6	5.5
	Indian	4	3.6
	Middle Eastern	2	1.8
	Native American	1	0.9
	Mixed ethnicity	9	8.2
Gender	Female	59	53.6
	Male	51	46.4
Year in College	First	20	18.2
	Second	21	19.1
	Third	34	30.9
	Fourth	33	30.0
	Fifth	2	1.8
Religion	Protestant (or "Just Christian")	44	40.9
	Catholic	14	12.7
	Jewish	14	12.7
	LDS	9	8.2
	Nonreligious/None	8	7.3
	Atheist	6	5.5
	Agnostic	6	5.5
	Buddhist	5	4.5
	Muslim	2	1.8
	Hindu	1	0.9
	Unification Church	1	0.9

trying to understand the experience of those being studied from the inside without placing prior conceptions on the subjects.

Furthermore, this approach seeks to capture the prereflective recollections and narratives that individuals can formulate regarding their experience. These stories and perceptions are important phenomena in and of themselves and prove essential when attempting to build further knowledge, wisdom, or theories. In this regard, our approach shared certain similarities to the approach employed by Freitas who argues, "it is only through providing an open-ended space for participant storytelling that one can begin to understand a student's unique experience and to piece together a 'master narrative' about an area of interest."[4] In our case, this area of interest was meaning and purpose.

Discovering the answer to our research question involved formulating interview questions that explored how students developed their purpose and in what college contexts this purpose was developed, discussed, examined, and so on. The interview guide can be found in appendix B. As can be seen from the long interview guide, the extended interview questions sought to explore students' experiences with discussing purpose in their family life, their precollege life, and then their college life. Besides asking the question about their purpose and meaning and life, we sought to ask questions that would allow them to share about the various ideological, social, and environmental influences on their development of purpose. To determine social influences, we asked questions about the influence of their parents, friends (high school and college), mentors (high school and college), and professors. To ascertain environmental and ideological influences, we asked about the role of various classes, books, extracurricular activities, and worldview beliefs (religious and nonreligious).

With regard to interview content, we asked students for their basic background, their understanding of the terms being studied (meaning and purpose), their own current views about them, the possible influence of their family, friends, educational institutions, other adult mentors, and religious/nonreligious beliefs on the development of their views about meaning and purpose. The major section included questions about student expectations regarding higher education with regard to purpose and their current experience regarding these topics in the curricular and co-curricular dimensions of student life. We also explored development of their worldview or religious tradition and how that related to purpose. Finally, we discussed their views of the future and their future goals.

The interviews were semistructured in that while we had a list of research questions, we would often take time to explore possible avenues that we had not anticipated. In fact, we occasionally added a question to the interviews when we realized we had failed to explore a particular area of importance. Interviews typically lasted from forty-five minutes to one hour. Students were paid thirty dollars on the successful completion of an interview.

Completed interviews were transcribed in the fall of 2012 and spring of 2013 by employees at the Center for Social Research at Calvin College and Baylor University. To analyze the data, we implemented the open coding approach used in grounded theory to analyze the responses since our desire was to generate themes from the particulars of student responses, rather than to impose theory on them.[5] In some cases, we used a two-cycle coding process through which descriptive categories could emerge (first cycle) and then be combined into thematic categories (second cycle).[6]

Gallup® Survey: National Quantitative Survey with 2,503 Students

Based on our qualitative findings, we devised a quantitative instrument that measured students' attitudes toward these particular purpose ingredients. We organized the particular purpose ingredients based on the theoretical framework derived from our qualitative findings above. We anticipated that the three different conceptual clusters of purpose ingredients would demonstrate important differences. The first cluster we linked to the Self-Achievers. This group included nine items (*make money; have a fulfilling career; be happy; produce new and original work, such as a book or piece of art; maintain a comfortable standard of living; live with no regrets; achieve success in my career; experience life to the fullest; discover new things about the world*). All of the items related to personal or self-oriented achievements. We made a couple adjustments from our qualitative findings categories in order to try and capture some nuances. With the "experiences," we broke the possible responses into two parts: (1) experience life to the fullest and (2) discover new things about the world. The reason for this division is that we discovered important subcodes that appeared to address two dimensions focused on a distinction between pleasure and curiosity. We also added "live with no regrets" to this group since we wanted to measure a possible self-oriented purpose that included a negative orientation. The second group, the Relationalists, consisted of three items: *help others, care for a family, and build lasting friendships*. All of these answers pertained to others focused purposes. The third group, the Transcendents, consisted of the following three responses: *make the world a better place, love God or a higher power, serve my community and/or country*. The common characteristic of this group is that they focused on a being, moral ideal, or group that was beyond-the-self and beyond one's immediate social group.

In collaboration with the Gallup® Organization, we then collected data from 2,503 college students, ages eighteen to twenty-three, in March 2014. Interviews were conducted with these respondents on landline telephones and cellular phones, with interviews conducted in Spanish for respondents who were primarily Spanish-speaking. Landline and cellular telephone numbers were selected using random-digit-dial methods. Landline respondents were chosen at random within each household on the basis of which member had the most recent birthday. Samples were weighted to correct for unequal selection probability, nonresponse, and double coverage of landline and cell users in the two sampling frames. The demographic items requested included age (18–20; 21–23), gender (M; F), Hispanic (Hispanic/Non-Hispanic), Black (Black; Non-Black), and Region (NE; MW; S; W). All levels of weighted demographic variables were very close to the target population (table A.2 on page 348). We also asked for self-identification regarding religion and family financial status.

One limitation we should note in our religious identity data is that 43.8 percent of respondents ended up belonging to "Other List." We had asked Gallup® Organization to ask for the specific religious identity of those who indicated "other," but due to a miscommunication, this result was not obtained. As a result,

Table A.2. Descriptive Statistics for Variables of Interest in National Quantitative Survey (N = 2,503)

Variable	Category	Frequency	Percentage
Gender	Male	1,451	58.0%
	Female	1,052	42.0%
Year in College	First Year	335	13.4%
	Second Year	692	27.6%
	Third Year	729	29.1%
	Fourth Year or Above	747	29.8%
Importance of Religion in One's Life	Very Important	795	31.8%
	Fairly Important	647	25.8%
	Not Very Important	1,061	42.4%
Financial Situation	Above Average	722	28.9%
	Average	1376	55.0%
	Below Average	405	16.1%
Race/Ethnicity	White	1,578	63.0%
	Black	300	12.0%
	Hispanic	402	16.1%
	Asian American	171	6.8%
	Other	33	1.3%
	Missing	19	0.8%
Political Affiliation	Republican	536	21.4%
	Democrat	1,057	42.2%
	Independent	105	4.2%
	Other party/others	805	32.2%
Institution Attended	Public Four-Year universities	1,319	52.7%
	Private Four-Year universities	596	23.8%
	Two-Year colleges	588	23.5%
Religious Service Attendances	Never	542	21.8%
	Less than once a year	158	6.3%
	Once or twice a year	493	19.8%
	Several times a year	340	13.7%
	Once a month	193	7.8%
	2-3 times a month	203	8.2%
	Weekly	403	16.2%
	Several times a week	159	6.4%
College Majors	Non-STEM non-Business majors	344	13.7%
	Health sciences majors	268	10.7%
	STEM majors	693	27.7%
	Social sciences majors	250	10.0%
	Humanities majors	395	15.8%
	Education-related majors	94	3.8%
	Business-related majors	380	15.2%
	Others	79	3.1%
Religious Affiliation	Catholic	293	11.7%
	Mainline Protestant	434	17.3%
	Evangelical Protestant	194	7.8%
	Nonreligious	381	15.2%
	Other religions	104	4.2%
	Other List	1,097	43.8%

readers should be cautious when interpreting the analytical results for those who indicated this identity, since it is very likely that this category contains a wide variety of students who did identify with the other religious categories.

The construct, *self-achiever-focused purpose in life* was measured by a total of nine items with five-point Likert scaled survey items, with 5 indicating strongly agree with the survey item and 1 indicating strongly disagree with the survey item. The Cronbach's alpha for self-achievement-focused purpose in life was 0.705. The construct, *relationalist-focused purpose in life* was measured by a total of three items with five-point Likert scaled survey items with 5 indicating strongly agree with the survey item and 1 indicating strongly disagree with the survey item. The Cronbach's alpha for relationalist-focused purpose in life was 0.585. Similarly, the construct, *transcendent-focused purpose in life* was measured by a total of three items with five-point Likert scale survey items with 5 indicating strongly agree with the survey item and 1 indicating strongly disagree with the survey item. The Cronbach's alpha for transcendent-focused purpose in life was 0.567 (see table A.3 on page 350).

There were three latent variables (endogenous variables) and a total of ten exogenous variables for this model. These ten variables included background characteristics, institutional characteristics, and religion associated variables. Specifically, Multiple Indicators Multiple Causes (MIMC) model was used to test the validity of the hypothesized model and present the associations between purpose in life constructs and observed variables in the model.[7] Given the unequal probability of selection in the selected sample, we accounted for the sampling weights when estimating the model.[8] We then utilized a two-step rule to identify the SEM model. The fit of the measurement model was assessed using confirmatory factor analysis (CFA) (see table A.3). Second, the structural equation modeling (SEM) was constructed and evaluated based on model fit indices (e.g., CFI, TLI, RMSEA, and SRMR) and path estimates (see table A.4 on page 351).

Gallup® Qualitative Interviews

From that quantitative sample above, Gallup® recruited 75 participants for the qualitative portion and managed the interviewing and transcribing of the data. Of the 75 participants, 53 attended public institutions, and 17 of these attended two-year institutions. The participants came from 35 different states. Twenty-six females and 49 males participated in the survey. The participants ranged from 18 to 23 years old with the following breakdown: 18 years old—1, 19 years old—6, 20 years old—13, 21 years old—21, 22 years old—25, and 23 years old—9. The racial identification included the following: White 40, missing 20,[9] Asian 7, Black 5, and Hispanic 3.

Table A.3. Confirmatory Factor Analysis of Purpose in Life Indicators

Variable	Factor Indicators		Estimate	SE	Est./SE
Self-Achievement-Focused Purpose in Life	Item 1	Make money	0.526	0.084	6.254***
	Item 2	Have a fulfilling career	0.495	0.045	11.023***
	Item 3	Be happy	0.466	0.041	11.307***
	Item 4	Produce new and original work, such as a book or a piece of art	0.163†	0.029	5.536***
	Item 9	Maintain a comfortable standard of living	0.619	0.055	11.205***
	Item 11	Live with no regrets	0.572	0.039	14.808***
	Item 13	Achieve success in my career	0.635	0.047	13.564***
	Item 15	Experience life to the fullest	0.424	0.047	9.050***
	Item 17	Discover new things about the world	0.379	0.033	11.339***
Relationalist-Focused Purpose in Life	Item 5	Help others	0.618	0.036	17.281***
	Item 8	Care for a family	0.566	0.037	15.505***
	Item 12	Build lasting friendships	0.418	0.039	10.693***
Transcendent-Focused Purpose in Life	Item 10	Make the world a better place	0.231†	0.026	8.842***
	Item 14	Love God or a higher power	0.957	0.022	44.206***
	Item 16	Serve my community and country	0.35	0.023	15.130***

Note: † indicates relatively low factor loadings.

*p < .05; **p < .01; ***p < .001.

Factor Analysis

Purpose in Life Factors	No. of Items	*M* (SD)	Skewness	Kurtosis	Chronbach's α
Self-Achievement-Focused Purpose in Life	9	35.689(4.963)	−0.947	1.65	0.705
Relationalist-Focused Purpose in Life	3	13.240(1.894)	−1.539	3.476	0.585
Transcendent-Focused Purpose in Life	3	11.412(2.710)	−0.421	−0.57	0.567

Table A.4. Model Fit Indices for Measurement Model and Structural Equation Model

Models	df	SRMR	RMSEA	CFI	TLI
Measurement Model	36	0.024	0.029	0.985	0.956
Structural Equation Model	363	0.027	0.025	0.937	0.907

We created a shorter guide for these telephone interviews (see appendix B) that would take each participant through various dimensions of his or her experiences with purpose development. The concepts covered included questions about life purpose, expectation of college experiences to guide or direct the purpose, guidance about life meaning, class discussions or assigned readings about meaning and purpose, and conversations outside of class with friends or professors regarding life purpose. Gallup® conducted the interviews from January 2014 through June 2014, and all of the interviews occurred by phone and lasted between twenty and thirty minutes.

After Gallup® finished the transcription, we analyzed the data. Again, to code the data we used an inductive approach to analyze the responses to the qualitative questions due to our desire to generate a framework from the particulars of student responses, rather than imposing prior categories on them.

The National Study of Youth and Religion (NSYR)

For some parts of our quantitative research, we drew on the National Study of Youth and Religion (NSYR) surveys. There are currently four waves of the NSYR survey, following the same youth from adolescence to late emerging adulthood. We use the first wave and the third wave in our research.

The first wave consists of a nationally representative telephone survey of 3,290 English- and Spanish-speaking adolescents (age 13 to 17) in the United States and one of their coresident parents. The data were collected between July 2002 and April 2003, using a random-digit-dial method by researchers at the University of North Carolina at Chapel Hill. The third wave was fielded between September 2007 and April 2008, when the respondents were age eighteen to twenty-three. In Wave 3, 2,532 original youth respondents participated in the survey for an overall Wave 1 to Wave 3 retention rate of 77.1 percent. The main source of attrition in the third wave was nonlocated respondents. Data are weighted using both household and census information to ensure that findings are as representative as possible. Readers interested in more on the NSYR survey methodology should consult http://youthandreligion.nd.edu/assets/102496/master_just_methods_11_12_2008.pdf.

For chapter 12 we also examined one part of the third wave of in-person interviews for the NSYR, which consisted of 230 in-depth personal interviews with eighteen to twenty-three-year-olds, a subset of emerging adults. These interviews provided a helpful database for a qualitative study that seeks to listen to the participants themselves and discern how they interpret and respond to questions about life purpose, future goals, and descriptions of a future good life. We did not conduct the interviews ourselves, but we received permission to access the interview database from the NSYR research team.

Conducted between May and September of 2008, respondents were offered a $75–$100 cash incentive to complete the interviews. The original interviews averaged approximately 135 minutes. Those conducting the interviews sought to include young emerging adults who represented a range of demographic and religious characteristics and took into account region, urban/suburban/rural, age, sex, race, household income, religion, and school type (for more detailed information about the method of this phase of the NSYR study and how it fit within the other NSYR studies, see http://youthandreligion.nd.edu/research-design/.) Thus, interviews were conducted in 35 different states in all geographic regions in the United States. The college students were nearly evenly divided by male (116) and female (114). With regard to race, the respondents identified as follows: 149 White, 33 Black, 25 Hispanic, 8 Asian, 4 Native American, 11 Other. With regard to education, 43 interviewees had completed a high school degree or below, 138 were in the process of completing a "four-year" degree (2 were actually fifth-year students, and 1 was a sixth-year student), 14 had completed an associate's degree, 30 had completed their bachelor's degree, and 5 did not provide their level of educational attainment.

The interviewers for the NSYR surveys asked two sets of questions related to the topic under discussion. The first question about purpose was generally asked in the following form:

> NSYR: Some people we talk with seem to have a very strong sense of purpose in life, they know exactly what is the value of life, what is important to be or do. Other people seem more disoriented or lost in life, not knowing exactly what their purpose is. How would you describe yourself when it comes to this question of purpose in life?

The second set of questions pertained to future accomplishments or experiences, which considered another way of addressing the topic of purpose. The young emerging adults were asked about these concepts using two or three questions. Often, these questions were asked consecutively; although, sometimes the interviewers split up the questions. The following is an example: "What ultimately do you want to get out of life? What would living a 'good life' look like to you?

Is there anything that you really want to accomplish or experience in your life before it's all over?" These questions do not specifically ask about life purpose, but they cover three concepts or terms usually understood as related or even equal to it. These questions were also asked in a way that downplayed the second component of the purpose definition offered by Damon et al.[10] For instance, "What do you want to get out of life" focuses on personal goals in a more self-focused manner. The second part of the question could also be taken to have a moral or evaluative aspect (i.e., good as in moral or ethical). The third concept again focuses on personal accomplishments or experiences. While we think it would have also been helpful to have asked participants about meaning in life, the research team did not do so.

While the original study accumulated 230 interviews, for reasons we do not know, one of the respondents did not address the topics covered in this study, so our sample was considered to be 229. We used an inductive approach to analyze the short-form responses since our desire was to generate themes from the particulars of young emerging adult responses rather than to impose prior frameworks on them. To do this, one author generated codes using a two-cycle coding process.[11] In the first cycle, he identified distinct categories of responses to the questions about purpose and the good life (see tables 1 and 2). In the second cycle process, he reexamined the first cycle subsets within the largest metacode categories and recoded them into either existing codes or new subcodes (see tables 1 and 2). A second author then used a similar process to validate the findings. Initially, they shared anywhere from 75 to 100 percent agreement among metacodes and the subcodes with a total interrater reliability rating of 86 percent for both levels of codes. Regarding both meta- and subcodes, the authors discussed and categorized the portions with which they found differences and came to an agreement regarding areas of difference.

Together, through the first round of coding, they found that the answers to the purpose question fit into one or more of five thematic categories, and answers to the second question addressing anticipated life goals, experience, and views of the good life produced four larger categories. This second-cycle coding produced the ten subcategories for the purpose question and the nine subcategories for the good life questions described in the findings.

College Students' Beliefs and Values Survey

We also use the College Students' Beliefs and Values (CSBV) surveys. The CSBV surveys were conducted by the Higher Education Research Institute at UCLA as part of the Spirituality in Higher Education project. The first survey consisted of a two-page addendum to the annual Cooperative Institutional Research Program (CIRP) Freshman Survey. The CIRP Freshman Survey has been administered annually since 1965. The CIRP survey and CSBV addendum included 159 items used to analyze the religious and spiritual experiences of college students. The survey was completed by 112,232 entering first-year students at 236 baccalaureate-granting institutions.

In the spring of 2007, 14,527 students completed a follow-up survey during their junior year. These students were selected as a subsample from 136 of the original 236 institutions. Most of the original questions were replicated so that change over time could be measured. Students from private nonreligious institutions, Catholic, evangelical, and mainline Protestant institutions were oversampled. Weights were created for both the 2004 and 2007 data to accurately estimate the characteristics of the entire population of incoming first-year students and junior-year students attending baccalaureate-granting institutions in the United States. In the research we present in this book, we use an approved subset of 93 variables from the 2004 and 2007 CSBV data. Additional information on methodology is available here: http://spirituality.ucla.edu/docs/results/freshman/2004_2007_Survey_Methodology.pdf.

Appendix B

____

Interview Guide

110 Students at 10 Campuses

A. Introduction

- Basics about the interview and confidentiality matters

B. About the Interviewee

- What year are you in college? Is this the only college you have attended, or have you gone elsewhere? Where?

- Have you declared a major or minor yet? What is it?

- Can you tell me a little bit about where you live during college? With whom do you live?

C. Family

- Tell me/us about your family situation growing up? Did you live with one parent, two parents, or some other arrangement?

- How close are you to your parents?

- What kinds of topics do you feel comfortable discussing with your parents? (e.g., moral dilemmas, politics, religion, meaning of life, relationships, and sex). Are there things you still don't like talking to them about?

- Growing up, did you perceive your parent(s)/guardian(s) as moral models for you? How so? Are there any ways you want to be different from your parents during your adult life?

- One of the things we are interested in is how young adults think about the purpose and meaning of their lives. We'll have some time to discuss this in more detail in just a few minutes, but first, can you tell me just a little bit about what you think?

  - Do you think there is a difference between finding "your purpose in life" and finding "the meaning of life"? If so, what is it?

  - What gives your life meaning? What makes life worth living for you?

  - Do you have a sense of purpose in your life, or is this something you are still trying to figure out? Or maybe questions of purpose just aren't all that important to you right now. [If they ask for a definition: *Purpose* has to do with your overall life goals.]

  - Can you talk a little bit about the role your parents have played in your [sense of purpose]/[search for purpose]/[lack of purpose]?

D. Friends

- Can you tell me about your close friends in high school and college (e.g., what group, how many)?

- What kinds of topics did you feel comfortable discussing with your close friends (e.g., moral dilemmas, politics, religion, meaning of life, relationships and sex)? Were there some things you didn't talk about with them?

- Did you perceive them as moral models for you or not? How so?

- Back to the question of purpose. Do you think your friends growing up have had any role in how you think about the meaning and purpose of your life? Or have they not really been important for this?

E. College Life

- Why did you choose this college/university?

- What do you see as the purpose of higher education?

- Did you expect it to help you think about issues of purpose and meaning in your life, or not? Do you now?

- What experiences in college have affirmed your sense of meaning in life? What experiences have shaken or disturbed your sense of meaning?

- Do you ever have discussions about the meaning or purpose of life in any of your classes? [If yes] Can you describe some of these discussions to me? Did you have any assigned readings that addressed purpose or meaning in life? Did it influence you in any way? Have any significant discussions with faculty about these topics outside of class?

- Have you read any books (fiction or nonfiction) in the last several years that changed the way you think about your life's direction? Which ones? How so? Do you look to any sacred book or books for guidance in this area?

- What sort of nonacademic activities are you involved in (e.g., theater, clubs, sports, "hanging out" with friends, etc.). What do you spend most of your free time doing while at college?

- Do you ever discuss ideas about the meaning and purpose of life in these group activities or with your friends? [If yes] Can you describe some of these discussions to me?

- Do you talk about the meaning or purpose of life with college friends, acquaintances, or even strangers through social media?

- Have you been in a romantic relationship in college? During that experience did you talk about purpose in life? Did the relationship cause you to think about life purpose differently?

- Are there any particular adult mentors at college with whom you have discussed this topic? How have they helped or influenced you in this area?

F. Religious/Spiritual Traditions

- [If not already discussed in section C] Would you describe your family as religious or spiritual? [If yes] Can you describe what that meant or looked like for me?

- Have your religious beliefs changed at all as you have gotten older? How about now that you are in college?

  - [If changed while in college] What is it about college that has made you change your belief?

- Is there a particular religious or spiritual label with which you identify? [If needs prompt] For example, some people say that they are Catholic, Jewish, Hindu, Protestant, evangelical, etc. Some others might say they are just Christian, Jewish or agnostics. Still others might think of themselves as spiritual but not really religious in any way. Do any of these types of labels describe you?

  - [If has a religious/spiritual identity] Are there any beliefs that you consider central to this identity?

  - [If has a religious/spiritual identity] What about practices? Are there any experiences or practices that you consider central to this identity?

- Back to the topic of meaning and purpose. [If has a religious/spiritual identity] Does being religious/spiritual help you think about questions related to the meaning and purpose of your life? Or does this not really play a role in how you think about your life? [If has no religious/spiritual identity] Do you think being nonreligious makes it easier or harder to think about these questions?

- Do you have any other identities that influence how you think about issues related to meaning and purpose in life?

G. The Future

- Five years from now, what would living a "good life" look like to you (e.g., family, living situation, job, as well as issues related to meaning and purpose in life)?

- What is it that you really want to accomplish or experience in life before it is all over?

- Do you believe in an afterlife? Does this belief influence how you think about meaning and purpose?

- Do you think your ideas about meaning and purpose will change in the future or are they pretty settled?

H. Conclusion

- Do you think these questions have become more or less important to you (or maybe the same importance) since you've been in college?

- Is there anything else you would like to talk about that we haven't covered?

Gallup® Qualitative Interview Guide

These questions were part of a larger interview that also explored issues of academic honesty and self-control.

1. Generally speaking, what gives your life meaning?

   a. IF NEEDED: For you, what makes life worth living?

2. Generally speaking, do you have a sense of purpose in your life, or is this something you are still trying to figure out? If so, what is it?

3. Have you ever received guidance about what gives your life meaning or what the purpose of your life is?

   a. IF YES: From whom?

4. Did you expect your experiences in college to help you think about purpose or meaning in your life?

   a. IF YES: How?

   b. IF NO: Why not?

5. Do you ever have discussions about the meaning or purpose of life in any of your classes?

   a. IF YES: Can you give me some examples?

6. Did you have any assigned readings that addressed purpose or meaning in life?

   a. IF YES: Can you give me some examples?

7. Have you ever had these types of conversations with faculty outside of class?

   a. IF YES: Did these discussions influence you in any way?

8. Do you ever have discussions about the meaning or purpose of life in your personal relationships?

   a. IF YES: Can you provide some examples?

   b. IF NOT MENTIONED IN ITEM 6: Are there any particular mentors at college with whom you have discussed this topic?

   c. IF YES: How have they helped or influenced you in this area?

9. Is there a particular religious or spiritual label with which you identify (PROBE FOR ACTUAL RELIGION)? IF NEEDED: For

example, some people say that they are Catholic, Jewish, Hindu, Protestant, evangelical, etc.

a. IF YES: How does being religious or spiritual influence how you think about questions related to the meaning and purpose of your life?

b. IF NO: How does being nonreligious influence how you think about meaning and purpose?

Purpose Question from the Gallup® Quantitative Survey

On a five-point scale, where 5 means strongly agree and 1 means strongly disagree, please rate your level of agreement with the following items. The purpose of my life is to ___________.

_____ Make money
_____ Have a fulfilling career
_____ Be happy
_____ Produce new and original work, such as a book or a piece of art
_____ Help others
_____ Change the way people think
_____ Do the right thing
_____ Care for a family
_____ Maintain a comfortable standard of living
_____ Make the world a better place
_____ Live with no regrets
_____ Build lasting friendships
_____ Achieve success in my career
_____ Love God or a higher power
_____ Experience life to the fullest
_____ Serve my community and country
_____ Discover new things about the world

Statistical Supplement to Chapters 3 and 10

Table C1. Odds Ratios from Logistic Regression Predicting Sense of Purpose in Life by Demographic, Family, and Religious Covariates among Eighteen- to Twenty-Three-Year-Olds, Weighted

	(1)	(2)	(3)
Demographic Background			
Female	1.359**	1.379**	1.333**
Race/ethnicity[a]			
Black	0.841	0.851	0.708
Hispanic	0.574***	0.573***	0.500***
Other	0.763	0.791	0.720
Age	1.048	1.044	1.057
Parents' income	1.133***	1.115***	1.127***
Parents' education	1.071**	1.079**	1.067**
Family Structure/Relationships			
Feels close to parents		1.216***	
Living with bio/adopted parents @ W1		1.265+	
Has experienced at least one par. breakup		0.925	
Religion			
Religious Tradition (W1)[b]			
Mainline Protestant			1.046
Black Protestant			1.110
Catholic			1.205
Jewish			3.746**
LDS			1.624
Not Religious			0.686+
Other religion			1.290
Indeterminate			1.783+
Closeness to/belief in God (W3)[c]			
Feels somewhat close			1.686***
Feels very/extremely close			2.801***
Does not believe in God			1.145
Parent church attendance (W1)			1.029
Importance of faith (W3)			0.875*
Frequency of Bible reading (W3)			1.042
Frequency of prayer (W3)			0.939+
Frequency of church attendance (W3)			1.068+
N	2,437	2,437	2,437
Pseudo R^2	0.062	0.071	0.09

Source: NSYR 2002–03, 2007–08.

Notes: [a]Reference category is White; [b]reference category is evangelical Protestant; [c]reference category is feels distant from God.

+ $p < .10$; *$p < .05$; **$p < .01$; ***$p < .001$.

Table C2. Odds Ratios from Logistic Regression Predicting Sense of Purpose in Life by Education, Sex/Relationships, and Finances/Employment among Eighteen- to Twenty-Three-Year-Olds, Weighted

	(1)	(2)[a]	(3)
Demographic Background			
Female	1.235*	1.408**	1.397**
Race/ethnicity[b]			
Black	0.824	0.791	0.810
Hispanic	0.537***	0.544***	0.618**
Other	0.731	0.716	0.775
Age	0.996	1.041	1.050
Parents' income	1.091***	1.092***	1.124***
Parents' education	1.015	1.038	1.071**
Education[c]			
Not Currently enrolled			
HS graduate	2.059***		
Some college	2.585***		
College graduate (bachelor's or more)	4.373***		
Currently enrolled			
High School	1.921*		
Religiously affiliated college/university	5.086***		
Elite university	5.371***		
Other college/university	5.364***		
Associate's degree institution	3.342***		
Finances, Employment, & Living Status			
Earnings (W3)		1.036**	
Personal debt (W3)		0.992+	
Living status[d]			
Lives with someone else (not parents)		0.997	
Lives in own place		1.246+	
Lives in group quarters (e.g., dorm, barracks)		1.592**	
Employment status[e]			
Employed only		1.574*	
Employed and in school		3.194***	
In school only		2.810***	
Active in armed forces		3.651***	
Sex & Relationships			
Ever cohabited			0.807+
Ever had oral sex			0.996
Ever had sexual intercourse			1.054
N	2,437	2,437	2,263
Pseudo R^2	0.092	0.095	0.060

Source: NSYR 2002–3, 2007–8.

Notes: [a]Model 3 is restricted to those who report never being married; [b]reference category is White; [c]all education categories are mutually exclusive. Reference category is not currently enrolled, did not graduate from high school; [d]reference category is lives with parents; [e]reference category is not in labor force or school.

$+ p < .10$; $*p < .05$; $**p < .01$; $***p < .001$.

Table C3. Odds Ratios from Logistic Regression Predicting Sense of Purpose in Life by Health, Helping Behavior, Deviant Behavior, and Materialism among Eighteen- to Twenty-Three-Year Olds, Weighted

	(1)	(2)	(3)	(4)
Demographic Background				
Female	1.501***	1.143	1.343**	1.293*
Race/ethnicity[a]				
Black	0.787	0.798	0.837	0.886
Hispanic	0.609**	0.532***	0.566***	0.572***
Other	0.796	0.755	0.728	0.810
Age	1.058	1.058	1.046	1.046
Parents' income	1.127***	1.127***	1.128***	1.129***
Parents' education	1.074**	1.063**	1.056*	1.061*
Health				
BMI categories[b]				
Underweight	1.264			
Overweight	1.080			
Obese	1.024			
Happiness with body	1.204***			
Self-rated general health	1.442***			
Deviant Behavior				
Frequency of binge drinking		0.946		
Frequency of cigarette smoking		0.926***		
Frequency of marijuana smoking		0.934*		
Frequency of fighting		0.893		
Frequency of pornography use		0.934		
Helping Behavior				
Volunteered in past year			1.306*	
Gave more than $50 in past year			1.210+	
Frequency of helping needy directly			1.006	
Materialism				
Admire people who own expensive things				0.989
Would be happier if could afford to buy more				0.783***
Shopping brings lots of pleasure				1.074
Things owned indicate success in life				1.000
N	2,437	2,437	2,437	2,437
Pseudo R^2	0.095	0.079	0.067	0.075

Source: NSYR 2002–3, 2007–8.

Notes: [a]Reference category is White; [b]reference category BMI normal.

+ $p < .10$; *$p < .05$; **$p < .01$; ***$p < .001$.

Table C4. Odds Ratios from Logistic Regression Predicting Sense of Purpose in Life for All Independent Variables, Only Statistically Significant Variables Shown, Weighted

Female	1.289+
Black[a]	0.665+
Hispanic[a]	0.511***
Parents' income	1.061*
Feels close to parents	1.174**
Jewish[b]	3.473*
LDS[b]	1.922*
Not Religious[b]	0.580**
Indeterminate[b]	1.760+
Feels somewhat close to God[c]	1.792***
Feels very/extremely close to God[c]	2.852***
Importance of faith (W3)	0.822**
HS graduate (not enrolled)[d]	1.776*
Some college (not enrolled)[d]	1.946*
College graduate (bachelors or more)[d]	2.671*
Religiously affiliated college/university (enrolled)[d]	2.383+
Elite university (enrolled)[d]	3.235*
Other college/university (enrolled)[d]	2.959**
Ever had sexual intercourse[e]	1.478*
Earnings (W3)	1.040**
Personal debt (W3)	0.990*
Employed only[f]	1.682*
Employed and in school[f]	2.812**
In school only[f]	2.560*
Active in armed forces[f]	4.429***
Underweight[g]	1.572+
Happiness with body	1.172**
Self-rated general health	1.351***
Frequency of binge drinking	0.869*
Would be happier if could afford to buy more	0.858**
N	2,437
Pseudo R^2	0.18

Source: NSYR 2002–3, 2007–8.

Notes: [a]Reference category is White; [b]reference category is evangelical Protestant; [c]reference category is feels distant from God; [d]reference category is not currently enrolled, did not graduate from high school; [e]coefficient from model restricted to never married ($N = 2,263$); [f]reference category is not in labor force or school.

+ $p < .10$, * $p < .05$, ** $p < .01$, *** $p < .0$.

Table C.5. The Effect of Exogenous Variables on Transcendent-Focused Purpose in Life

Transcendent-Focused Purpose in Life ON:		Estimate	SE	Est./SE	*p*
Religion importance (reference group: not very important)	Very important	0.725	0.027	27.005	0.000***
	Fairly important	0.448	0.022	20.433	0.000***
Religious Services Attendance (reference group: attends several times a year or less)	Several times a month	0.064	0.016	3.956	0.000***
	Several times a week	0.107	0.018	5.946	0.000***
Religious affiliation (reference group: other list)	Catholic	0.030	0.015	2.039	0.041*
	Protestant	0.004	0.001	2.622	0.009**
	Evangelical	0.057	0.011	5.036	0.000***
	Nonreligious	−0.109	0.016	−6.766	0.000***
	Other religions	0.020	0.017	−1.144	0.253

*$p < 0.05$; **$p < 0.01$; ***$p < 0.001$.

Table C.6. The Effect of Exogenous Variables on Relationalist-Focused Purpose in Life

Relationists-Focused Purpose in Life ON:		Estimate	SE	Est./SE	*p*
Religion importance (reference group: not very important)	Very important	0.218	0.041	5.342	0.000***
	Fairly important	0.121	0.032	3.734	0.000***
	Private 4-yr. university	-0.050	0.033	−1.502	0.133
Religious Services Attendance (reference group: attends several times a year or less)	Several times a month	0.033	0.027	1.250	0.211
	Several times a week	0.054	0.034	1.600	0.109
Religion Affiliation (reference group: other list)	Catholic	0.018	0.026	0.685	0.493
	Protestant	0.001	0.002	0.789	0.430
	Evangelical	0.067	0.020	3.361	0.001***
	Nonreligious	−0.107	0.030	−3.534	0.000***
	Other religions	−0.006	0.025	−0.247	0.805

*$p < 0.05$; **$p < 0.01$; ***$p < 0.001$.

Table C.7. The Effect of Exogenous Variables on Self-Achievement-Focused Purpose in Life

Self-Achievement-Focused Purpose in Life ON:		Estimate	SE	Est./SE	*p*
Religion importance (reference group: not very important)	Very important	0.083	0.040	2.044	0.041*
	Fairly important	0.097	0.028	3.461	0.001***
Religious Services Attendance (reference group: attends several times a year or less)	Several times a month	−0.050	0.025	−2.002	0.045*
	Several times a week	−0.182	0.034	−5.308	0.000***
Religion Affiliation (reference group: other list)	Catholic	0.072	0.023	3.109	0.002**
	Protestant	0.000	0.002	0.142	0.887
	Evangelical	0.083	0.022	3.719	0.000***
	Nonreligious	−0.039	0.027	−1.468	0.142
	Other religions	−0.037	0.022	−1.701	0.089

*$p < 0.05$; **$p < 0.01$; ***$p < 0.001$.

Notes

Introduction

1. C. John Sommerville, *The Decline of the Secular University* (New York: Oxford University Press, 2006), 8.

2. Aristotle, *Nichomachean Ethics*, trans. and ed. Roger Crisp (New York: Cambridge University Press, 2000), 4.

3. For an explanation of why psychology tended to avoid this topic see William Damon, Jenni Menon, and Kendall Cotton Bronk, "The Development of Purpose during Adolescence," *Applied Developmental Science* 7, no. 3 (2003): 119–28.

4. For a summary of this research, see Kendall C. Bronk, *Purpose in Life: A Critical Component of Optimal Youth Development* (New York: Springer, 2014). For additional examples see Anthony L. Burrow and Patrick L. Hill. "Purpose as a Form of Identity Capital for Positive Youth Adjustment," *Developmental psychology* 47, no. 4 (2011): 1196; Lisa Kiang, "Deriving Daily Purpose through Daily Events and Role Fulfillment among Asian American Youth," *Journal of Research on Adolescence* 22, no. 1 (2012): 185–98; Kendall Cotton Bronk, Patrick L. Hill, Daniel K. Lapsley, Tasneem L. Talib, and Holmes Finch, "Purpose, Hope, and Life Satisfaction in Three Age Groups," *Journal of Positive Psychology* 4, no. 6 (2009): 500–10; Anthony L. Burrow, Amanda C. O'Dell, and Patrick L. Hill, "Profiles of a Developmental Asset: Youth Purpose as a Context for Hope and Well-Being," *Journal of Youth and Adolescence* 39, no. 11 (2010): 1265–73; Kendall Cotton Bronk, "The Role of Purpose in Life in Healthy Identity Formation: A Grounded Model," *New Directions for Youth Development* 2011, no. 132 (2011): 31–44; Ann S. Masten and Marie-Gabrielle Reed, "Resilience in Development," *Handbook of Positive Psychology*, (2002): 74–88.

5. Ibid.

6. Warren Nord, *Does God Make a Difference? Taking Religion Seriously in Our Schools and Universities* (New York: Oxford University Press, 2010).

7. Anthony T. Kronman, *Education's End: Why Our Colleges and Universities Have Given Up on the Meaning of Life* (New Haven: Yale University Press, 2007), 7.

8. Alexander W. Astin, Helen S. Astin, and Jennifer Lindholm, *Cultivating the Spirit: How College Can Enhance Students' Inner Lives* (San Francisco: Jossey-Bass, 2011), 37.

9. Kronman, *Education's End*, 123.

10. Robert J. Nash and Michelle C. Murray, *Helping College Students Find Purpose: The Campus Guide to Meaning-Making* (San Francisco: Jossey-Bass, 2010), xiv–xv.

11. Astin, Astin, and Lindholm *Cultivating the Spirit.*

12. For more information about the methodology for these interviews, see appendix A.

13. Astin, Astin, and Lindholm, *Cultivating the Spirit.*

14. Ibid., 3.

15. Ibid., 36.

16. U.S. Department of Education, *Digest of Educational Statistics*, table 301.10, Enrollment, Staff, and Degrees/Certificates Conferred in Degree-Granting and Non-Degree-Granting Postsecondary Institutions, by Control and Level of Institution, Sex of Student, Type of Staff, and Level of Degree: Fall 2013 and 2012–13 (Washington, DC: U.S. Department of Education, 2014) [online].

17. See for example, Kathleen M. Goodman, Katie Wilson, and Z Nicolazzo, "Campus Practice in Support of Spirituality, Faith, Religion, and Life Purpose," in *Making Meaning: Embracing Spirituality, Faith, Religion, and Life Purpose in Student Affairs*, ed. Jenny L. Small (Sterling, VA: Stylus Press, 2015), 134–35.

18. Tim Clydesdale, *The Purposeful Graduate: Why Colleges Must Talk to Students about Vocation* (Chicago: University of Chicago Press, 2015), 216.

19. Ibid., 216–17.

20. Numerous scholars in the various disciplines of psychology, sociology and higher education have proposed a variety of ways of differentiating and defining meaning, purpose, and the good life when undertaking empirical study. William Damon, Jenni Menon, and Kendall Cotton Bronk, "The Development of Purpose during Adolescence," *Applied Developmental Science* 7, no. 3 (2003), 119–28; Logan S. George and Crystal L. Park, "Are Meaning and Purpose Distinct? An Examination of Correlates and Predictors," *Journal of Positive Psychology* 8, no. 5 (2013): 365–75; Patrick L. Hill, Anthony L. Burrow, and Rachel Sumner, "Addressing Important Questions in the Field of Adolescent Purpose," *Child Development Perspectives* 7, no. 4 (2013): 232–36. One of these scholars concluded we need empirical research that differentiates purpose from similar constructs "such as meaning in life and eudemonic well-being." Hill, Burrow, and Sumner, "Addressing Important Questions," 234.

21. Kronman, *Education's End.*

Chapter 1

1. Palmer Parker and Arthur Zajonc, *The Heart of Higher Education: A Call to Renewal* (San Francisco: Jossey Bass, 2010), 3.

2. Anthony Kronman, *Education's End: Why Our Colleges and Universities Have Given Up on the Meaning of Life* (New Haven: Yale University Press, 2007), 42–43.

3. See for example Tim Clydesdale, *The Purposeful Graduate: Why Colleges Must Talk to Students about Vocation* (Chicago: University of Chicago Press, 2015); Anthony Kronman, *Education's End*; Robert J. Nash and Michelle C. Murray, *Helping College Students Find Purpose: The Campus Guide to Meaning-Making* (San Francisco: Jossey-Bass,

2010); Palmer and Zajonc, *The Heart of Higher Education*; Jon C. Dalton and Pamela C. Crosby, "When Faith Fails: Why Nurturing Purpose and Meaning Are So Critical to Student Learning and Development in College," *Journal of College and Character* 11, no. 3 (2010) [online] doi: 10.2202/1940-1639.1720; Sharon Parks, *Big Questions, Worthy Dreams: Mentoring Young Adults in Their Search for Meaning, Purpose and Faith* (San Francisco: Jossey Bass, 2001); Harry R. Lewis, *Excellence without a Soul: How a Great University Forgot Education* (New York: Public Affairs, 2006).

4. Harry R. Lewis, *Excellence without a Soul*, xii. We find it interesting that this quote is quite similar to that offered by Palmer and Zajonc.

5. Samuel E. Morison, *The Founding of Harvard College* (Cambridge: Harvard University Press, 1935), 333.

6. Kronman, *Education's End*, 58.

7. Donald H. Meyer, *The Instructed Conscience: The Shaping of the American National Ethic* (Philadelphia: University of Pennsylvania Press, 1972), 24–25.

8. Donald Tweksbury, *The Founding of American Colleges and Universities before the Civil War* (New York: Teachers College, Columbia University, 1932).

9. Alexander W. Astin, Helen S. Astin, and Jennifer A. Lindholm, *Cultivating the Spirit: How College Can Enhance Students' Inner Lives* (San Francisco: Jossey-Bass, 2011); Nash and Murray, *Helping College Students Find Purpose*; Palmer and Zajonc, *The Heart of Higher Education*.

10. Kronman, *Education's End*, 65.

11. John Thelin, *A History of American Higher Education*, 2nd ed. (Baltimore: Johns Hopkins University Press, 2011).

12. Kronman, *Education's End*, 66.

13. Ibid., 71.

14. Ibid., 74.

15. Julie Reuben, *The Making of the Modern University: Intellectual Transformation and the Marginalization of Morality* (Chicago: University of Chicago Press, 1996), 139.

16. Ibid., 170.

17. John Dewey and James Tufts, *Ethics*, rev. ed. (New York: Holt, Rinehart, and Winston, 1932), 151.

18. Ibid., 151.

19. Ibid., 212.

20. Reuben, *The Making of the Modern University*, 176.

21. Christian Smith, *The Secular Revolution: Power, Interests, and Conflict in the Secularization of American Public Life* (Berkeley: University of California Press, 2003).

22. Douglas Sloan, "The Teaching of Ethics in the American Undergraduate Curriculum, 1876–1976," in *Ethics Teaching in Higher Education*, eds. Daniel Callahan and Sissela Bok (New York: Plenum Press, 1980), 1–57; Meyer, *The Instructed Conscience*.

23. Sloan, "The Teaching of Ethics in the American Undergraduate Curriculum, 1876–1976."

24. Ibid.

25. Michael Davis, *Ethics and the University* (New York: Routledge, 1999).

26. Robert Anderson, *European Universities from the Enlightenment to 1914* (New York: Oxford University Press, 2004).

27. *Digest of Educational Statistics*, table 303.10, Total Fall Enrollment in Degree-Granting Institutions, by Attendance Status, Sex of Student, and Control of Institution: Selected Years, 1947 through 2025 (Washington, DC: U.S. Department of Education, 2016) [online].

28. Sloan, "The Teaching of Ethics in the American Undergraduate Curriculum, 1876–1976," 44.

29. Warren Nord, *Does God Make a Difference? Taking Religion Seriously in Our Schools and Universities* (New York: Oxford University Press, 2010). Astin, Astin, and Lindholm, *Cultivating the Spirit*, 141.

30. Nord, *Does God Make a Difference?*

31. Sloan, "The Teaching of Ethics in the American Undergraduate Curriculum, 1876–1976"; George Marsden, *The Soul of the American University: From Protestant Establishment to Established Nonbelief* (New York: Oxford University Press, 1994).

32. Richard Hofstadter and Wilson Smith, eds., *American Higher Education: A Documentary History*, vol. 2 (Chicago: University of Chicago Press, 1961), 957–58.

33. Robert M. Hutchins, *The Higher Learning in America* (New Brunswick: Transaction, 1995), 66. First published 1936 by Yale University Press.

34. John Dewey, "President Hutchins' Proposals to Remake Higher Education," *Social Frontier* 3 (1937): 104.

35. Mark U. Edwards, "Why Faculty Find It Difficult to Talk about Religion," in *The American University in a Postsecular Age*, eds. Douglas Jacobsen and Rhonda Jacobsen (New York: Oxford University Press, 2008).

36. Astin, Astin, and Lindholm, *Cultivating the Spirit*, 141.

37. *Digest of Educational Statistics*, table 310, Degrees Conferred by Degree-Granting Institutions, by Level of Degree and Sex of Student: Selected Years, 1869–70 through 2021–22 (Washington, DC: U.S. Department of Education, 2012) [online]; table 318.20 Bachelor's, Master's, and Doctor's Degrees Conferred by Postsecondary Institutions, by Sex of Student and Discipline Division: 2013–14 (Washington, DC: U.S. Department of Education, 2015) [online].

38. *Digest of Educational Statistics*, table 303.10, Total Fall Enrollment in Degree-Granting Postsecondary Institutions, by Attendance Status, Sex of Student, and Control of Institution: Selected Years, 1947 through 2025 (Washington, DC: U.S. Department of Education, 2016) [online].

39. *Digest of Educational Statistics*, table 303.60, Total Fall Enrollment in Degree-Granting Postsecondary Institutions, by Control and Level of Institution and State or Jurisdiction: 2013 and 2014 (Washington, DC: U.S. Department of Education, 2015) [online].

40. *Digest of Educational Statistics*, table 303.10, Total Fall Enrollment in Degree-Granting Postsecondary Institutions, by Attendance Status, Sex of Student, and Control of Institution: Selected Years, 1947 through 2025; table 306.10, Total Fall Enrollment in Degree-Granting Postsecondary Institutions, by Level of Enrollment, Sex, Attendance Status, and Race/Ethnicity of Student: Selected Years, 1976 through 2013 (Washington, DC: U.S. Department of Education, 2014) [online].

41. *Digest of Educational Statistics*, table 306.10, Total Fall Enrollment in Degree-Granting Postsecondary Institutions, by Level of Enrollment, Sex, Attendance Status, and

Race/Ethnicity of Student: Selected years, 1976 through 2014 (Washington, DC: U.S. Department of Education, 2015) [online].

42. Nash and Murray, *Helping College Students Find Purpose*, xxvii–xxviii

43. Astin, Astin and Lindholm, *Cultivating the Spirit*, 140.

44. Robert J. Panos, Alexander W. Astin, and John A. Creager, *National Norms for Entering College Freshman—Fall 1967* (Los Angeles: American Council on Education, 1967), 18; Kevin Eagan et al., *The American Freshman: National Norms Fall 2013* (Los Angeles: Higher Education Research Institute, UCLA, 2014), 44.

45. Kronman, *Education's End*, 194.

46. Nash and Murray, *Helping College Students Find Purpose*.

47. Joseph Bottum, *An Anxious Age: A Post-Protestant Ethic and the Spirit of Capitalism* (New York: Image, 2014).

48. Roger Finke and Rodney Stark, "Why Mainline Denominations Decline" (chapter 7) in *The Churching of America, 1776–2005* (New Brunswick, NJ: Rutgers University Press, 2005).

49. Ross Douthat, *Bad Religion: How We Became a Nation of Heretics* (New York: Free Press, 2013).

50. Tim Clydesdale, "Wake Up and Smell the New Epistemology," *Chronicle of Higher Education*, January 23, 2009, accessed July 15, 2015, http://chronicle.com/article/Wake-UpSmell-the-New/4568.

51. Evan Schofer and John W. Meyer, "The Worldwide Expansion of Higher Education in the Twentieth Century," *American Sociological Review* 70, no. 6 (December 2005): 898–920.

52. *Digest of Educational Statistics*, table 220, Total Fall Enrollment in Degree-Granting Institutions, by Attendance Status, Sex of Student, and Control of Institution: Selected Years, 1947 through 2011 (Washington, DC: U.S. Department of Education, 2012) [online].

53. *Digest of Educational Statistics*, tables 220–83 (Washington, DC: U.S. Department of Education, 2012) [online].

54. Nord, *Does God Make a Difference?*

55. Dalton and Crosby, "When Faith Fails," 5.

56. Paul Froese, *On Purpose: How We Create the Meaning of Life* (New York: Oxford University Press, 2015), 48.

57. Marcia B. Baxter Magolda, *Creating Contexts for Learning and Self-Authorship* (Nashville: Vanderbilt University Press, 1999), 268.

58. Astin, Astin, and Lindholm, *Cultivating the Spirit*, 139

59. Jennifer A. Lindholm, *The Quest for Meaning and Wholeness: Spiritual and Religious Connections in the Lives of College Faculty* (San Francisco: Jossey-Bass, 2014), 213.

60. Higher Education Research Institute, *Results from the 2014 HERI Faculty Survey Spirituality Module* (Los Angeles: Higher Education Research Institute, 2014).

61. Kendall C. Bronk, *Purpose in Life: A Critical Component of Optimal Youth Development* (New York: Springer, 2014); William Damon, *The Path to Purpose: Helping Our Children Find Their Calling in Life* (New York: Free Press, 2008); William Damon, Jenni Menon, and Kendall Cotton Bronk, "The Development of Purpose during Adolescence,"

Applied Developmental Science 7, no. 3 (2003): 119–28; Prem S. Fry, "The Development of Personal Meaning and Wisdom in Adolescence: A Reexamination of Moderating and Consolidating Factors and Influences," in *The Human Quest for Meaning: A Handbook of Psychological Research and Clinical Applications*, eds. Paul T. P. Wong and Prem S. Fry (London: Routledge, 1998), 91.

Chapter 2

1. Justin Barrett, *Born Believers: The Science of Children's Religious Belief* (New York: Free Press, 2012), 43–55.

2. Karen L. De Vogler and Peter Ebersole, "Young Adolescents' Meaning in Life," *Psychological Reports* 52 (1983): 427–31.

3. Prem S. Fry, "The Development of Personal Meaning and Wisdom in Adolescence: A Reexamination of Moderating and Consolidating Factors and Influences," in *The Human Quest for Meaning: A Handbook of Psychological Research and Clinical Applications*, eds. Paul T. P. Wong and Prem S. Fry (London: Routledge, 1998), 91.

4. William Damon, Jenni Menon, and Kendall Cotton Bronk, "The Development of Purpose during Adolescence," *Applied Developmental Science* 7, no. 3 (2003): 119–28.

5. Ibid., 126.

6. For a critical review of the literature on purpose, see Damon, Menon, and Bronk, "The Development of Purpose during Adolescence," 119–28. For an article addressing meaning see Fry, "The Development of Personal Meaning and Wisdom in Adolescence," 91–110.

7. Damon, Menon, and Bronk, "The Development of Purpose during Adolescence," 119, 123.

8. R. H. DuRant, et al., "Factors Associated with the Use of Violence among Urban Black Adolescents," *American Journal of Public Health* 84 (1994): 612–17.

9. Anthony L. Burrow and Patrick L. Hill, "Purpose as a Form of Identity Capital for Positive Youth Adjustment," *Developmental Psychology* 42, no. 4 (2001): 1196–1206; Jane E. Pizzolato, Elizabeth L. Brown, and Mary A. Kanny, "Purpose Plus: Supporting Youth Purpose, Control, and Academic Achievement," *New Directions for Youth Development* 132 (2011): 75–88; Kendall C. Bronk, et al., "Purpose, Hope, and Life Satisfaction in Three Age Groups," *Journal of Positive Psychology* 4 (2009): 500–10.

10. See, for example, Burrow and Hill, "Purpose as a Form of Identity Capital for Positive Youth Adjustment," 1196–206; Anthony L. Burrow, Amanda C. O'Dell, and Patrick L. Hill, "Profiles of a Developmental Asset: Youth Purpose as a Context for Hope and Well-Being," *Journal of Youth Adolescence* 39 (2010): 1265–73.

11. Fry, "The Development of Personal Meaning and Wisdom in Adolescence," 93. Italics in original.

12. Heather Malin et al., "Adolescent Purpose Development: Exploring Empathy, Discovering Roles, Shifting Priorities, and Creating Pathways," *Journal of Research on Adolescence* 24, no. 1 (2014): 186–99; Jennifer Menon and William Damon, "The Role Spirituality and Religious Faith Play in Supporting Purpose in Adolescence," in *Positive*

Youth Development and Spirituality: From Theory to Research, eds. R. M. Benson, R. W. Roeser, and E. Phelps (West Conshoshocken, PA: Templeton Foundation Press, 2008), 210–30.

13. Kendall C. Bronk, *Purpose in Life: A Critical Component of Optimal Youth Development* (New York: Springer, 2014).

14. Damon, Menon, and Bronk, "The Development of Purpose during Adolescence," 123.

15. In four of these six cases, the conflicts clearly emerged from the divorce and resulting difficult family situation (which was the case with Lauren). In light of the unusual marital stability of most of our interview sample (84 percent came from intact families), we wonder whether a sample with a higher divorce rate would produce additional examples of purpose arising out of parental conflict. In the two other situations of conflict, both women were female Indian women who now had much different morals (more liberal) or a different religion (Christian) than their family.

16. Barbara Schneider and David Stevenson, *The Ambitious Generation: Motivated but Directionless* (New Haven: Yale University Press, 2000), 8.

17. See also William Damon, *The Path to Purpose: Helping Our Children Find Their Calling in Life* (New York: Free Press, 2008), 100–01.

18. This term is taken from the book by Amy Chua, *The Battle Hymn of the Tiger Mother* (New York: Penguin Press, 2011).

19. Malin, et al., "Adolescent Purpose Development," 192.

20. Holly H. Schiffrin et al., "Helping or Hovering? The Effects of Helicopter Parenting on College Students' Well-Being," *Journal of Child and Family Studies* (2014) 23:548–57; T. LeMoyne and T. Buchanan (2011). "Does 'Hovering' Matter? Helicopter Parenting and Its Effect on Well-Being," *Sociological Spectrum* 31 (2011): 399–418; L. M. Padilla-Walker and L. J. Nelson, "Black Hawk Down? Establishing Helicopter Parenting as a Distinct Construct from Other Forms of Parental Control During Emerging Adulthood," *Journal of Adolescence* 35 (2012): 1177–90.

C. Segrin, A. Woszıdlo, M. Givertz, A. Bauer, and M. T. Murphy, "The Association between Overparenting, Parent-Child Communication, and Entitlement and Adaptive Traits in Adult Children," *Family Relations* 61 (2012): 237–52.

21. Schiffrin et al., "Helping or Hovering?" 548; For an understanding of self-authorship theory see Marcia B. Baxter Magolda, *Making Their Own Way: Narratives for Transforming Higher Education to Promote Self-Development* (Sterling, VA: Stylus Press, 2001).

22. Fry, "The Development of Personal Meaning and Wisdom in Adolescence," 98.

23. Jenni Menon Mariano, "Introduction to Special Section: Understanding Paths to Youth Purpose—Why Content and Contexts Matter," *Applied Developmental Science* 18, no. 3 (2014): 144. See also, William Damon, "The Why Question: Teachers Can Instill a Sense of Purpose," *Education Next* 9, no. 3 (2009). http://educationnext.org/the-why-question-2/#; S. I. Koshy and J. M. Mariano, "Promoting Youth Purpose: A Review of the Literature," *New Directions for Youth Development* 132 (2011): 13–30.

24. Malin et al., "Adolescent Purpose Development."

25. Ibid., 192.

26. For an overview of these studies see Kendall C. Bronk, *Purpose in Life*.

27. Nancy J. Evans et al., *Student Development in College: Theory, Research and Practice*, 2nd ed. (San Francisco: Jossey Bass, 2010).

28. B. R. Johnson and J. Clifton (2010). "Younger Generations Less Likely to Join Boy Scouts: Boy Scouts Go on to Gain More Education, Make More Money," with Jon Clifton. Gallup® Online. Gallup® Organization.

29. Kendall C. Bronk, "A Grounded Theory of the Development of Noble Youth Purpose," *Journal of Adolescent Research* 27, no. 1 (2012): 78–109.

30. Sharon Parks, *Big Questions, Worthy Dreams: Mentoring Young Adults in Their Search for Meaning, Purpose and Faith* (San Francisco: Jossey Bass, 2001), 70.

31. Ibid., 77.

Chapter 3

1. Kendall Cotton Bronk, *Purpose in Life: A Critical Component of Optimal Youth Development* (New York: Springer, 2014), 91.

2. For a review of this literature, please consult Anthony L. Burrow and Patrick L. Hill, "Purpose as a Form of Identity Capital for Positive Youth Adjustment," *Developmental Psychology* 47, no. 4 (2011): 1196; Lisa Kiang, "Deriving Daily Purpose through Daily Events and Role Fulfillment among Asian American Youth," *Journal of Research on Adolescence* 22, no. 1 (2012): 185–98; Kendall Cotton Bronk, Patrick L. Hill, Daniel K. Lapsley, Tasneem L. Talib, and Holmes Finch, "Purpose, Hope, and Life Satisfaction in Three Age Groups," *Journal of Positive Psychology* 4, no. 6 (2009): 500–10; Anthony L. Burrow, Amanda C. O'Dell, and Patrick L. Hill, "Profiles of a Developmental Asset: Youth Purpose as a Context for Hope and Well-Being," *Journal of Youth and Adolescence* 39, no. 11 (2010): 1265–73; Kendall Cotton Bronk, "The Role of Purpose in Life in Healthy Identity Formation: A Grounded Model," *New Directions for Youth Development* 2011, no. 132 (2011): 31–44; Ann S. Masten and Marie-Gabrielle Reed, "Resilience in Development," *Handbook of Positive Psychology* (2002): 74–88; Kendall Cotton Bronk, *Purpose in Life: A Critical Component of Optimal Youth Development* (New York: Springer, 2014), 91.

3. Michael J Shanahan, "Pathways to Adulthood in Changing Societies: Variability and Mechanisms in Life Course Perspective," *Annual Review of Sociology* (2000): 667–92.

4. Jeffrey Jensen Arnett, *Emerging Adulthood: The Winding Road from the Late Teens through the Twenties* (New York: Oxford University Press, 2004).

5. Christian Smith with Kari Christoffersen, Hilary Davidson, and Patricia Snell Herzog, *Lost in Transition: The Dark Side of Emerging Adulthood* (New York: Oxford University Press, 2011).

6. Technical details about the National Study of Youth and Religion are available in the appendix.

7. The latter two are both from Ryff's Purpose in Life subscale. Carol D. Ryff, "Happiness Is Everything, or Is It? Explorations on the Meaning of Psychological Well-Being," *Journal of Personality and Social Psychology* 57, no. 6 (1989): 1069.

8. William Damon, *The Path to Purpose: Helping Our Children Find Purpose in Life* (New York: Free Press, 2008).

9. The 60 percent is a bit lower than the 65 percent we find in our qualitative samples of college students that we interviewed. In one sense, the bar was set higher for these quantitative survey questions. The respondents were required to affirm they have a purpose in life across three separate questions. They reported a consistent presence of purpose in life. Moreover, our sample of interviewees was taken from college students. As we show in this chapter, those who are in college are more likely to report having a life purpose than other emerging adults.

10. Several further methodological issues are worth considering here. First, the predicted probabilities we present are based on linear predictions from our models. We recognize that many continuous and ordinal variables might have nonlinear impacts on purpose. Space simply prohibits the full exploration of all of these nonlinear possibilities. Also, our predicted probabilities are not modeled on the possibility of certain factors interacting with one another. In the real world, many factors undoubtedly work in complex, nonadditive ways, to influence purpose. Although the mapping we do here necessarily simplifies this, we still believe that it helps to identify the most important social factors that impact a sense of purpose.

11. Kara Joyner, and J. Richard Udry. "You Don't Bring Me Anything but Down: Adolescent Romance and Depression," *Journal of Health and Social Behavior* (2000): 369–91; Peggy C. Giordano, "Relationships in Adolescence," *Annual Review of Sociology* (2003): 257–81; Mark D. Regnerus, *Forbidden Fruit: Sex and Religion in the Lives of American Teenagers* (New York: Oxford University Press, 2007); Mark Regnerus and Jeremy Uecker, *Premarital Sex in America: How Young Americans Meet, Mate, and Think about Marrying* (New York: Oxford University Press, 2010); Linda Smolak, "Body Image in Children and Adolescents: Where Do We Go from Here?" *Body Image* 1, no. 1 (2004): 15–28.

12. We used standardized odds ratios to measure effect size. For standardized coefficients less than one (which indicate a negative effect with odds ratios), we calculated the inverse of the coefficient to accurately compare effect size to the coefficients that were greater than one.

13. For example, see Lisa Kiang and Andrew J. Fuligni, "Meaning in Life as a Mediator of Ethnic Identity and Adjustment Among Adolescents from Latin, Asian, and European American Backgrounds," *Journal of Youth and Adolescence* 39, no. 11 (2010): 1253–64.

14. See John Bynner, "Rethinking the Youth Phase of the Life-Course: The Case for Emerging Adulthood?" *Journal of Youth Studies* 8, no. 4 (2005): 367–84.

15. Claude S. Fischer and Michael Hout, *Century of Difference: How America Changed in the Last One Hundred Years* (New York: Russell Sage Foundation, 2006).

16. Bill Marsh, "Why People Marry," *New York Times*, April 27, 2013. Accessed August 24, 2015, http://www.nytimes.com/interactive/2013/04/28/sunday-review/Why-People-Marry.html.

17. Paul Froese, "On Purpose: How We Create the Meaning of Life" (New York: Oxford University Press, 2015), 5. Interestingly, Froese found that self-described liberals were "less likely to know their purpose in life."

Chapter 4

1. Charles Taylor, *Sources of the Self: The Making of the Modern Identity* (New York: Harvard University Press, 1989), 3.

2. Marcia B. Baxter Magolda, *Making Their Own Way: Narratives for Transforming Higher Education to Promote Self-Development* (Sterling, VA: Stylus Press, 2001); Marcia B. Baxter Magolda, *Creating Contexts for Learning and Self-Authorship: Constructive-Developmental Pedagogy* (Nashville: Vanderbilt University Press, 1999); Marcia B. Baxter Magolda and Patricia M. King, *Theories and Models of Practice to Educate for Self-Authorship* (Sterling, VA: Stylus, 2004). See also Robert J. Nash and Michelle C. Murray, *Helping College Students Find Purpose: The Campus Guide to Meaning-Making* (San Francisco: Jossey-Bass, 2010).

Chapter 5

1. Alexander W. Astin, Helen S. Astin, and Jennifer Lindholm, *Cultivating the Spirit: How College Can Enhance Students' Inner Lives* (San Francisco: Jossey-Bass, 2011); Tim Clydesdale, *The Purposeful Graduate: Why Colleges Must Talk to Students about Vocation* (Chicago: University of Chicago Press, 2015); Anthony T. Kronman, *Education's End: Why Our Colleges and Universities Have Given Up on the Meaning of Life* (New Haven: Yale University Press, 2007); Robert J. Nash and Michelle C. Murray, *Helping College Students Find Purpose: The Campus Guide to Meaning-Making* (San Francisco: Jossey-Bass, 2010); Sharon Parks, *Big Questions, Worthy Dreams: Mentoring Young Adults in Their Search for Meaning, Purpose and Faith* (San Francisco: Jossey Bass, 2001); Jenny Small, ed., *Making Meaning: Embracing Spirituality, Faith, Religion, and Life Purpose in Student Affairs* (Sterling, VA: Stylus, 2015).

2. William Damon, Jenni Menon, and Kendall Cotton Bronk, "The Development of Purpose during Adolescence," *Applied Developmental Science* 7, no. 3 (2003): 119.

3. Ibid.

4. Victor Frankl, *Man's Search for Meaning: An Introduction to Logotherapy*, 3rd ed. (New York: Simon & Schuster, 1984/1959).

5. James C. Crumbaugh and Leonard Maholick, "An Experimental Study in Existentialism: The Psychometric Approach to Frankl's Concept of Noogenic Neurosis," in *Psychotherapy and Existentialism*, ed. Victor E. Frankl (New York: Washington Square Press, 1967); Karen De Vogler and Peter Ebersole, "Categorization of College Students' Meaning in Life," *Psychological Reports* 46 (1980): 387–90; Carol D. Ryff, "Happiness Is Everything, or Is It? Explorations on the Meaning of Psychological Well-Being," *Journal of Personality and Social Psychology* 57, no. 6 (1989): 1069–81.

6. James Fowler, *Stages of Faith: The Psychology of Human Development and the Quest for Meaning* (San Francisco: Harper San Francisco, 1981), xii.

7. Ibid., 92–93 (italics added).

8. Michael Barnes, Dennis Doyle, and Byron R. Johnson (1989). "The Formulation of a Fowler Scale: An Empirical Assessment Among Catholics," *Review of Religious Research* 30: 412–20.

9. Craig Dykstra, "Faith Development and Religious Education," in *Christian Perspectives on Faith Development*, eds. Jeff Astley and Leslie Francis (Grand Rapids: Eerdmans, 1992), 251–71; Jenny L. Small, *Understanding College Students' Spiritual Identities: Different Faiths, Varied Worldviews* (New York: Hampton Press, 2011).

10. Dykstra, "Faith Development and Religious Education," 55.

11. Elizabeth J. Tisdell, "The Spiritual Dimension of Adult Development," *New Directions for Adult and Continuing Education* 84 (1999): 87–95.

12. Paul Froese defined purse as "the personal meaning we give to any experience" (p. 3). In *On Purpose: How We Create the Meaning of Life* (New York: Oxford University Press, 2015).

13. Damon, Menon, and Bronk, "The Development of Purpose during Adolescence," 121.

14. See for example, the essays in Paul T. P. Wong, ed., *The Human Quest for Meaning: Theories, Research and Applications*, rev. ed. (New York: Routledge, 2012).

15. Arthur Chickering and Linda Reisser, *Education and Identity* (San Francisco: Jossey-Bass, 1993), 212.

16. Parks, *Big Questions, Worthy Dreams*, 14.

17. Ibid., 19.

18. Nash and Murray, *Helping College Students Find Purpose*, xx.

19. Ibid.

20. Damon, Menon and Bronk, "The Development of Purpose during Adolescence," 120–21.

21. Karen De Vogler and Peter Ebersole, "Categorization of College Students' Meaning in Life," *Psychological Reports* 46 (1980): 387–90.

22. Ibid., 427–31.

23. Christian Smith with Patricia Snell, *Souls in Transition: The Religious and Spiritual Lives of Emerging Adults* (New York: Oxford University Press, 2009), 267.

24. David Brooks, "The Problem with Meaning," *New York Times*, January 5, 2015, A23.

25. William Damon, Jenni Menon, and Kendall Cotton Bronk, "The Development of Purpose during Adolescence," 121.

26. Ibid.

27. Charles Taylor, *Sources of the Self: The Making of the Modern Identity* (Cambridge: Harvard University Press, 1989), 3.

28. Ibid., 28.

29. Marcia B. Baxter Magolda, *Making Their Own Way: Narratives for Transforming Higher Education to Promote Self-Development* (Sterling, VA: Stylus Press, 2001); Marcia B. Baxter Magolda, *Creating Contexts for Learning and Self-Authorship: Constructive-Developmental Pedagogy* (Nashville: Vanderbilt University Press, 1999); Marcia B. Baxter Magolda and Patricia M. King, *Theories and Models of Practice to Educate for Self-Authorship* (Sterling, VA: Stylus, 2004). See also Robert J. Nash and Michelle C. Murray, *Helping College Students Find Purpose: The Campus Guide to Meaning-Making* (San Francisco: Jossey-Bass, 2010).

30. Marcia B. Baxter Magolda, "Self-Authorship as the Common Goal of Twenty-First-Century Education," in *Learning Partnerships: Theory and Models of Practice to Edu-

cate for Self-Authorship, eds., Marcia B. Baxter Magolda and Patricia M. King (Sterling, VA: Stylus, 2004), 8.

31. Baxter Magolda, *Creating Contexts for Learning and Self-Authorship*, 6.

32. Baxter Magolda, *Making Their Own Way*, 101–15.

33. Ibid., 93.

34. Ibid., 93, 102, 104, 108.

35. Parks, *Big Questions, Worthy Dreams*, 88–89.

36. Paul Froese, *On Purpose: How We Create the Meaning of Life* (New York: Oxford University Press, 2015), back jacket.

37. Gary Reker and Paul T. P. Wong, *The Human Quest for Meaning: Theories, Research and Applications*, ed. Paul T. P. Wong, rev. ed. (New York: Routledge, 2012), 437.

38. Gary T. Reker and Paul T. P. Wong distinguish between global meaning and situational meaning. See Gary T. Reker and Paul T. P. Wong, "Personal Meaning in Life and Psychosocial Adaptation in the Later Years," in *The Human Quest for Meaning: Theories, Research and Applications*, ed. Paul T. P. Wong, rev. ed. (New York: Routledge, 2012), 433–56.

39. Reker and Wong, *The Human Quest for Meaning*, 433.

40. Ibid., 434.

41. Ibid., 433–56.

42. Ibid.

43. Ibid., *The Human Quest for Meaning*, 437.

44. Paul T. P. Wong, "Toward a Dual-Systems Model of What Makes Life Worth Living," in *The Human Quest for Meaning: Theories, Research and Applications*, ed. Paul T. P. Wong, rev. ed. (New York: Routledge, 2012), 3.

45. Reker and Wong, *The Human Quest for Meaning*, 437.

46. Ibid., 437–38.

47. Ibid., 437.

Chapter 6

1. William Damon, Jenni Menon, and Kendall Cotton Bronk, "The Development of Purpose during Adolescence," *Applied Developmental Science* 7, no. 3 (2003): 121.

2. Ibid.

3. Ibid.

4. Ibid.

5. Ibid. Italics in original source.

6. Kendall Cotton Bronk, "A Grounded Theory of the Development of Noble Youth Purpose," *Journal of Adolescent Research* 27, no. 1 (2012): 78–109. doi: 10.1080/17439760903271439. Kendall Cotton Bronk et al., "Purpose, Hope, and Life Satisfaction in Three Age Groups," *Journal of Positive Psychology* 4, (2009): 500–10. doi: 10.1177/0743558411412958; Anthony Burrow and Patrick L. Hill, "Purpose as a Form of Identity Capital for Positive Youth Adjustment," *Developmental Psychology* 42, no. 4 (2011): 1196–1206: doi: 10.1037/a0023818.; Anthony Burrow, Amanda O'Dell, and Patrick Hill,

"Profiles of a Developmental Asset: Youth Purpose as a Context for Hope and Well-Being," *Journal of Youth Adolescence* 39, (2010): doi: 10.1007/s10964-009-9481-1; Brandy Quinn, "Other-Oriented Purpose: The Potential Roles of Beliefs about the World and Other People," *Youth & Society* 46, no. 6 (2014): 779–800. doi: 10.1177/0044118X12452435.

    7. Damon, Menon, and Bronk, "The Development of Purpose during Adolescence."

    8. Patrick L. Hill, Anthony L. Burrow, Amanda C. Dell, Meghan A. Thornton, "Classifying Adolescents' Conceptions of Purpose in Life," *Journal of Positive Psychology* 5, no. 6 (2010): 466.

    9. Alice Schroeder, *The Snowball: Warren Buffett and the Business of Life* (New York: Bantam Books, 2008), 826.

    10. Kendall Cotton Bronk, *Purpose in Life: A Critical Component of Optimal Youth Development* (New York: Springer, 2014). doi 10.1007/978-94-007-7491-9_6.

    11. Seana Moran, "What 'Purpose' Means to Youth: Are There Cultures of Purpose?" *Applied Developmental Science* 18, no. 3 (2014): p. 167. doi: 10.1080/10888691.2014.92435.

    12. Ibid., 163.

    13. Alexander W. Astin, Helen S. Astin, and Jennifer Lindholm, *Cultivating the Spirit: How College Can Enhance Students' Inner Lives* (San Francisco: Jossey-Bass, 2011).

    14. Interviews were conducted with respondents on landline and cellular phones. Samples were weighted to correct for selection probability, nonresponse, and coverage of landline and cell users. They were weighted to match the national demographics of gender, age, race, Hispanic ethnicity, education, region, population density, and phone status, which enable us to generalize results to the population (table 1).

    15. We are grateful for the assistance of Hongwei Yu, a postdoctoral fellow at Baylor with this analysis.

    16. Carol Ryff, Corey M. Keyes, and Diane L. Hughes, "Status Inequalities, Perceived Discrimination, and Eudaimonic Well-Being: Do the Challenges of Minority Life Hone Purpose and Growth?" *Journal of Health and Social Behavior* 44 (2003): 275–91.

    17. Bronk, *Purpose in Life*, 137.

    18. Christian Smith with Kari Christoffersen, Hillary Davidson, and Patricia Snell Herzog, *Lost in Transition: The Dark Side of Emerging Adulthood* (New York: Oxford, 2011).

    19. Ibid.

    20. Arthur Chickering and Linda Reisser, *Education and Identity* (San Francisco: Jossey-Bass, 1993).

    21. William G. Perry, *Forms of Intellectual and Ethical Development in the College Years: A Scheme* (San Francisco: Jossey-Bass, 1999/1968).

    22. Ibid., 238.

    23. Ibid., 239.

    24. Peter L. Hill et al., "Collegiate Purpose Orientations and Well-Being in Early and Middle Adulthood," *Journal of Applied Developmental Psychology* 31, (2010): 173–79.

    25. Ibid., 173.

    26. M. J. Bundick, D. Y. Yeager, P. King, and W. Damon, "Thriving across the Life Span," in W. F. Overton and R. M. Lerner (eds.), *Handbook of Lifespan Human Develop-*

ment (New York: Wiley, 2010). Burrow and Hill, "Purpose as a Form of Identity"; Burrow, O'Dell, and Hill, "Profiles of a Developmental Asset."

27. Burrow and Hill, "Purpose as a Form of Identity"; Bronk, *Purpose in Life*; Jane E. Pizzolato, Elizabeth L. Brown, and Mary A. Kanny, "Purpose Plus: Supporting Youth Purpose, Control, and Academic Achievement," *New Directions for Youth Development* 2011, no. 132 (2011): 75–88; Bronk et al., "Purpose Hope and Life Satisfaction."

Chapter 7

1. Paul Froese, *On Purpose: How We Create the Meaning of Life* (New York: Oxford University Press, 2015), 63.

2. Christian Smith with Patricia Snell, *Souls in Transition: The Religious and Spiritual Lives of Emerging Adults* (New York: Oxford University Press, 2009), 268.

3. William Damon, *The Path to Purpose* (New York: Free Press, 2008), 33; See also Heather Malin, Timothy S. Reilly, Brandy Quinn, and Seana Moran, "Adolescent Purpose Development: Exploring Empathy, Discovering Roles, Shifting Priorities, and Creating Pathways," *Journal of Research on Adolescence* 24, no. 1 (2013): 186–99. doi: 10.1111/jora.12051.

4. Ibid., 60.

5. Ibid.

6. William G. Perry, *Forms of Intellectual and Ethical Development in the College Years: A Scheme* (San Francisco: Jossey-Bass, 1999/1968).

7. Ibid.

8. Ibid.

9. Alexander W. Astin, Helen S. Astin, and Jennifer Lindholm, *Cultivating the Spirit: How College Can Enhance Students' Inner Lives* (San Francisco: Jossey-Bass, 2011): 27–48.

10. Ibid., 28.

11. Ibid.

12. Jeffrey J. Arnett, "Emerging Adulthood: A Theory of Development From the Late Teens Through the Twenties," *American Psychologist*, 55 (2000): 469–480; Jeffrey J. Arnett, *Emerging Adulthood: The Winding Road from the Late Teens through the Twenties* (New York: Oxford University Press, 2004).

13. Arnett, *Emerging Adulthood*, 8.

14. Ibid., 13.

15. Ibid., 10.

16. Ibid., 10–11.

17. Damon, *The Path to Purpose*, 18.

18. James C. Crumbaugh and Leonard Maholick, "An Experimental Study in Existentialism: The Psychometric Approach to Frankl's Concept of Noogenic Neurosis," in *Psychotherapy and Existentialism*, ed. Victor E. Frankl (New York: Washington Square Press, 1967), 183–97; D. L. Debats, "Measurement of Personal Meaning: The Psychometric Properties of the Life Regard Index," in *The Human Quest for Meaning: A Handbook of Psychological Research and Clinical Application*, ed. Paul T. P. Wong (Mahwah: Lawrence Earlbaum, 1998), 237–59; George B. Kish and David R. Moody, "Psychopathology and

Life Purposes," *International Forum for Logotherapy* 12, no. 1 (1989): 40–45; Daniel T. Shek, "The Chinese Purpose-in-life Test and Psychological Well-Being in Chinese College Students," *International Forum for Logotherapy* 16, no. 1 (1993): 35–42.

19. Damon, *The Path to Purpose*, 33.

20. Christian Smith with Kari Christoffersen, Hilary Davidson, and Patricia Snell Herzog, *Lost in Transition: The Dark Side of Emerging Adulthood* (New York: Oxford, 2011). While Smith's book is about eighteen- to twenty-three-year-old emerging adults who are not all college students, the vast majority of the National Study of Youth and Religion (NSYR) qualitative sample (82 percent) were attending some kind of higher education.

21. Ibid., 60.

22. Ibid., 69.

23. Tim Clydesdale, *The Purposeful Graduate: Why Colleges Must Talk to Students about Vocation* (Chicago: University of Chicago Press, 2015); see also Colleen Flaherty, "Why 'Vocation' Isn't a Dirty Word," *Inside Higher Education*, June 24, 2015, accessed July 24, 2015, https://www.insidehighered.com/news/2015/06/24/author-new-book-purposeful-graduates-says-colleges-must-talk-students-about-making.

24. *Oxford English Dictionary*. 2nd ed. 20 vols. Oxford: Oxford University Press, 1989. Also available at http://www.oed.com/.

25. Clydesdale, *The Purposeful Graduate*.

26. Smith with Snell, *Lost in Transition*, 269.

27. Damon, *The Path to Purpose*, 64.

28. Clydesdale, *The Purposeful Graduate*, 108.

29. One of us expands on this critique in Perry L. Glanzer and Todd C. Ream, *Christianity and Moral Identity in Higher Education* (New York: Palgrave Macmillan, 2009).

Chapter 8

1. Mark Edmundson, "When I Was Young at Yale," *Chronicle Review*, 27 January 2014, accessed July 27, 2015, http://chronicle.com/article/Beauty-BonesTheory-at/144201/.

2. Sharon Daloz Parks, *The Critical Years: The Young Adult Search for a Faith to Live By* (San Francisco: Harper & Row, 1987); Sharon Daloz Parks, *Big Questions, Worthy Dreams: Mentoring Young Adults in Their Search for Meaning, Purpose and Faith* (San Francisco: Jossey Bass, 2000).

3. Fry, "The Development of Personal Meaning and Wisdom in Adolescence: A Reexamination of Moderating and Consolidating Factors and Influences," in Paul T. P. Wong and Prem S. Fry (Eds.), *The Human Quest for Meaning: A Handbook of Psychological Research and Clinical Applications* (Mahwah, NJ: Lawrence Erlbaum Associates, Inc.), 91–110.

4. William G. Perry, *Forms of Intellectual and Ethical Development in the College Years: A Scheme* (San Francisco: Jossey-Bass, 1999), 206.

5. Parks, *Big Questions, Worthy Dreams*, 129.

6. Parks, *The Critical Years*.

7. Ibid., 134.

8. Parks, *Big Questions, Worthy Dreams*, 168.

9. Robert J. Panos, Alesxander W. Astin, and John A. Creager, *National Norms for Entering College Freshman—Fall 1967.* (Los Angeles: American Council on Education, 1967), 18; Kevin Eagan et al., *The American Freshman: National Norms Fall 2015* (Los Angeles: Higher Education Research Institute, UCLA, 2015), 53.

10. Ibid.

11. Ibid.

12. Tim Clydesdale, *The Purposeful Graduate: Why Colleges Must Talk to Students about Vocation* (Chicago: University of Chicago Press, 2015), 87.

13. Kevin Eagan et al., *The American Freshman*, 44.

14. Ibid., 31.

15. Ibid.

16. Ray Franke et al., *Findings from the 2009 Administration of the College Senior Survey (CSS): National Aggregates* (Los Angeles: Higher Education Research Institute, 2010), 33. Interestingly, the HERI institution's most recent survey of seniors found that the third-largest change between freshman and seniors concerned those who considered developing a meaningful philosophy of life an "essential" or "very important" life goal. While 50.7 percent of freshman indicated it was, 58.8 percent of seniors indicated that it was a change of 8.1 percent.

17. Anthony T. Kronman, *Education's End: Why Our Colleges and Universities Have Given Up on the Meaning of Life* (New Haven, CT: Yale University Press, 2007), 7.

18. Kronman, *Education's End*, 242–65.

19. Clydesdale, *The Purposeful Graduate*.

20. See A. J. Conyers, *The Listening Heart: Vocation and the Crisis of Modern Culture* (Waco, TX: Baylor University Press, 2009); William C. Placher, *Callings: Twenty Centuries of Christian Wisdom on Vocation* (Grand Rapids, MI: Eerdmans, 2005); Mark R. Schwehn and Dorothy C. Bass, eds., *Leading Lives that Matter: What We Should Do and Who We Should Be* (Grand Rapids, MI: Eerdmans, 2006); Lee Hardy, *The Fabric of This World: Inquiries into Calling, Career Choice, and the Design of Human Work* (Grand Rapids, MI: Eerdmans, 1990).

21. One odd contrast of these types of classes as opposed to great texts classes, which is perhaps why the great texts are great, is that students could not always remember the name of the course or the books or authors that they found interesting, as these two students tried to recall, but they still found them influential:

- In that one class we had to read . . . Oh goodness, it's something about your calling, like a calling or purpose. It talks about vocation. Uh, I can't remember. . . . It went in depth about your relation to God, how you know things you experience in life, what's your vocation, what's your calling, [and] what's the purpose, what's the meaning . . . I mean it got me thinking about it for sure and it kind of planted the seed in my head.

- I took a servant leadership course in my sophomore year of college and we did discuss it to an extent, like: What is your purpose? What is your calling? What is the purpose and calling of human being? We read a book called, Something Something Purpose. Um, I can't remember the title. But it was, yeah, it had a lot of short little excerpts about people who had done these great things, and what their leadership skills looked like, and things like that.

22. Alexander W. Astin, Helen S. Astin, and Jennifer Lindholm, *Cultivating the Spirit: How College Can Enhance Students' Inner Lives* (San Francisco: Jossey-Bass, 2011), 27.

23. Ibid., 40.

24. Ibid., 37.

25. Ibid.

26. Please consult Appendix C for additional information about our analysis using this data.

27. These include public, public charter, public magnet, private religious, private nonreligious, and home school.

28. We don't include the institutional mean-level values for faculty responses from figure 8.4 because it reduces the sample size without adding anything substantive to our final interpretation.

29. Max Weber, "The Vocation of Science," in *The Essential Weber: A Reader*, ed. Sam Whimster (New York: Routledge, 2004), 283. Part of the reason for Weber's position, it should be noted, pertained to the fact that the professor may abuse his power when teaching a captive audience. Weber noted of this situation, "it is far too easy for him to demonstrate the courage of his convictions where those present, who perhaps think differently, are condemned to silence" (p. 283).

30. Astin, Astin and Lindholm, *Cultivating the Spirit*, 30.

31. Ibid.

32. Parks, *Big Questions, Worthy Dreams*, 129.

33. Clydesdale, *The Purposeful Graduate*.

Chapter 9

1. In the introduction to his autobiography, *The Story of My Experiments with Truth*, Gandhi relates the story of a friend who had a unique concern about his effort to write an autobiography, "What has set you on this adventure?" he asked. "Writing an autobiography is a practice peculiar to the West. I know of nobody in the East having written one, except amongst those who have come under Western influence." Gandhi's friend had a conception of the future similar to that of Kelsey that led him to raise concerns about the autobiographical project:

And what will you write? Supposing you reject tomorrow the things you hold as principles today, or supposing you revise in the future your plans of today, is it not likely that the men who shape their conduct on the authority of your word, spoken or written, may be misled. Don't you think it would be better not to write anything like an autobiography, at any rate just yet?

Gandhi, *An Autobiography: The Story of My Experiments with Truth* (Boston: Beacon Press, 1997), xxv–xxvi.

2. Alexander W. Astin, *Achieving Educational Excellence: A Critical Assessment of Priorities and Practices in Higher Education* (San Francisco: Jossey-Bass, 1985); Richard P. Keeling, ed. *Learning Reconsidered: A Campus-Wide Focus on the Student Experience* (The National Association of Student Personnel Administrators, The American College Personnel Association, 2004); Richard P. Keeling, *Learning Reconsidered 2: Implementing a Campus-Wide Focus on the Student Experience* (American College Personnel Association [ACPA], Association of College and University Housing Officers–International [ACUHO-I], Association of College Unions–International [ACUI], National Academic Advising Association [NACADA], National Association for Campus Activities [NACA], National Association of Student Personnel Administrators [NASPA], and National Intramural Recreational Sports Association [NIRSA], 2006).

3. Julie Reuben, *The Making of the Modern University: Intellectual Transformation and the Marginalization of Morality* (Chicago: University of Chicago Press, 1996).

4. Anthony T. Kronman, *Education's End: Why Our Colleges and Universities Have Given Up on the Meaning of Life* (New Haven: Yale University Press, 2007).

5. Tim Clydesdale, *The Purposeful Graduate: Why Colleges Must Talk to Students about Vocation* (Chicago: University of Chicago Press, 2015), 87.

6. Kronman, *Education's End.*

7. Alexander W. Astin, Helen S. Astin, and Jennifer Lindholm, *Cultivating the Spirit: How College Can Enhance Students' Inner Lives* (San Francisco: Jossey-Bass, 2011).

8. Parker Palmer, Arthur Zajonc, and Megan Scribner, *Heart of Higher Education: A Call to Renewal* (San Francisco: Jossey Bass, 2010), 55.

9. Kronman, *Education's End.*

10. More information on the data and our method can be found in the appendix.

11. Ideally, we would have liked to have additional measures that were not exclusively focused on religion and spirituality, but they were not available to us in the data.

12. Sharon Daloz Parks, *Big Questions, Worthy Dreams: Mentoring Young Adults in Their Search for Meaning, Purpose and Faith* (San Francisco: Jossey Bass, 2000).

13. Larry A. Braskamp, Lois Calian Trautvetter, and Kelly Ward, *Putting Students First: How Colleges Develop Students Purposefully* (San Francisco: Anker, 2006).

14. Clydesdale, *The Purposeful Graduate.*

15. Astin, Astin, and Lindholm, *Cultivating the Spirit*, 27.

16. Alexander W. Astin, *Achieving Educational Excellence* (San Francisco: Jossey-Bass, 1985), p. 298.

17. Ibid.

18. Marcia B. Baxter-Magolda, "Self-authorship as the Common Goal of Twenty-First Century Education," in *Learning Partnerships: Theory and Models of Practice to Educate for Self-Authorship*, eds. Marcia B. Baxter-Magolda and Patricia M. King (Sterling, VA: Stylus Press, 2004), xxii.

19. See also Nash and Murray, *Helping College Students Find Purpose.*

20. Stephen G. Post, *The Hidden Gifts of Helping: How the Power of Giving, Compassion, and Hope Can Get Us Through Hard Times* (New York, NY: Jossey-Bass, 2011); Stephen G. Post and Jill Neimark, *Why Good Things Happen to Good People: How to Live a Longer, Healthier, Happier Life by the Simple Act of Giving* (New York, NY: Broadway Books, 2008).

21. Matthew T. Lee et al., (2014). "Daily Spiritual Experiences and Adolescent Treatment Response," *Alcohol Treatment Quarterly* 32 (2): 271–98; Michael Hallett and Byron R. Johnson (2014). "The Resurgence of Religion in America's Prisons," *Religions* 5 (3): 663–83; Sung Joon Jang et al., (2014). "Structured Voluntary Youth Activities and Positive Outcomes in Adulthood: An Exploratory Study of Involvement in Scouting and Subjective Well-Being," *Sociological Focus* 47: 238–67; Maria E. Pagano et al., (2015), "Social Anxiety and Peer-Helping in Adolescent Addiction Treatment," *Alcoholism: Clinical and Experimental Research* 39 (5): 887–95.

Chapter 10

1. Paul Froese, *On Purpose: How We Create the Meaning of Life* (New York: Oxford University Press, 2015), pp. 4–5; Kendall Cotton Bronk, *Purpose in Life: A Critical Component of Optimal Youth Development* (New York: Springer, 2014), 103.

2. Froese, *On Purpose*; Steve Crabtree and Brett Pelham, "The Complex Relationship Between Religion and Purpose," *Gallup*, December 24, 2008 accessed August 3, 2015. http://www.gallup.com/poll/113575/complex-relationship-between-religion-purpose.aspx.; Stephen Cranney, "Do People Who Believe in God Report More Meaning in Their Lives? Existential Effects of Belief," *Journal for the Scientific Study of Religion* 52, no. 3 (2013): 638–46; Leslie J. Francis, "The Relationship between Bible Reading and Purpose in Life among 13–15 Year Olds," *Mental Health, Religion and Culture* 3, no. 1 (2000): 27–36; Leslie J. Francis and Thomas E. Evans, "The Relationship between Personal Prayer and Purpose in Life Among Church-Going and Non-Church-Going 12–15 Year Olds in the UK," *Religious Education* 9 (1996): 9–21; Kris Tirri and Brandon Quinn, "Exploring the Role of Religion and Spirituality in the Development of Purpose: Case Studies of Purposeful Youth," *British Journal of Religious Education* 32, no. 30 (2010): 201–14.

3. Leslie Francis and Linda Burton, "The Influence of Personal Prayer on Purpose in Life among Catholic Adolescents," *Journal of Beliefs and Values* 15 (1994): 6–9; Katie Byron and Cindy Miller-Perrin, "The Value of Life Purpose: Purpose as a Mediator of Faith and Well-Being," *Journal of Positive Psychology* 4, no. 1 (2009): 64–70; Christian Smith with Patricia Snell, *Souls in Transition: The Religious and Spiritual Lives of Emerging Adults* (New York: Oxford University Press, 2009); Kerry Chamberlain and Sheryl Zika, "Religiosity, Life Meaning, and Well-Being: Some Relationships in a Sample of Women," *Journal for the Scientific Study of Religion* 27 (1988): 411–20.

4. Smith with Snell, *Souls in Transition*, 296.

5. Cranney, "Do People Who Believe in God Report More Meaning in Their Lives?" 638.

6. James C. Crumbaugh and Leonard Maholick, "An Experimental Study in Existentialism: The Psychometric Approach to Frankl's Concept of Noogenic Neurosis," in

Psychotherapy and Existentialism, ed. Victor E. Frankl (New York: Washington Square Press, 1967), 183–87; Carol C. Molcar and Daniel W. Steumpfig, "Effects of World View on Purpose in Life, *Journal of Psychology* 122, no. 4 (1988): 365–71.

7. Doug Soderstorm and E. Wayne Wright, "Religious Orientation and Meaning in Life," *Journal of Clinical Psychology* 33 (1977): 65–68.

8. David Myers, "The Funds, Friends, and Faith of Happy People," *American Psychologist* 55, no. 1 (2000): 56–67.

9. Cranney, "Do People Who Believe in God Report More Meaning in Their Lives?" 644.

10. Christopher Peterson and Martin Seligman, *Character Strengths and Virtues: A Handbook and Classification* (New York: Oxford University Press, 2004), 621.

11. Alexander W. Astin, Helen S. Astin, and Jennifer Lindholm, *Cultivating the Spirit: How College Can Enhance Students' Inner Lives* (San Francisco: Jossey-Bass, 2011), 27.

12. For more on this survey, please consult the Appendix.

13. More on the components of this measure can be found here: http://spirituality.ucla.edu/docs/results/freshman/CSBV04.FactorScales.8.28.WEBSITE.pdf.

14. Jenni M. Mariano and William Damon, "The Role Spirituality and Religious Faith Play in Supporting Purpose in Adolescence," in *Positive Youth Development and Spirituality: From Theory to Research,* eds. R. M. Benson, R. W. Roeser, and E. Phelps (West Conshohocken, PA: Templeton Foundation Press, 2008), 216, 218–20.

15. The one non-theistic exception to this outlook was Hao, a Buddhist Vietnamese student. When Hao was asked about how he connected his religious identity with his view of purpose, Hao responded by placing his life story in a religiously inspired metaphysical narrative, although not necessarily a theistic one:

> One of my purposes is to try and be a better person. That's what Buddhism teaches you, to be a better person. Because in Buddhism they believe in reincarnation, so I don't want to be reincarnated into a dung beetle. So my purpose in life is to be a better person so I can be reincarnated into a human being, because that's pretty much the best thing you can reincarnate to. So I guess religion plays in a part of how I strive myself to be in the future.

Hao's larger metaphysical belief in reincarnation does not draw on any sense of God's design of the universe, but it does provide a way of understanding the moral order of the universe. Ultimately, the universe leads toward a kind of eternal justice. This belief also compels him to engage in a certain kind of moral striving that the nontheists in the next chapter have found restraining, since it comes from the nature of the universe and not one's own creation.

16. Bronk, *Purpose in Life.*

17. Mariano and Damon, "The Role Spirituality and Religious Faith Play in Supporting Purpose in Adolescence."

18. Astin, Astin, and Lindholm, *Cultivating the Spirit,* 42.

19. Jonathan P. Hill, "Faith and Understanding: Specifying the Impact of Higher Education on Religious Belief," *Journal for the Scientific Study of Religion* 50, no. 3 (2011): 533–551; Damon Mayrl and Jeremy E. Uecker. "Higher Education and Religious Liberalization among Young Adults." *Social Forces* 90, no. 1 (2011): 181–208.

20. Mariano and Damon, "The Role Spirituality and Religious Faith Play in Supporting Purpose in Adolescence."

21. Ibid., 218.

22. Ibid., 219.

23. Tim Clydesdale, *The Purposeful Graduate: Why Colleges Must Talk to Students about Vocation* (Chicago: University of Chicago Press, 2015).

24. Robert Nash and Michelle Murray, *Helping College Students Find Purpose: The Campus Guide to Meaning-Making* (San Francisco: Jossey-Bass, 2010).

25. Douglas Jacobsen and Rhonda Hustedt Jacobsen, *No Longer Invisible: Religion in University Education* (New York: Oxford, 2012).

26. Nash and Murray, *Helping College Students Find Purpose*, 57.

27. Ibid.

28. Ibid.

29. Ibid., 62.

30. Ibid., 74–75.

31. Ibid., 77.

32. Gary Reker and Paul T. P. Wong, *The Human Quest for Meaning: Theories, Research and Applications*, ed. Paul T. P. Wong, rev. ed. (New York: Routledge, 2012).

Chapter 11

1. Steve Stewart-Williams, *Darwin, God and the Meaning of Life: How Evolutionary Theory Undermines Everything You Thought You Knew* (New York: Cambridge University Press, 2010), 195.

2. HERI data we received, 2007, CSBV.

3. Robert N. Bellah et al., *Habits of the Heart: Individualism and Commitment in American Life* (San Francisco: Harper & Row, 1985), 221.

4. Alexander W. Astin, Helen S. Astin, and Jennifer Lindholm, *Cultivating the Spirit: How College Can Enhance Students' Inner Lives* (San Francisco: Jossey-Bass, 2011).

5. Ibid., 113. Interestingly, evangelical college students experience some of the greatest increases in religious struggle (but not religious skepticism).

6. Jenny L. Small, *Understanding College Students' Spiritual Identities: Different Faiths, Varied Worldviews* (New York: Hampton Press, 2011); Jenny L. Small, *Making Meaning: Embracing Spirituality, Faith, Religion, and Life Purpose in Student Affairs* (Sterling, VA: Stylus, 2015).

7. Tim Clydesdale, *The Purposeful Graduate: Why Colleges Must Talk to Students about Vocation* (Chicago: University of Chicago Press, 2015); Tricia A. Siefert, "What's So Funny about Peace, Love and Understanding? Or, Why Higher Education Is Finally

Talking about Faith, Belief, Meaning and Purpose," in *Making Meaning: Embracing Spirituality, Faith, Religion, and Life Purpose in Student Affairs* (Sterling, VA: Stylus Press, 2015), 58–80.

Chapter 12

1. Kendall Cotton Bronk et al., "Purpose, Hope, and Life Satisfaction in Three Age Groups," *Journal of Positive Psychology* 4 (2009): 507. doi: 10.1177/0743558411412958.

2. William Damon, Jenni Menon, and Kendall Cotton Bronk, "The Development of Purpose during Adolescence," *Applied Developmental Science* 7, no. 3 (2003): 123.

3. Patrick L. Hill et al., "Collegiate Purpose Orientations and Well-Being in Adulthood," *Journal of Applied Developmental Psychology* 31 (2010): 173–79; Patrick L. Hill et al., "Classifying Adolescents' Conceptions of Purpose in Life," *Journal of Positive Psychology* 5, no. 6, (2010): 466–73.

4. Kendall Cotton Bronk, *Purpose in Life: A Critical Component of Optimal Youth Development* (New York: Springer, 2014); William Damon, Jenni Menon, and Kendall Cotton Bronk, "The Development of Purpose during Adolescence," *Applied Developmental Science* 7, no. 3 (2003); Todd B. Kashdan and Patrick E. McKnight, "Origins of Purpose in Life: Refining Our Understanding of a Life Well Lived," *Psychological Topics* 18, (2009): 303–16.

5. Patrick L. Hill, Anthony L. Burrow, and Rachel Sumner, "Addressing Important Questions in the Field of Adolescent Purpose," *Child Development Perspectives* 7, no. 4 (2013): 234.

6. These were *not* interviews we conducted ourselves; rather, they were part of large, ongoing project on the religious and spiritual lives of adolescents and emerging adults in the United States. For more detailed information about the method of this phase of the NSYR study and how it fit within the other NSYR studies see: http://youthandreligion.nd.edu/research-design/ and http://youthandreligion.nd.edu/assets/102493/wave-3methods_11_5_08_final_with_iv_guide.pdf).

7. Christian Smith with Patricia Snell, *Lost in Transition: The Dark Side of Emerging Adulthood* (New York: Oxford, 2011).

8. Alice Schroeder, *The Snowball: Warren Buffett and the Business of Life* (New York: Bantam Books, 2008), 623.

9. Smith with Snell, *Souls in Transition*, 122.

10. Ibid.

11. Ibid.

12. Katariina Salmela-Aro and Jari-Erik Nurmi, "Goal Contents, Well-Being, and Life Context during Transition to University: A Longitudinal Study," *International Journal of Behavioral Development* 20 (1997): 471–91.

Conclusion

1. Margaret Mead, *Blackberry Winter: My Earlier Years* (New York: William Morrow & Co., 1972), 90.

2. Tim Clydesdale, *The Purposeful Graduate: Why Colleges Must Talk to Students about Vocation* (Chicago: University of Chicago Press, 2015), 96.

3. George Marsden, *The Outrageous Idea of Christian Scholarship* (New York: Oxford University Press, 1996), 19.

4. Craig Dykstra, "Faith Development and Religious Education," in *Christian Perspectives on Faith Development*, eds. Jeff Astley and Leslie Francis (Grand Rapids: Eerdmans, 1992), 251–71; Jenny L. Small, *Understanding College Students' Spiritual Identities: Different Faiths, Varied Worldviews* (New York: Hampton Press, 2011); and various essays in Jenny Small, ed. *Making Meaning: Embracing Spirituality, Faith, Religion, and Life Purpose in Student Affairs* (Sterling, VA: Stylus, 2015).

5. Warren Nord, *Does God Make a Difference? Taking Religion Seriously in Our Schools and Universities* (New York: Oxford University Press, 2010).

6. Perry L. Glanzer, "Taking the Tournament of Worldviews Seriously in Education: Why Teaching about Religion Is Not Enough," in *Education and Religion: Major Themes in Education*, eds. Philip Barnes and James Arthur (New York: Routledge Taylor Francis, 2016).

7. Robert J. Nash and Michelle C. Murray, *Helping College Students Find Purpose: The Campus Guide to Meaning-Making* (San Francisco: Jossey-Bass, 2010), 39.

8. Ibid., 227.

9. Ibid., 36.

10. Ibid., 43.

11. Ibid., 44.

12. John Eldredge, *Epic: The Story God Is Telling* (Colorado Springs: Thomas Nelson, 2007), 25–26.

13. Palmer Parker and Arthur Zajonc with Megan Scribner, *The Heart of Higher Education: A Call to Renewal* (San Francisco: Jossey Bass, 2010), 10.

14. Ibid., 98.

15. Ibid., 122–23.

16. Clydesdale, *The Purposeful Graduate*, 55.

17. William Damon, Jenni Menon, and Kendall Cotton Bronk, "The Development of Purpose during Adolescence," *Applied Developmental Science* 7, no. 3 (2003): 121.

18. Ibid.

19. William Damon, *The Path to Purpose* (New York: Free Press, 2008); Kendall Cotton Bronk, *Purpose in Life: A Critical Component of Optimal Youth Development* (New York: Springer, 2014).

20. Clydesdale, *The Purposeful Graduate*; Jenny Small, ed., *Making Meaning: Embracing Spirituality, Faith, Religion, and Life Purpose in Student Affairs* (Sterling, VA: Stylus Press, 2015); Jon C. Dalton and Pamela Crosby, "When Faith Fails: Why Nurturing Purpose and Meaning Are So Critical to Student Learning and Development in College," *Journal of College and* Character 11, no. 3 (2010): 1–6.

21. Clydesdale, *The Purposeful Graduate*, xvii.

22. Anthony T. Kronman, *Education's End: Why Our Colleges and Universities Have Given Up on the Meaning of Life* (New Haven: Yale University Press, 2007).

23. Clydesdale, *The Purposeful Graduate*; Small, *Understanding College Students' Spiritual Identities: Different Faiths, Varied Worldviews* (New York: Hampton Press, 2011),

24. Alexander W. Astin, Helen S. Astin, and Jennifer A. Lindholm, *Cultivating the Spirit: How College Can Enhance Students' Inner Lives* (San Francisco: Jossey-Bass, 2011), 137.

25. Clydesdale, *The Purposeful Graduate*; Sharon Daloz Parks, *Big Questions, Worthy Dreams: Mentoring Young Adults in Their Search for Meaning, Purpose and Faith* (San Francisco: Jossey Bass, 2000).

26. Warren Nord, *Does God Make a Difference? Taking Religion Seriously in Our Schools and Universities* (New York: Oxford University Press, 2010), 269.

27. Anthony T. Kronman, *Education's End*.

28. Christian Smith with Patricia Snell, *Lost in Transition: The Dark Side of Emerging Adulthood* (New York: Oxford, 2011).

29. For more about what this might mean see Perry L. Glanzer, "Building the Good Life: Using Identities to Frame Moral Education in Higher Education," *Journal of College and Character* 14, no. 2 (2013): 177–84.

30. Kathleen M. Goodman, Katie Wilson, and Z Nicolazzo, "Campus Practice in Support of Spirituality, Faith, Religion, and Life Purpose," in Small, ed., *Making Meaning*, 133–34; M. M. Kocet and D. L. Stewart, "The Role of Student Affairs in Promoting Religious and Secular Pluralism and Interfaith Cooperation," *Journal of College and Character* 12 (1): online.

31. Goodman, Wilson, and Nicolazzo, "Campus Practice in Support of Spirituality, Faith, Religion, and Life Purpose," 136.

32. Glanzer, "Building the Good Life."

33. M. Bundick, "The Benefits of Reflecting on and Discussing Purpose in Life in Emerging Adulthood," Jenni Menon Mariano, ed., *New Directions for Youth Development* 132 (2011): 89–103; Jane E. Pizzolato, Elizabeth L. Brown, and Mary A. Kanny, "Purpose Plus: Supporting Youth Purpose, Control, and Academic Achievement," *New Directions for Youth Development* 132 (2011): 75–88; B. J. Dik et al., "Make Your Work Matter: Development and Pilot Evaluation of a Purpose-Centered Career Education Intervention, *New Directions for Youth Development* 132 (2011): 59–73.

34. Eboo Patel and Mary Ellen Giess, "Bring Muslims, Evangelicals and Atheists Together on Campus," *The Chronicle of Higher Education.* November 3, 2015. Retrieved from http://chronicle.com/article/Bring-Muslims-Evangelicals/234018.

35. Clydesdale, *The Purposeful Graduate*; Larry A. Braskamp, Lois Calian Trautvetter, and Kelly Ward, *Putting Students First: How Colleges Develop Students Purposefully* (San Francisco: Anker, 2006).

36. Michele M. Welkner and Amanda Bowsher, "Soul-binding: Students' Perspectives on Meaning, Purpose, and College Experience," *Journal of College and Character* 13, no. 3 (2012). doi.10.1515/jcc-2012-1881.

37. Kendall C. Bronk, "A Grounded Theory of the Development of Noble Youth Purpose," *Journal of Adolescent Research* 27, no. 1 (2012): 78–109; D. Shamah, "Supporting a Strong Sense of Purpose: Lessons from a Rural Community," *New Directions for Youth Development* 132 (2011): 45–58.

38. Clydesdale, *The Purposeful Graduate*; Braskamp, Trautvetter, and Ward, *Putting Students First.*

39. William G. Perry, *Forms of Intellectual and Ethical Development in the College Years: A Scheme* (San Francisco: Jossey-Bass, 1999).

40. Parks, *Big Questions, Worthy Dreams*.

41. Sharon Daloz Parks, *The Critical Years: The Young Adult Search for a Faith to Live By* (San Francisco: Harper & Row, 1986); Parks, *Big Questions, Worthy Dreams*.

42. Perry, *Forms of Intellectual and Ethical Development in the College Years*, 206.

43. Parks, *Big Questions, Worthy Dreams*, 129.

44. Ibid., 134.

45. Ibid., 168.

46. Clydesdale, *The Purposeful Graduate*, 16.

47. Small, *Understanding College Students' Spiritual Identities*, 15.

48. Clydesdale, *The Purposeful Graduate*, 97.

49. John Dewey, *Democracy in Education* (1916; reprint., New York: Free Press, 1966), 97.

50. Stephen L. Carter, *God's Name in Vain: The Rights and Wrongs of Religion in Politics* (New York: Basic Books, 2000), 116.

51. Alasdair MacIntyre, *After Virtue, A Study in Moral Theory*, 3rd ed. (Notre Dame: University of Notre Dame Press, 2007).

52. Joel Carpenter, Perry L. Glanzer and Nicholas S. Lantinga, *Christian Higher Education: A Global Reconnaissance* (Grand Rapids: Wm. B. Eerdmans Publishing Company, 2014).

53. Clydesdale, *The Purposeful Graduate*, 67.

54. Ibid., 68.

55. Ibid., 69.

56. Perry L. Glanzer, "Building the Good Life: Using Identities to Frame Moral Education in Higher Education," *Journal of College and Character* 14, no. 2 (2013): 177–84.

57. Ibid., 216.

58. Centre for Civil Society, "What Is Civil Society?" London School of Economics (July 30, 2010), http://www.lse.ac.uk/collections/CCS/what_is_civil_society.htm. By civil society, we mean "the arena of uncoerced collective action around shared interests, purposes and values. In theory, its institutional forms are distinct from those of the state, family and market, though in practice, the boundaries between state, civil society, family and market are often complex, blurred and negotiated. Civil society commonly embraces a diversity of spaces, actors and institutional forms, varying in their degree of formality, autonomy and power. Civil societies are often populated by organisations such as registered charities, development non-governmental organisations, community groups, women's organisations, faith-based organisations, professional associations, trades unions, self-help groups, social movements, business associations, coalitions and advocacy group." Centre for Civil Society (2010), retrieved 7/30/2010.

59. We think private institutions with a particular mission can treat student groups different. After all, they are not legally bound, nor do we believe they should be, to follow state institutions in the same way. Respect for pluralism requires a respect for pluralistic institutions.

60. John Dewey, "My Pedagogic Creed," *John Dewey: The Early Works, 1882–1898*, vol. 5 (Carbondale, IL: Southern Illinois University Press, 1972), 87.

61. Clydesdale, *The Purposeful Graduate*, 98.

Appendix A

1. William Damon, Jenni Menon, and Kendall Cotton Bronk, "The Development of Purpose During Adolescence," *Applied Developmental Science* 7, no. 3 (2003): 123.

2. Anthony T. Kronman, *Education's End: Why Our Colleges and Universities Have Given Up on the Meaning of Life* (New Haven: Yale University Press, 2007).

3. Juliet Corbin and Anselm Strauss, *Basics of Qualitative Research: Grounded Theory Procedures and Techniques*, 3rd ed. (Thousand Oaks, CA: Sage, 2008).

4. Donna Freitas, *Sex and the Soul: Juggling Sexuality, Spirituality, Romance, and Religion on America's College Campuses* (New York: Oxford University Press, 2008), 246.

5. Corbin and Strauss, *Basics of Qualitative Research*.

6. Johnny Saldana, *The Coding Manual for Qualitative Researchers*, 2nd ed. (London: Sage, 2013).

7. Alyssa Bryant Rockenbach, Tara D. Hudson, and Jeremy B. Tuchmayer, "Fostering Meaning, Purpose, and Enduring Commitments to Community Service in College: A Multidimensional Conceptual Model," *Journal of Higher Education* 85, no. 3 (2014): 312–38.

8. Ibid.

9. Unfortunately, Gallup® reported that twenty-one students did not respond to the questions that were required to report race/ethnicity, so they are missing a race value in the data set.

10. William Damon, Jenni Menon, and Kendall Cotton Bronk, "The Development of Purpose during Adolescence."

11. Johnny Saldana, *The Coding Manual for Qualitative Researchers*.

Bibliography

Aristotle. *Nichomachean Ethics.* Trans. and ed. Roger Crisp. New York: Cambridge University Press, 2000.

Anderson, Robert. *European Universities from the Enlightenment to 1914.* New York: Oxford University Press, 2004.

Arnett, Jeffrey. "Emerging Adulthood: A Theory of Development from the Late Teens through the Twenties." *American Psychologist* 55 (2000): 469–80.

———. *Emerging Adulthood: The Winding Road from the Late Teens through the Twenties.* New York: Oxford University Press, 2004.

Astin, Alexander. *Achieving Educational Excellence: A Critical Assessment of Priorities and Practices in Higher Education.* San Francisco: Jossey-Bass, 1985.

Astin, Alexander W., Helen S., Astin, and Jennifer A. Lindholm. *Cultivating the Spirit: How College Can Enhance Students' Inner Lives.* San Francisco: Jossey-Bass, 2011.

Barrett, Justin. *Born Believers: The Science of Children's Religious Belief.* New York: Free Press, 2012.

Baxter Magolda, Marcia B. *Creating Contexts for Learning and Self-Authorship: Constructive-Developmental Pedagogy.* Nashville: Vanderbilt University Press, 1999.

———. *Making Their Own Way: Narratives for Transforming Higher Education to Promote Self-Development.* Sterling, VA: Stylus Press, 2001.

Baxter Magolda, Marcia B., and P. M. King (eds.). *Learning Partnerships: Theory and Models of Practice to Educate for Self-Authorship.* Sterling, VA: Stylus Press, 2004.

Braskamp, L. A., L. C. Trautvetter, and Kelly Ward. *Putting Students First: How Colleges Develop Students Purposefully.* San Francisco: Anker Publishing Co, 2006.

Bronk, Kendall Cotton. "Humility among Adolescent Purpose Exemplars." *Journal of Research on Character Education* 6, no. 1 (2008): 35–51.

———. *Purpose in Life: A Critical Component of Optimal Youth Development.* New York: Springer, 2014. doi: 10.1007/978-94-007-7491-9_6.

———. "The Role of Purpose in Life in Healthy Identity Formation: A Grounded Model." *New Directions for Youth Development* 132 (2011): 31–44. doi: 10.1002/yd.426.

———. "A Grounded Theory of the Development of Noble Youth Purpose." *Journal of Adolescent Research* 27, no. 1 (2012): 78–109. doi: 10.1177/0743558411412958.

Bronk, Kendall Cotton, Patrick Hill, Daniel K. Lapsley, Tasneem L. Talib, and Holmes Finch. "Purpose, Hope, and Life Satisfaction in Three Age Groups." *Journal of Positive Psychology* 4, no. 6 (2009): 500–10. doi: 10.1080/17439760903271439.

Brooks, Arthur C. *Who Really Cares: America's Charity Divide*. New York: Basic Books, 2006.

Brooks, David. "The Problem with Meaning." *New York Times*, January 5, 2015, A23.

———. *The Road to Character*. New York: Random House, 2015.

———. "The Streamlined Life." *New York Times*, May 6, 2014, A25.

Bundick, M. J., Yeager, D. Y., King, P., and Damon, W. "Thriving across the Life Span." In *Handbook of Lifespan Human Development*, edited by W. F. Overton and R. M. Lerner. New York: Wiley, 2009.

Burrow, Anthony and Patrick L. Hill. "Purpose as a Form of Identity Capital for Positive Youth Adjustment." *Developmental Psychology* 42, no. 4 (2011): 1196–1206. doi: 10.1037/a0023818.

Burrow, Anthony, Amanda C. O'Dell, and Patrick Hill. "Profiles of a Developmental Asset: Youth Purpose as a Context for Hope and Well-Being." *Journal of Youth Adolescence* 39 (2010): 1265–73. doi: 10.1007/s10964-009-9481-1.

Bynner, John. "Rethinking the Youth Phase of the Life-Course: The Case for Emerging Adulthood?" *Journal of Youth Studies* 8, no. 4 (2005): 367–84.

Byron, Katie and Cindy Miller-Perrin, "The Value and of Life Purpose: Purpose as a Mediator of Faith and Well-Being." *Journal of Positive Psychology* 4, no. 1 (2009): 64–70. doi: 10.1080/17439760802357867.

Carpenter, Joel, Perry L. Glanzer, and Nicholas, S. Lantinga. *Christian Higher Education: A Global Reconnaissance*. Grand Rapids: Wm. B. Eerdmans Publishing Company, 2014.

Chamberlain, Kerry and Sheryl Zika. "Religiosity, Life Meaning, and Well-Being: Some Relationships in a Sample of Women." *Journal for the Scientific Study of Religion* 27 (1988): 411–20.

Chickering, Art W. and Linda Reisser (1993). *Education and Identity*. San Francisco: Jossey-Bass.

Chickering, Art W., Jon C. Dalton, and Liesa Stamm. *Encouraging Authenticity and Spirituality in Higher Education*. San Francisco: Jossey-Bass, 2005.

Chua, Amy. *The Battle Hymn of the Tiger Mother*. New York: Penguin Press, 2011.

Clydesdale, Tim. *The Purposeful Graduate: Why Colleges Must Talk to Students about Vocation*. Chicago: University of Chicago Press, 2015.

Colby, Anne, Thomas Ehrlich, Elizabeth Beaumont, and Jason Stephens. *Educating Citizens: Preparing America's Undergraduates for Lives of Moral Responsibility*. San Francisco, CA: Jossey-Bass, 2003.

Corbin, Juliet M. and Anselm Strauss. *Basics of Qualitative Research: Techniques and Procedures for Developing Grounded Theory*, 4th ed. Sage Publishers: London, 2015.

Cranney, Stephen. "Do People Who Believe in God Report More Meaning in Their Lives? The Existential Effects of Belief." *Journal for the Scientific Study of Religion* 52, no. 3 (2013): 638–46.

Creswell, John W. *Educational Research: Planning, Conducting, and Evaluating Quantitative and Qualitative Research*. Upper Saddle River, NJ: Pearson: Merrill Prentice Hall, 2008.

Crumbaugh, James C. and Leonard Maholick. "An Experimental Study in Existentialism: The Psychometric Approach to Frankl's Concept of *Noogenic* Neurosis." In *Psychotherapy and existentialism,* edited by V. E. Frankl, 183–97. New York: Washington Square Press, 1967.

Dalton, John C. and Pamela Crosby. "When Faith Fails: Why Nurturing Purpose And Meaning Are So Critical to Student Learning and Development in College." *Journal of College and Character* 11, no. 3 (2010): 1–6.

Damon, William. *The Path to Purpose: Helping Our Children Find Their Calling in Life.* New York: Free Press, 2008.

Damon, William and Kendall Cotton Bronk. "Taking Ultimate Responsibility." In *Responsibility at Work: How Leading Professionals Act (Or Don't Act) Responsibly,* edited by Howard Gardner, 21–42. San Francisco: Jossey-Bass, 2007.

Damon, William, Jenni Menon Mariano, and Kendall Cotton Bronk. "The Development of Purpose during Adolescence." *Applied Developmental Science* 7, no. 3 (2003), 119–28.

Davis, Michael. *Ethics and the University.* New York: Routledge, 1999.

Debats, D. L. "Measurement of Personal Meaning: The Psychometric Properties of the Life Regard Index." In *The Human Quest for Meaning: A Handbook of Psychological Research and Clinical Application,* edited by Paul T. P. Wong, 237–59. Mahwah: Lawrence Earlbaum, 1998.

De Vogler, Karen L., and Peter Ebersole. "Categorization of College Students' Meaning of Life." *Psychological Reports* 46 (1980): 387–90.

Dewey, John. *Democracy in Education.* New York: Free Press, 1966/1916.

Dewey, John and James Tufts, *Ethics,* rev. ed. New York: Holt, Rinehart, and Winston, 1932.

Digest of Educational Statistics. Washington, DC: U.S. Department of Education, 2014 [online].

Dykstra, Craig. "Faith Development and Religious Education." In *Christian Perspectives on Faith Development,* edited by J. Astley and L. Francis, 251–71. Grand Rapids: Eerdmans, 1992.

Eagan, Kevin, Ellen Bara Stolzenberg, Joseph J. Ramirez, Melissa C. Aragon, Maria Ramirez Suchard, and Sylvia Hurtado. *The American Freshman: National Norms Fall 2014.* Los Angeles: Higher Education Research Institute, UCLA, 2014.

Edwards, Mark U. "Why Faculty Find It Difficult to Talk about Religion." In *The American University in a Postsecular Age,* edited by Douglas Jacobsen and Rhonda Jacobsen. New York: Oxford University Press, 2008.

Eldredge, John. *Epic: The Story God Is Telling.* Colorado Springs: Thomas Nelson, 2007.

Fischer, Claude S. and Michael Hout. *Century of Difference: How America Changed in the Last One Hundred Years.* New York: Russell Sage Foundation, 2006.

Fowler, James W. *Stages of Faith: The Psychology of Human Development and the Quest for Meaning.* San Francisco: HarperOne, 1981.

Francis, Leslie and Linda Burton. "The Influence of Personal Prayer on Purpose in Life among Catholic Adolescents." *Journal of Beliefs and Values* 15 (1994): 6–9.

Francis, Leslie J. "The Relationship between Bible Reading and Purpose in Life among 13–15 Year Olds." *Mental Health, Religion and Culture* 3, no. 1 (2000): 27–36.

Francis, L. J. and T. E. Evans. "The Relationship between Personal Prayer and Purpose in Life among Church-Going and Non-Church-Going 12–15 Year Olds in the UK." *Religious Education* 9 (1996): 9–21.

Franke, Ray, Sylvia Ruiz, Jessica Sharkness, Linda DeAngelo, and John Pryor. *Findings from the 2009 Administration of the College Senior Survey (CSS): National Aggregates*. Los Angeles: Higher Education Research Institute, UCLA, 2010.

Frankl, Victor. *Man's Search for Meaning: An Introduction to Logotherapy*. 3rd ed. New York: Simon & Schuster, 1984/1959.

Fry, Prem S. "The Development of Personal Meaning and Wisdom in Adolescence: A Reexamination of Moderating and Consolidating Factors and Influences." In *The Human Quest for Meaning: A Handbook of Psychological Research and Clinical Applications*, edited by Paul T. P. Wong and Prem S. Fry. London: Routledge, 1998.

George, Logan S. and Crystal L. Park, "Are Meaning and Purpose Distinct? An Examination of Correlates and Predictors." *The Journal of Positive Psychology* 8, no. 5 (2013): 365–75.

Gandhi. *An Autobiography: The Story of My Experiments with Truth*. Boston: Beacon Press, 1997.

Glanzer, Perry L. and Todd C. Ream. *Christianity and Moral Identity in Higher Education*. New York: Palgrave Macmillan, 2009.

Grant, Adam. *Give and Take: Why Helping Others Drives Our Success*. New York: Penguin Books.

Hardy, Lee. *The Fabric of This World: Inquiries into Calling, Career Choice, and the Design of Human Work*. Grand Rapids, MI: Eerdmans, 1990.

Higher Education Research Institute. (2003). *The Spiritual Life of College Students: A National Study of College Students' Search for Meaning and Purpose*. Retrieved from http://spirituality.ucla.edu/docs/reports/Spiritual_Life_College_Students_Full_Report.pdf (accessed 17 July 2015).

Hill, Patrick L., Anthony L. Burrow, Jay W. Brandenberger, Daniel K. Lapsley, and Jessica Collado Quaranto. "Collegiate Purpose Orientations and Well-Being in Adulthood." *Journal of Applied Developmental Psychology* 31 (2010): 173–79. doi:10.1016/j.appdev.2009.12.001.

Hill, Patrick L., Anthony L. Burrow, Amanda C. Dell, and Meghan A. Thornton. "Classifying Adolescents' Conceptions of Purpose in Life." *Journal of Positive Psychology* 5, no. 6 (2010): 466–73. doi: 10.1080/17439760.2010.534488.

Hill, Patrick L., Anthony L. Burrow, and Rachel Sumner. "Addressing Important Questions in the Field of Adolescent Purpose." *Child Development Perspectives* 7, no. 4 (2013): 232–36. doi: 10.1111/cdep.12048.

Hofstadter, Richard and Wilson Smith, eds., *American Higher Education: A Documentary History*, vol. 2. Chicago: University of Chicago Press, 1961.

Hutchins, Robert M. *The Higher Learning in America*. New Brunswick: Transaction, 1995/1936.

Kashdan, Todd B. and Patrick E. McKnight. "Origins of a Purpose In Life: Refining Our Understanding of a Life Well Lived." *Psychological Topics* 18 (2009): 303–16.

Kiang, Lisa. "Deriving Daily Purpose through Daily Events and Role Fulfillment among Asian American Youth." *Journal of Research on Adolescence* 22 (2012): 185–98. doi:10.1111/j.1532-7795.2011.00767.x

Kiang, Lisa and Andrew Kuligni. "Meaning in Life as a Mediator of Ethnic Identity and Adjustment among Adolescents from Latin, Asian, and European American Backgrounds." *Journal of Youth and Adolescence* 39, no. 11 (2010): 1253–64.

Kish, George and David R. Moody. "Psychopathology and Life Purposes." *International Forum for Logotherapy* 12, no. 1 (1989): 40–45.

Kohlberg, Lawrence. *The Philosophy of Moral Development: Moral Stages and the Idea of Justice, Essays on Moral Development, Vol. 1.* San Francisco, CA: Harper and Row Publishers, 1981.

Koshy, S. I. and Jenni Menon Mariano. "Promoting Youth Purpose: A Review of the Literature." *New Directions for Youth Development* 132 (2011): 13–30.

Kronman, Anthony. T. *Education's End: Why Our Colleges and Universities Have Given Up on the Meaning of Life.* New Haven, CT: Yale University Press, 2007.

Lewis, Harry. *Excellence without a Soul: How a Great University Forgot Education.* New York: Public Affairs, 2006.

Lindholm, Jennifer A. *The Quest for Meaning and Wholeness: Spiritual and Religious Connections in the Lives of College Faculty.* San Francisco: Jossey-Bass, 2014.

MacIntyre, Alasdair. *After Virtue, A Study in Moral Theory*, 3rd ed. Notre Dame: University of Notre Dame Press, 2007.

Malin, Heather, Timothy S. Reilly, Brandy Quinn, and Seana Moran. "Adolescent Purpose Development: Exploring Empathy, Discovering Roles, Shifting Priorities, and Creating Pathways." *Journal of Research on Adolescence* 24, no. 1 (2013): 186–99. doi: 10.1111/jora.12051

Mariano, Jenni M. and George E. Vaillant. "Purpose among the 'Greatest Generation.'" *Journal of Positive Psychology* 7, no. 4 (2012): 281–93. doi: 10.1080/13598130903358501.

Mariano, Jenni Menon. "Introduction to Special Section: Understanding Paths to Youth Purpose—Why Content and Contexts Matter." *Applied Developmental Science* 18, no. 3 (2014): 139–47.

Mariano, Jenni Menon and William Damon. "The Role Spirituality and Religious Faith Play in Supporting Purpose in Adolescence." In *Positive Youth Development and Spirituality: From Theory to Research*, edited by R. M. Benson, R. W. Roeser, and E. Phelps, 210–30. West Conshoshocken, PA: Templeton Foundation Press, 2008.

Marsden, George. *The Soul of the American University: From Protestant Establishment to Established Nonbelief.* New York: Oxford University Press, 1994.

Marsh, Bill. "Why People Marry." *New York Times*, April 27, 2013. Accessed August 24, 2015, http://www.nytimes.com/interactive/2013/04/28/sunday-review/Why-People-Marry.html.

McKnight, Patrick and Todd Kashdan. "Purpose in Life as a System That Creates and Sustains Health and Well-Being: An Integrative, Testable Theory." *Review of General Psychology* 13 (2009): 242–51. doi: 10.1037/a0017152.

Mead, Margaret. *Blackberry Winter: My Earlier Years.* New York: William Morrow & Co., 1972.

Meyer, Donald H. *The Instructed Conscience: The Shaping of the American National Ethic.* Philadelphia: University of Pennsylvania Press, 1972.

Molcar, Carol C. and Daniel W. Steumpfig. "Effects of World View on Purpose in Life." *Journal of Psychology* 122, no. 4 (1988): 365–71.

Moran, Seana. "What 'Purpose' Means to Youth: Are There Cultures of Purpose?" *Applied Developmental Science* 18, no. 3 (2014): 163–75, doi: 10.1080/10888691.2014.92435.

Morison, Samuel E. *The Founding of Harvard College.* Cambridge: Harvard University Press, 1935.

Myers, David. "The Funds, Friends, and Faith of Happy People." *American Psychologist* 55, no. 1 (2000): 56–67.

Nash, Robert J. and Michelle Murray. *Helping College Students Find Purpose: The Campus Guide to Meaning-Making.* San Francisco: Jossey-Bass, 2010.

Nord, Warren A. *Does God Make a Difference? Taking Religion Seriously in Our Schools and Universities.* New York: Oxford University Press, 2010.

Paddleford, B. L. "The Relationship between Drug Involvement and Purpose in Life." *Journal of Clinical Psychology* 41, no. 6 (1974): 1153–60.

Palmer, Palmer. J. and Arthur Zajonc (with Megan Scribner). *The Heart of Higher Education: A Call to Renewal.* San Francisco: Jossey Bass, 2010.

Panos, R. J., Alexander W. Astin, and Creager, J. A. *National Norms for Entering College Freshman—Fall 1967.* Los Angeles: American Council on Education, 1967.

Parks, Sharon D. *Big Questions, Worthy Dreams: Mentoring Young Adults in Their Search for Meaning, Purpose and Faith.* San Francisco: Jossey Bass, 2000.

———. *The Critical Years: The Young Adult Search for a Faith to Live By.* San Francisco: Harper & Row, 1986.

Perry, William G., Jr. *Forms of Intellectual and Ethical Development in the College Years: A Scheme.* San Francisco: Jossey-Bass, 1999/1968.

Placher, William C. *Callings: Twenty Centuries of Christian Wisdom on Vocation.* Grand Rapids, MI: Eerdmans, 2005.

Peterson, Christopher and Martin Seligman. *Character Strengths and Virtues: A Handbook and Classification.* New York: Oxford University Press, 2004.

Pizzolato, Jane, Elizabeth L Brown, and Mary A. Kanny. "Purpose Plus: Supporting Youth Purpose, Control, and Academic Achievement." *New Directions for Youth Development* 132 (2011): 75–88. doi: 10.1002/yd.429.

Quinn, Brandy. "Other-Oriented Purpose: The Potential Roles of Beliefs about the World and Other People." *Youth and Society* 20, no. 10 (2012): 1–22. doi: 10.1177/0044118X12452435.

Reuben, Julie. *The Making of the Modern University: Intellectual Transformation and the Marginalization of Morality.* Chicago, IL: University of Chicago Press, 1996.

Rockenbach, Alyssa B., Tara D. Hudson, and Jeremy B. Tuchmayer. "Fostering Meaning, Purpose, and Enduring Commitments to Community Service in College: A Multidimensional Conceptual Model." *Journal of Higher Education* 85, no. 3 (2014): 312–38.

Ryff, Carol, Corey Keyes, and Diane Hughes. "Status Inequalities, Perceived Discrimination, and Eudaimonic Well-Being: Do the Challenges of Minority Life Hone Purpose and Growth?" *Journal of Health and Social Behavior* 44 (2003): 275–91.

Ryff, Carol. "Happiness Is Everything, or Is It? Explorations on the Meaning of Psychological Well-Being." *Journal of Personality and Social Psychology* 57, no. 6 (1989): 1069–81.

Saldaña, Johnny. *The Coding Manual for Qualitative Researchers*, 2nd ed. London: Sage, 2013.

Schneider, Barbara and David Stevenson. *The Ambitious Generation: Motivated but Directionless*. New Haven: Yale University Press, 2000.

Schofer, Evan and John W. Meyer, "The Worldwide Expansion of Higher Education in the Twentieth Century." *American Sociological Review* 70, no. 6 (December 2005): 898–920.

Schroeder, Alice. *The Snowball: Warren Buffett and the Business of Life*. New York: Bantam Books, 2008.

Schwehn, Mark R. and Dorothy C. Bass, eds., *Leading Lives that Matter: What We Should Do and Who We Should Be*. Grand Rapids, MI: Eerdmans, 2006.

Shanahan, Michael J. "Pathways to Adulthood in Changing Societies: Variability and Mechanisms in Life Course Perspective." *Annual Review of Sociology, 26* (2000): 667–92.

Shek. Daniel T. "The Chinese Purpose-in-life Test and Psychological Well-Being in Chinese College Students." *International Forum for Logotherapy* 16, no. 1 (1993): 35–42.

Sloan, Douglas. "The Teaching of Ethics in the American Undergraduate Curriculum, 1876–1976." In *Ethics Teaching in Higher Education*, edited by Daniel Callahan and Sissela Bok, 1–57. New York: Plenum Press, 1980.

Small, Jenny L. *Understanding College Students' Spiritual Identities: Different Faiths, Varied Worldviews*. New York: Hampton Press, 2011.

———, ed. *Making Meaning: Embracing Spirituality, Faith, Religion, and Life Purpose in Student Affairs*. Sterling, VA: Stylus Press, 2015.

Smith, Christian. *The Secular Revolution: Power, Interests, and Conflict in the Secularization of American Public Life*. Berkeley. University of California Press, 2003.

———. *What Is a Person? Rethinking Humanity, Social Life, and the Moral Good from the Person Up*. Chicago: University of Chicago Press, 2010.

——— (with Kari Christoffersen, Hilary Davidson, and Patricia Snell Herzog). *Lost in Transition: The Dark Side of Emerging Adulthood*. New York: Oxford University Press, 2011.

——— (with P. Snell). *Souls in Transition: The Religious and Spiritual Lives of Emerging Adults*. New York: Oxford University Press, 2009.

Soderstorm, Doug and E. Wayne Wright. "Religious Orientation and Meaning in Life." *Journal of Clinical Psychology* 33 (1977): 65–68.

Sommerville, C. John. *Religion in the National Agenda: What We Mean by Religious, Spiritual, and Secular*. Waco, TX: Baylor University Press, 2009.

Steger, Michael F., Shigehiro Oishi, and Todd B. Kashdan. 2009. "Meaning in Life Across the Life Span: Levels and Correlates of Meaning in Life from Emerging Adulthood to Older Adulthood." *Journal of Positive Psychology* 4, 1 (2009): 43–52. doi: 10.1080/17439760802303127.

Stewart-Williams, Steve. *Darwin, God and the Meaning of Life: How Evolutionary Theory Undermines Everything You Thought You Knew*. New York: Cambridge University Press, 2010.

Taylor, Charles. *Sources of the Self: The Making of the Modern Identity*. Cambridge: Harvard University Press, 1989.

Thelin, John. *A History of American Higher Education*, 2nd ed. Baltimore: Johns Hopkins University Press, 2011.

Tirri, Kris and Brandon Quinn. "Exploring the Role of Religion and Spirituality in the Development of Purpose: Case Studies of Purposeful Youth." *British Journal of Religious Education* 32, 30 (2010): 201–14.

Tweksbury, Donald. *The Founding of American Colleges and Universities before the Civil War*. New York: Teachers College, Columbia University, 1932.

Welkener, Michelle and Amanda Bowsher. "Soul-Building: Students' Perspectives on Meaning, Purpose, and the College Experience." *Journal of College and Character* 13, 3 (2012): 1–12. doi:10.1515/jcc-2012-1881.

Wong, Paul T., ed. *The Human Quest for Meaning: Theories, Research and Applications*, rev. ed. New York: Routledge, 2012.

Index